ROMANTIC SOCIABILITY

Challenging the assumptions which underlie an understanding of the 'Romantics' as solitary and anti-sociable, and Romanticism as representing the rejection of Enlightenment sociability, this volume introduces sociability to the field of Romantic literary and cultural studies. The volume engages with Jürgen Habermas's model of the 'public sphere' which emphasizes the coffee-house and club as models of an older, masculine eighteenth-century sociability, focussing on the changing nature of sociability in British radical culture of the 1790s and on the gendered nature of sociability. In a range of essays which examine modes of sociability as diverse as circles of sedition, international republicanism, Dissenting culture, Romantic lecturing, theatre and shopping, the volume transforms our understanding of Romanticism by exploring the social networks of such central Romantic figures as Anna Barbauld, Frances Burney, Samuel Taylor Coleridge, William Godwin, William Hazlitt, Anne Lister, Robert Merry, Joseph Priestley, John Thelwall and Mary Wollstonecraft.

Gillian Russell is Senior Lecturer in English at the Australian National University. She is author of *The Theatres of War: Performance, Politics and Society, 1793–1815* (1995) and an associate editor of *An Oxford Companion to the Romantic Age: British Culture 1776–1832*, ed. Iain McCalman (1999). Her articles have appeared in *Eighteenth-Century Life, British Journal for Eighteenth-Century Studies, Eighteenth-Century Studies* and *The Eighteenth-Century: Theory and Interpretation*.

Clara Tuite is Lecturer in English at the University of Melbourne. She is the author of *Romantic Austen* (Cambridge, 2002) and an associate editor of *An Oxford Companion to the Romantic Age: British Culture 1776–1832*.

ROMANTIC SOCIABILITY

Social Networks and Literary Culture in Britain
1770–1840

EDITED BY

GILLIAN RUSSELL AND CLARA TUITE

CAMBRIDGE
UNIVERSITY PRESS

PUBLISHED BY THE PRESS SYNDICATE OF THE UNIVERSITY OF CAMBRIDGE
The Pitt Building, Trumpington Street, Cambridge, United Kingdom

CAMBRIDGE UNIVERSITY PRESS
The Edinburgh Building, Cambridge CB2 2RU, UK
40 West 20th Street, New York, NY 10011-4211, USA
477 Williamstown Road, Port Melbourne, VIC 3207, Australia
Ruiz de Alarcón 13, 28014 Madrid, Spain
Dock House, The Waterfront, Cape Town 8001, South Africa

http://www.cambridge.org

© Cambridge University Press 2002

First published 2002

Printed in the United Kingdom at the University Press, Cambridge

Typeface Baskerville Monotype 11 / 12.5 pt.   *System* LATEX 2$_\varepsilon$ [TB]

A catalogue record for this book is available from the British Library

Library of Congress Cataloguing in Publication data

Romantic sociability : social networks and literary culture in Britain, 1770–1840 / edited by
Gillian Russell and Clara Tuite.
p. cm.
Includes bibliographical references and index.
ISBN 0 521 77068 8
1. English literature – 18th century – History and criticism.   2. Literature and
society – Great Britain – History – 18th century.   3. Literature and society – Great Britain –
History – 19th century.   4. Social networks – Great Britain – History – 18th century.
5. Social networks – Great Britain – History – 19th century.   6. Authors, English – Friends
and associates.   7. Romanticism – Great Britain.   I. Russell, Gillian.   II. Tuite, Clara, 1964–
PR448.S64 R66   2002
820.8'0355 – dc21   2001043955

ISBN 0 521 77068 8 hardback

To Benjamin Penny
and Susan Conley

Contents

Illustrations

Contributors

JUDITH BARBOUR has been an Honorary Research Associate at the University of Sydney since her retirement from teaching in the Department of English. She has published articles on Mary Shelley, Mary Wollstonecraft and William Godwin. She is currently editing an electronic edition of Mary Shelley's biography of her father, William Godwin, from the Abinger Manuscripts at the Bodleian Library, Oxford, and researching the topic of eighteenth-century women actors of Shakespeare.

JULIE A. CARLSON is Associate Professor of English at the University of California, Santa Barbara. She is the author of *In the Theatre of Romanticism: Coleridge, Nationalism, Women* (1994) and guest editor of *Domestic / Tragedy (SAQ* 98 (1999)). She has written essays on Romantic theatre, sexuality and politics with particular focus on Coleridge and Baillie. Currently she is working on the Godwin–Wollstonecraft–Shelley family and collaborating on a project about Romantic medievalism.

DEIRDRE COLEMAN teaches in the School of English, University of Sydney. She is the author of *Coleridge and 'The Friend' (1809–1810)* (1988) and has recently edited *Maiden Voyages and Infant Colonies: Two Women's Travel Narratives of the 1790s* (1999). She is currently writing a book on colonization in Sierra Leone and Botany Bay for Cambridge University Press's 'Studies in Romanticism' series.

JAMES EPSTEIN is Professor of History at Vanderbilt University. He has written extensively on radical politics in the late eighteenth and nineteenth centuries. His most recent book is *Radical Expression: Political Language, Ritual and Symbol in England, 1790–1850* (1994). He is also co-editor of *Journal of British Studies.*

MARGARET C. JACOB is Professor of History at the University of California, Los Angeles, and past President of the American Society for Eighteenth-Century Studies. She has worked on Newtonianism, industrialization, freemasonry, and now on British radicals of the 1790s with Lynn Hunt. Her most recent book is *The Enlightenment. A Brief History with Documents* (2001).

ANNE JANOWITZ is Professor of Romantic Poetry at Queen Mary College, University of London. She is the author of *England's Ruins* (1990) and *Lyric and Labour in the Romantic Tradition* (1998).

DEIDRE SHAUNA LYNCH, Associate Professor of English at Indiana University, is the author of *The Economy of Character: Novels, Market Culture, and the Business of Inner Meaning* (1998) and the editor of, most recently, *Janeites: Austen's Disciples and Devotees* (2000).

JON MEE is Margaret Candfield Fellow in English at University College, Oxford. He is the author of *Dangerous Enthusiasm: William Blake and the Culture of Radicalism in the 1790s* (1992) and an associate editor of *An Oxford Companion to the Romantic Age: British Culture 1776–1832*, ed. Iain McCalman (1999). As well as writing on recent Indian fiction in English, he has written numerous essays on different aspects of the cultural politics of the Romantic period and is currently completing a monograph under the title *Enthusiasm, Romanticism, and Regulation: The Policing of Culture in the Romantic Period*.

GILLIAN RUSSELL is Senior Lecturer in English at the Australian National University, Canberra. She is the author of *The Theatres of War: Performance, Politics, and Society, 1793–1815* (1995) and an associate editor of *An Oxford Companion to the Romantic Age: British Culture 1776–1832*, ed. Iain McCalman (1999).

CLARA TUITE is Lecturer in English at the University of Melbourne. She is an associate editor of *An Oxford Companion to the Romantic Age: British Culture 1776–1832*, ed. Iain McCalman (1999), and the author of *Romantic Austen: Sexual Politics and the Literary Canon*, forthcoming in Cambridge University Press's 'Studies in Romanticism' series.

Acknowledgements

This project was supported by a grant from the Australian Research Council. Gillian Russell would like to thank especially Paul Campbell, who aided in research for her chapter and in preparation of the volume for publication. Joan Sussler of the Lewis Walpole Library, Erin Chase of the Huntington Library, John Powell of the Newberry Library and Alastair Laing at the National Trust, UK, were extremely helpful in obtaining illustrations. Clara Tuite would like to thank Iain McCalman for a fellowship at the Humanities Research Centre, Australian National University, which enabled the editors an extended period of *in situ* sociability and collaboration on the project. We are grateful to Josie Dixon for initial encouragement and shepherding of the volume in its early stages: our editor at Cambridge University Press, Linda Bree, has been a trusted guide in its completion.

This volume has been produced in its own sociable contexts: we would like to note the companionable discussions with Judith Barbour and Deirdre Coleman, Sarah Lloyd, Jon Mee and Iain McCalman, that have been so important in shaping its development. We are enormously grateful to our contributors for the lively spirit of international sociability, dialogue and discussion that energizes the volume and makes it so much more than just the sum of its parts. Our greatest debts, as always, are to Benjamin Penny and Susan Conley.

Introducing Romantic sociability

Gillian Russell and Clara Tuite

On the night of 28 December 1817, the painter Benjamin Robert Haydon held a dinner in the painting room of his studio at 22 Lisson Grove, London. The centrepiece of the room, illuminated by the flickering light of a winter's day fire, was *Christ's Entry into Jerusalem*: the occasion was partly marking a completion of a phase in the painting which had involved Haydon's portrait of William Wordsworth witnessing Christ between the figures of Voltaire and Milton. Present at the party were Wordsworth himself, John Keats, who was meeting Wordsworth for the first time, Charles Lamb and Thomas Monkhouse. The evening soon became exceedingly convivial. There was a vigorous debate on the merits of Homer, Shakespeare, Milton and Virgil, and toasts were made to Voltaire and Newton. Others joined the party in the course of the evening – the surgeon Joseph Ritchie, who was about to embark on a trip of exploration in Africa, and John Kingston, comptroller of the Stamp Office and a man with some pretensions in *belles lettres*. According to Haydon, Kingston had been curious to meet Wordsworth partly because of the latter's literary celebrity but also because, as distributor of stamps for Westmorland, Wordsworth was Kingston's inferior in the civil service. 'The moment he was introduced he let Wordsworth know *who* he officially was', writes Haydon in his diary. This produced an awkward moment of self-consciousness for Wordsworth, who was exposed before the company as a placeman, subject to the authority of men like Kingston. The latter's attempt to enter into the world of these artists and writers by talking to Wordsworth about poetry was ridiculed by a drunk Charles Lamb, who countered Kingston's sage remarks with the nursery rhyme 'Diddle diddle don', an assertion of the infantile and the ludic against the bureaucratic intruder. 'There is no describing this scene adequately', Haydon commented.

There was not the restraint of refined company, nor the vulgar freedom of low, but a frank, natural license, such as one sees in an act of Shakespeare, every man expressing his natural emotions without fear. Into this company, a little heated with wine, a Comptroller of the Stamp Office walked, frilled, dressed, & official, with a due awe of the powers above him and a due contempt for those beneath him.

He goes on:

There was something interesting in seeing Wordsworth sitting, & Keats & Lamb, & my Picture of Christ's entry towering up behind them, occasionally brightened by the gleams of flame that sparkled from the fire, & hearing the voice of Wordsworth repeating Milton with an intonation like the funeral bell of St Paul's & the music of Handel mingled, & then Lamb's wit came sparkling in between, & Keats's rich fancy of Satyrs & Fauns & doves & white clouds, wound up the stream of conversation. I never passed a more delightful day & I am convinced that nothing in Boswell is equal to what came out from these Poets. Indeed there were no such Poets in his time. It was an evening worthy of the Elizabethan age, and will long flash upon "that inward eye which is the bliss of Solitude."[1]

The 'immortal dinner', as it was described in Haydon's *Autobiography*, was a sociable event staged by the painter in what was both a private and a professional space – his studio – and before a work in progress which was not merely a kind of theatrical backdrop but another kind of guest in dialogic relationship with the drama before it.[2] *Christ's Entry* was a heroic vindication and, indeed, sanctification, of the capacity of men of genius to transcend the age. The dinner has been restaged on a number of occasions in biographies of the principals and has recently been the subject of a study in its own right which uses the event as a centrepiece of biographical accounts of the protagonists and a survey of metropolitan culture in 1817, but it has not received any sustained critical attention within Romantic studies, like 'Romantic sociability' as a whole.[3] The turn to history in Romantic studies has given us some glimpses into the sociability of men and women of the Romantic period – for example, the dense network comprised by the reform societies, publishers' dinners, theatre-going and supper parties of the Godwin circle in the 1790s; the suburban sociality of sonnet-writing contests, tea-drinking and music-making of the Hunt circle in the 1810s and 1820s; the 'Italianate salon' of William Roscoe at Liverpool; John Clare's scrutiny of Coleridge, Lamb and Hazlitt at the *London Magazine* dinners of the 1820s; the freneticism of Thomas Moore's conversational commerce; Helen Maria Williams's anglicization of French salon sociability – but in only a few of these cases has sociability actually been the focus of the analysis and there has certainly been no work which has attempted to define 'Romantic sociability' or map a possible field of study in such terms.[4]

Within the social history of the long eighteenth century it would be true to say that sociability has received more substantial attention in work by scholars such as Peter Borsay, John Money, Kathleen Wilson and Peter Clark.[5] Tim Hitchcock and Michèle Cohen's *English Masculinities* uses sociability as a sub-category in which to group two of the chapters of that collection while both John Brewer's *Pleasures of the Imagination* and Amanda Vickery's *The Gentleman's Daughter* deal extensively with the topic, without explicitly foregrounding it.[6] Paul Langford's essay 'Manners and the Eighteenth-Century State: the Case of the Unsociable Englishman' tackles the subject more directly, culminating in a sub-section entitled 'English sociability'. Langford's essay exemplifies a general tendency in eighteenth-century history, literary studies and social and political theory to regard sociability ahistorically as a given of social interaction which does not require explanation.[7] For example, the two essays in *English Masculinities* grouped under the rubric 'Sociability' which address plebeian male sociability and gendered constructions of conversation for upper-middle class and elite males, suggest that sociability varied according to class and social rank, but the editors do not directly address how they are using the category nor how their essays might inflect its meaning. Leslie Mitchell's *TLS* review of Peter Clark's monumental *British Clubs and Societies* speculated that the willingness of Britons to associate in clubs and societies could be explained by urbanization and a non-interventionist state post 1688 but 'must also owe something to what was innate in the British character', a universalizing perspective also apparent in Langford's essay which develops into what is in effect a polemic about English national character.[8] Rejecting the Habermasian model of the public sphere, Langford defines 'English sociability' as 'distinct from sociability as extended kinship and sociability as the divided or alienated self, as public' and concludes with a quote from a Victorian, George Gissing, to the effect that English sociability has never been 'ceremonial' or 'mirthful' but 'as regards every prime instinct of the community . . . [the English] social instinct is supreme'. Glossing this quotation, Langford concludes: 'If, at last, [English sociability] is an illusion, it is one that has entranced the English themselves. Its most lasting legacy is surely the potent image of the gentleman as the authentic representative of Englishness, in the character which the eighteenth century bestowed on him.'[9] Langford's essay illustrates the continuing discursive potency of sociability, how it can articulate particular constructions of gender, class and national identity. As this volume will outline, this discursive potency is not just a feature of current academic discourse on sociability but was apparent in the eighteenth century.

The comparative neglect of events such as Haydon's account of the 'immortal dinner' is a reflection of the marginal status of texts such as the essay, diaries and letters in Romantic literary studies, which have had considerable ideological investment in canonical genres and forms such as the lyric, as well as in a narrow text-based definition of the Romantic public sphere. As Paul Magnuson states: 'The public space of Romanticism is the book and the periodical', which suggests that it is not to be found in the theatre, the debating club, the bookshop or the dining room.[10] An argument of this volume is that we need to re-cover the significance of sociability, not simply for biographical studies of Romantic writers or in order to contextualize their work, but as a kind of text in its own right, a form of cultural work – sometimes play-fully convivial as at 22 Lisson Grove – which was a fundamental part of the self-definition of Romantic writers and artists. Another reason why events such as Haydon's 'immortal dinner' have been neglected is the apparent incompatibility of such convivial and theatrical social oc-casions with Romanticism's traditional identification with the lone poet, withdrawn into productive introspection, with individualism rather than collective activity, and with the cultivation of the authentic rather than the performative self.[11] These emphases have been given a historical inflection in Mark Philp's claim that in the 1790s 'the ideals nurtured by sociability collapsed . . . leaving the stage free for the isolationism of the Romantics', a statement which appropriately highlights the crucial significance of the 1790s but which also proposes the 'Romantics' as anti-sociable and Romanticism as a whole as representing the rejection of Enlightenment sociability.[12] The chapters in this volume will attempt to challenge these assumptions. It is our contention that the solitary self has stood for Romanticism for too long: this volume will investigate its sociable other.

If the sociable occupies the position of the other of a solitary or inte-riorized Romanticism, this is partly because there has been no critical tradition of representing a Romanticism in which sociability is a value. As Lawrence Klein has pointed out, '[i]t is often observed that a reaction against emphatic sociability took shape in the form of a rehabilitation of solitude'.[13] Before we move on to survey the heterogeneous forms that could be said to constitute Romanticism's sociable others, it might be worth mapping the move from what Klein refers to as the 'emphatic' sociability of the earlier eighteenth century to the Romantic moment of solitude, which is engaged in Haydon's dialectic between solitude and sociability. In *British Clubs and Societies*, Peter Clark refers to 'an intricate tessellation' of social activity in the Georgian period of which he distinguishes three broad categories: the 'private' sociability of the home, where 'the greatest volume of social contact took place'; an 'old-style' sociability based around the church, parliament, court and the street; and a 'new-style' sociability engendered by the commercialization of culture in venues such as the coffee-house, the inn, tavern, alehouse, the proliferation of forms of voluntary association, theatres, pleasure-gardens, dancing assemblies and so on. Within this last category Clark notes but does not substantively analyze distinct gender differences between what he calls 'fashionable sociability', 'influenced by sensibility and the public presence of women', and the sociability of the club, coffee-house and tavern, which was strongly identified with male homosociality.[14] The predominance of the coffee-house and the club as models of sociability, both within eighteenth-century representations and contemporary readings of the period, has functioned to produce a paradigmatic model of sociability that is implicitly male and homosocial. It is one of the aims of this volume to re-examine this model in order to account for a more diverse range of sites of sociability, in particular, sites which are more inclusive of female modes of sociability, and to account for forms of female participation in the public sphere more generally, as part of a larger investigation of gender and Romantic-period sociability.[15]

The coffee-house and the club are the primary sites and practices of the conversational model of culture which starts to gain ground in the eighteenth century.[16] A vital cultural formation in this respect is the early periodicals, in particular, Richard Steele's *The Tatler* (1709–11) and Joseph Addison's *The Spectator* (1711–12, 1714).[17] Whilst *The Tatler* and *The Spectator* exist for us as edited 'texts', they began their lives as 'papers', circulating within the heterogeneous worlds of the actual sites of sociability with which they conducted their sociable traffic. There are a number of ways in which the early eighteenth-century public sphere might be said to announce sociability as a value:

(1) in the modelling of culture as a conversation, and the cultivation of the sociable virtues of laughter, clubbability, conviviality, taste and politeness;[18]

(2) in the modelling of culture as object of spectatorship (a less participatory yet more theatrical model than (1) above);

(3) in the use of sociability to ground moral judgements in Enlightenment moral philosophy;

(4) and in the production of sociability as a value through its absence, i.e., in the satirical production of the absence of sociability or through the sentimental conventions of melancholy and pathos.

Written from particular coffee-houses (*The Spectator* was written from Lloyd's, for many years), where the editors reported on the passing sociable world they saw and heard, and where they were known (at least to begin with) to their audience of readers, the periodical papers are significant in attesting to the importance of sociability as a fact in eighteenth-century public culture, and in producing this sociability as a value. *The Tatler* and *The Spectator* produce sociability as both a fact, as anecdote, topic, as part of the 'motley' of 'Whate'er men do, or say, or think, or dream' (*The Tatler*, motto for No. 1, p.15) and as a value. Part of what is distinctive about this early eighteenth-century public discourse, then, at least as it is manifested in *The Tatler* and *The Spectator*, is its utopic heterogeneity, and a certain Menippean satirical and carnivalesque inclusiveness. If these papers strike William Godwin as 'strikingly loose and unsystematical',[19] it is because they are intended to be, in that a certain looseness keeps the model of conversation in view of the reader. In *The Tatler*, conversation provides a model of democratic exchange: 'Equality is the Life of Conversation' (*The Tatler* No. 225, p. 174). And if equality is the life of conversation, it is also the life of business exchange:

Man is said to be a Sociable Animal, and, as an instance of it, we may observe, that we take all Occasions and Pretences of forming our selves into those little Nocturnal Assemblies, which are commonly known by the Name of Clubs ... When Men are thus knit together, by a Love of Society, not a Spirit of Faction, and don't meet to censure or annoy those that are absent, but to enjoy one another: When they are thus combined for their own Improvement, or for the Good of others, or at least to relax themselves from the Business of the Day, by an innocent and chearful Conversation, there may be something very useful in these little Institutions and Establishments. (*The Spectator* No. 9, p. 39, p. 42)

Part of what is at stake here is the integration of politics and business into sociable practice. Here, sociability is produced as a naturalizing feature of business, as the clubbable man eases into 'innocent and chearful Conversation' at the end of the 'Business of the Day'. The assertion that the spirit of the club is 'not a Spirit of Faction' also registers the erasure of political interest as a key feature of early Hanoverian modes of politeness and sociability: politics and sociability do not go hand in hand. Our volume seeks to examine what happens to this model which keeps politics and sociability separate in a period such as the 1790s which is marked, we argue, by highly charged combinations of politics and sociability. Jon Mee's chapter, in particular, examines the nature of precisely this kind of transformation of an early eighteenth-century mode of sociability, elaborated in the work of Shaftesbury, within the radical political cultures of the 1790s in the circles of Robert Merry.

Another significant model of sociability is the theatrical, performative or what John Dwyer has referred to as the 'spectatorial model'[20] of culture. This model intersects with the conversational model, but can diverge from it in that it can involve a less participatory model of culture and sociability. As *The Spectator* No. 1 says: 'I have acted in all the parts of my Life as a Looker-on, which is the Character I intend to preserve in this paper.' (*The Spectator* No. 1, p. 5). The figure of the spectator is a significant sociable presence in the writings of the Scottish Enlightenment, a crucial cultural form of the classical eighteenth-century public sphere. Adam Smith founds the Scottish Enlightenment tradition of what John Dwyer has referred to as 'spectatorial ethics', exemplified by Smith's invocation of the 'cool and impartial spectator' (in *Theory of Moral Sentiments* (1749, revised 1790)). As Dwyer has also suggested, sociability is an 'imperative' of Enlightenment moral philosophy in general.[21] According to Adam Smith, the best model of society is a conversational one in which pleasure arises 'from a certain correspondence of sentiments and opinions, from a certain harmony of minds, which like so many musical instruments coincide and keep time with one another'.[22] This moral philosophy is exemplary in its elaboration of sociability as a value. Moral philosophy and journalism are not separate realms, though. Indeed, the bringing together of journalism and philosophy – the open and critical discussion of modes of behaviour and everyday life – is a critical impulse of the bourgeois public sphere. As Addison's speaker in *The Spectator* No. 10 says: 'I shall be ambitious to have it said of me, that I have brought Philosophy out of Closets and Libraries, Schools and Colleges, to dwell in Clubs and Assemblies, at tea-Tables, and in Coffee-Houses' (*The Spectator* No. 10, p. 44).

And just as Scottish Enlightenment philosophy is characterized by a focus on emphatically social and sociable relations, so too does this new coffee-house sociability involve both a democratization of philosophy and an enactment of the ideal of philosophy as a mode of sociable

interchange. *The Tatler* and *The Spectator* papers popularize the philosophical ideals of the Scottish Enlightenment, self-consciously promulgating
sociability as a virtue.

In *The Spectator*'s reading of Thomas Hobbes's *Discourse of Human Nature*
(1650), its satirical reproduction of Hobbes's misanthropic reading of
laughter as pride – '[a]ccording to this Author therefore, when we hear
a Man laugh excessively, instead of saying he is very Merry, we ought
to tell him he is very Proud' (*The Spectator* No. 47, p. 200) – produces
the sociable virtue of laughter, thereby offering another example of the
early eighteenth-century public sphere's production of sociability as a
value. Running counter to the pessimistic and mechanistic model of
civil society offered by Hobbes, produced out of a seventeenth-century
background of religious and civil conflict, this reading offers a moment
at which *The Spectator* foregrounds its own ideological implication within
the Enlightened Hanoverian Whig regime in its valuing of social order
and harmony, free of the 'Spirit of Faction', and of an order of 'Merry'
sociability. Even the categories of melancholy and pathos are pressed
into sociable service in the culture of the early eighteenth-century public
sphere. The discourse of sentiment, for example, involved the category
of catharsis, which relies on the sympathy of spectators. As Addison
writes in *The Spectator*, it is by contemplating the 'greater miseries of others
[that] a man forgets his own and obtains the needed mental catharsis'
(*The Spectator* No. 387). A literature of pathos is a primary tool also in
this training of feeling. Dwyer has referred, for example, to the Ossian
poems of James Macpherson as attempts to 'increase humanity through
the skilful manipulation of pathos'.[23]

In this context, the political overdetermination of sentiment and sensibility in the 1790s as signifiers, on the one hand, of Jacobin revolutionary excess, and on the other, of counter-revolutionary chivalry and
loyalism (most notably in Edmund Burke's *Reflections on the Revolution in
France* (1790)), offer a measure of what is distinctive about Romantic-
period sociability in contrast with the earlier period. In the 1790s, one
of the primarily contested set of associations with sentiment is sociability
and anti-sociability. In Jane Austen's *Sense and Sensibility*, written in the
late 1790s though not published until 1811, the sensibility embodied in the
character of Marianne Dashwood is represented as emphatically anti-
sociable. This is inflected in the novel through the counter-revolutionary
perception of sensibility as a form of excess which threatens social and
familial stability. John Mullan's important *Sentiment and Sociability: The
Language of Feeling in the Eighteenth Century* (1988) frames a discussion of the

relations between solipsism and sociability in the moral philosophy of Shaftesbury, Adam Smith and David Hume with a play on the title of Austen's novel and passing references to Austen. For Mullan, Austen's identification of sensibility with anti-sociability is invoked as though Austen transcends the struggles over the definition of sociability and sentiment that Mullan is describing in the book, rather than participating in the contestation of the meaning of both sociability and sentiment that characterized the 1790s. Furthermore, Mullan both endorses the conventional literary-historical narrative which reads the Austen novel as a sociable cure for sentimental excesses, and relies on an idea of sociability as a given which does not require explanation.[24] Our project, on the other hand, understands sensibility and sociability to be heavily contested terms and practices critically implicated in the cultural politics of the 1790s, with often highly unstable meanings.

The culture of sentiment is a vital part of what Jürgen Habermas in his *Structural Transformation of the Public Sphere* refers to as the 'audience-oriented privacy' which develops in the early eighteenth century.[25] Genres such as the letter and the diary, as well as the epistolary novel[26] – sentiment's primary literary genre – all participate in the particular *frissons* of this new culture of 'audience-oriented privacy', in which forms of intimacy are staged in public. A similar recognition of the public and socially oriented production of the individual underlies Niklas Luhmann's investigation of the 'codification of intimacy', and the culture of 'affect-management',[27] which is predicated upon an understanding of the individual not as an isolate, but as a socially recognized entity who is required to *perform* his or her individuality within a repertoire of codes and modes of affect. Such conventions break down any absolute distinction between the solitary and the sociable. Similarly, such a culture of 'audience-oriented privacy' suggests a complicated version of the so-called public and private distinction, which has been such a significant category of cultural, social and historical analysis since the English translation in 1989 of *The Structural Transformation of the Public Sphere*. Here the public sphere is used to account for the ways in which modern European democracies are distinguished from their centralizing absolutist predecessors, and refers to a democratic space of discursive interaction in which citizens participate in a public culture of critique. Implicated in the economic, social and cultural developments of *laissez-faire* capitalism, the public sphere is nonetheless distinct in principle from both apparatuses of state and from economic markets. The distinction between the so-called private and public spheres has been a critical distinction for cultural history, for the study of gender and for politically oriented studies of culture, and for our rubric of sociability. Within this field of debate on the public and the private, as in the social and literary history of this period, the category of sociability is engaged regularly but fleetingly, never elaborated in its own right. When sociability does make an appearance, it is often used as a term of differentiation from the political, as a site of mere play or of a purposeless form of performance or theatricality. Influential in this respect is the work of the German sociologist Georg Simmel, whose 1911 essay 'On Sociability' identifies sociability as any social interaction which exists primarily 'for its own sake and for the fascination which in its own liberation from [social] ties it diffuses'. It is a 'play-form' of interaction which need have 'no extrinsic results'. 'Sociates feel that the formation of a society as such is a value; they are driven toward this form of existence.' For Simmel, sociability's 'aim is nothing but the success of the sociable moment and, at most, a memory of it'.[28] A similar ahistoricizing construction of sociability is apparent in more recent accounts of the public sphere, for example in Jeff Weintraub's reference to: 'The approach, exemplified . . . by the work of Ariès (and other figures in social history and anthropology), which sees the "public" realm as a sphere of fluid and polymorphous sociability, and seeks to analyze the cultural and dramatic conventions that make it possible.'[29]

Weintraub's tag of 'fluid and polymorphous' underplays the complexity of the historical and social specificities that might be said to be played out in sociable practices. And Bruce Robbins's summary of Weintraub's model, in his introduction to *The Phantom Public Sphere*, emphasizes the theatricality of sociability, its 'symbolic display and theatrical self-representation [which] has little if anything to do with collective decision making or state power'.[30] Here, sociability is opposed both to political power and to rational communality; it is fully comprehended by a model of theatricality which is associated with individualistic impulses of 'display' and 'self-representation'.

Similarly problematic in this respect is Nancy Fraser's reading of the public as 'a theater in modern societies in which political participation is enacted through the medium of talk'.[31] The pure metaphoricity of this relation between the theatre and the public sphere – by which an abstracted model of the theatre and of the public sphere become mutually signifying – works to evacuate both of any real material meaning. The public sphere is not simply a theatre, and sociability is not purely dramatic. The theatre is one particular form of material site of the public and of the sociable, with specific and changing conventions of sociable behaviours. To elaborate this materiality (as against a kind of abstractedness) is one of the projects which will be conducted in this volume. Performativity and publicity are vital defining categories for the public sphere, and for understanding the social and the sociable. They are also particularly important categories in terms of the possibilities of making sexuality a central category for social theory, rather than the marginal one it often is. As Michael Warner has pointed out, 'it remains depressingly easy to speak of "social theory" and have in mind whole debates and paraprofessional networks in which sexuality figures only peripherally or not at all'.[32] Critical figures within social theory such as Jürgen Habermas, Anthony Giddens, Ernesto Laclau and Chantal Mouffe, Niklas Luhmann and Pierre Bourdieu, all elaborate important social-theory models in which sexuality is either a marginal category or an unproblematically heteronormative one. As Warner further points out, '[s]ocial theory as a quasi-institution for the past century has returned continually to the question of sexuality, but almost without recognizing why it has done so, and with an endless capacity to marginalize queer sexuality in its descriptions of the social world'.[33] The work of Judith Butler has been enormously important in theorizing performativity as a critical category both of social and textual analysis, and in relation to gender and sexuality. As Butler suggests, '[p]erformativity is neither free play nor theatrical self-representation; nor can it simply be equated with performance'. Performativity is both a self-conscious or literalized form of social performance, and a 'repetition of norms [that is] not performed by a subject [but] what enables a subject'.[34] The nuanced and theorized mode of performativity that Butler brings to the study of subjectivity, gender and sexuality in contemporary culture offers enormous scope also for the historical study of sexuality, and for the more specific theorization of social performance and sociability, enabling, for example, a theoretical inflection of that historical model of sociability associated with modernity that Peter Clark identifies as 'fashionable sociability'. Just how the idea of the performative might be used to inform a sense of a fashionable sociability that is both embodied and discursively produced is examined in Clara Tuite's chapter on the relations between style, sociability and sexuality – and what we might call a 'queer' and Tory cultural politics and sociable style – in the diaries of the landed gentry heiress, Anne Lister.

The most influential account of the public sphere, Habermas's *Structural Transformation*, also participates in social theory's view of sociability and the performative as essentialized forms of human behaviour which are distinct from political or historical engagement. For Georg Simmel, the category of conversation was important in precisely those ways in which it is 'merely' sociable, not critical: 'In purely sociable conversation, the topic is merely the indispensable medium through which the lively exchange of speech itself unfolds its attractions . . . Talk [is] its own purpose.' Here, the 'purely sociable conversation' of a phatic sociability in which '[t]alk [is] its own purpose' is distinct from a 'talk' that is geared to critique. However, in Habermas's narrative of the 'transformation' from a courtly to a public model of culture his phatic sociability – analogized to the phatic modes of performativity that characterize courtly modes of behaviour – functions as the courtly other of what bourgeois culture of critique surpasses. What distinguishes the bourgeois public sphere from an aristocratic culture, where talk is its own medium, is the way in which an urban culture begins to 'shed its dependence on the authority of the aristocratic noble hosts and to acquire that autonomy that turns conversation into criticism and *bon mots* into arguments'.[35] For Habermas, then, it is precisely the *transformation* of conversation away from the ideal form into critique that is important. But what of Simmel's 'purely sociable conversation'? Does it have another function besides being this courtly other? How is sociability critical to these modes of critique? Do we have to sacrifice the *bon mot* for the rational argument? Margaret C. Jacob's chapter, 'Sociability and the international republican conversation', engages precisely these issues in its examination of the sociable production of the democratic subject which occurred in printed periodicals, letters and drawing rooms across Europe, as well as in the colonies. This question – what function has sociability in a culture of critique? – becomes even more pressing when we move the focus, as this volume does, from the earlier half of the eighteenth century – the golden Habermasian age of the bourgeois public sphere – to the end of the century, the 1790s, when the public sphere becomes politicized. And this is a primary question of the volume: what happens to this influential Habermasian model of the public sphere, and of sociability, in the Romantic period?

Habermas does not address 'Romanticism' as such, but nonetheless traces a development whereby the late eighteenth-century public, 'England after 1750', 'grows out' of 'early institutions' such as the coffee-house. The 'medium of the press and its professional criticism . . . formed the public sphere of a rational-critical debate in the world of letters within which the subjectivity originating in the interiority of the conjugal family, by communicating with itself, attained clarity with itself'.[36] In this model the conversation within print and between writer and reader 'grows out' of, implicitly displacing or exceeding the actual conversation of the coffee-house and the kind of print culture which in Addisonian terms models itself on and evokes that 'talk'. The Habermasian public sphere as it applies to England therefore has two aspects, an early eighteenth-century phase in which cultural production is primarily conceived in sociable terms and a post-1750 phase in which the 'imagined community' of print takes precedence.[37] This phase initiates what is a movement of decline for Habermas, staged in his chapter title as 'From a Culture-Debating to a Culture-Consuming Public'. As Deidre Lynch puts it in her chapter in the volume, 'Habermas . . . narrativizes the relationship between commerce and the public sphere – outlining a process in which commercialization represents the sad, feminized sequel to public sphere conversation' (p. 214). Lynch's chapter seeks to challenge Habermas's model which links consumption and femininity against political activism, and re-examines the relations between commerce, the public sphere and women's historical agency, by considering shopping as a model of sociability and an occasion for the rational articulation of public issues.

The most influential applications of Habermas to the Romantic period in Britain have been those of Terry Eagleton and Jon Klancher, both of which engage the genre of the periodical as a paradigmatic formation of the public sphere constituted by and through print culture.[38] Klancher's *The Making of English Reading Audiences, 1790–1832* (1987) 'explains how eighteenth-century writers used the periodical to organize audiences, but also why their "widening circle" of readers perceptibly fragmented in the political crises of the 1790s'. Klancher argues that Habermas's ' "public sphere" was deeply compromised from the start, no sooner projected than transformed into an image to consume by readers who did not frequent it'.[39] Eagleton's critique of Habermas's model of the public sphere similarly notes its 'severe problems of historical periodization' and its 'nostalgic', 'idealizing' connotations. The consensual model of the public sphere was exploded from within, Eagleton argues, by the emergence in the 1790s of a counter public sphere of 'the Corresponding Societies, the radical press, Owenism, Cobbett's *Political Register* and Paine's *Rights of Man*, feminism and the Dissenting churches, a whole oppositional network of journals, clubs, pamphlets, debates and institutions'. Periodical criticism registered 'fissiparousness' rather than consensus: 'Sir Roger de Coverley and Sir Andrew Freeport were no longer drinking companions at the same club, but deadly rivals.'

Eagleton argues that the 'function of criticism' in the Romantic period moves from the press and its professional criticism to 'poetry itself' because 'the depth and span of critique which would be equal to a society wracked by political turmoil is altogether beyond the powers of criticism in its traditional sense'. The force of that criticism lay in the Romantics' elaboration of 'disinterestedness as a revolutionary force, the production of a powerful yet decentred human subject which cannot be formalized within the protocols of rational exchange'.[40] The latter phrase – 'protocols of rational exchange' – indicates but does not name Addisonian sociability as a set of rules or the particular cultural space of the coffee-house encoding an interaction of the discursive and non-discursive, material and theoretical, which Romanticism by implication had to 'grow out' of or exceed. Eagleton's more historically nuanced account of the public sphere as it applies to Britain in this period therefore basically recapitulates Habermas's two-phase model of the public sphere. However, while Habermas's 'world of letters' that subsumed the world of the coffee-house includes periodical criticism and forms such as the novel (by implication allowing a place for a writer such as Austen), Eagleton limits the function of criticism to poetry. His emphasis on the counter public sphere is also problematic insofar as he represents it as the source of a 'turmoil' which fragments and 'invades' the ideal of the consensual public sphere but which implicitly cannot function as the sphere of critique in itself – that honour is given to poetry as a reaction to the crisis which the counter public sphere had exposed.

Rather than interpreting 1790s radical culture as a counter public sphere revealing the self-interest and untenability of the earlier model of consensus between gentlemen as a synecdoche of civil society, it might be more useful to see this decade as representing an intensified politicization and expansion of the boundaries of the public sphere in which sociability as a value – encoding principles of free debate, openness, harmony between equals – is amplified by the French Revolution and its impact on Britain. The chapters in this volume by James Epstein, Margaret C. Jacob, Jon Mee and Gillian Russell address this phenomenon in a variety of ways. Eagleton's description of the counter public sphere refers to print culture in the form of Cobbett, Paine, journals and pamphlets but interestingly he situates these as part of a range of activities and institutions, such as the corresponding societies, which had a significant sociable dimension.[41] To Eagleton's definition of the counter public sphere we might add political lecturing, ultra-radical tavern culture, radical dining and the circles of Horne Tooke, William Godwin and publishers such as Joseph Johnson.[42] Such a sociable culture does not suggest a simple eclipse of the coffee-house model of the public sphere but what might be described as its apotheosis as critique. As James Epstein's chapter in this volume suggests, the political potency of the ideals of unfettered expression and mutual openness and trust expressed through companionability, the right of a man to discourse with his friends, made the coffee-house more significant than ever in the 1790s. The ludic or performative dimensions of sociability which scholars as diverse as Simmel, Sennett, Habermas and Fraser have sought to distinguish from the political or rational also came into their own in the 1790s as part of the parodic or subversive strategies of radical culture. An example is John Thelwall's 'King Chaunticlere' in *Politics for the People*, for which its publisher, Daniel Isaac Eaton, was prosecuted in 1793. The title registers its origins as a sociable performance, stating that 'King Chaunticlere' was 'An Anecdote, related by Citizen Thelwall, at the Capel Court Society', a debating club, and the text itself notes the audience response, how it produced 'applause', a fracas, and ultimately Thelwall being 'conducted away with shouts of triumph by the greater part of the company'.[43] In this case the function of criticism emerges out of Thelwall's elaboration of the sociable art of telling stories in company; the ideal of unfettered exchange (which also allows for the possibility of contention and even the unsociable) underpins his political performance.

As Paul Hamilton states in relation to Godwin's emphasis on the value of 'unreserved communication', 'such a meeting of idealism and empiricism is the political consequence of a utopian moment which Augustan literary culture had contained and postponed for so long'.[44] We might extend this 'meeting' to include 1790s radical culture as a whole. One of the aims of the counter-revolution was to close down the spaces in which texts such as 'King Chaunticlere' could be enacted and subsequently disseminated in the form of print, spaces such as the debating clubs, lecture-rooms and taverns. But more effective in many respects was the use of the spy-system to place in doubt the very principles of mutual confidence and trust on which social intercourse was based. The coffee-house was a site of surveillance, not by Mr Spectator, whose role encodes and enables a sympathetic social relationship, but by a spy masquerading as a true companion in order to betray and punish. (The counter-revolution of the 1790s accentuates what might be described as the fear of the anti-sociable – the 'Spirit of Faction' – underlying sociable relations, particularly between men, throughout the eighteenth century.)[45]

The threat posed by counter-revolution to the sociable ideals of the Enlightenment public sphere is the subject of Godwin's *Caleb Williams*. Trying to escape from his persecutor Falkland, the eponymous hero 'disappears' in multi-cultural London by taking on the identity of a Jew. The metropolis is represented as a place of alienation, loneliness, isolation and pretence (Caleb regards himself as a 'counterfeit'). In short, it is anti-sociable: 'I dared not look for the consolations of friendship; but, instead of seeking to identify myself with the joys and sorrows of others, and exchanging the delicious gifts of confidence and sympathy, was compelled to centre my thoughts and my vigilance in myself. My life was all a lie.'[46] Caleb tries to support himself financially by producing journalism in the style of 'Addison's Spectators', an index of the difference between the early eighteenth-century public sphere and its 1790s version.[47] The sociable conception of literary production, based on the ideals of free interchange as well as actual social interchange between individuals is shown to be impossible. 'Counterfeited' as a Jew, Caleb uses his servant as an intermediary between himself and his publisher, whom he never sees: his writing, moreover, is not a disinterested expression of a secure gentlemanly identity but a mode of 'subsistence', with mechanistic overtones. Caleb's imitation of *The Spectator* to earn a living anticipates Klancher's claim that the public sphere was 'no sooner projected than transformed into an image to consume by readers who did not frequent it'.[48] The allusion to *The Spectator* also suggests how the 'spectatorial ethics' of the Enlightenment public sphere, implying communality and sympathy, have mutated into spectatorship as police: ironically Williams, 'counterfeiting' as Mr Spectator, is himself being traced by Falkland's agent Gines. It suggests a suspicion of the products of a commodity print culture as inherently 'counterfeit'. Textuality itself – in its printed form – is problematic for Godwin. Print culture is counterfeiting because it is subject to the invisible workings and secret machinations by which the dominant classes can appropriate the energies and audiences of a popular form such as the handbill and redirect them to its own ends. For Godwin, only face-to-face contact unmediated by textuality can ensure free and open communication. However, at the same time he distrusted the licentiousness of the ludic, performative sociability in which men like Thelwall and Merry indulged. 'Truth', he claimed, 'could never be properly communicated in theatres and halls of assembly'. Godwin saw the elaboration of radical culture as subversive laughter, the giving way of politeness to the carnivalesque inherent in the looseness of the Addisonian model of the public sphere, as having the potential to unleash the dangerous enthusiasm of the mob: 'the conviviality of the feast may lead to the depredations of a riot'.[49]

Godwin's emphasis on the importance of conversation in *Political Justice* was an attempt to reconfigure the terms of trust inherent in the Addisonian public sphere, constructing a space that might be more secure from the attentions of government but which would also serve to monitor the dangers of conviviality's 'loose talk'. His ideal of conversation was based on his own sociable circles, a company of friends, 'private sociability', in terms of Peter Clark's categorization. In the wake of the 1790s this version of sociability came to sustain literary culture in Romantic-period Britain in ways that have been only partially recognized. Sociable practices which were hitherto not part of the coffee-house model of the public sphere as critique, practices such as home visiting, private dinners (often under the auspices of publishers) and walking, played an increasingly important part in the validation of a distinctively literary public culture. This is apparent, for example, in Benjamin Haydon's careful delineation of his dinner party in 1817 as occupying a space between the 'restraint of refined company' and 'the vulgar freedom of low' (reminiscent of Godwin's conviviality). Moreover, the 'frank, natural license' which the event exemplifies is qualitatively different from the model of literary culture as conversation represented by Boswell and Johnson: 'I am convinced that nothing in Boswell is equal to what came out from these Poets. Indeed there was no such Poets in his time.' The men at Haydon's assume public representativeness not in terms of class or social status, or even as cultural arbiters on the Addisonian or Johnsonian model, but as a company of 'Poets'. Similar occasions, lubricated by alcohol, enlivened by highly performative conversational strategies such as Charles Lamb's punning or Samuel Taylor Coleridge's monologues, formed the sociable contexts in which literary production was discussed, circulated and sometimes created. The participants also worked to constitute this form of sociability textually, particularly through periodical publication (apparent in titles such as *The Companion*, *Table Talk*, *The Round Table* or *The Ambulator*), in letters and also in poetry. As Nicholas Roe and Jeffrey Cox have shown, the cultural politics of the Hunt–Keats circle and that of the attack against them in magazines such as *Blackwood's* was at base a struggle over what Hunt described as 'sociality' – a particular idealization of friendship and group interaction as an exemplary model of social organization in general.[50] In the context of post-Waterloo Britain such an emphasis on the transcendent and redemptive capacities of the bonds of brotherhood and companionship had distinct political connotations. As Cox says: 'Against violence in society and despondency in culture [the Hunt circle] pitted sociability: the bonds between them offered the hope of a society unbound.'[51] Anne Janowitz's chapter explores such possibilities of friendship and radicalism in the movement from an 'amiable' to a 'radical' model of sociability in the Dissenting circles of Anna Laetitia Barbauld, a milieu with which Deirdre Coleman also engages in her chapter on Barbauld's friendships with Joseph Priestley and his wife Mary Priestley, seared as they were by the violence of the Birmingham riots of 1791. The theme of 'old friends' is also the topic of Julie Carlson's chapter on William Hazlitt, Thomas Holcroft and the sociability of theatre. As Carlson's chapter explores, Hazlitt, recognizing the barriers of class and gender that make the Godwinian ideal of culture as conversation impossible, nonetheless retains an attachment to the utopian possibilities of unfettered interchange between rational beings, and therefore a model of culture which is based in sociability.

The sociability of figures such as Leigh Hunt was not encompassed by the activities of his circle in the Vale of Health in Hampstead: as editor of *The Examiner* he was intimate with the coffee-houses, the taverns, theatres and indeed the prisons of the Regency.[52] Hunt attempted to categorize his periodicals in terms of these different modes of sociability, describing *The Examiner* as 'his tavern-room for politics, for political pleasantry, for criticism upon the theatres and living writers. The Indicator is his private room, his study, his retreat from public care and criticism, with the reader who chuses to accompany him.'[53] Hunt's statement, like the elaboration of 'sociality' in the poems collected in *Foliage*, demonstrates the orientation of Romantic literary culture away from the ludic, convivial and spy-infiltrated tavern world towards the 'private' and domestic sociability of *The Indicator*, a move not without its risks in both gender and class terms, insofar as it made the boundaries of the public sphere more permeable to groups such as women and servants. The elaboration of Huntian sociality, and other kinds of literary sociability in the period, courts effeminization in both positive and negative terms: hence the attacks on Hunt, Keats and Hazlitt for guilt by association with 'superannuated governesses', footmen and washerwomen.[54] These attacks were partly a sign of the way in which the reconfiguration of the public entailed in the move from the tavern room to the drawing-room inevitably entailed a reconfiguration of the gender and class dimensions of that public. The pressure exerted upon this masculine and homosocial coffee-house model of Romantic literary sociability by the active presence of women as writers and participators within the literary public sphere is examined in Judith Barbour's chapter on the relations between sociability and literary textuality in the correspondence of William Godwin. Barbour examines the fraught relations between the more recognizably 'public' and masculine homosocial model of literary sociability of the coffee-house and the more domestically oriented form of literary sociability, by tracking a 'repertoire of sociability' in Godwin's relationship with Mary Wollstonecraft, the latter mediated by sociable and quasi-sexual relations with other women writers such as Mary Hays, Elizabeth Inchbald and Amelia Alderson.

As many critics have acknowledged, Romantic-period Britain is notable as the era in which imaginative literature assumes a fully-fledged cultural and political authority. It is our contention that sociability as both fact and value, reconfigured and realigned as a result of the repressed utopian moment of the 1790s, was a crucial element in the shaping of that authority. The process of reconfiguration and realignment considerably expanded and in some cases threatened the literary public sphere by incorporating others – women, servants, the lower orders – which the paradigmatic coffee-house model of the public sphere could more easily ignore. A lesson of this for our own definition of 'Romantic sociability' is not to focus solely on the sociability of literary circles but to recognize its fluid interplay with other modes of sociability within British society as a whole. We need to be alert to the contexts in which sociability is taking place and also to its potential to be constructed discursively as a value both then and now. As editors of a volume that emanates from Australia we find it interesting to note that the part that the Antipodes had to play in the Romantic discourse of sociability was for Charles Lamb, at least, in defining the limits of sociability. In a letter to Barron Field in New South Wales he contemplates the difficulty of conducting an epistolary relationship as sociable interchange: at one point he says to Field, 'Your "now" is not my "now"; and again, your "then," is not my "then"; but my "now" may be your "then," and vice versa.'[55] Lamb later used this letter as the basis of an essay for the *London Magazine*, 'Distant Correspondents', thereby staging his lost intimacy with his friend in a more public context:

I am insensibly chatting to you as familiarly as when we used to exchange good-morrows out of our old contiguous windows, in pump-famed Hare-court in the Temple. Why did you ever leave that quiet corner? – Why did I? ... My heart is as dry as that spring sometimes proves in a thirsty August, when I revert to the space that is between us; a length of passage enough to render obsolete the phrases of our English letters before they can reach you.[56]

Lamb's letter is typical of a certain Romantic discourse of sociability in which occasions of companionship, conviviality and friendship are nostalgically commemorated by a speaker writing from a standpoint of isolation or self-willed solitude. His correspondence with Field in Australia suggests that in a period when the British sphere of influence was wider than ever before, due to global war, empire and exploration, sociable networks and communities had to be reconfigured and reimagined. A history of sociability in this period might therefore also function as an alternative history of war and empire, a topic towards which we can only gesture.

Conversation being a predominant trope of the volume, we seek to engage the topic of Romantic sociability in a spirit of open dialogue and discussion. The volume is not exhaustive or comprehensive – we are aware of too much ground to be covered in this vast field to set out to do this – but rather seeks to extend our exercise here of introducing sociability to the field of Romantic literary and cultural studies. The 1790s and the sociability of radical circles are foregrounded in the collection because of what we regard as the crucial significance of this decade and these sociable milieus in the shaping of a distinctively 'Romantic' sociability. William Hazlitt's 1820 essay, 'On the Conversation of Authors', which recognizes that conversation can no longer be universalized as a model for culture, contains a fascinating metaphor which inscribes imaginative literature as the evanescent tracings of a sociability which always exceeds its textual representation. Writing, he claims, is 'like the chalk-figures drawn on ballroom floors to be danced out before morning!'[57] In the spirit of Hazlitt's sense of the hopelessness of the task, the aim of this book is to attempt to retrace some of these figures, restoring to our sense of Romantic period culture the sociable contexts in which it was lived and inscribed.

NOTES

For full citations see Bibliography.

1 Haydon, *Diary*, vol. II, pp. 174, 175, 176.
2 Taylor, *Life*, vol. I, p. 354.
3 Hughes-Hallett, *Immortal Dinner*. Despite having the dinner as its subject, Hughes-Hallett's book does not contextualize the event in relation to Romantic and eighteenth-century sociability as a whole. See also Olney, *Haydon*, pp. 131–4; Moorman, *Wordsworth*, pp. 316–18; George, *Life*.
4 Philp, *Godwin's Political Justice*, pp. 122–9; Roe, *Culture of Dissent*, esp. chapter 4; Cox, *Poetry and Politics*; Sweet, '"Lorenzo's" Liverpool'; Swartz, '"Their

terrors"'; Chandler, *England*, pp. 282–4; Leask, 'Salons'. Relevant work also includes Aske, 'Critical Disfigurings'.

5 Borsay, *English Urban Renaissance*; Wilson, *Sense of the People*, esp. chapter 1; Money, *Experience and Identity*; Clark, *British Clubs*.

6 Hitchcock and Cohen, *English Masculinities*; Brewer, *Pleasures*; Vickery, *Gentleman's Daughter*. Similarly, the related category of 'social reputation' is used as a section to group two essays in Barker and Chalus (eds.), *Gender*.

7 Langford, 'Manners'. See also his *Englishness Identified*. See also Whyman's *Sociability and Power*, which, despite using 'sociability' in the title of the volume, does not explicitly address the term as an analytical category.

8 *TLS*, 20 March 2000, p. 10.

9 Langford, 'Manners', pp. 314, 316.

10 Magnuson, *Reading Public Romanticism*, p. 5. A similar criticism could be made of the articles in the forum 'Romanticism and its Publics', in *Studies in Romanticism* 33 (1994), pp. 523–88.

11 For the performativity of literary production in the Romantic period see Pascoe, *Romantic Theatricality*.

12 Philp, *Godwin's Political Justice*, p. 164.

13 Klein, 'Sociability, Solitude', p. 156. Klein signals the movement away from an 'emphatic' sociability to a Romantic solitude, but does not engage this at any length.

14 Clark, *British Clubs*, pp. 192, 39, 451.

15 The gendered dimension of accounts of the public sphere is addressed by Eger *et al.*, *Women, Writing*. While a number of chapters by Ellis, Kelly and Leask refer to sociability (often extensively), the use of the term as an analytical category is not explicitly foregrounded by either these writers or the editors: the term receives no entry in the index, for instance. See essays by Ellis, 'Coffee-women', Kelly, 'Bluestocking Feminism', Leask, 'Salons'. See also Cowan, 'What was Masculine about the Public Sphere?'.

16 See Borsay, *English Urban Renaissance*, pp. 150–62.

17 References to these works taken from Bond (ed.), *The Tatler*, and Bond (ed.), *The Spectator*. Subsequent references are included in parentheses in the text.

18 See Klein, *Shaftesbury*.

19 Godwin, 'Of English Style', p. 439.

20 See 'Enlightened Spectators and Classical Moralists', in Dwyer and Sher (eds.), *Sociability*, esp. p. 96.

21 Dwyer, 'The Imperative of Sociability'. On Scottish Enlightenment philosophy and sociability, see also Hont, 'The Language of Sociability and Commerce'.

22 Smith, *Theory*, p. 337.

23 Dwyer, 'Enlightened Spectators', p. 109.

24 For a further discussion of Austen, sensibility and sociability, see Tuite, *Romantic Austen*, chapter 2.

25 Habermas, *Structural Transformation*, p. 51.

26 For Habermas on these genres, see *ibid.*, pp. 48–51.
27 This is formulated in Luhmann, *Love as Passion*, p. 17.
28 Simmel, 'Sociability', pp. 50, 45, 43–4, 45.
29 Weintraub, 'The Public/Private Distinction', p. 7.
30 Robbins, *Phantom Public Sphere*, p. xiii.
31 Fraser, 'Rethinking the Public Sphere', p. 2.
32 Warner, 'Introduction', p. viii.
33 *Ibid.*, p. ix.
34 Butler, *Bodies*, p. 95.
35 Simmel, 'Sociability', p. 52; Habermas, *Structural Transformation*, p. 31.
36 *Ibid.*, p. 51.
37 The phrase 'imagined community' derives from Anderson's *Imagined Communities*, which has been a major influence on theories of the public sphere. For a challenge to Habermas's (and Anderson's) emphasis on the importance of print in constituting that public sphere see Landes, 'The Public and the Private Sphere'. Landes's argument that 'a theory of "public representations" needs to account for the culturally variant ways that humans produce and make use of multiple representations' (p. 155) can be extended to justify our focus on sociability.
38 Eagleton, *Function of Criticism*; Klancher, *Making*. More recent applications of Habermas to Romantic-period Britain include Gilmartin, *Print Politics*; McCann, *Cultural Politics*; Keen, *Crisis*; and Eger *et al.*, *Women, Writing*.
39 Klancher, *Making*, p. 15.
40 Eagleton, *Function of Criticism*, pp. 8, 36, 39, 38, 41.
41 See Thale, *Selections*, for references to toasting and songs.
42 For the sociability of ultra-radicalism see McCalman, *Radical Underworld*; for radical dining see Epstein, 'Radical Dining'; for Godwin see Philp, *Godwin's Political Justice* and St Clair, *Godwins and the Shelleys*; for Horne Tooke see Bewley, *Gentleman Radical*.
43 Butler (ed.), *Burke, Paine, Godwin*, pp. 186, 188.
44 Hamilton, 'Coleridge and Godwin', p. 46.
45 For an account of how this fear of relations between men takes its most extreme or quasi-homophobic form in our period in the paranoia of the Gothic novel, see Sedgwick's *Between Men*, esp. pp. 83–117.
46 Godwin, *Caleb Williams*, p. 265.
47 *Ibid.*, p. 268.
48 Klancher, *Making*, p. 15.
49 'Conviviality' has distinct gendered connotations, being linked with male homosociality and the enduring influence of what Peter Clark describes as 'the older cultures of honour (with its stress on masculine conviviality, heavy drinking, and reputation)': *British Clubs*, p. 450. For an account of the gender politics of the sociability of philanthropy see Lloyd, 'Pleasing Spectacles'.
50 Roe, *John Keats*; Cox, *Poetry and Politics*.
51 Cox, *Poetry and Politics*, p. 60.

52 For prison sociability see McCalman, 'Newgate'.
53 *The Indicator* 2 (20 October 1819), p. 9, quoted in Cox, *Poetry and Politics*, p. 73.
54 See Hofkosh, *Sexual Politics*.
55 Lamb, *Letters*, vol. III, p. 252.
56 Lamb, *Works*, vol. II, p. 108.
57 Hazlitt, *Complete Works*, vol. XII, p. 27.

2

Sociability and the international republican conversation

Margaret C. Jacob

The new sociability of the eighteenth century offered political awakening and personal awareness that often goes under-reported in our various histories of Enlightened practices. The fashion of sociable gatherings opened a new space, one that facilitated the discussion of public events; in some social venues, learning the arts of governance itself took centre-stage. In *Living the Enlightenment* (1991) I examined masonic practices in various European countries from the 1720s to the 1780s and drew out the political implications of lodges having become in effect 'schools' in the art of governing.[1] Of the many forms of sociability the lodges were by far the most formal and the most overtly interested in governance, in constitutions, voting, taxes, rules of decorum, etc. By contrast the scientific societies, salons, reading clubs and literary and philosophical societies seldom concerned themselves directly with rituals, systems of governance, or with policing moral behaviour. They practised self-improvement without casting it as an ethical enterprise to be directed by group pressure. Yet, however informal, being sociable offered the opportunity for group discussion that could ignite new thoughts; possibly, as I will argue at the end of this chapter, new affections and actions.

Most important, local conversations could turn remarkably international. By the 1770s, and oftentimes inspired by upheaval in the American colonies, British and Continental clubs, societies and lodges display a heightened awareness of issues defined as corruption, or as tyranny and oppression. That awareness only deepened as events in Paris unfolded in the summer of 1789. The ensuing establishment of corresponding societies in the 1790s and the radicalization of existing clubs and organizations on both sides of the Channel – even on both sides of the Atlantic – provide continuity with the developments from the 1770s onward. By the 1790s the political stakes had risen considerably, and for a time French events became the universal idiom for analysis.

There is as much continuity – as there is rupture – between Enlightened social practices and the heated fraternizing of the 1790s, between the Enlightenment as lived earlier in the clubs and salons and the political socializing of radicals and Romantics. In the last decades of the century one theme seemed to dominate the international conversation in sociable circles: the meaning and nature of democratic republics, and after 1789, the kind of personal transformation needed to create the democratic subject. Whether experienced in the privacy of the study, or amid the distraction of the lodge or the salon, all reformers participated in what I would describe as an international republican conversation. It took place in printed periodicals and private letters as well as in drawing-rooms, largely written or spoken in English or French (the former was also used by Dutch and German correspondents). For a brief time early in the 1790s the conversation transcended national identities just as it provided some consolation to the like-minded. Helen Maria Williams, the British ex-patriot and revolutionary loyalist, told her friends back home how much she missed them in these terms:

The société des amis de la Constitution at Rouen sent me a very flattering letter of thanks for my french journal, and ordered three Thousand copies of an answer I sent them, to be printed – these honors I find 'play round the head but come not to the heart,' nor do I feel any pleasure from the Democrats which at all compensates to my heart for this cruel separation from my friends at home.[2]

Decades earlier, Enlightened authors had proclaimed an international republic of letters, an imaginary place where tolerance and freedom of expression reigned supreme. As the century waned, republicanism reclaimed its overtly political associations. In places as diverse as Brussels and Buenos Aires, the call to establish a republic, with democratic associations, became the only practical direction available to the critics of both oligarchy and monarchy.[3] In Britain, foreign revolutions experienced vicariously, hence inwardly, also called forth the necessity for personal transformation as much as they demanded an alteration of corrupt electoral practices. By the 1790s radicals were asking themselves: if the democratic republic had become the ideal, how would men and women conduct themselves in such an imagined place? But before that question could be posed on either side of the Channel, disillusionment with the existing regimes had to occur.

In the second half of the century many factors – some of them ostensibly contradictory – played into the shift towards practical reform with a republican tinge. In some places in Europe the policies of Enlightened absolutists sowed unintended seeds. In the southern Netherlands during the 1750s and 1760s, the Austrian regime fostered reform wherever possible. Cobenzl's strategy was intended to break the authority of the old ruling elites, the landed nobility and the ultramontane clergy. Inevitably the Austrians wound up enlisting the assistance of minor *philosophes*, men like Pierre Rousseau and Rousset de Missy. Their religious and political views were far to the left of anything the monarchy and its ministers had in mind, but they had the requisite journalistic skills.[4] As the career of Rousset de Missy illustrates, agents enlisted to do the work of kings can sometimes turn against their paymasters. By 1747 to 1748, Rousset had evolved from being a client of the House of Orange and its British–Austrian allies – what has been called a 'Dutch Whig' – into a fomenter of revolution, a zealot in the cause of reforming a corrupt republic. By 1750 he had been sent into exile.[5] Decades after his death, in 1793 the Amsterdam masonic lodge he had founded, with its gaze cast towards Paris, celebrated the demise of 'the tyrant Tarquin and his damnable wife Tullia'. In 1795 the brothers rejoiced in the French Revolution and feasted with its invading army, addressing them as 'liberators'.[6] Most European lodges throughout the eighteenth century were loyalist, or at least conforming. But official corruption occasionally pushed them into a posture of opposition that could continue for decades.

British political life also offers other examples of official authority acting with unintended consequences and providing the impetus for radical socializing. In the 1760s the heavy-handed repression of John Wilkes by ministers of party and crown fuelled discontent that arguably would have remained more dormant had Wilkes been allowed to take his seat and rail as he pleased. The fact that the high-living Wilkes proved open to bribery in return for staying exiled in France suggests that his understanding of politics had an opportunistic side that would be harder to find a mere decade later.[7] Throughout the 1760s there were prim Real Whigs like Catharine Macaulay who found him to be 'a man guilty of so many excesses & inconsistencies'. Richard Price said that Wilkes was 'an immoral patriot'.[8] In part the heavy hand of government created this creature; the populace and the clubs that rallied round him – including masonic lodges in the Midlands – did the rest.

In arguing for a new era of radicalism that takes root in the second half of the eighteenth century I do not want to imply that during the previous decades the discontent were simply asleep at the helm. But the radicalism of the later decades has a different and more moralistic tone from the aggressive freethinking found among republicans of the generation associated with the names of Trenchard and Gordon, or Toland and Collins. Many forces contributed to this mid- to late-century shift in the political consciousness of the educated: print culture, growing urban literacy and most important, in northern and western Europe and the American colonies, the triumph of a liberal, socially focussed, more emotive version of Protestantism. By mid-century its benign face can be seen among the middling classes in Birmingham, or Philadelphia, or Geneva. In the 1770s moral pronouncements of Protestant origins about virtue and the vitality of republics flourished. Also in that decade, as James Bradley has shown, Dissenters and liberal Anglicans made common electoral causes in districts from Bristol to Manchester.[9] The clergy were vital to these electoral efforts. Even deists like Benjamin Franklin could give assistance to fellow radicals in search of a universal and socially anchored religiosity. With Franklin's aid, the cleric David Williams wrote *A liturgy on the universal principles of religion and morality* (1776). The message was zealous for the cause of reform, in language that recalled the Protestant enthusiasts of an earlier age. Not surprisingly in 1792 Williams made his way to France along with Thomas Paine.[10] Paine's pen in turn could preach in the homiletic style made famous in the colonies by clerics like Ezra Stiles and Jonathan Mayhew.[11]

The distinctively Protestant cast to the international republican conversation, however secular in its orientation, meant that the language of morality and the language of political reform became inextricably united. In addition co-religionists networked across the Atlantic. The Congregational minister in Rhode Island, Ezra Stiles, had contact with over forty like-minded radicals in England. On 30 January 1749, when Massachusetts citizens were called upon to observe and mourn the hundredth anniversary of the execution of Charles I, Mayhew rose in his pulpit to celebrate the Puritans who proclaimed that 'Britons will not be slaves'. Among the worshippers was the young Paul Revere, soon to become an ardent republican and freemason.[12] Within the setting provided by liberal Protestantism, piety, social morality and political principles fused, or as Raymond Williams puts it, 'a conclusion about personal feeling became a conclusion about society'.[13] There is a continuity provided by liberal Protestantism between the politics of Joseph Priestley in the 1770s and the democratic Unitarianism of Samuel Taylor Coleridge in the 1790s.[14]

The American colonists deserve a great deal of credit for putting the republican vocabulary forward as the passionate and international idiom of the age. But then so too do the English radicals to whom the colonists were so deeply indebted. The Club of Honest Whigs in London welcomed rebels like Franklin and Josiah Quincy, while as Pauline Maier and Bernard Bailyn have argued, English radicals from Harrington to Trenchard and Gordon and Mrs Macaulay provided the colonists with their reading matter. In the 1770s men like Arthur and William Lee of Virginia acted also as go-betweens, and in this hot-house of conversation of the like-minded it became possible for the Americans to imagine that insurrection in the mother country might also be possible.

Once again, as with the clandestine literature of the early century, the raising of the rhetorical and political temperature could not be imagined without the services of publishers like Edward and Charles Dilly, James Ridgway and Daniel Isaac Eaton.[15] To discuss the motives of such publishers is beside the point. What is important is the appearance in Western publishing, as early as the seventeenth century, of publishers with a subversive 'voice': the so-called 'Pierre Marteau of Cologne' published after 1660 from The Netherlands, but in French, and produced a string of books against absolutism. Edmund Curll in London during the reign of Anne specialized in the scandalous and irreverent while a full half century later, Marc Michel Rey in Amsterdam published Rousseau and d'Holbach. In Britain the Dillys, et al. issued dozens of texts in support of the American revolution or constitutional reform. The political implications of print culture acquire a clearer meaning when we can see certain presses used systematically for specific types of largely unacceptable literature. Would there have been a High Enlightenment in Paris if Rey had not been plying his trade in Amsterdam? He gave the world Rousseau along with a host of anonymous books, previously clandestine, once in manuscript only.

Thus in the 1760s and 1770s, thanks to Rey, there was Rousseau. The sources of his appeal were multiple and varied. Emphasis needs to be placed upon the moralizing quality of his political idealism and its compatibility with the liberal Protestantism I have just described. In 1762, at its publication, the *Social Contract* joined an already inaugurated, international and largely abstract conversation, much of it quite heated, about the nature of the best form of government, about republics, or the possibilities for reform as promoted by Enlightened 'despots'. Rousseau's debt to classical republican thought was obvious; indeed he saw Geneva as a once pure republic that had been corrupted by its elite.

What is most important about Rousseau's vision, I would suggest, is the fact that unlike the earlier freethinkers, or for that matter Wilkes, Rousseau entertained no ribald hostility to religion *per se*. Indeed his youth had been saturated in a newer and far more liberal brand of Calvinism current in Geneva at the time. As a result both Catholics and Protestants all over Europe could read him in preference to many of the other, far more irreligious philosophes.[16] In Italy Cosimo Amidei and Carlantonio Pilati, inspired by Rousseau, came to see that the work of reform had to be Europe-wide; it was not simply an Italian problem. Rousseau's universalist emphasis on purity and virtue, on the goodness of man, resonated especially well with the liberal Protestantism. Then too it appealed to freemasons, who had long used republican and moralizing language to describe the constitutionally imposed discipline and the equalitarian ideals of a lodge. As an Amsterdam masonic orator put it in 1766, 'The main reason why freemasonry was so well received among the enlightened: the Natural state of humanity is therein restored perfectly, no disguise will be tolerated.'[17] The transparency of affect that enabled the Enlightened to see through the disguise created by effete luxury and politeness lay at the heart of Rousseau's message. He made republicans seem to be naturally, if vaguely religious. Piety turned outwards, towards the social or towards nature, became remarkably fashionable. Rousseau deserves considerable credit for the intense moralizing about republics commonplace by the 1770s, and he popularized the prudish republicanism so beloved by Anglo-American men and women of Dissenting background.

Rousseau also generated ferocious critics. The *Parlement* of Paris, the main French judicial body, condemned the *Social Contract* in 1762, and even some of Rousseau's closest friends backed away from him. Yet, arguably, his novels were far more subversive than his technical treatise on the theory of political liberty. Written for a general audience, *La nouvelle Héloise* and *Emile* gloried in the fictional search for transparency between men and women, for the absence of duplicity and formal coldness. Each advocated self-discipline within the framework of sentiment and a longing to return to nature. Despite the obvious piety of Richardson, novels had always been suspect among the conservative. By the 1790s they came to blame Rousseau for fomenting the French Revolution. Edmund Burke saw novels as part of the rot that had undermined authority. He declared that they were 'part of a systematic scheme by Rousseau to destroy all social and family relationships, thus enabling the French revolutionaries to take power'.[18] Burke was nothing if not succinct. By 1789 the very name, Rousseau, had come to symbolize subversion.

By the 1770s the political stakes for European reformers seemed to rise by the year. In France the courts or *parlements* thwarted the crown and prevented fiscal reform. They revealed the impotence of the monarchy to effect meaningful reform. In Sweden royal authority was reasserted against the claims of the English-style parliament. In the same decade the Polish Commonwealth was dismantled by its imperialist neighbours, and in 1776 no one could say how the tumultuous events in the American colonies would progress. In the German-speaking lands the secret Illuminati rose to prominence, and the authorities responded with fury. Throughout the West everything political took on a new urgency. Letters and people traversed the Atlantic and the Channel with reports of new defeats or victories.

None of this radicalism, or simply the new political awareness, can be explained without a nod towards sociability and print culture. In the German-speaking lands absolutist princes ruled in every principality with the exception of a few free cities. Yet in both Germany and Austria by the last quarter of the eighteenth century the new public sphere was plainly visible. Journals, books and newspapers – although censured – flourished. At the same time, probably close to 300 masonic lodges had sprung up, found in almost every medium-sized town.[19] Although they often enjoyed the sponsorship of kings like Frederick the Great of Prussia, the lodges were nonetheless controversial, especially in Catholic areas. In general the German lodges were deeply hierarchical, far more so than their counterparts further to the west. The association of German freemasonry with the absolutist monarchy of Frederick did not, however, make the lodges off-bounds for Enlightened intellectuals like the young poet Goethe, the renegade Lutheran Lessing, and the secular, but devout Jew, Moses Mendelssohn.

Many others in Germany found the goals of freemasonry to be inspirational. By the 1780s German freemasonry had spawned a radical offshoot, the famous (or infamous) Illuminati. Founded by Adam Weishaupt (born 1748), a twenty-eight-year-old professor, the League of the Illuminati was strongest in Munich. Its leaders wanted to use it as a vehicle for the reform of freemasonry and then to extend its influence throughout Germany. At the height of its fame the League had no more than 600 members, of whom the majority were court and administrative officials, clergymen and military officers. They swore an oath to such vagaries as: 'The order of the day is to put an end to the machinations of the purveyors of injustice.'[20] They too had been deeply impressed by the American Revolution.

The Illuminati of the 1780s provided an excuse. The danger they supposedly posed enabled the authorities in every Continental European country to conjure up the fear of subversion and to crack down on the supporters of Enlightenment. In the Austrian kingdom the supposedly Enlightened, but worried, Joseph II closed down all but one masonic lodge in every town, and the surviving one had to be approved by the Grand Lodge in Vienna or Brussels. In Germany men were arrested as Illuminati just on the suspicion of membership. In response ordinary freemasons defended themselves by noting that their only offence had been that they welcomed men of all religions, and even then they claimed to be (on the whole) devout Christians.[21] From this distance we might ask, had the Continental Enlightenment devolved into a collection of men playing at a private game of secrecy where posturing passed for political engagement? If a reformer were to answer 'yes' to that question, the antidote for the ailment might be imagined to lie across the Channel, in the model of parliamentary government, however corrupt and oligarchic.

Decades before the conservative reaction of the 1790s in Britain the creation of a reform parliament preoccupied sections of the urban middle class. In the throes of Anglophilia a young Frenchman, Jean Paul Marat, decided to see for himself how 'liberty' fared in the land of its birth. Informed by Voltairean idealism, Marat witnessed political agitation at first hand in England during the 1760s and early 1770s – during the so-called 'Wilkes and Liberty' movement. Wilkes and his followers had demanded reforms in the system of elections. Marat saw Wilkes imprisoned on charges that his supporters found to have been invented for the occasion. Like so many others, Marat too turned to reading Rousseau to find out why liberty, even in Britain, possessed so many enemies. He had graduated from Voltaire and advanced to republicanism and Rousseau. Then Marat took up his own pen and produced a devastating attack on the power of princes, on oppression and slavery, *Chains of Slavery* (1774).[22] We may only wonder if he discussed its contents with his masonic brethren when he turned up in Amsterdam and signed the visitors' book of Rousset de Missy's original lodge.

Marat, and later Paine, fittingly captured the mood among British liberals and radicals. By the 1780s they had made reform, in particular the abolition of the African slave trade, a live subject for debate. In the movement against slavery, secular ideas associated with the Enlightenment were complemented, indeed augmented, by religious fervour of a Quaker and Methodist variety.[23] And there was no shortage of stories in print about the conditions of the slave trade and the brutality of the plantation system. Some were written by men who had been slaves. The international republican conversation could focus on concrete domestic issues like the nature of parliamentary representation, but it could also think globally, and attack the human misery inflicted by European imperial expansion.

In the land of its birth, the Enlightenment returned to England with renewed vigour, largely under the impact of the American Revolution. The cause of heterodoxy and reform was taken up in the 1770s and 1780s by the Dissenting Unitarian minister, Joseph Priestley. To a man and woman – the feminist Mary Wollstonecraft came out of the same liberal Protestant circles – Dissenters (non-Anglican Protestants) tended to support the American Revolution, just as they had supported the parliamentary rebel John Wilkes. Once again, the link was forged between political and intellectual radicalism. Just when the Church of England thought it had put the twin genies of radicalism and heresy back in the bottle, 'the infidel spirit of the times' – as the Dean of Canterbury put it – wafted out again.[24] From his grave, Hume (died 1776) even got into the fray as his executors saw to it that his deistic religious views finally made their way into print.

In France reading and travel had convinced Denis Diderot of the injustice and corruption of the society in which he was born and had to live. He deplored European colonialism, and in a silent collaboration with the Abbé Raynal, a bestseller was born: *Histoire philosophique et politique des établissements et du commerce des Européens dans les deux Indes (Philosophical and Political History of the European Establishments and Trade in the Two Indies)*, 1770, enlarged in 1774, with many subsequent editions. Along with works by Marat and others, the book addressed the moral issue raised by European hegemony as it never had been raised before. Inexorably, Diderot was moving in the direction of believing in democracy – for all the peoples of the world. Although their friendship had died in bitterness many decades previously, Diderot and Rousseau had begun to walk the same path in their political theory. Rousseau held the torch.

By the 1780s the new American republic, no longer a colony, rejoined the international conversation at the heart of the Enlightenment. One northern American state after the other – with New Jersey the last in 1804 – abolished slavery within its domain. Southern plantation owners had to take care when they ventured north with their human chattel in tow. This was the first time a legislative body anywhere in the world had turned its back on centuries of Western (and non-Western) practice. The effect on European liberals was inspirational. In Belfast the republican newspaper of the 1790s, *The Northern Star*, denounced the attack on the Unitarian and supporter of the French Revolution, Joseph Priestley. A pro-king, pro-church mob in Birmingham had burned down his home and laboratory. In the mind of the Irish radicals Negro slavery stood as yet another example of the British imperial oppression that Priestley had experienced.[25] For a brief moment, from Philadelphia to Berlin, it seemed as if a consensus had formed about a set of universal principles, of inalienable human rights upon which all Enlightened people could agree. As late as 1815 the British supporter of the French Revolution, Helen Maria Williams, could fantasize about going to America where she would 'pass my days in composing [visions?] in praise of liberty'.[26]

By no means were all the voices associated with Enlightened opinion articulate on the subject of slavery. Hume, as we know, had been plainly racist in his assumptions about non-Western peoples. When British and French *émigré* radicals of the 1790s went to the new American republic quite a few succumbed to the lure of slave-owning once it became possible for them legally to own other men and women. In the French Caribbean, writers of mixed racial ancestry like Moreau de Saint-Méry, who came to hold high office in the colonies, knew enough about the Enlightenment that they could identify with its scientific spirit and detail the abuses of the mercantilist and slave system. But they never pulled away from the entire institution and its injustices. In the end they offered more criticisms of Versailles than they did of the planters.[27] A Spanish Jesuit, Francisco Javier Clavigero attempted to write the history of Mexico from an Enlightened perspective. His *Historia Antigua de México* (1781–2) rejected diabolical intervention and addressed Mexican civilization by reference to its own assumptions. Yet in the end Clavigero could not embrace the secular and moral vision of the Enlightenment. He argued that the Mexicans must accept their conquest and virtual enslavement as a punishment for their sins.[28]

Decisively, slavery came on to the international agenda by the 1780s. There were good reasons for this late-century disaffection. The same century that produced the Enlightenment witnessed a hardening of slave laws and institutions, particularly in the British and French colonies. Plantation life had become socially respectable for the often-absent owners who reaped its benefits. In the British West Indies killing a slave was punishable only with a fine. In the French colonies the repressive *Code Noir* had been promulgated by Louis XIV in 1685, the same year that he began the persecution of French Protestants. In the course of the eighteenth century the situation of the slaves in the French colonies had actually worsened, as more and more plantations were established and the black population came to vastly outnumber their white overseers, who ruled with increasing harshness. And slavery, as well as racial stereotyping, had plenty of apologists.[29] Yet remarkably, given the bias against Africans found in much of the travel literature, around 1780 an emotional sea-change occurred in literate European circles.

No entirely adequate account has been offered for the emotional shift against slavery, but one piece in the puzzle must be the writings and testimonies given by blacks themselves. Men like Ignatius Sancho and Olaudah Equiano, both freed slaves who made their way to England, raised their voices to oppose the slave system. Many abolitionists entertained stereotypes about blacks, about the lethargy imagined as the inevitable result of the African heat. Yet they also hated slavery, and inspired first by the American revolution – then by the French – they launched a moral crusade that slowly led to victory. At the same time a disillusionment with the amateurish and stereotypical quality of travel literature caused reformers to demand a more exacting and scientific account of the world's peoples.[30] Some of the new accounts would harden racial categories, others would seek to write from the inside, from the values and assumptions of distant and foreign peoples.

By 1789 political events within Europe, and globally, were to make slavery a burning issue. More than any other event in Western history the French Revolution galvanized international opinion against slavery and around the issue of universal human rights.[31] Helen Maria Williams effortlessly saw the linkage, 'respecting the rights of man in Europe we shall always agree in wishing that a portion of those same rights were extended to Africa'.[32] By 1791 even the translator of a vast collection of Moslem law was shocked by how much legal energy had been spent in Moslem countries defining slavery and the rights of owners.[33] Street-corner lecturers harangued London and provincial audiences about the evils of the slave trade, and Quakers and Methodists prayed in their chapels for the victims of enslavement.

Historians have long debated the exact relationship between the Enlightenment and the French Revolution. In the minds of contemporaries, supporters as well as opponents of the Revolution, the Enlightenment had laid the groundwork for its most important ideas and agendas. Within two years of its outbreak in 1789, the Revolution had galvanized a radical movement in the British Isles, in Haiti, and finally in Ireland and Egypt. The Haitian revolution of slaves against their French masters forced the French revolutionaries back in Paris to confront the meaning of the principles they had decreed for themselves. In 1794 the National Assembly abolished slavery and the slave trade in the French colonies. Napoleon would reinstitute it, and the issue remained fraught until finally in 1833 Britain abolished slavery in its colonies. In 1848 a new revolution in France reinstated the principles of the French Revolution with regard to slavery. Around the issue of human rights in general, and slavery in particular, the links between the Enlightenment and the highest ideals articulated during the French Revolution seem incontrovertible.[34]

A British radical who had gone to Paris in 1792, James Watt, Jr – the son of the famous perfecter of the steam engine – wrote to his perplexed father in Birmingham and tied the warp of the Enlightenment to the woof of revolution:

My hatred is not against individual kings, but against the system of Royalty, for I think kings in general far less blameable than the people that submit to them. The abolition of that source of all our evils in this country is a more deadly blow to the prejudices of mankind, than would be the destruction of all the monarchs of Europe ... The principles upon which their thrones were founded are now disavowed by an Enlightened age and mankind awakened from their lethargy are everywhere shaking off a system founded upon force and Priestcraft.

The young James had cast his lot with the Jacobins, and in his letters he took to lecturing his long-suffering father on the evils of monarchy, and on his own hatred for the 'crimes of tyrants'.[35] When he arrived in Paris in March 1792 James Jr brought greetings from the Manchester Constitutional Society to the Mayor of Paris, and Robespierre presented him and his travelling companion, Thomas Cooper, to the Jacobin society. With Watt and Cooper went a letter from Thomas Walker that 'hinted at the imminent collapse of the British monarchy and aristocratic society'.[36] Enthused by the writings of Thomas Paine, and by the heady exaltation of a revolution in full throttle, Cooper would remember those months as the happiest of his life.[37] Fraternizing had become so intense – in Paris but also in Manchester – that lives came to be shaped by it.

Watt's youthful reading had been heavily laden with works by the *philosophes* and with the latest scientific writing. His politics and his books complemented one another, and we would be hard pressed to say which had come first. In addition, Watt, like so many followers of Enlightened ideas in England, had joined one of the many 'corresponding societies' that had sprung up after 1789. They sought to offer moral support to the revolutionaries in Paris, and to import their reformist spirit. Decades earlier, Watt's father had been a pivotal figure in the Lunar Society of

Birmingham, one of the most famous and liberal literary-philosophical societies of the 1770s. During the 1790s the corresponding societies in England and the Jacobin clubs in France built upon the foundations of civic and social life created in the course of the eighteenth century. In every major American and European city, civil society expanded along with literacy, and even more books were published. If one single thread united most of these new disparate, unconnected, even informal groups, it was their interest in utility, in the practical, in progress and in intense self-improvement.

Perhaps most typical were the societies of 'usefulness', *Het Nut*, as each was called in town after town in the Dutch Republic. They channelled discontent, inspired charitable efforts, built libraries, sponsored lectures, published weekly journals and in general cast a cold eye on a situation about which there was considerable general agreement: the Dutch Republic had gone into decline and was in need of reform. A participant in the international republican conversation, the Baron Van der Capellen, emerged as a leader among the Dutch critics of the *stadholderate*. In the early 1780s a misguided war with Britain over commercial rights exposed the sad condition of the Republic's army and navy. Van der Capellen seized on these failings and the need for truly representative institutions in the Republic. The Estates General that met in The Hague represented each province, not the general population, and it was dominated by old families drawn from local elites, the so-called regents. Van der Capellen privately wrote to Benjamin Franklin about his personal 'right to vote' in the assembly of the various Dutch states. In an address *To the Netherlands People* (1781) – soon translated into French, German, and English – Van der Capellen proclaimed himself the prophet who would lead his people out of bondage and 'make them free'.[38] Predictably the new societies to promote usefulness took up Van der Capellen's call. So too did the leading masonic lodge of Amsterdam where Rousset and then Marat had fraternized.

The temperature of politics in the 1790s everywhere in Western Europe made usefulness the least of all the evils now imagined by the authorities in church and state. Spying became the order of the day as did sexual innuendo aimed particularly at the radical clubs. Fraternizing elicited paranoia about the homoerotic, and while sociability had been suspect before, in the 1790s conservatives unleashed an unprecedented torrent of abuse. Yet no side entirely cornered the market on sexual taunts. In Sheffield in 1793 the corresponding society wrote to its counterpart in Edinburgh and claimed that 'male prostitutes' and 'venal hirelings', the sycophants of courts, 'would fell their country and its liberties for a mess of potage' and they have 'gone so far as to sap and destroy every prop and pillar' supporting the constitution.[39] But in the genre of print, as opposed to private conversation, the Tories and the opponents of the French Revolution deserve the prize for viciousness and sexual innuendo, much of it anonymous. Take the following poem aimed at the free-living Charles James Fox and the Whigs:

> Thus *Satan* leads, as artfully, his Clan,
> As F [o]x, not *Guy Faux*, but as *dark* a man,
> Leads his *thin'd pack*, whipp'd in by Sh [e]r[ida]n –
> A Clan, so *naked*, that 'twas apt enough,
> E'en then to've stiled the corps – not Blue – but Buff;
> For tho' the *Diaboliads* cou'd make Speeches,
> They, doubtless, had of old – not any *Breeches*.
> How soon our MODERN DIABOLIADS' *STATE*
> May lit'rally be *in buff*, is known to Fate;
> Tho'thus much speak already their sad faces,
> From their *long fasting*, from a *want of Places*,
> Eyes sunk, with haggard looks, and shrivell'd skin,
> While keen vexation gnaws their hearts within[40]

The intimation of sexual deviance, nasty though it is, may not have been entirely without foundation. By this I mean it is possible to see in the circles of radicals and Romantics that emerge in the 1790s new forms of personal experimentation, the attempt to create new genres of affect and freedom. Clubs of male reformers took up the feminist cause and embraced Wollstonecraft as well as the women revolutionaries in France.[41] Irish republicans like Mary Ann McCracken thought that 'the present Era will produce some women of sufficient talents to inspire the rest with genuine love of Liberty . . . I think the reign of prejudice is nearly at an end.'[42] At the same moment William Blake sang of free love between the sexes.[43] Even animals had their moment of liberation with the British radical, John Oswald, raising the issue of humane treatment.[44] And as if this sort of theorizing were not enough, the pied piper of the radical and Romantic left, William Godwin, gave the world a reasoned argument against marriage and monogamy and in favour of complete freedom in matters sexual.[45]

In Whig lives as lived, the meaning of this revolt against authority could become visible and concrete. By 1800 the King of Clubs in London constituted the fashionable club for Whig reformers, and into the circle moved Tom Wedgwood, Gregory Watt (the son of James), James

Mackintosh (after 1803 Sir James), the Smith brothers and the Scottish poet, Thomas Campbell. Southey, Coleridge, Humphry Davy, James and John Tobin – overlapping with Gregory Watt – made yet another related circle.[46] Among the members of these loose clubs or associations, many like Mackintosh became celebrated Whigs while the Reverend Sydney Smith sealed his credentials by being one of the founders of the *Edinburgh Review* and a major contributor to it. He too had been deeply influenced by the principles of the French Revolution about which he had learned, he said, in 1798.[47] Smith's life exemplified the intense personal meaning of revolutions lived vicariously, and the importance of being able to consort with like-minded associates.

Smith believed that in both fiction and non-fiction philosophers like Godwin had been 'impelled and directed' by the progress of the Revolution: 'The fearful convulsion ... agitated the world of politics and of morals ... burst open the secret springs of imagination and of thought ... roused [Godwin] not into action but into thought.' Smith said that the effect upon readers like himself was transformative: 'passions which have not usually been thought worthy to agitate the soul, now first seem to have their most ardent beatings, and their tumultuous joys'.[48] If Smith knew joy and likened it to the effects of the French Revolution, he came to happiness by a most circuitous route. In contrast to the liberty he found in Godwin, Smith experienced what he called 'the tyranny, trouble and folly' of his own father.[49] They had poisonous relations complicated by tension about money and ideology, with the freethinking Smith even defending the right to commit suicide. Eventually his father told him in 1797 to go away and never darken his door.[50]

Father and son sputtered on for years in this vein. Significantly, when Smith and his wife finally established a family of their own they raised their children in an atmosphere of such freedom that one governess after the other fled in despair. He 'purposely indulged' his own children in 'the liberty [which will] accustom a young man gradually to be his own master'. They saw their marriage as companionate and sought to set a very different emotional tone in the household from that which Smith had known as a child.[51] In the 1790s, even the devout Anglican Anna Maria Larpent thought that what ailed the French and their revolution could be analyzed in terms of men and women there being too distant one from the other.[52] Radicals like the Smiths, Romantics like Wordsworth and Coleridge, dreamed of eliminating personal distance, of finding emotional transparency.

Same-sex experimentation, as well as intense friendships between the sexes, characterized these circles of radicals and Romantics. The Wordsworth–Dorothy Wordsworth–Coleridge triangle, for example, has long defied any sort of simple characterization. To say that each in his or her way was in love with the other, while leaving open the nature of that love, is probably the best that anyone at this distance can do.[53] Southey was also smitten by his male friends, particularly Coleridge. Long after they had abandoned their plan to migrate to Pennsylvania and join Priestley – there to set up a utopian community on the egalitarian principles of pantisocracy – Southey longed for Coleridge's company: 'the man, to whom, in all the ups and downs of six years, my heart has clung with most affection, despite even its own efforts'.[54]

At the root of the utopian and (*avant la lettre*) socialist scheme stood the passionate figure of George Dyer. More than the other utopians who wanted to find personal and gender equality in Pennsylvania, Dyer possessed a deep concern for the poor and disadvantaged. For a time the circle of Dyer, Southey, Wordsworth and Coleridge became intensely involved one with the other. Dyer knew poverty first-hand, having seen his father committed to the poorhouse.[55] He wrote and spoke about social conditions for much of his life. Yet Dyer also shared in the experimentally erotic milieu of the Romantics. In 1800 he suppressed a book of poetry that contains these lines addressed to Robert Anderson: 'But, no, my friend: I read thy candid page, / . . . / Oh! May I view again with ravish's sight, / As when with thee, Anderson, I stray'd, / And all the wonder-varying scene survey'd.'[56] Dyer also knew his Anacreon well, and the ancient poet had long been associated with same-sex intimacy.[57] A barely suppressed eroticism infused Dyer's memories of his youthful Cambridge days. In his *Ode To the Cam* the picture evokes 'nature's living power' and the 'new-born joys' of 'bard, the lover, and the jocund swain'. Yet it also makes clear that 'All must be left, tho' friendly to the Muse; / And man, poor man, lie down in cheerless gloom.'

The vision shared by Dyer and his circle of radical Romantics held them together for a time in London and the Lake District, all bound by a labile affection. The circle endorsed the philosophic and revolutionary traditions of the seventeenth century. Dyer entered 'in converse sweet with Locke, immortal sage; / So too by Cam with him, whose bosom glow'd / With thy pure raptures, and the Muse's rage' [i.e. Milton]. Algernon Sidney was also invoked by them as they cursed 'those murd'rers of the world', the Austrians and the Prussians. Whether in alliance with the French revolutionaries, or with the Poles led by Kosciusko, Dyer and his friends wooed 'Thee, Liberty'.[58]

Other seekers were drawn to the Romantic flame, and Tom Wedgwood, the son of the famous potter, became Coleridge's bosom companion. They both shared an addiction to opium, and aided by Coleridge, the young Wedgwood and possibly his brother also tried a form of hemp leaves known as 'bang'.[59] Tom had early on developed a disdain for 'the pleasures of the family & having a great disgust to large mixed company'.[60] After a series of male companions, many of them also associated with the King of Clubs,[61] the young Wedgwood succumbed to his addictions. Telling his brother in 1804 that his 'present sufferings [are] too intolerable & they are beyond all alleviation . . . my pains & extreme feebleness & depression are now unceasing', Tom was dead by the summer of 1805.[62] His youthful dalliance with Godwin and radicalism, and with science, did not save him from the depression that stalked the Wedgwood family. It is little wonder that they also sought liberty in their personal lives, emboldened again by their shared intimacies with poets and philosophers. By 1800 the politics found amid the sociability of republicans and radicals had become intensely personal. Decades of sociability, politics observed or lived, had loosened old restraints and thrown up new cautions. In the midst of the Terror, Helen Maria Williams said that 'the scenes which have lately been acting at Paris . . . have . . . been such that scarcely can my conviction that this temporary evil will produce permanent good at all reconcile my mind to that profusion of blood, that dismal waste of life of which I have been witness'.[63] Living on the edge of a more democratic era could bring exhilaration as well as fear and foreboding.

NOTES

For full citations see Bibliography.
1 Jacob, *Living*.
2 Bloom and Bloom (eds.), *Piozzi Letters*, vol. I, p. 371.
3 On the Spanish colonies and rebellion in the late eighteenth century see McFarlane, 'Identity'.
4 De Boom, *Les Ministres*.
5 See Jacob, *Radical Enlightenment*.
6 The Library of the Grand Lodge of The Netherlands, The Hague, MS 41:10 for 1795 and discussed in Jacob, 'Radicalism', pp. 233, 234.
7 Thomas, *Wilkes*, p. 63.
8 Hill, *Republican Virago*, pp. 56, 57.

9 Bradley, *Religion*.
10 Hans, *New Trends*, pp. 164–5.
11 Fruchtman, *Paine*, p. 10.
12 Triber, *True Republican*, p. 20.
13 Williams, *Culture*, p. 30.
14 Cf. Ryan, *Romantic Reformation*.
15 Davis, '"That Odious"'.
16 See Van Kley, *Religious Origins*, pp. 296–7.
17 The Library of the Grand Lodge, The Hague, MS 41:8, fo. 26.
18 *The Anti-Jacobin*, quoted in Barker-Benfield, *Culture of Sensibility*, p. 260.
19 See Dülmen, *Society*.
20 See Abbott (ed.), *Fictions*, and Neugebauer-Wölk, *Esoterische Bünde*.
21 [Anon] *Freymaureren*.
22 See Conner, *Marat*, pp. 23–4.
23 Turner, 'Limits'.
24 Aston, 'Horne'.
25 *Northern Star*, Belfast, 25 April 1792, 'The Negroe's Complaint'.
26 Huntington Library, MS BN 454, 16 June 1815, Helen M. Williams to her friend in America, Ruth Baldwin Barlow.
27 Lewis, *Main Currents*, pp. 131–3.
28 See Cervantes, *Devil*, pp. 153–4.
29 Goveia, *West Indian*, pp. 20–1, pp. 44–5.
30 Marshall and Williams, *Great Map*, pp. 300–1.
31 See Hunt (ed.), *French Revolution*. Cf. Durey, *Transatlantic*, pp. 282–5.
32 John Rylands Library, Manchester, MS 570, 26 February 1792, to Mrs Piozzi.
33 Ali Ibn Abi Bakr, Burhan al-Din, al-Marghinani, *The Hedàya*, pp. xlii–xliii.
34 Hunt (ed.), *French Revolution*.
35 Birmingham City Library, MS letter written from Nantes, 17 October 1792, James Watt Jr to his father, JWP, w/6.
36 I quote Durey, *Transatlantic Radicals*, p. 34, who is paraphrasing Godwin. The groundbreaking work on James Watt, Jr was done by Robinson, 'English Jacobin'. Cf. Erdman, *Commerce*, pp. 50–5.
37 Durey, *Transatlantic Radicals*, p. 33.
38 Capellen, *Brieven*, pp. 387–8.
39 *The First and Second Report*, p. 166.
40 [Anon], *Secession*.
41 See *The Cabinet*.
42 McNeill, *McCracken*, p. 127, quoting a letter of 16 March 1797.
43 Blake, *Sexes*.
44 Oswald, *Cry*.
45 Godwin, *An Enquiry*, vol. II, pp. 844–51.
46 Paris, *Davy*, p. 62. William Clayfield was also in this circle.
47 Smith, *Works*, preface. On the club see Litchfield, *Wedgwood*, p. 97. On conversations in this circle see Smith (ed.), *Letters*, vol. I, p. 63; letter of June 1801.
48 Smith, *Works*, vol. III, p. 16, from the *New Monthly Magazine*.

49 Smith (ed.), *Letters*, vol. I, p. 103, letter of April 1805 to Francis Jeffrey.

50 Huntington Library, Sydney Smith MSS, HM 30430, 26 June 1796 to his father, Robert Smith, wanting money, and it is clear there has been an estrangement: 'I hope my dr father you will do me the favor of writing to me – as it will be a proof that you begin to feel a returning regard for me.' See also HM 30431, 9 July 1796; HM 30433, 5 November 1797, Smith to his brother Bobus, saying that his father has told him to go away and stay away; 25 November 1797 to his father: 'I hope the conversation upon suicide which pass'd between us, has produced no other unpleasant sensation in your mind than the want of respect to you, of which I am sorry to say, you have a right to accuse me.' He says that they have quarrelled about metaphysical 'nonsense'. HM 30449, from Edinburgh, 25 December 1801.

51 Smith (ed.), *Letters*, vol. I, p. 69, letter to Mrs Beach, wife of his patron, March 1802.

52 Huntington Library, HM 31201, Anna Maria Larpent's diary, entry for 2 December 1796, in which she claims that French men and women are too separate and sees Montaigne as the culprit.

53 Certainly contemporaries were made uneasy by the attachment between Wordsworth and Coleridge; British Library MSS ADD 35345, Josiah Wedgwood, Jr to Tom Poole, 1799 February 1, hoping that Wordsworth and Coleridge will remain separated; Coleridge will benefit from 'mixed society'.

54 Huntington Library, HM 4829, 27 July 1800, Southey to William Taylor.

55 New York Public Library, uncatalogued Dyer letter, no. 101, 5 February, n.d.

56 Dyer, *Poems*, Preface, vol. I, p. xxxvii, 'the principles of freedom are too sacred, to be surrendered to trifles'; 'Ode addressed to Dr Robert Anderson', vol. II, p. 91. The Huntington Library's copy belonged to Southey.

57 Dyer, *Poems*, vol. I, p. 17. My thanks to Bernie Frischer on matters classical and Anacreon.

58 *Ibid.*, pp. 44–5, *Ode on Liberty: Written on a Public Anniversary*, and at the time of the Polish uprising.

59 Keele University, Wedgwood MSS, W/M 1112, fo. 159 Coleridge to Wedgwood (possibly Josiah), 17 February 1803; on Tom's addictions see same call number, 24 June 1804, Tom to Josiah, Jr; on the family's reserve see Sarah to Tom, 3 July 1804, her letter to him attributed 'to the inveterate bad habit of not expressing our feelings which so many of our family have & I amongst the rest . . . my taciturnity has really been owing partly to the family infirmity'.

60 Keele University, Wedgwood MS W/M21, 27 April 1790, Tom to his brother, Josiah Jr, on his going off to live with John Leslie.

61 Keele University, Wedgwood MS W/M21, same to same, 18 November 1800 and 1 April 1802, 'I am just going to the King of Clubs.'

62 *Ibid.*, letter of 12 November 1804, same to same, on his suffering; letter of condolence, 16 July 1805, Thomas Campbell to Josiah, Jr.

63 John Rylands Library, Manchester, MS 570, 4 September 1794 to Mrs Piozzi.

3

'Equality and No King': sociability and sedition: the case of John Frost

James Epstein

On the evening of 6 November 1792, John Frost dined at the tavern above the Percy coffee-house in Marylebone. As he left the building through the coffee-house, an acquaintance who knew Frost as a commissioner of the watching and lighting of streets engaged him in conversation about the situation in France from where Frost had recently returned. Frost responded by proclaiming for all to hear, 'I am for equality; I can see no reason why man should not be upon a footing with another; it is every man's birthright.' He defended this proposition when challenged by various persons, adding when pressed that by 'equality' he meant 'no kings'. Asked specifically if he meant no king 'in this country', he responded, 'Yes, no king, the constitution of this country is a bad one'. It was this encounter that took Frost from a site of sociability, dining and conversation to King's Bench and eventually to Newgate Prison – sites of law, 'justice', majesty and punishment.[1] Frost's case provides a point of departure for thinking about the nexus among sites of sociability, politics and law, and the behaviour and language appropriate to each. His case also marks the historical moment at which the boundaries between sociability and sedition, polite conversation and political commitment, became extremely difficult to negotiate, particularly for a certain brand of gentleman radical.

The tavern and coffee-house are, of course, classic sites of the 'bourgeois' public sphere, places for the reading of newspapers, conversing among friends and other informed citizens, sometimes hosting formal debating clubs, a space of conviviality where ideas circulate freely among supposed equals.[2] It was here that Britain's other political nation gathered to form and to express 'political opinion' on the events of the day; it was here that private individuals traded information and formed commercial and social bonds.[3] Indeed, before leaving the Percy, Frost had been deep in dinner conversation about questions of agricultural improvement. This was predominately, if not exclusively, male space; it was also space marked off, at least ideally, not only from the controls of royal government but also from the street, the fair and the low tavern culture of the metropolis.[4] In certain respects, therefore, the belief in some form of 'equality' would seem appropriate to coffee-house culture, and the demand for 'no king' would seem to affirm the status of the public sphere itself, a zone removed from royal authority.

And yet the consideration of the public sphere and the norms of sociability cannot be separated so neatly from other spaces and sites of discourse and power. Thus Frost's claim to equality and no king raised the issue, on the one hand, of disconnecting this space from norms of social hierarchy which in the last instance resided in the figure of the king and, on the other hand, threatened to connect the coffee-house to the street and the raucous alehouse culture of artisans and the labouring poor. The classic manifestation of coffee-house culture as a site of bourgeois sociability continued to be founded on a double denial of, or separation from, both aristocratic and plebeian culture. The Percy was a well-known coffee-house and tavern located in a socially exclusive part of town, at Rathbone Place off Oxford Street, where a generation earlier James Boswell had dined with literary friends.[5] The distinction still maintained in residual form at the Percy between its upstairs tavern and lower-floor coffee-house had, in fact, broken down earlier in the century: coffee-houses often served good food and wine, distinguishing features of the gentleman's tavern. The equal footing of the Percy was that between gentlemen of a certain social standing.

As Terry Eagleton argues, the hallmark of such discursive space was its consensual character, embodying common standards of taste and conduct that were first and most famously articulated by Joseph Addison and Richard Steele in their *Tatler* and *Spectator* essays. The suspension of social status, if not political difference, at such sites of sociability was predicated on shared standards of the sayable, on norms of politeness, good behaviour, restrained conversation and good writing. The blending of 'grace and gravitas, urbanity and morality, correction and consolidation' was, as Eagleton writes, directly linked to the production of a 'polite' reading public and to the growing legitimacy of essay-writing, to the republic of *belles lettres*.[6] In addition, it was thought that the coffee-house might play a moral role equivalent to that played by the 'polis' in ancient Athens and Rome, functioning as a breeding ground for citizens and civic virtue – or 'virtue' reconstituted in terms of politeness and manners.[7] The coffee-house was a self-regulating republic of urban civility. However, this civility was always subject to a series of tensions: between the permissive pleasures of heavy drinking and good order, between accessibility to customers of varying social backgrounds and distinction based on the appearance of good taste and manners, between free conversation and the hazardous subjects of politics and religion.

By the late eighteenth century, the ideals of civility associated with coffee-house culture had become at best tenuous. While taverns and coffee-houses had from the late seventeenth century been contentious political sites, in the wake of the American and French Revolutions consensual norms of 'bourgeois' conduct, of politeness and sociability, could not withstand the disruptions of revolutionary politics. Taverns and coffee-houses were hardly safe havens for those committed to the principles of the French Revolution. If, as Jürgen Habermas proposes, the rationality of the public sphere was in the first instance the product of private subjectivity originating within the conjugal family (and later extended into the market), by 1792 the capacity for private individuals to exchange views with a measure of security was in jeopardy. The watchfulness of government spies, and perhaps more significantly that of private individuals responding to the royal proclamation of May 1792 against sedition, now policed the space of the tavern and coffee-house, their rooms, boxes and tables. Taverns and alehouses, it should be remembered, were subject to the control of licensing by local magistrates; many proprietors were, in fact, pressured to ban supporters of Thomas Paine from their premises.[8] Moreover, the 'publicness' of the coffee-house and tavern was not of a piece: Frost had been dining in a 'private' box in the tavern before entering the more 'public' space of the coffee-house below. John Binns, who had himself faced trial for his revolutionary activities, recalled that the 'Jacobin' orator John Thelwall never felt comfortable even in 'private' conversation. 'If he went into an oyster house, or an *à-la-mode* beef-shop, he would conceit that one-half of the boxes in the room had government spies in them, whose especial business was to watch and report, as far as possible, all he said and all he did.'[9]

In light of his own trial for high treason, Thelwall's paranoia was understandable, and as the case of Charles Pigott and William Hodgson illustrates, it was not entirely misplaced. Both men were leading members of the London Corresponding Society. Pigott was a prominent radical author of gentry background who specialized in scurrilous exposés of the sexual morals of the aristocracy and Hodgson was a hatter.[10] The two men had dined 'convivially together' at a London coffee-house; they called for newspapers which they read and discussed. Hodgson spoke freely of the Duke of York's 'bad private character', commenting that he 'respected no man however exalted by rank, unless dignified by virtue'. Less decorously, he called the Elector of Hanover (i.e. George III) and Landgrave of Hesse Cassell 'German Hog Butchers'. While in private conversation – conversing with an 'openness and freedom' natural to their surroundings – Pigott and Hodgson were accosted by a gentleman, a member of John Reeves's Association for Preserving Liberty and Property against Republicans and Levellers, who had been eavesdropping on their conversation. Joined by fellow loyalists who 'laid siege' to their table, these men attempted to force the two radicals to drink a loyal toast to 'the King and the Royal Family'. On the basis of notes taken by informers, Pigott and Hodgson were arrested and eventually brought to trial. According to Pigott's account, in prison they were told that they were arrested because 'we were TOM PAINE's Men, and rebels; that he [the gaoler] had been told we were GENTLEMEN, but it was a lie, we were d___d BLACKGUARD RASCALS'. Stripped of the social garb of being 'gentlemen', and unable to meet the exorbitantly high bail set at £500 each, the two men remained for over three weeks in Newgate prison before being brought to trial.[11]

When the two men were finally brought before a grand jury the legal issue turned, according to Pigott, on whether words 'passing between two friends in a public coffee-house, at a table where they were sitted [sic] by themselves' could be the subject of an indictment; did freeborn Englishmen have a right as to their own thoughts and private words? 'Till, now', declared Pigott, 'it had been supposed, that the table or box in a coffee room, was as sacred and inviolable as a private room, nay, even as our house.' There was, however, a paradox to Pigott's argument since he maintained not merely that he and Hodgson were in 'private' conversation but that the 'publicness' of the coffee-house and the freedom and loudness with which they spoke – including toasting 'the French Republic' – demonstrated that they were not engaged in seditious activity. Rather than conspiring sedition – sedition being characterized by 'silence and concealment', shunning 'the light' – they appeared and spoke together openly at one of the most frequented coffee-houses in the city of London. It was precisely the 'publicness' of their 'private' conversation that guaranteed the good intent of their actions and words; they had not sought the protections of secrecy.[12] As it turned out, Pigott's indictment was discarded (he had been indicted *ex-officio* by the attorney general) while Hodgson was sentenced to two years' imprisonment and fined £200. From Newgate, where he languished beyond his sentence due to his inability to pay the fine, Hodgson reiterated his sentiments in print: 'for I am neither ashamed of the language I held, nor do I feel the slightest contrition for having used it; I here, in the face of the whole world, avow my opinion to be, that a REPUBLIC is the best suited to the happiness of the French people'.[13]

Frost's situation was, of course, not strictly analogous to that of Pigott and Hodgson (a point Pigott made) in that he had been challenged to state his views 'publicly' and had voluntarily obliged. On the other hand, like Pigott and Hodgson, Frost had almost certainly been set up by vigilant fellow citizens who knew him for his radical sympathies. A site of sociability had been transformed into 'AN INQUISITION', to quote Pigott. Furthermore, after refusing to back down, one witness related that Frost was told that he was fortunate not to be kicked out of the coffee-house into the street where he would be unprotected by the protocols of the coffee-house. Frost responded by asking whether his opponents 'doubted his courage'. The incident, as reported, tested not merely Frost's republicanism but his commitment to a code of male honour. Such situations had to be carefully negotiated if one were successfully to maintain face without leading to serious altercation or prosecution. For instance, in the heated conditions following the Priestley riots – which were themselves an organized loyalist response to an occasion of radical dining and sociability – Samuel Parr, 'the Whig Dr Johnson', was compelled to toast church and king while dining out in the vicinity of Birmingham. He boldly added his own gloss: 'Church and King. – Once it was the toast of Jacobites; now it is the toast of incendiaries. It means church without the gospel – and king above the law.'[14] John Binns, who was in Birmingham as the delegate of the London Corresponding Society in 1796, courageously paid a visit to the 'Church and King' tavern where the Priestley riots were believed to have been planned; the panel of plate glass on the entrance door displayed in 'large polished gilt letters, the words, "NO JACOBINS ADMITTED HERE"'. Entering loyalist territory, Binns was apparently recognized as a LCS delegate and in an attempt to smoke him out, he was greeted by the toast 'Church and King', followed by 'Damn all Jacobins'. After Binns refused to drink the second toast, customers shouted for him to be thrown out of the tavern. According to Binns's account, he then defended his political principles in a conciliatory speech; he was allowed to finish his drink and retire at his own discretion.[15] A victory of sorts.

The tavern and coffee-house were arenas for testing the courage of men's political convictions; male honour thus was bound up with politics and sociability. The challenges and counter-challenges to drink particular toasts or to stand by one's words and allegiances were in certain important respects analogous to the code of the duel. Standing by one's word had been crucial to an earlier regime of truth based on the presumed reliability of a gentleman's utterances – gentlemen being independent and thus honest.[16] The code of the duel was, however, also linked to upper-class bouts of massive drinking and rowdiness, and was increasingly seen as an atavistic expression of aristocratic manliness in a commercial age.[17] As sites of sociability, commerce and conversation, coffee-houses were thus subject to persuasive conditions that in practice fell short of Enlightenment notions of truthful discourse or for that matter norms of 'bourgeois' propriety. They represented an ideal of rational sociability while at the same time housing emotions and behaviour that might undermine that ideal.

Despite the less than ideal realization of the norms of rational sociability, it is nonetheless important to recognize that Enlightenment-based concepts of conversation, free discussion and 'truth' were crucial to a distinct strain of British radicalism deeply influenced by the overlapping traditions of Puritanism and eighteenth-century rationalism. In William Godwin's *Caleb Williams* (1794), the aristocratic Falkland's major character flaw is his overriding, and ultimately self-destructive, regard for his honour and reputation over truth and benevolent understanding. Written in the shadow of the government's campaign against the likes of Frost, the novel is itself a commentary on the conditions governing rational persuasion and truthful representation.[18] In Godwin's *Enquiry Concerning Political Justice*, the section on the 'utility of social communication' provides the model of the 'ideal speech situation' – what Godwin calls 'candid and unreserved conversation'. 'Let us suppose', writes Godwin, unimpaired conversation between two sensitive truth seekers, 'desirous extensively to communicate the truths with which they are acquainted' and distinguished by 'mildness of their temper, and a spirit of comprehensive benevolence'. Unlike the 'cold' encounter with the printed page, vigorous private conversation provides a variety of views, stimulating 'freedom and elasticity to our disquisitions'.

Moreover, for the followers of Paine and Godwin, rational communication, whether through discussion or reading, stood in striking opposition to aristocratic and royal spectacle, and the appeal to the senses and emotions. Royal pomp, splendour and ornamental display were calculated 'to bring over to its party our eyes and our ears'. Godwin argued, as did Paine, that kings set out with 'every artifice' to 'dazzle our SENSE, and mislead our judgement'.[19] It was against the 'artifice' of spectacle and theatrical display that reasoned conversation stood. Despite radicals' own extensive use of ritual and symbolic expression – the planting of liberty trees, demands to illuminate, displaying of caps of liberty, revolutionary songs and toasts – there was a lingering suspicion that such gestures pandered to popular irrationality, appealing to the senses rather than the mind. Similarly, public oratory, particularly rabble-rousing, was suspect since it did not allow for deliberation.[20] Radicals often contrasted the decorum of their own proceedings to the drunken spectacle of loyalist mobs burning Paine in effigy or to the disorder of heavy-drinking and liberally bribed election crowds.

As Mark Philp comments, 'sociability is the basic fabric of late eighteenth-century intellectual life'; Godwin and his friends 'lived in a round of debate and discussion, in clubs, associations, debating societies, salons, taverns, coffee houses, bookshops, publishing houses and in the street'.[21] This was the social and intellectual milieu that nurtured radical ideas extolling the value of conversation and sociability, the power of reason and opinion; this was also the social world in which Frost moved. He was a close friend of Horne Tooke, whose house at Wimbledon was a centre of continuous dining, drinking, conversation and conviviality. Leading figures of London's radical intelligentsia, generally drawn from the middling social ranks, gathered at Tooke's table – including Paine, Thelwall, Godwin, the playwright Thomas Holcroft, the publisher Joseph Johnson, the engraver William Sharp, Robert Merry, the sculptor Thomas Banks, Archibald Hamilton Rowan of the United Irishmen, the radical lawyer Felix Vaughan, and the republican Thomas Cooper, among others.[22] At these gregarious sessions politics were mixed with wide-ranging discussion and the forging of networks of friends and future dining companions.

But while Godwin was wary of popular political associations, preferring conversation to formal organizations and enforced programmes, Frost was a leading member of the Society for Constitutional Information; his reform credentials dated back to the period of the famous Thatched House resolutions of 1782.[23] As a prominent lawyer who had been educated at Winchester School, Frost assisted Tooke in coordinating communications among provincial associations of artisans and tradesmen, offering editorial advice in the drawing up of their constitutions and rules. Thomas Hardy, the radical shoemaker who founded the LCS, consulted Tooke and Frost when he established the society.

In the early 1790s, radicals were organized across a spectrum of socially differentiated associations each offering their own brand of sociability: ranging from the aristocratic Foxite Whigs of the Friends of the People, to the largely middle-class members of the revived Society for Constitutional Information, to the shoemakers and tailors who joined the LCS with its policy of 'members unlimited' (although even the LCS's weekly membership fee of one penny excluded the lower ranks of London's labouring poor).[24] The boundaries separating members of these radical groups were not fixed; moreover, places like Daniel Isaac Eaton's bookstore and his journal *Politics for the People* provided fluid sites of social and literary contact between polite and plebeian culture.[25] Nonetheless, the social distinctions separating democrats of the 1790s were quite real, as were the differences separating varying sites and styles of radical sociability. The raucous, irreverent 'free and easies' held at alehouses frequented by ultra-radical artisans constituted a masculine world of plebeian sociability quite distinct from that of Horne Tooke's Wimbledon dinner parties. The SCI's annual subscription of one guinea ensured a 'polite' membership. At the dinner celebrating the fourteenth anniversary of the SCI, in May 1794, free tickets were given to members of the LCS unable to afford the seven shillings and six pence price for dinner, several of whom were reported to have behaved 'improperly'.[26] Frost was among the few gentlemen, along with Tooke, Thelwall and Joseph Gerrald, to directly associate himself with the LCS. Thus a government spy reported that at a division meeting of the LCS held at the 'Green Dragon', Frost had delivered an impassioned speech to several hundred members, adding that he was 'almost the only decent Man I have seen in any of their Divisions'.[27] Frost was a bridging figure, and was for that reason particularly vulnerable; he was a gentleman out of place.

He also was a hunted man. In December 1792, *The London Gazette*, the government's official journal, announced that the commissioners of the Treasury were offering a reward of £100 for anyone apprehending or aiding in the apprehension of Frost, 'late of Westminster', who had been indicted on charges of sedition in King's Bench and who 'now absconds from justice'.[28] Frost had in fact accompanied Paine as he fled to France. In a letter to Tooke, he described Paine's reception at Calais where a young woman presented Paine with the national cockade. Paine proceeded to Paris as the elected deputy of Calais to the National Convention. Frost attended the Convention as the delegate of the SCI; he and Joel Barlow, the American democrat, were sent to present the SCI's address to the Convention along with a promise to send one thousand pairs of shoes for France's republican armies.[29] Barlow and Frost were voted 'the honours of the session' and were hailed as generous republicans. From Paris Frost wrote a defiant letter to William Pitt, dated 29 December, '1st Year of the Republic', claiming that he had only learned of his indictment and that he would return to stand trial armed with Pitt's own letters in hand from 1782, declaring his support for political reform.[30] Frost remained in Paris long enough to attend the trial of Louis XVI.

Having refused to retract his statement for equality and no king, Frost's case was settled not in the street or by a duel, but in a court of law. The conditions of discursive exchange and symbolic power were now constructed quite differently; the space of the coffee-house was reiterated within the determining place of the trial and the law, its language and protocols. In contrast to the relatively 'open' or fluid space of the coffee-house-tavern – a freewheeling zone of political, cultural and commercial interchange – the courtroom was hierarchically ordered. Certain speakers, judges and lawyers, spoke with the law's authority.[31] Space was demarcated; bodies were placed in their assigned places: the bench, the bar, the jury box and public gallery. Within the visual register of the court, wigged and sumptuously robed judges, barristers and costumed court officials were distinguished from the defendant, jurors and spectators dressed in their ordinary clothes. Wigs and robes formed part of the law's ensemble of visual effects aimed at inspiring terror and awe. Thus the courtroom was predicated on norms of stability.[32] As officially sanctioned discursive space, it was constructed ideally as anything but an occasion for free speech among equals.

It is important to recognize, however, that such pretensions to stability were not realized in practice; they constituted an ideal or limit rather than a reality. The law's ambition to completely fill or produce its own social reality was constantly challenged and occasionally undone by its own contradictions, particularly by the gap between law and its own legitimating rhetoric of justice.[33] Moreover, counter-notions of British citizenship were partly founded on the participatory experience of what Margaret Somers terms the 'national legal sphere'.[34] Courtrooms were often sites of disorder and subversion. In fact, the potential for delinquency, for making a stand against governmental injustice, was enhanced by the law's very own ambitions and measures to command space, bodies and speech. Unlike other European countries, in England the courtroom was a 'public' space; there was a popular audience for key trials. Not only were trial texts published but courtrooms were open to the public at large – on occasion tickets were even sold. Attending court could be a form of sociability or leisure entertainment. The central courts of King's Bench, Common Pleas and Chancery were located in the open interior of Westminster Hall, where there was constant noise and milling about of strollers, booksellers, witnesses, jurymen and others.[35] Like the coffee-house, the courtroom was gendered space, all those who spoke were men, although public galleries were open to women. As a young woman, Amelia Alderson, subsequently Opie, was a frequenter of the assize courts at Norwich, her home town, 'delighting in the excitement of trials there'. As a visitor to London, she attended the treason trial of John Horne Tooke, sending home full accounts of the proceedings to her radical father.[36]

In May 1793 the press reported that Westminster Hall 'was prodigiously crowded' for Frost's trial.[37] The government in the person of the Attorney-General, Sir John Scott (the future Lord Eldon), took over what had been initiated as a private prosecution. Frost was tried before a special jury, which meant, in effect, that it was packed. Despite being a lawyer, he 'spoke' only by proxy, through his attorney Thomas Erskine. For radicals facing trial, the decision whether to represent themselves or to engage counsel was often a tough one. Radicals were generally suspicious of lawyers and the language of the law. Pigott, for example, roundly denounced the 'chicanery' of lawyers and the law; although ignorant of the law 'and wholly unpractised in the meretricious arts of elocution, thank Heaven! I am perfectly acquainted with *equity and right* . . .'[38] Pigott's popular *Political Dictionary* defines 'barrister' as 'loquacity, impudence, presumption, vanity, consequence, sophistry, inconsistency, and self-interest. Erskine, Garrow.'[39] The language and practice of the law were seen as contrary to the communication of truth, the antithesis to the truth-bearing properties of unrestricted conversation among equals. To be represented by legal counsel was, at least for the moment, to be reduced to silence. Radicals often resorted to publishing the defences that they 'would have' given: the social world of the text substituting for that of the courtroom.

It was Erskine who read to the court Pitt's correspondence with Frost from 1782 in which the future Prime Minister had stated his support of the Thatched House resolutions. And it was Erskine who devised a defence that turned on a somewhat cowardly dodge and one that did not work. Erskine, the most brilliant trial lawyer of his day, endeavoured to show that Frost had been 'in liquor'; he had spoken 'in the heat and levity of wine'. As Erskine told Frost's story, the company of diners 'did not retire till the bottle had made many merry circles; and it appears . . . that Mr Frost, *to say the least*, had drunk very freely'. In his drunken state, Frost was entrapped. Erskine asked the jury to consider whether 'an English gentleman in future [must] fill his wine by a measure', lest he risk having his character 'blasted' and his person carried off to prison. 'Does any man', asked Erskine, 'put such constraint upon himself in the most private moment of his life, that he would be contented to have his loosest and lightest words recorded' and presented against him in court? If such an invasion of privacy and polite sociability were to be allowed, 'scarcely a dinner would end without a duel and an indictment'. While presenting an eloquent plea for the rights of free speech and private conscience, Erskine, at least implicitly, defended the manly pleasures of heavy drinking. Privacy was defined in homosocial terms; the rights of masculinity were asserted rather than the rights of man. Erskine also opened the possibility that Frost had not been himself and thus not meant what he had said – equality and no king were reduced to the 'loosest and lightest words'. Indeed, the trial text includes a long extract from Locke's *Essay Concerning Human Understanding*, discussing whether since punishment is annexed to personality, and personality to consciousness, drunkenness should excuse a criminal act.[40] Leaving aside the legal and philosophical niceties of the case, Erskine had found a way for Frost to retract or excuse his statement favouring equality. Moreover, rather than sociability leading to rational, free exchange, and therefore a version of 'truth', due to his dining and wining Frost had spoken without proper regard for himself and others. The court had called the equality and sociability of the coffee-house to account. The narrative logic of Frost's story was transformed by the space of the trial and by Erskine's defence – a defence which the *Monthly Review* and *Critical Review*, literary journals sympathetic to reform, found to be among 'his most eloquent', 'able and ingenious'.[41]

In the event Frost was sentenced to six months in Newgate Prison, struck from the Court rolls, and was also condemned to stand in the pillory at Charing Cross for one hour. Henry 'Redhead' Yorke, who had been with Frost and Paine in Paris, framed his Paineite tract *These are the Times That Try Men's Souls!* as a letter to 'John Frost Prisoner in Newgate'. He assured Frost that his case was now before 'the most solemn tribunal upon the earth': 'the judgment of an enlightened public' would deliver a final 'verdict of truth'.[42] Newgate was itself an extraordinary site of radical sociability and literary production: 'a microcosm of enlightened republican civility and morality'. Here Frost was united with 'Jacobin' comrades, including the radical publishers James Ridgway (publisher of Frost's trial), Henry Symonds, Daniel Holt and Daniel Isaac Eaton, William Winterbotham, who was engaged in compiling his four-volume *Philosophical View of the United States*, Hodgson, Joseph Gerrald, who was waiting to be transported and 'mad' Lord George Gordon. Godwin, Thomas Holcroft (before his own imprisonment on treason charges), William Sharp, Robert Southey, Samuel Taylor Coleridge and the writer Maria Reveley were among those paying regular visits to Newgate's republic of letters to dine and converse with suffering friends.[43] Ironically, Newgate allowed radical prisoners and their guests to produce a strikingly autonomous version of Enlightened sociability, an ideal staging of the 'public sphere' and its principles.

At the conclusion of his sentence, Frost was condemned to stand in the pillory; street spectacle was to speak over and against the discourse of the coffee-house. He was, however, excused this final indignity due to ill health, although radical handbills circulated through London announcing that 'Living or Dead' Frost would be condemned to stand on the pillory for 'supporting the Rights of the People'. The following day the ailing Frost was released from Newgate wrapped in blankets, put into a coach and taken to the house of a local magistrate to enter into sureties. He was accompanied from prison by the gentleman radicals Horne Tooke, Thelwall and Sharp. The *Morning Chronicle* reported that 'As soon as he was at liberty the multitude' took the horses out of his carriage and drew him along the streets stopping at 'every marked place, particularly St James's Palace, Carlton House, Charing Cross [where the pillory was set up] . . . to shout and express their joy'.[44] The crowd responded to those in power, countering the ritual of public shame with a carnivalesque remapping of urban, royal space; the radical crowd extended the call for 'equality' from the confines of the coffee-house to the more raucous, levelling zone of the street. Outside Frost's house in Spring Gardens, Thelwall addressed the crowd, entreating them to separate peaceably. Twenty years later, as if to add retrospective commentary on the interactions between royal power and the private citizen, government authority and the public sphere, the Prince Regent, acting in the name of the King, granted Frost a free pardon.

Certain points can be grasped from this brief summary of Frost's case. We might chart, for instance, a discursive and spatial trajectory. As Frost moved successively from dining at Marylebone, to trial at Westminster, to imprisonment at Newgate and back into the streets of the fashionable

West End, we can see precisely how meaning is dependent on spatial circuits, and on the balance between power and delinquency governing different sites: a spatial economy is evident. The tavern, coffee-house, courtroom, prison, the pillory and the street are not merely backgrounds to the production of meaning, passive contexts within which utterance takes place. Rather as Lynda Nead comments, social space is part of an 'active ordering and organizing' of subjective identities, social relations and meaning.[45] In order to understand Frost's case, we must know something about how the sites of assembly through which his story circulates came into being. 'Patterns of discourse are regulated through the forms of corporate assembly in which they are produced', write Peter Stallybrass and Allon White. And they continue,

the formation of new kinds of speech can be traced through the emergence of new public sites of discourse and the transformation of old ones. Each 'site of assembly' constitutes a nucleus of material and cultural conditions which regulate what may and may not be said, who may speak, how people may communicate and what importance must be given to what is said ... in large part, the history of political struggle has been the history of the attempts made to control significant sites of assembly and spaces of discourse.[46]

In large part the history of early nineteenth-century popular radicalism can, indeed, be written as a contest to gain access to, and to appropriate, sites of assembly and expression, to produce, at least potentially, a 'plebeian counter-public sphere'.[47]

However, to understand political struggles for control of such sites and the meanings attached to these struggles, we must also consider the relationship between sites of assembly and the historical transformations in these relationships. The sociability of the coffee-house or tavern was never independent of other sites of assembly or the controls of government and law. As we have noted, the polite culture of the coffee-house was organized in contradistinction to both aristocratic and vulgar forms of conviviality. The norms and spaces of bourgeois sociability were situated within a shifting field of social, political and discursive forces. In addition, the relationship between reading and sites of assembly was hierarchically governed. Certain kinds of texts were closely connected to particular spaces: the handbill joins the street; the quarterly journal lodges in the coffee-house and gentleman's private library; Jacobin journals, Daniel Isaac Eaton's *Politics for the People* and Thomas Spence's *Pig's Meat*, are read aloud in low taverns and alehouses, the haunts of radical artisans and the labouring poor.[48] As for Frost's trial and his subsequent story, it was of course the medium of print culture that freed the event from a particular moment and place. Frost's trial was reported in the press; it was published as a pamphlet by the radical bookseller James Ridgway and it eventually made its way into the collection of *State Trials*.[49]

By the early 1790s, the culture of the coffee-house and tavern had come under intensified political pressure. For Edmund Burke the French Revolution represented a bout of insane linguistic and ideological disorder – 'the political nonsense of . . . licentious and giddy coffee-houses' undoing the silent 'work of ages'.[50] The babble of coffee-house conversation symbolized the broader danger to the state and its silent design, whereas for Paine the politics of the coffee-house offered a truthful indication of the state of public opinion; here one could read the mind of the nation. Refusing to return from Paris to London to stand trial for publishing the second part of his *Rights of Man*, Paine wrote to Sir Archibald Macdonald, the Attorney General, so that his opinions would not be misrepresented. In his letter, he taunted the Attorney General with being unable to get convictions without the aid of packed juries; he appealed to the opinion of the coffee-house in direct opposition to that of the law court and jury: 'I have gone into coffee-houses and places where I was unknown, on purpose to learn the currency of opinion, and I never yet saw any company of twelve men that condemned the book [*Rights of Man*]; and this I think is a fair way of collecting the natural currency of opinion.' The Attorney General responded by asking the special jury of 'merchants' to decide 'whether the sense of this nation is to be had in some pot-houses and coffee-houses'.[51]

The sociability of the coffee-house could no longer be secured against sedition. Indeed, in 1790 the *Bee*, an Edinburgh journal, proposed that the gentleman's journal might displace the coffee-house altogether; the 'society of the text' might permit a retreat from sociability to domesticity. 'A man, after the fatigues of the day are over, may thus sit down in his elbow chair, and together with his wife and family, be introduced, as it were, into a spacious coffee-house, which is frequented by men of all nations.'[52] Polite society's retreat from the coffee-house and tavern to the home, from homosocial carousing to the domestic safety of wife and family, was indicative of the times.[53] And if wealthy men often paid mere lip service to idealized notions of the home and family, the nineteenth-century gentleman's club offered a surrogate 'family', a homosocial home away from home. If sociability is among the key terms for understanding the social and literary world of the eighteenth century, respectability is among the key terms for understanding the nineteenth century: the shift is an important one.

In conclusion, we can return to Frost's statement, his declaration for equality and no king. The 1790s witnessed an acute crisis in representation, including a contest over how and where meanings were legitimately to be articulated.[54] As the National Convention abolished the French monarchy in September 1792, tried and then executed Louis XVI in January 1793, the declaration for 'equality and no king' became supercharged. The month following the incident at the Percy coffeehouse, the Manchester Society for Constitutional Information insisted that 'equality' meant equality of rights not property or wealth. They blamed loyalists for propagating a 'perversion of terms', warning that by the continual repetition that 'equality' referred to property, 'the uninformed, or as they are now arrogantly styled, the SWINISH MULTITUDE' might attempt to enforce 'so dangerous a doctrine'.[55] But by late 1792, just as it became increasingly difficult to protect the term 'equality' from being perversely understood, it was impossible to seal off the coffee-house from the street and plebeian tavern or to host polite debating clubs and public lectures without raising the spectre of democracy and alarming those in authority.[56]

And what about the phrase 'no king'? Frost's utterance was easily confused with that of the less celebrated, but perhaps no less inebriated, Edward Swift. Swift was convicted at the Berkshire summer assizes in 1794 for having declaimed, 'Damnation, blast the King I would as soon shoot the King as a Mad dog', going on to say that he would go down to Birmingham 'and bring up a set of rioters and make Windsor worse than ever France was'.[57] How was Frost's proposition to be distinguished from regicidal handbills selling in metropolitan streets and alehouses, such as the mock-theatre advertisement announcing a performance for the benefit of John Bull at the 'FEDERATION THEATRE in EQUALITY SQUARE' of the farce 'LA GUILLOTINE or GEORGE'S HEAD IN THE BASKET!'? This anonymous handbill was presented in prosecution evidence at Thomas Hardy's trial for high treason.[58]

As middle-class radicals retreated from the political fray (not Frost, as it happens), they retreated from both the language of 'equality' and the spaces that had bred and sustained such language.[59] Crucial distinctions could no longer be maintained: the spaces and language of polite sociability and reform sentiment had to be more clearly demarcated from the raucous, dangerous places and tones of plebeian culture. Social and political ambiguities became less ambiguous. As Jon Klancher argues, it was in the 1790s that alehouses displaced coffee-houses as centres of 'insurgent public discourse'.[60] While the odd *declassé* gentleman drifted into the underworld of low alehouses and taverns, of debating clubs and blasphemous sing-songs, this masculine world of anti-authoritarian conviviality described so brilliantly by Iain McCalman belonged to artisans and small tradesmen.[61] The appeal to 'equality and no king' – along with those supporting such views – was banished from polite society and had found its proper nineteenth-century home.[62]

NOTES

My thanks to Michelle Hawley, Gillian Russell and Clara Tuite for their careful comments on an earlier draft of this chapter.
For full citations see Bibliography.

1 Howell and Howell (eds.), *State Trials*, vol. XXII (1792–3), 'Proceedings against John Frost for Seditious Words', cols. 471–522, cited hereafter as 'Proceedings'. Given that the politically charged anniversary of the 'glorious' revolution (4 November) had only just passed, feelings may still have been riding high.
2 Habermas, *Structural Transformation*, particularly pp. 51–67; Brewer, 'Commercialization'; Brewer, *Pleasures*, pp. 34–41; Wilson, *Sense of the People*, chapter 1; Pincus, '"Coffee Politicians"'; Herzog, *Poisoning*, chapter 2; Thale, 'London Debating Societies'.
3 See Wahrman's discussion of 'public opinion' in 'Public opinion', particularly pp. 93–9.
4 Wilson, *Sense of the People*, pp. 47–54; Langford, *Polite and Commercial People*, pp. 101–2; for female participation in debating clubs, see Andrew, 'Popular Culture'.
5 Lillywhite, *London Coffee Houses*, pp. 445–6; Clark, *English Alehouse*, pp. 6–14, for the hierarchy of inn, tavern and alehouse.
6 Eagleton, *Function of Criticism*, pp. 9–30. Also see Porter, 'Enlightenment in England'; and cf. Klancher, *Making*, chapter 1, for an important revision to thinking on the 'public sphere'.
7 Phillipson, 'Scottish Enlightenment'; Pocock, 'Virtues'; Shields, *Civil Tongues*, chapters 2 and 3.
8 Habermas, *Structural Transformation*, p. 51; Rogers, *Crowds*, pp. 192–210. For provincial loyalist coercion, see Booth, 'Popular Loyalism'. For prosecutions see Emsley, 'Repression' and his 'An Aspect of Pitt's "Terror"'.
9 Binns, *Recollections*, p. 44.
10 See Rogers, 'Pigott's Private Eye'.
11 My account is based on Pigott, *Persecution*.
12 For the protection offered by secret association, see Jacob, *Radical Enlightenment*. It is misleading to view the 'private' and 'public' spheres during this

period in terms of strict opposition. On this point, see Goodman, 'Public Sphere'; Brewer, 'This, That and the Other'.

13 Hodgson, *Case*, p. 9. Hodgson was released after the fine was paid by a public subscription. He also wrote *Commonwealth of Reason*, an interesting utopian tract, while he was in Newgate.

14 Field, *Memoirs*, vol. II, p. 309. For the Priestley riots, see Rose, 'Priestley Riots' and Deirdre Coleman's chapter in this volume.

15 Binns, *Recollections*, pp. 69–72.

16 Shapin, *Social History*, particularly chapter 3.

17 See Moore, *Full Inquiry*, vol. II; Andrew, 'Code of Honour'; Kiernan, *The Duel*, pp. 2–21; Langford, *Polite and Commercial People*, pp. 587–90; and Elster, *Alchemies*, pp. 203–38.

18 Leaver, 'Pursuing Conversations', argues that Godwin uses the novel form as a means of 'private conversation' between text and reader.

19 Godwin, *Enquiry*, Priestley (ed.), vol. II, pp. 49–50. For Paine, see Epstein, *Radical Expression*, pp. 111–12.

20 Rogers, *Crowds*, p. 211. Thus at the outdoor meeting at Copenhagen Fields in 1795 several rostra were set up, so that there could be deliberations. See *Account of the Proceedings* (London, 1795).

21 Philp, *Godwin's Political Justice*, p. 127. Also see Butler, *Romantics*, pp. 25–6; Roe, *Wordsworth and Coleridge*, pp. 9–10, 169, 243.

22 Bewley, *Gentleman Radical*, p. 85.

23 'Proceedings', cols. 492–4; *DNB*, vol. VII, pp. 727–8.

24 Thompson, *Making*, chapter 5; Goodwin, *Friends of Liberty*.

25 This point is made forcefully by Davis, '"That Odious"'.

26 Bewley, *Gentleman Radical*, pp. 104–5, 147; Hone, *For the Cause*, p. 15.

27 Public Records Office (hereafter PRO), London, TS 11/959/3505, report of Munro, cited in Thale (ed.), *Selections*, pp. 27–8.

28 *London Gazette*, 11–15 December 1792, p. 933.

29 PRO, TS 11/962/3508, SCI Minute Book, vol. II, 1791–4; TS 11/3505/2; 'J. F.'[John Frost] to Horne Tooke, Paris, 20 September 1792, in TS 11/951/3495; *The Complete Reports*, p. 5, Appendix C to 'Second Report ... of the House of Commons' reprints the society's address to the National Convention; Keane, *Paine*, pp. 343, 349–50; Goodwin, *Friends of Liberty*, pp. 253–5.

30 *Morning Chronicle*, 1 January 1793.

31 As Pierre Bourdieu remarks, 'Legal discourse is a creative speech which brings into existence that which it utters. It is the limit aimed at by all performative utterances.' Bourdieu, *Language*, p. 42. Also see Hay, 'Property.'

32 The courtroom thus conforms to De Certeau's concept of a 'place'. See De Certeau, *Practice*, p. 117.

33 The point is a complicated and contested one, but among other works, see Derrida, 'Force of Law'; Cornell, 'Violence'; cf. Fish, *Doing What Comes Naturally*, particularly 'Force', pp. 503–24.

34 Somers, 'Citizenship'; Somers, 'Rights'.
35 See, for example, Oldham, *Mansfield Manuscripts*, vol. I, pp. 119–21. I am grateful to Margot Finn for bringing this reference to my attention.
36 Brightwell, *Memoir*, pp. 9–10; Vickery, 'Golden Age', p. 411; Finn, 'Women, Consumption and Coverture', for women's active manipulation of the law and courtrooms.
37 *Morning Chronicle*, 28 May 1793; *Evening Mail*, 29 May 1793.
38 Pigott, *Persecution*, pp. 1–2. Cf. Thelwall, *Natural and Constitutional Right*, pp. iii–iv. Both Pigott and Thelwall's tracts purported to be defences that they would have given. Representation by counsel in criminal cases was, in fact, a fairly recent development. See Beattie, 'Scales'.
39 Pigott, *Political Dictionary*, p. 6. In the same vein, see Anon., *Advice*.
40 'Proceedings', cols. 499–502, 520–1. On the pleasures of drink and eighteenth-century hedonism more generally, see Porter, 'Material Pleasures'.
41 *Monthly Review*, October 1794, vol. 15, pp. 200–01; *Critical Review*, January 1795, vol. 13, p. 107.
42 Yorke, *These are the Times*, p. 3.
43 McCalman, 'Newgate'. For Godwin's visits to Newgate, see Godwin's diary, Abinger Collection; also Philp, *Godwin's Political Justice*, appendix B.
44 Scrapbook of Political Broadsides, British Library (pressmark 648.c. 26), handbills, fol. 29; *Morning Chronicle* 20 December 1793; *Public Advertiser* 19 December 1793; *Annual Register*, 1793, pp. 50–1; Bewley, *Gentleman Radical*, p. 134. It is possible that the authorities decided that they did not want to risk placing Frost in the pillory, fearing the response of the crowd.
45 Nead, 'Mapping the Self', p. 167.
46 Stallybrass and White, *Politics and Poetics*, p 80.
47 Gilmartin, *Print Politics*, introduction; Eley, 'Nations'.
48 See Klancher, *Making*, chapter 1; Raven, 'New Reading Histories'.
49 *The Trial of John Frost*, published by J. Ridgway and H. D. Symonds, copies in Bodleian Library, Oxford and at Yale University. The text published in *State Trials* is based on this pamphlet edition which sold for 1s/6d.
50 Burke, *Reflections*, ed. O'Brien, p. 160.
51 *The Genuine Trial*, p. 36. Paine was represented by Erskine who argued against allowing Paine's letter to be read to the jury.
52 Quoted in Klancher, *Making*, pp. 23–4.
53 On this point, see Davidoff and Hall, *Family Fortunes*, particularly part 1.
54 See Barrell, *Imagining*, introduction, pp. 1–46.
55 *Manchester Herald*, 8 December 1792; also reprinted as a handbill, copy in PRO, TS 11/3505/2. Cf. *Equality*, a loyalist tract published for the Hackney Association for the Preservation of Peace, Liberty and Property. For popular loyalism, see Philp, 'Vulgar Conservatism'. For the debate over 'equality', see the editor's Introduction, Claeys (ed.), *Political Writings*, vol. I, pp. xxx–xliii.
56 Thale, 'London Debating Societies', pp. 64–6.
57 PRO, TS 11/944 [3433], crown brief.

58 Howell and Howell, *State Trials*, 24 (1794), cols. 682–3.
59 For Frost's later political activity, see Hone, *For the Cause*, pp. 134, 141.
60 Klancher, *Making*, pp. 26–7.
61 McCalman, 'Ultra-Radicalism'; McCalman, *Radical Underworld*. Also see Borsay, '"All the Town's a Stage"', documenting a longer-term growth of 'two autonomous cultures' in terms of polite and popular urban spatial practice.
62 In this sense, Thelwall's fate is perhaps relevant, as is Wordsworth's transposition of the figure of the Solitary in the *Excursion*. See Thompson, 'Hunting the Jacobin Fox'.

4

Amiable and radical sociability: Anna Barbauld's 'free familiar conversation'

Anne Janowitz

This chapter traces the intellectual path taken by Anna Barbauld from her poetic apprenticeship in the setting of provincial Dissenting sociability to her activist interventions as poet and polemicist in the print culture of 1790s radical London. Using Barbauld as an exemplary case, I consider two models of sociability in the late eighteenth century. The first model is that epitomized by the 'free familiar conversation' advocated by her father, the Dissenting educationalist John Aikin, D.D. and instanced in the pedagogy and manners of the Warrington Academy (1757–86).[1] This pedagogy to produce 'a well-tuned mind' was practised through the Warrington Academy's educational method, and it was formative for the poetic style of the young Anna (Aikin) Barbauld in the 1760s and 1770s. At Warrington tutors aimed to incarnate the ideal of social intercourse conceived of as informal, familiar and amiable, teaching the virtues of 'candid manners' and an 'active mind'.[2]

The second model was shaped from a more urban and militant notion of sociability linked to political activism, in which benevolence is evinced through political activity and analytical perspicacity, and which structured an interventionist poetic in the early 1790s. This version of sociality is linked more directly to the radical strand of the urban print network: in this case, the intellectual circle of Dissenters and radical reformers who made up the list of the publisher, Joseph Johnson. The associated poetic aimed to eschew manners for the power of analysis, to pierce through 'The plausive argument, the daring lye,/The artful gloss' (87: 28–9) of those eloquent sophists who use rhetoric to perpetrate injustice.

The personalities in the two social circles overlap. Warrington tutors who were also published by Johnson included John Aikin, William Enfield, Gilbert Wakefield and Joseph Priestley.[3] Johnson himself had been associated with the Warrington Academy from the 1760s, first as a conduit for its publications, but in the later 1770s and in the 1780s his press became a route by which the declining fortunes of the Academy might be recovered through the development of a more general dissenting intellectual print culture.[4] From the late 1780s, the revolution debates brought Johnson closer to a more pointed political edge. From this period, Johnson's circle thinned numerically and hardened out politically, and he was linked to Paine, Wollstonecraft, Godwin and a more radical version of republicanism, drawing his Warrington authors into a new radical intellectual milieu. Pivoting politically around the rising radicalism of Nonconformist English intellectuals in response to both the defeat of the repeal of the Test and Corporation Acts and to the success of the first years of the French Revolution, the Warrington and Johnson circles were also geographically distinguished. Though not rural, Warrington having long been a trading and manufacturing town, it was nevertheless quite different from the cultural cacophony of London's radical and reform milieus.[5]

Anna Barbauld was intellectually formed during her years in the provincial Warrington circle. She lived there from the ages of fifteen to thirty-one as the brilliant and beautiful daughter of a beloved tutor. She internalized the values of Warrington sociability and in turn gave them a poetic, public form in her *Poems* (1773). After marrying Rochemont Barbauld in 1774 she moved from Warrington to Suffolk, where the couple spent some years running a boys' school, punctuated by winter breaks to London and travels to the Continent, after which she and her husband settled in Hampstead in 1787.[6]

The transit from Warrington to London can be described as Anna Barbauld's shift from sensibility to Romanticism, from 'amiability' to 'ardour', from 'the social hours/Which charm'd us once' (20:16) to the echoes of 'shrieks and yells' of African slaves which disrupt and move into action the 'lone Poet' who no longer can rest protected from those sounds by the benign 'hum of village talk'(87: 82, 74).[7] Having served an apprenticeship in amiable poetics and consciousness in the Warrington circle, and having gained practical experience in running a boys' school at Palgrave and publishing as an educationalist herself, Barbauld blossomed as poet and pamphleteer in Hampstead and London, forging an autonomous public identity through the intellectual and cultural freedoms offered by Johnson's press. In her urban poetry of the late 1780s and early 1790s, Barbauld concretized and dialectically criticized the abstractions of Warrington values and manners. Her experience of freedom emerged from the engagement of her provincial Dissenting background with radical urban print culture. In London

Anna Barbauld was no longer principally either the pleasing daughter of the house, nor the wife and partner of the schoolmaster, but an intellectual involved with the contemporary political issues of slavery, religious toleration and the consequences of the French Revolution.

Isobel Armstrong has recently made the decisive case for the analytical autonomy of Romantic women poets, using Anna Barbauld as her test-case.[8] And both John Guillory and William Keach have discussed Barbauld with reference to her Dissenting environment: Guillory by showing how her topographical poetry participated in the larger Dissenting claim to cultural authority; and Keach by explaining Barbauld's contradictory assertion of both political freedom and female domesticity through the class configuration of Dissenting culture, and in particular, via the influence of Joseph Priestley.[9] The present chapter builds on their work by discussing the particular texture of Barbauld's experience of Dissenting social circles and their impact on her intellectual development.

The Dissenting Academy at Warrington was founded as one of a series of establishments to train Nonconformist clergy. But the strength of the institution was in science and letters: there was a strong secular strain to the curriculum, and it drew from a wide social base of sons of planters, professionals and manufacturers.[10] After its demise, Warrington's reputation served as an emblem of what liberal pedagogy might rise to, 'distinguished by sound learning, just and liberal principles, and virtuous manners'.[11] This renown was developed as public history in the former Warrington student William Turner's narrative of the Academy, which ran over many numbers of the *Monthly Repository* in 1813, while it had first been enshrined as personal history in the sermon William Enfield delivered at John Aikin, D.D.'s funeral. It was Aikin who had introduced many of the informal norms of instructional life there; as a result, the history of Warrington Academy is closely tied up with the Aikin family history. Warrington's reputation in the nineteenth century was decided through Lucy Aikin's memoir of her father (Anna Barbauld's brother), John Aikin, M.D. and it was further brought into the literary arena through memoirs of Anna Barbauld herself by both Lucy Aikin and her great-niece, Anna Le Breton.[12] The foundational Warrington sociable norms promoted by its network of male Dissenting clerics, which even the cranky Gilbert Wakefield recalled in his *Memoirs* as a 'feast of reason and of soul', were codified in the historicizing of that experience through the memoirs of their female descendants, an aspect of Warrington's self-conscious assimilation of the schoolroom to the parlour. Anna Barbauld's insistence upon the value of the family and familiar bonds was reiterated by Lucy Aikin as the domesticity of an extended family: 'I have often thought with envy of that society', she wrote in a letter to the Lancashire historian Henry Bright, 'they [the tutors] and theirs lived together like one large family'.[13] This domesticity linked tutors, students and families via an idealized notion of intellectual freedom: a familiarity in which 'pleasing fires of lively fancy play,/And wisdom mingles her serener ray' (1:47–8). The narrative of Warrington is one which recalled that 'The most cordial intimacy subsisted among the tutors and their families, with whom also the elder students associated on terms of easy and affectionate intercourse'.[14]

But the Warrington Academy was not a family: it was a pioneering provincial Dissenting institution. It numbered some of the most significant educationalists among the Dissenting branches of Presbyterians and Congregationalists, and from it emerged important scientific, radical and reform thinkers and publications. Warrington provided the intellectual counterpart to the commercial and technological growth sponsored by Quakers.[15] By the 1780s these Nonconformists felt themselves to be on the cusp of fully entering into English social and political life, anticipating the repeal of the Test and Corporation Acts, which continued to debar them from university degrees and from holding public political office. Having developed the economic infrastructure for political power through their commercial and industrial interests as well as producing scientific and literary innovation outside of Oxbridge, the Dissenting milieu could claim a pristine intellectual and moral authority – not holding public office meant they could not be accused of corruption, and the intellectual self-confidence inspired by such a position runs through the rhetoric of various Warringtonians. Warrington's discourse of politics was principled and enlightened, shaped by Aikin and Gilbert Wakefield, and Joseph Priestley: anti-slavery sentiments ran high, and Barbauld's poem on 'Corsica' suggests that current political issues were part and parcel of everyday discussion and enthusiasms. Students, who included Malthus, Harriet Martineau's father, later M.P.s, and a large number of scientists and writers, at moments even outflanked their tutors, and the tutors: 'were alarmed and terrified at the anti-English zeal, which, during the American war, was displayed by several of the students. One of them, who boarded at Dr Enfield's, insisted on his right to illuminate *his own* windows for an American victory; but this the Doctor declined to allow, as it committed himself, the master of the house.'[16]

All of which is to suggest something of the intellectual and social world within which the young Anna Aikin led her charmed, if also circumscribed, life as John Aikin's daughter. She had been recognized as brilliant from childhood. Newcome Cappe recalled hearing her as a precocious four-year-old correct her father on a piece of religious doctrine.[17] Having persuaded her father to allow her to learn Greek and Latin, she was a ready interlocutor for the Warrington students and tutors.[18] But if Warrington served her as an idyll it did not suggest to her that it might serve as a model institution for other young women, and readers of Anna Barbauld's letters will know that she turned down Elizabeth Montagu's request to help start a 'kind of Academy' for young women, arguing instead that the 'best way for a woman to acquire knowledge is from conversation with a father or brother'. She asserted: 'my own situation has been peculiar, and would be no rule for others'.[19] In fact, her own education *was* undertaken through conversation with father and brother, but within an institutional setting that itself aimed in its ethos to blend together the familial and the educational. She might well have had an idealized notion of how pliable were the boundaries of the domestic scene, and her early poems suggest her special place and her equanimity within that 'peculiar' extended family.

The poems Barbauld wrote as a young woman at Warrington – those that were published in 1773 and those that remained unpublished but were circulated in the Warrington circle – taken as a group formulate her notions of intellectual friendship, weaving together the values of sentiment and intellect. Her praise of Mary Wilkinson Priestley is precisely that she embodies a balance of mind and feeling: 'So cool a judgment, and a heart so warm' (1: 26). When visiting the Priestleys at home,

> Oft have I there the social circle joined
> Whose brightening influence raised my pensive mind,
> For none within that circle's magic bound,
> But sprightly spirits move their chearful round.
>
> (1: 41–4)

Barbauld praises the individual autonomy and group cohesion of the members of the 'social circle': they are not 'bound' by a charm, but shaped through voluntary association, and notably, though ornamented by 'easy smiles', no 'dark unfriendly passions enter there'(1: 46). The principle connects sociality and morality: it is 'ev'ry social tye that binds the good' (7:40). In his pedagogic experiments at the Academy, John Aikin had fostered a set of informal 'societies', urging tutors and students to voluntarily join associations to help them with elocution and composition.[20] The sense of freedom within propriety structures many of Anna Barbauld's images: demonstrating the elasticity of a necessary boundary: although 'On A Lady's Writing' has not yet been precisely dated, it conveys this as the addressee's lines are praised for being 'Correct though free, and regular though fair'(51: 3–4).

The interpenetrating of the sociable and the pedagogic at Warrington is condensed into the notion of 'friendship' – that informal polite manner which allows for rational discourse to take place, and for it to wander between the study and the garden, assimilating domestic affection and mental exercise, and apparently drawing women and men together within the circle. This ideal was of course not singular to Warrington; it formed part of a more general movement of middle-class consolidation through the promotion of a coherent ideology of polite manners.[21] But in the freedom of this particular community with its intimate ties of family, religion and aspiration, we find an exemplary site of such an ideal. In a genealogy of sociability, we might locate in Warrington the intellectual precursor to the early twentieth-century Bloomsbury group, whose convergence of male Cambridge education with the Stephens daughters' accomplishments and talents also strove towards a rigorous intellectual life, both polite and informal. As Priestley later recalled of the Warrington group's teas: 'our conversation was equally instructive and pleasing'.[22] In a poem addressed to William Enfield, tutor of Belles Lettres and Rector Academiae from 1770 until its demise, Barbauld presents a rule of pedagogy based on 'the friendly heart'(47: 1).[23] She reminds him to 'cease the task by precept to inform' (47: 8) since it is an intrinsic amiability that will better do the job: 'Thy candid manners and thy active mind / With more prevailing force the will shall bind'(47: 10–11). Friendship not only links feeling with mind, it 'better than a Muse inspires' (3: 4).

These early poems suggest that Barbauld's youthful poetic career was both bounded and authorized by her role as a privileged daughter and sister. Her brother was particularly instrumental in the publication of her 1773 *Poems*. When he returned to Warrington after finishing his medical studies in Aberdeen, 'by his persuasion and assistance her Poems were selected, revised, and arranged for publication'.[24] The appearance of the 1773 *Poems* was mutually beneficial for the Warrington Academy and for Anna Barbauld herself. William Woodfall's discussion of the *Poems* in the *Monthly Review* reminds its readers of Barbauld's place within the informal familial-pedagogic network of Dissenting intellectuals, suggesting her indebtedness to her social circle: 'The pupils of that very useful

seminar [Warrington] ... celebrated her genius, and diffused her praises
far and wide; and some of her compositions have been read and admired
by persons of the first taste and judgment in the republic of letters.'[25]
The volume signalled a step away from the world of the private circulation of poems into a public print culture, but advertising the boundaries of Warrington sociability. For if Warrington gave fame to Barbauld,
the volume also promoted the Academy. One of the central poems of
the volume, 'The Invitation', serves as an advertisement for the institution, describing its pedagogic aims – 'Beneath [the Mersey's] willows
rove th'inquiring youth,/And court the fair majestic forms of truth';
picturing its pleasant surrounds – 'Here bath'd by frequent show'rs
cool vales are seen,/Cloath'd with fresh verdure, and eternal green';
and enacting its polite rhetoric – 'where science smiles, the Muses join
the train;/And gentlest arts and purest manners reign' (4: 95–6, 55–6,
109–10). John Guillory has shown how Barbauld's landscape poetry participates (however unselfconsciously) in the project of cultural advance-
ment by Dissenters through taking on and forwarding what he describes
as 'vernacular literacy', suggesting that 'culture can be acquired like
property' – acquisition being available to the bourgeoisie rather than the
entitlement correspondent with the aristocracy.[26] 'The Invitation', written in the later 1760s, distils the benevolence of the Warrington ethos,
and its central place in the *Poems* suggests as well how that volume served
as evidence of the delights and accomplishments of the Warrington
Academy itself. To take the measure of its self-confident self-portrait
against Barbauld's more critical and mature poetry, it is worth jumping
ahead to a comparison with her late poem, *Eighteen Hundred and Eleven*.
'The Invitation' projects forward from 1773 a future in which the Test and
Corporation Acts have been repealed, and the students of Warrington
fully integrated into civil society. Realizing their youthful ambitions, they
are called by their country 'To fix her laws, her spirit to sustain,/And
light up glory through her wide domain!' (4: 137–8). 'The Invitation'
appears quite naive next to the later poem's dystopic view of London in
ruins, a poem which investigates and aims to make sense of the dialectics
of empire and commerce, where 'Arts, arms and wealth destroy the fruits
they bring' (124: 315). [27]

And against Barbauld's prospectus for Warrington, we need also to
place the hints from the Warrington Academy papers that the reality
of life there was actually very fraught. Henry Bright, a nineteenth-
century Lancashire historian found documents amongst the papers of
the Academy's founder John Seddon that attest to ongoing emotional

and financial tumult. Love affairs begun with the daughters of tutors, rowdy nights in local taverns, and bad behaviour by students who could not be properly disciplined for fear of losing their fees, meant a continual state of psychological and financial difficulty at Warrington: 'The beautiful Miss Rigbys made wild work with the students' hearts; and the trustees had to insist that they must be removed from the house if any students stayed there'; A memorandum from Gilbert Wakefield suggests the problem: 'The Academy is neither school nor college; it is without the supervision exercised in the one, and it wants the influence and authority of the other, – the students are treated as men, while they are but a set of wild and reckless boys.'[28]

So, when William Woodfall in the *Monthly Review* criticized her volume of *Poems* 1773 for lacking 'passion', there is a rational kernel to the rebuke.[29] The problem is not that Barbauld is unfeminine, and 'cold' as Coleridge would scurrilously insult her many years later; but that the boundaries of amiable sociability upon which Warrington was built and needed to stabilize itself, had to be rhetorically made firm if it were not to call attention to the troubles of a small community which had no 'real sanctions against bad behaviour, except expulsion', which it was financially difficult to enforce.[30] This is what Lucy Aikin later called Warrington's 'long struggle against [the finally] incurable disease' of operating in a buyer's educational market.[31] So, though Anna Barbauld's Warrington poetry does perhaps exhibit, as William McCarthy suggests, a defence against passion, this is in keeping with a poetry that is fundamentally aiming at assimilation, not at subversion.[32]

In her Warrington poetry, Barbauld displays the good poetic manners of a sister and daughter that endorse the sexual division of intellectual labour that paradoxically unites the Aikin family enterprise: to her brother she writes, 'To thee, the flute and sounding lyre decreed,/Mine, the low murmurs of the tuneful reed' (7:92–3). This voice will be sharply altered as she comes to know more about the passions of both politics and domesticity, and as her poetry is built from that passionate knowledge. Her political understanding was both sharpened and concretized in the urban milieu of 1790s radical London where the abstractions of Warrington were brought to bear on actual political events and decisions. And her husband's developing madness, which ended in his estrangement from his wife and his subsequent suicide, made visible to her the interior vistas of violent eccentricity. But amongst the Warrington poems, 'A Summer Evening's Meditation' does give an intimation of a point beyond the elasticity of Warrington boundaries. Here she lets her mind soar way above and beyond her vernal surroundings, where 'I launch into the trackless deeps of space' (58:82) exploring the furthest extent of the universe, though landing again to seek 'the known accustom'd spot' until 'the hour will come / when all these splendours bursting on my sight / Shall stand unveil'd, and to my ravish's sense / Unlock the glories of the world unknown' (58: 119–22). That world as yet unknown would come to be seen by many of Barbauld's peers as potential in the material apocalypse of the French Revolution. If the *Poems* of 1773 poetically publicized the familiarity of Warrington, the volume nonetheless drew Anna Aikin out towards that glorious world which would allow her both anonymity and autonomy, the world of writers associated with her publisher in London, Joseph Johnson.

For Woodfall in his review, passion is unproblematically linked to femininity and to romantic love; but in the post-1789 period, passion was becoming an increasingly political word, and the ardour that Anna Barbauld began to show in both prose and poetry might well have appeared to Woodfall to be just as unfeminine as earlier, though freighted with fervour. Not that she was oblivious to romantic love. Lucy Aikin wrote about it to Bright, giving a light and literary account: 'Rousseau's "Heloise" too, had much to answer for, and at its appearance (so Miss Aikin tells me), "everybody instantly fell in love with every body" and then it was that Mr Barbauld won his bride.'[33] Rochemont Barbauld came from a Huguenot family, intended for the Established clergy, but became a Dissenter while at Warrington.[34] He and Anna married in 1774, and after twelve years with their boys' school, Rochment was invited to take on the Dissenting congregation in Hampstead.[35] At the Palgrave school Barbauld became as polished an educationalist as she had been a polite daughter at Warrington. William Turner writes in his memorial article of 1825 that 'during this whole period her muse did not favour the public with any of her productions; although some exquisite gems were occasionally dug from the poetic vein'.[36] Instead, she turned to pedagogic writings, and from this period come *Lessons for Children of Two to Three Years Old* (1778), *Lessons for Children of Three Years Old* (1778), *Lessons for Children from Three to Four Years Old* (1779) and her *Hymns in Prose for Children* (1781). As with her volume of *Poems* (1773), these writings were published by Joseph Johnson, and it was during the Palgrave period that the Barbaulds began to attend Johnson's dinners when they were in London. Anna Barbauld described those evenings to her brother in a letter after a trip to London in 1784: 'Our evenings, particularly at Johnson's, were so truly social and lively, that we protracted them sometimes till – but I am not telling tales. Ask – at what time we used to separate.'[37] The circle she would have met in the 1780s at Johnson's was less politically homogeneous than it would come to be in the post-1789 period. Anglicans and Dissenters, political moderates and radicals were published by Johnson in this period, and entertained by him at his weekly dinners.[38] Here Anna Barbauld encountered Sarah Trimmer, also writing on education for children and also published by Johnson; a few years later, Trimmer would break with the publisher over the partisanship of his author and dinner list.[39]

But when the Barbaulds moved to Hampstead in 1787, the move precipitated the beginning of a new literary and personal identity for Anna Barbauld. Horace Walpole had been pleased, in 1774, to show Anna and Rochemont around Strawberry Hill, and a few years later to praise her poetry in a letter to William Mason. But in 1790, with the storm raging in the Dissenting and Reform milieus about both the disaster of the defeat of the Repeal of the Test and Corporation Acts and the marvellous explosion of the French Revolution, Walpole called her the 'virago Barbauld'; and in 1791, she had become a 'poissionière' 'prophetess' ready to exercise her 'talons', a republican 'disciple of Paine'.[40]

Though we are used to thinking of later eighteenth-century London as being a centre with the borough as a self-enclosed village, literary and political Hampstead residents such as Anna Barbauld and her friend Joanna Baillie felt themselves to be both members of the locality and part of the metropolis. Access to town might often be made difficult by bad roads and weather, but there was an ongoing traffic in and out of the centre, with a daily coach between Hampstead and Oxford Street. And in the later 1780s and 1790s, the Aikin family and the Warrington community had dispersed to various areas of London. While Rochemont and Anna Barbauld lived in Church Row, Priestley and Wakefield were living in Hackney, and John Aikin lived first in Broad Street in London, and later moved permanently to Stoke Newington.[41] But the print culture fostered through Johnson's press and its linked social circle knitted together in print what might appear disparate over space, and also reinforced the connections between suburbs and centre in his dinner parties. In London Barbauld moved in more than one social circle: for example, she often dined at the house of bluestocking Elizabeth Montagu where she observed 'the imposing union of literature and fashion'; but it was while 'under the humbler roof of her friend and publisher, Joseph Johnson' that she saw 'a chosen knot of lettered equals'.[42] Johnson's building in St Paul's Churchyard served him as both office and home: right in the centre of London, the intelligentsia passed by and through. Mary Wollstonecraft worked for him in the 1780s, being supplied by him with plenty of literary work, and it was at Johnson's table that she found love as well as literary interest in Fuseli. There is no doubt but that Johnson's circle was lively, daring, artistic as well as politically radical, and that it exerted a powerful influence on rationalist women such as Wollstonecraft and Barbauld, and later Mary Hays.[43] The move to Hampstead brought Barbauld into closer physical and political proximity to her brother than she had been at Palgrave, and the links to Johnson had been long-standing and familial. Johnson's friendship with Joseph Priestley helped to cultivate a geographically wide range of authors: as his biographer points out, 'By publishing with Johnson . . . they enjoyed a kind of proximity to one another that complemented their closeness in thought' as liberal Dissenters.[44] And amongst the now explicitly *radical* Johnson circle, amiability was of much less concern than political passion. Anna Barbauld turned to these public issues – religious toleration, the slave trade and the French Revolution – and made passionate claims for them in both poetry and prose.

She made a significant intervention into the pamphlet war around the French Revolution. Barbauld's *Address to the Opposers of the Repeal* was reprinted by Johnson twice in 1790. Her pamphlet explicitly linked the domestic political questions of religious toleration that had originated in the English Revolution of the 1640s with the international ones of 1789. Johnson's pamphlet press offered anonymity – he published over fifty pamphlets on the issue of toleration – and this anonymity cut across the sexual division of intellectual labour that Barbauld had endorsed whilst at Warrington.[45] Her argument was printed within end papers advertising other republican Dissenting pamphleteers, including the Warrington tutors Gilbert Wakefield and Joseph Priestley. Before the year was out, Barbauld's address had itself become the object of a set of 'strictures' by William Keate, Rector of Laverton.[46] She was thus fully engaged in the public debate. In her address, Barbauld speaks the enlightened rationality that aims for a universal constituency: 'We wish to bury every name of distinction in the common appellation of Citizen.'[47] The pamphlet modulates from an ironic criticism of those who opposed the Repeal into a passionate advocacy of the French Revolution, drawing on the millenarian rhetoric associated with the spectrum of radicalism in the early 1790s:

Can you not discern the signs of the times? The minds of men are in movement from the Borysthenes to the Atlantic. Agitated with new and strong emotions, they swell and heave beneath oppression, as the seas within the Polar Circle, when, at the approach of Spring, they grow impatient to burst their icy chains; when what, but an instant before, seemed so firm, spread for many a dreary league like a floor of solid marble, at once with a tremendous noise gives way, long fissures spread in every direction, and the air redounds with the clash of floating fragments, which every hour are broken from the mass.[48]

This address is grounded in a sense of intellectual entitlement, as Barbauld claims her right to speak of a 'certain, sure operation of increasing light and knowledge'.[49] Against the manners of polite society as structurally moral by virtue of their amiability, Barbauld insists 'Truth is of a very intolerant spirit. She will not make any compromise with Error.'[50] She has brought with her from her Warrington education her focus on the universal and the rational, but it is now ignited by the excitement of current events, and eschews her earlier discourse of domestic sociability – its mental mode is that of intervention now rather than meditation.

In his 'strictures', William Keate groups together pamphlets by Priestley and Price and Barbauld as all belonging to a single persuasion and intellectual formation, and he singles out Barbauld's for its 'intemperance' and 'arrogance'; rebuking the author for not allowing 'himself time to cool' while admitting that the pamphlet's prose is 'animated'.[51] A postscript (which may be disingenuous) adds: 'since the above was at the press, the author hears, with infinite surprise, not unmixed with concern', that the pamphlet 'is from a female pen! "And in soft bosoms dwells such mighty rage?"'.[52]

In 1791, Johnson published Barbauld's poem about the slave trade under her own name – it was one of many abolitionist poems written by women throughout the debate.[53] Her description in the poem of the life of 'voluptuous ease' amongst the plantations may have been in part learned from the stories of the sons of planters who were educated and disciplined at the Warrington Academy. Bright found evidence in the Seddon papers that 'the West Indians were bewailing their native islands, and shocking the tutors by declaring that the earliest request of a planter's child was always for a "young nigger to kick"'.[54] Righteous indignation is the tone of the poem, and in it Barbauld makes an assault upon the corrupt rhetoric of current politics: she excoriates the 'flimsy sophistry' (87:27) of Parliamentary debate. With the publication of the signed *Epistle to*

Wilberforce and the anonymous pamphlets of 1790–3, which included *Civic Sermons to the People*, and an essay on Gilbert Wakefield, Barbauld fully engaged the public arena of republican intervention. Walpole counted Barbauld as a republican poet, grouping her with Robert Merry and Helen Maria Williams as a Painite elegist.[55] She was now being acknowledged as part of a circle defined politically, rather than familiarly, and whose rhetoric was passionate rather than amiable.

And this was not only a public persona; in her privately circulated poems of the period, Barbauld is proudly self-conscious of her shift. Her 'Lines to Samuel Rogers in Wales on the Eve of Bastille Day, 1791' link the urban and the revolutionary, and point away from the Warrington manner:

> Hanging woods and fairy streams,
> Inspirers of poetic dreams,
> Must not now the soul enthrall,
> While dungeons burst, and despots fall.
> (89: 4–7).

Her letter adds: 'what have you to say in your defence for rambling amongst fairy streams & hanging woods instead of being at the "Crown and Anchor" as you and every good patriot ought to be on the 14th of July?'[56] Walpole recorded that the event was broken into by government agents, and 'Eleven disciples of Paine [taken into] custody': 'Mrs Merry, Mrs Barbauld, and Miss Helen Maria Williams will probably have subjects for elegies.' Gillian Russell and Clara Tuite have interestingly characterized Barbauld's importance to the event without actually being present at it (Walpole writes that she did not turn up, even though she had 'let her nails grow accordingly') as 'virtual sociability'.[57] The Warrington world which, as Lucy Aikin saw epitomized in the tutor William Enfield, aimed at 'rendering mankind not only mutually serviceable, but mutually agreeable', had given way to a world which was turning upside down, and in which to have a character 'in essence amiable' was no longer the desideratum: 'To please all the world . . ./Is no passion of mine' writes John Aikin in his *Poems* of 1791.[58]

While Anna Barbauld was gathering rhetorical energy in the Johnson milieu, her fellow Warringtonian, Gilbert Wakefield, had also become increasingly radicalized. Wakefield held the Warrington image up to a somewhat tarnishing gaze in his *Memoirs* of 1792. In his acerbic reminiscences of the Academy, Wakefield looks back to the Warrington of the 1760s and 1770s with a demystifying eye, providing an irascible counterpart to the Aikin family narrative. Of John Aikin he writes that he could be very cruel to students, telling tales of 'mortifying instances of severity in the castigation of his pupils'.[59] Wakefield strips apart the apparently seamless links between amiability and rationality: of the Hebrew tutor at Warrington, John Taylor, he writes, he was 'very learned, liberal and rational', but as well, 'peevish and angry' as a disputant, 'utterly impatient of contradiction, and dictatorial even to intolerance'.[60] Wakefield argues that principle and friendship may often part company: he says that his pursuit of 'religious truth' could only be undertaken 'in opposition to the sensibilities of domestic influence' and 'the restraints of friendship'.[61] In the same year he published a pamphlet arguing against any kind of public worship and Anna Barbauld published, again through Johnson's press, a set of 'strictures' against Wakefield's polemic. Her pamphlet shows her thoughtfully addressing the continuum of the domestic and the public: 'The sentiments of admiration, love, and joy, swell the bosom with emotions which seek for fellowship and communication. The flame may indeed be kindled by silent musing; but when kindled it must infallibly spread.'[62] In this pamphlet which is itself very passionate about the goods brought about by public worship, we may be facing an argument which is motivated by the exigencies of Barbauld's own daily life, for these two pathways of print culture and the quasi-public sociality of congregational worship were the ones through which Anna Barbauld presented herself as an autonomous intellectual woman. She points to the democracy of public worship: 'Public Worship is a *civic* meeting. The temple is the only place where human beings, of every rank and sex and age, meet together for one common purpose.'[63] She might only 'virtually' attend radical celebrations, but she would regularly attend the congregation. But the essay also shows Barbauld's astute psychological analysis of Wakefield, a man who fell out with almost all his colleagues: 'Separating through the purest motives from one church, he has not found another with which he is inclined to associate . . . he worships alone because he stands alone.'[64]

Barbauld's periodical publications of the early 1790s included 'To a Great Nation, Written by a Lady' in Benjamin Flower's *Cambridge Intelligencer*. While the Johnson pamphlets use anonymity to allow Barbauld to enter fully into the debate without reference to gender, the prominence given to the gender of the writer here seems quite pointed as a juxtaposition of polite and passionate rhetoric: perhaps there is a place, after all, for 'dark unfriendly passions' (1: 46). The poem suggests that a lady can, without shame, write in the passionately analytical language of

politics, rather than love: 'nor virgin's plighted hand, nor sighs / just now
the ardent youth detain' from the dealing round of 'dreadful vengeance'
(93: 11–12, 2). It is worth noting that Johnson cultivated both the Godwin
and the Aikin families, and opened a space for both Anna Barbauld and
Mary Wollstonecraft to develop as intellectuals. But they both played very
different roles, and the tension between them can be cited in Barbauld's
occasional poem 'The Rights of Woman'. The difference between the
two may be seen as that between Dissenting and radical sensibilities.[65]
Wollstonecraft had criticized Barbauld's 'To a Lady, with some painted
Flowers' in her *Vindication of the Rights of Woman*, and Craft and McCarthy
argue that Barbauld's response is the work of a momentary irritation,
rather than a programmatic argument about women's rights. It is certainly the case that Barbauld aims in this poem to make the universal case
overwhelm any sexual division of labour or love, and hierarchy of gender
is recouped into a 'mutual love' that confounds the rationality of 'separate
rights' (90: 32). There is a hint of Barbauld's Warrington naivete in this
poem, and it is not surprising that she never intended it for publication.[66]
Amongst the Aikin female historians, the anti-Wollstonecraft–Godwin
tendency became a family inheritance: 'The ladies of my family, though
great admirers of Mrs Godwin's writings, were too correct in their conduct to visit her, and the same objection was felt to Mrs Shelley.'[67] The different trajectories of the Aikins and the Wollstonecraft–Godwin–Shelleys
mark out different lines in the politics of radicalism and republicanism
in the late eighteenth and early nineteenth centuries. The Aikins' liberalism was rooted deeply in and bounded by their religious convictions;
the Godwin–Shelleys pressed their radicalism further until, bursting the
bounds of piety and convention, it fostered a version of political and aesthetic radicalism that looked towards the democratic secular radicalism
of the later nineteenth century. And we can see how distasteful the close-
knit Aikins would have found Godwin's public positions on domesticity:
in 1793 Godwin had vigorously argued against the priority of familiar, in
the sense of the familial, ties: 'My wife or mother may be profligate or a
prostitute, malicious, lying or dishonest. If they be, of what consequence
is it that they are mine?'[68]

    The mid to late 1790s saw, as we know, the retreat from interventionist
politics on many fronts. Mary Wollstonecraft was dead by 1797, and
her legacy is one which is unblemished by any fall from radical principle. Joseph Johnson found himself tried and imprisoned for publishing
Gilbert Wakefield's excoriation of Bishop Llandaff.[69] Wakefield spent
a year in prison and died soon after in 1801. Just after his release from

prison, John Aikin wrote a poem to him in the temper of anti-Jacobinism, in which he invited Wakefield to put aside his politics and return to a more amiable muse: 'Cease then, my Friend, thy generous hopeless aim ... And in the soothing voice of friendship drown / The groans and shouts, and triumphs of the world.' The passionate radical and internationalist aim of '*fraternité*' has relaxed into a more local and familiar idea of friendship. Wakefield replied in a poem, also published in Aikin's *Monthly Magazine*, in which he refused to take that route, vowing still to 'front the grim visage of despotic power, / lawless, self-will'd, fierce, merciless, corrupt'. He died before the next year was over.[70]

Anna Barbauld, on the other hand, continued to make poetry out of her experience. Like her fellow poets, Wordsworth and Coleridge, in the mid-decade retreat Barbauld meditated on her earlier poetic and polemical interventions. Her 1795 'Autumnal Thought' offers a poignant retrospective of her period of political passion. The autumn here presents that moment of the mid-1790s, 'when the fervid Passions cool, / And Judgment, late, begins to rule; / When Reason mounts her throne serene, And social friendship gilds the scene' (99: 15–17). But for that loss, she cannot find Wordsworth's 'abundant recompense'; at the very moment of equanimity, 'But O, the swiftly shortening day! Low in the west the sinking ray!' The balance is hard to maintain, and her intimation of the afterlife when 'The flames that drank our vital strength' are 'at length assuaged' recognizes the declension of 'failing spirits [that] prompt no more' (99: 27).

In the break-up of the radical urban print milieu, Anna Barbauld turned increasingly to the more private sociability of her family: she and her now very unstable husband moved to Stoke Newington in 1802, to be with her brother, who had moved there in ill health in 1798. There the family became involved in local activities – Rochemont held the ministry at the Newington Green chapel, while Anna founded the local book society – and distanced from national issues.[71] John Aikin set the tone when he wrote in a letter of 1802, 'I am cured of all theoretical ideas of reform.'[72] In her first years in Stoke Newington, Barbauld wrote little that indicated either the poetic of passion or the active link to the urban social groups she had associated with in the early 1790s. She wrote rather as an editor, collating materials from *The Spectator* and *The Tatler*, and editing Richardson's *Letters*.

There is agreement amongst contemporary interpreters of Barbauld's work that her Juvenalian satire, *Eighteen Hundred and Eleven*, is one of her strongest intellectual pieces, and displays a poetic maturity perhaps glimpsed but certainly not achieved in her Warrington poems.[73] After her husband's severe illness and suicide, which she may be alluding to when she writes in a fragment of how 'All that can wake the love of [her] soul' 'wrecked around thee sink' (123: 5–6), she found a renewed strain of independence and analytical passion out of which she made *Eighteen Hundred and Eleven*. Perhaps most revealing in that poem is her presentation of London, the site of her emancipation into intellectual discourse and personal autonomy, now projected into the future, buffeted by time and the course of empire into a ruin. Barbauld first presents the ideal of London that was hers when she arrived in the late 1780s. This is a city startlingly unlike that Warrington ideal of the balance of freedom and regularity; instead, London's walls are 'irregularly great' (124: 161). The metropolis is a great estate of diversity and possibility, with 'No jealous drawbridge, and no closing gate' (124: 162). Unlike many of Barbauld's early 'conversation' poems, intimately addressed to a friend or relative (a style Coleridge brilliantly adopted), this is a very public poem, whose interlocutor is Britain the 'island Queen' (124: 40). But if its elevated stance marks one difference from Barbauld's early poems, it nonetheless evinces a personal isolation through a narrating voice more vulnerable and idiosyncratically subjective than the 'good daughter' benignity of many of her Warrington poems. Despite the obvious links to the tradition of the urban and rural moralized ruin poem of the eighteenth century, this is a poem which reiterates Romanticism's appeal to freedom while also acknowledging the defeats of the previous decade. Both the imaginary ruin of London and the imagined empire of Columbus issue from a speaking self who has been unmoored from her previous circles of sociability. There is a poignant identification between Barbauld and the city; she is elegiac in her evocation of the fading city whose 'glories pass away' (124: 314). Mary Wollstonecraft had criticized Barbauld for her linking of flowers and ladies, but by making the metaphoric link between the metropolis and the flower, 'But fairest flowers expand but to decay', Barbauld presents the life of the city on the model of a beautiful woman, who 'knows no second spring' (124: 313, 316), and so doing, she both dignifies the problem of female ageing and also infuses London's ruins with humanity. *Eighteen Hundred and Eleven* might well be Barbauld's revision of her 'Autumnal Thought' of 1795. The sense of loss that permeates the earlier poem is here attached to a more politically astute understanding of the pathways of defeat and regeneration. While the earlier poem could offer only the recompense of the social circle, *Eighteen Hundred and Eleven* compels its speaker into the visionary mode, where she is, as prophetess, both utterly isolated and the medium through which others might see how 'to other climes the genius soars/. . . And swears – Thy world, Columbus, shall be free' (124: 321, 334).

NOTES

For full citations see Bibliography.

1 The phrase was used by William Turner to describe the pedagogic style of John Aikin D.D., in his 'Historical Account', *Monthly Repository* 8 (1813), 169.

2 'A Character', '[William Enfield]', Barbauld, *Poems*, (50: 1) p. 69, (47: 11) p. 68. All further references to Anna Barbauld's poems will be keyed to this, authoritative edition, by poem number and line number, in parenthesis.

3 Tyson, *Johnson*, p. 226.

4 *Ibid.*, p. 39.

5 McLachlan, *Warrington Academy*, p. 3.

6 Le Breton, *Memoir*, pp. 46, 62; Rodgers, *Georgian Chronicle*, pp. 98–9.

7 'A Character of Joseph Priestley' and 'Epistle to William Wilberforce, Esq. On the Rejection of the Bill for abolishing the Slave Trade'.

8 Armstrong, 'Gush of the Feminine'.

9 Guillory, 'English Common Place'; Keach, 'Barbauld'. See also Ross, 'Configurations'.

10 MacLachlan, *Warrington Academy*, p. 23.

11 Enfield, *Funeral Sermon*, p. 18.

12 Aikin, *Memoir*; Aikin, *Works*; Le Breton, *Memoir*; Le Breton, *Memories*; a twentieth-century descendant has continued the tradition: Rodgers, *Georgian Chronicle*.

13 Wakefield, *Memoirs*, p. 215; Aikin quoted in Le Breton, *Memoir*, p. 35; for a different reading of the meaning of Barbauld's interest in the domestic, see McDonagh, 'Barbauld's Domestic Economy'.

14 Aikin, *Memoir*, vol. I, p. 10.

15 Watts, *Dissenters*, vol. I, p. 366.

16 Rodgers, *Georgian Chronicle*, p. 50; Bright, 'Historical Sketch', p. 22.

17 Cappe, *Discourses*, p. xiv.

18 Aikin, *Works*, vol. I, p. vii.

19 Le Breton, *Memoir*, p. 47.

20 McLachlan, *Warrington Academy*, p. 82.

21 Langford, *Polite and Commercial People*, pp. 59–122.

22 Bright, 'Historical Sketch', p. 12.

23 *Ibid.*, p. 15.

24 Aikin, *Works*, vol. I, p. xiii.

25 Woodfall, *Monthly Review* 48 (1773), p. 54.

26 Guillory, 'English Common Place', p. 18.

27 For two very different and impressive readings of *Eighteen Hundred and Eleven*, see Keach, 'Regency Prophecy' and Newlyn, *Reading, Writing*, pp. 134–69.

28 Bright, 'Historical Sketch', pp. 22, 28.

29 Woodfall, *Monthly Review*, pp. 54–9, 133–7, 133.

30 Coleridge, *Table Talk*, vol. I, pp. 564–5; Bright, 'Historical Sketch', p. 21.

31 Aikin, *Memoir*, vol.II, p. 297.

32 Elizabeth Eger, on the other hand, finds Barbauld to be 'an outsider in a community of outsiders' at Warrington; see, Eger 'Nine Living Muses', p. 214; McCarthy, '"We Hoped the Woman"'.

33 Bright, 'Historical Sketch', p. 22, p. 28.

34 McLachlan, *Warrington Academy*, p. 87.

35 Rodgers, *Georgian Chronicle*, p. 98.

36 Turner, 'Mrs Barbauld', *The Newcastle Magazine* 4 (1825), p. 230.

37 Ellis, *Memoir*, vol. I, p. 117.

38 Chard, 'Joseph Johnson'.

39 Tyson, *Johnson*, p. 84; Beloe, *The Sexagenarian*, vol. I, p. 345.

40 Walpole, *Letters*, vol. IX, p. 10; vol. XIV, p. 345; vol. XV, p. 25.

41 Ellis, *Memoir*, vol. I, p. 176.

42 Aikin, *Works*, vol. I, pp. xxxii–xxxiii.

43 Tyson, *Johnson*, pp. 67–8, 143–4.

44 *Ibid.*, p. 56.

45 *Ibid.*, p. 93.

46 Keate, *Free Examination*, pp. 55–64.

47 Barbauld, *Address*, p. 17.

48 *Ibid.*, pp. 31–2.

49 *Ibid.*, p. 31.

50 *Ibid.*, p. 15.

51 Keate, *Free Examination*, p. 55.

52 *Ibid.*, p. 64.

53 See Ferguson, *Subject to Others*.

54 Bright, 'Historical Sketch', p. 22.

55 Walpole, *Letters*, vol. XV, p. 25.

56 Rodgers, *Georgian Chronicle*, p. 115.

57 Gillian Russell and Clara Tuite, letter to author. See also Jon Mee's chapter in this volume on Robert Merry's role in this event.

58 'Counter-Remonstrance', Aikin, *Poems*, p. v.

59 Wakefield, *Memoirs*, p. 204.

60 *Ibid.*, p. 211.

61 *Ibid.*, p. 2.

62 Barbauld, *Remarks*, p. 18.

63 *Ibid.*, p. 43.

64 *Ibid.*, p. 57.

65 Keach, 'Barbauld', p. 56.

66 But see Newlyn, *Reading, Writing*, pp. 134–69, for an interesting vindication of the poem.

67 Rodgers, *Georgian Chronicle*, p. 189.

68 Godwin, *Enquiry*, ed. Priestley, vol. III, p. 146.

69 Tyson, *Johnson*, p. 163; see also Smyser, 'Trial'; Chard, 'Joseph Johnson'.
70 Aikin, 'To Gilbert Wakefield', p. 422; Wakefield, 'To John Aikin', p. 513. See also Aikin, 'To the Memory of Gilbert Wakefield', pp. 220–1.
71 Rodgers, *Georgian Chronicle*, pp. 129–30.
72 Aikin, *Memoir*, vol. I, p. 247.
73 Mellor, 'The Female Poet', p. 271; Newlyn, *Reading, Writing*, pp. 134–69; Keach, 'Regency Prophecy'.

5

Firebrands, letters and flowers: Mrs Barbauld and the Priestleys

Deirdre Coleman

A year after the tremendous success of her *Poems*, and *Miscellaneous Pieces in Prose*, both published in 1773, the Dissenter Anna Letitia Aikin received a charming letter from the patrician bluestocking Elizabeth Montagu. As part of Montagu's ploy for opening up 'a more intimate correspondence' with Aikin, she launches into a meditation on the sociability of 'polite letters' and the exclusions of the public sphere, both in the literary world and in the political realm:

> The genuine effect of polite letters is to inspire candour, a social spirit, and gentle manners; to teach a disdain of frivolous amusements, injurious censoriousness, and foolish animosities. To partake of these advantages and to live under the benign empire of the muses, on the conditions of a naturalized subject, who, not having any inherent right to a share of office, credit, or authority, seeks nothing but the protection of the society, is all I aim at.[1]

The modesty, deference and self-deprecation of the woman writer is a familiar rhetorical ploy. Montagu appears to argue that, when it comes to genius and inspiration – 'the benign empire of the muses' – she does not enjoy by birthright the rights and privileges of a native; she can only be admitted to such after long residence and acculturation. But if womanly modesty entails self-exclusion, Montagu's discourse of citizenship – the use of terms such as 'empire', 'naturalized subject', 'inherent right' and 'authority' – is primarily concerned with exclusions imposed on women from without. The world of polite letters is a gentlemanly, homosocial one, she implies, a world which, if it does not exclude women completely, only tolerates them as 'naturalized' foreigners; and of course this exclusion from the world of letters mirrors the wider exclusion of women from political life. Thus, Montagu's modesty cloaks an appeal to the shared experience of women's marginal position within the public sphere. This bid for solidarity with her new Dissenting friend is then cleverly consolidated by Montagu's allusion to the function and status of the Dissenting public sphere within the national republic of letters, manifest in her appeal to a minimalist model of the state, whose sole purpose is the protection of the individual and his/her rights. Montagu's alignment of the literary woman's marginalization with the civic disabilities suffered by Dissenters was an astute gambit, calculated to woo and flatter her correspondent.[2]

In a recent article on Barbauld and Dissent, Daniel E. White describes the Dissenting public sphere as a sub-category of the classical public sphere, a 'fragment that exerted critical pressure from within'. His focus is on the Warrington Academy, and his model is familial literary collaboration, his readings centring on Barbauld's co-authored productions with her brother, John Aikin, *Miscellaneous Pieces in Prose* (1773) and *Evenings at Home* (1792–6). Arguing that readings of Barbauld as feminist or anti-feminist are off-target, White presents Barbauld as a moderate whose writings attempt to '"domesticate" the oppositional and rigorous identities of rational Dissent, to colour its austere religious and civil values with familial and domestic hues that would endear virtue, piety, and commerce to the affections of her readers'. There are many excellent aspects to White's article, such as his probing of the constituent elements of Barbauld's 'moderation', and his examination of the dialectical movement in her writings between establishment and sects, but his focus on familial collaboration and on 'the intimate plenitude of the home' obscures the extent to which women writers like Barbauld challenged private/public distinctions through their longing for equal participation in the world of knowledge and learning.[3]

In Barbauld's own case, despite a loving relationship with her father and brother, filial and fraternal bonds brought their own particular demands, requiring some dexterous negotiations, as can be seen in Barbauld's unpublished poem to her brother, 'To Dr Aikin on his Complaining that she neglected him' (1768).[4] The poem is notable for its regret that, whereas in early youth, brother and sister pursued the same studies, they are now assigned quite different paths, according to cultural prescription. Embittered by this exclusion from 'masculine' pursuits, the challenge for Barbauld is to recreate the 'bounded sphere' of women as a positive – a challenge she meets by describing it as the realm of fancy, or poetry, and domestic virtue. In order to arrive at this resolution, Barbauld mobilizes various modalities of 'friendship'. Initially 'friendship' is enlisted as the basis of her sibling relationship, but as the poem develops 'friendship' breaks free from familial ties to assume the shape of a socially useful and healing skill which, with its non-specialized,

universal language of words and gestures, transcends the (masculine) 'art'
of medicine and pharmacology:

> Beyond thy art thy friendship shall prevail
> And cordial looks shall cure, when drugs would fail:
> Thy words of balm shall cure the wounds of strife,
> And med'cine all the sharper ills of life. (*Poems*, p. 19)

By means of an all-inclusive social friendship, Barbauld inscribes the
'bounded sphere' within the wider world of her brother's knowledge.
Furthermore, by the end of the poem, her earlier elaboration of the
overlapping familial and public meanings of 'friendship' licenses her
poetic voice to participate in the public and social realm: 'when fair
friendship will unloose my tongue,/My trembling voice shall ne'er refuse
the song' (*Poems*, p. 19).

Thus, missing from White's model of collaboration is Barbauld's experience and understanding of knowledge as a gendered issue, requiring
careful negotiation through language of the terms on which she is permitted to participate in the world of polite letters. His essay also rests
upon a somewhat tame reading of the woman whose 'unfilial' politics
distressed some of her most ardent admirers.[5] Henry Crabb Robinson,
for instance, rereading her earlier writings, and looking back on the
hostile reception of her *Eighteen Hundred and Eleven, a Poem* (1812), was
disturbed by the 'unqualified jacobinism of her politics'.[6] Similarly, after her death in 1825, the anonymous reviewer of her collected writings
regretted that her 'fiery democracy sometimes carried her almost the
length of profanation' (*Poems*, p. 295).

This chapter goes beyond domestic and familial collaboration to focus
on Barbauld's close but argumentative relationship with Joseph Priestley,
the eminent scientist, theologian, philosopher and controversialist. Much
as she admired, and was influenced by, the eminent Priestley, Barbauld
was never a disciple, holding strongly in her early writings to a belief in
the virtues ascribed to her sex, such as sympathy and affection, sociability and conversation, and innate delicacy of taste.[7] In the 1770s, under
the influence of an emerging language and culture of sentiment and
sensibility, Barbauld took it upon herself to soften and temper Priestley's
masculine rigour by subjecting it to an aesthetic discourse of beauty
and sentimental standards of morality – an ambition which found her
treading dangerously upon 'enchanted ground', travelling towards 'the
regions of chivalry and romance' (*Works*, vol. II, p. 246). Her critique of

Priestleyan rationalism here anticipates that of Edmund Burke fifteen years later, in *Reflections upon the Revolution in France* (1790), where he lampoons Dissent as a '*hortus siccus*' (dry garden),[8] his brilliant and enduring emblem for the Unitarians' dead, dry, theoretical language of science, against which he so fulsomely pits 'the flowers of rhetoric' (as Mary Wollstonecraft in her turn so contemptuously characterized his style[9]), together with a chivalric code associating women with flowers, beauty, innocence and passivity.

Priestley took Barbauld's strictures seriously. Indeed, he was so disturbed by the drift of her opposition to him in the 1770s that he accused her of siding with the Papists in holding that 'ignorance is the mother of devotion'; he also charged her with giving cover and comfort to Dissenters defecting to the Establishment.[10] By the 1790s, however, Barbauld was firmly back inside the fold, celebrating the Establishment's opposition for the 'mark of separation' it placed upon Dissenters like herself, and heroically recommitting her sect to internal exile and persecution (*Works*, vol. II, p. 365). The regulation of her earlier emphasis on the primacy of feeling over intellect ('few can reason, but all can feel', *Works*, vol. II, p. 172) is further evident after the Birmingham riots of 1791, when the scale and level of intimidation against Dissenters escalated, and friends like the Priestleys lived under the shadow of a return of the mob's mindless ferocity.[11] With formerly close-knit communities of Dissenters splintering under renewed popular hostility, and many blaming Priestley for inciting the rioters, the Enlightenment sociability represented by Warrington in the 1760s and 1770s suddenly seemed a thing of the past. Rising to the occasion, undaunted, Barbauld wrote her magnificent *Civic Sermons to the People* (1792). Celebrating reason, or 'discourse', as the faculty distinguishing humans from brutes, she boldly throws wide the doors of civic and political participation to all men and women, regardless of class, so long as their actions are governed by reason.

JOSEPH PRIESTLEY AND MRS BARBAULD

All his life, and well before he earned the nickname 'Gunpowder Joe', Priestley revelled in controversy.[12] A couple of years after leaving Warrington he wrote gleefully to Barbauld that the Academy was lucky to have severed its connexion with him, for he was 'about to make a bolder push than ever for the pillory, the King's Bench Prison, or something worse' (Le Breton, *Memoir*, p. 37), a reference to his *View of the Principles and Conduct of the Protestant Dissenters* (London: J. Johnson, 1769), 'the freest and boldest thing' he had written to date, he claimed (Rutt, *Theological*, vol. I:I, p. 103). Priestley had been appointed tutor in languages and *belles lettres* at Warrington in 1761, when Anna Aikin was eighteen. The following year he married Mary Wilkinson, a year younger than Aikin, to whom the poet addressed a number of verses, calling her 'Amanda', a poetical name meaning 'beloved'. Altogether, Barbauld addressed eight poems to Mary or Joseph Priestley, and at least a half dozen other poems arise out of her relationship with this couple. Indeed, Barbauld's first known poem was entitled 'On Mrs P[riestley]'s Leaving Warrington', thrown into the chaise as the Priestleys left Warrington for Leeds in 1767.[13] This departure occasioned a significant rupture in the social circle so lovingly evoked in Barbauld's early poetry, and it is from this point onwards that her more concerted criticism of Priestley begins.

Priestley was proud of his own and his wife's involvement with Barbauld's literary career. In his *Memoirs*, published posthumously, he boasted:

Mrs Barbauld has told me that it was the perusal of some verses of mine that first induced her to write any thing in verse, so that this country is in some measure indebted to me for one of the best poets it can boast of. Several of her first poems were written when she was in my house, on occasions that occurred while she was there. (Rutt, *Theological*, vol. I:I, p. 54)

This insertion of himself into the poet's fame was a long-standing habit. In 1782, on the publication of *Two Discourses: 1. On Habitual Devotion: 2. On the Duty of not living to ourselves*, Priestley announced that, though ignorant of it, the public was already under considerable obligations to his first sermon, 'On Habitual Devotion' (1767), 'as it was the occasion of that excellent poem of Mrs Barbauld's, entitled *An Address to the Deity*, which was composed immediately after'. The intimate relationship between Barbauld and Priestley, advertised by the latter in 1782, had, in fact, been long known to the public, for in 1773, upon the publication of Barbauld's 'The Mouse's Petition' (*Poems*, pp. 36–7), the two friends found themselves somewhat unexpectedly pitted against each other in the controversy arising out of this playful poem about a mouse doomed to suffocate as a result of the scientist's experiments with different gases. The mouse's humble and plaintive petition to Priestley – 'Let not thy strong oppressive force/A free-born mouse detain' – stirred a hornet's nest in the public press, with reviewers fervently espousing the mouse's sentimental plea and denouncing the cruelty of experimental philosophers. Such was the furore that, in subsequent editions, Barbauld appended a note to the poem defending Priestley from the charge of cruelty: 'what was intended as the petition of mercy against justice, has been construed as the plea of humanity against cruelty ... cruelty could never be apprehended from the Gentleman to whom this is addressed ... the poor animal would have suffered more as the victim of domestic economy, than of philosophical curiosity' (*Poems*, p. 245). Despite her assertion that the mouse would have suffered more in a mouse-trap than through Priestley's experiments on it 'with different kinds of air' (*Poems*, p. 36), Barbauld had unwittingly bequeathed a hostage to Priestley's later enemies and persecutors. In Burke's propaganda war against revolutionaries in the 1790s, the association of chemistry and experimental science with unfeeling, hard-hearted metaphysics immediately called to mind the figure of Priestley; in 1796, for instance, raging against experimental philosophers as indifferent to 'those feelings and habitudes, which are the supports of the moral world', Burke thundered: 'These philosophers, consider men in their experiments, no more than they do mice in an air pump, or in a recipient of mephitic gas.'[14]

Despite her public defence of Priestley in 1773, and the latter's assertion in 1782 of the profound influence of his sermon 'On Habitual Devotion' on Barbauld's *Address to the Deity*, there remained serious differences between the two friends, differences which flared out in 1775, with Barbauld's 'Thoughts on the Devotional Taste, on Sects, and on Establishments'. Written the year after her marriage, Barbauld argues that the language of love, with all its 'exaggerated expressions' and 'romantic excesses' (*Works*, vol. II, p. 245), is the ideal language for religious devotion, a belief which may have reflected the 'exaggerated passion' upon which her own marriage was built, to the disapproval of her family, who resented Rochemont Barbauld's 'crazy demonstrations of amorous rapture, set off with theatrical French manners' (Le Breton, *Memoir*, p. 43). A less speculative explanation of the essay's thrust and general temper is to read it as Priestley read it, as a directly personal attack on him.[15] Philosophy, 'metaphysical subtleties', 'a disputatious spirit, and fondness for controversy': Barbauld argued that all these had given the mind 'a sceptical turn, with an aptness to call in question the most established truths' (*Works*, vol. II, p. 235). Barbauld's stand is not only on behalf of religion, however; as her title 'Devotional Taste' makes clear, she is also arguing for the primary importance of literature, taste and the fine arts. Devotion, properly called, is 'a taste, an affair of sentiment and feeling ... Its seat is in the imagination and the passions, and it has its source in that relish for the sublime, the vast, and the beautiful, by which we taste the

charms of poetry and other compositions that address our finer feelings'
(*Works*, vol. II, p. 232). Priestley's low opinion of aesthetics and the fine
arts, his scorn for 'the elegant enjoyments of life' are writ large in his sermons and published writings. When a tutor at Warrington he encouraged
his students to write poetry, 'not with any design to make them poets, but
to give them a greater facility in writing prose', a pedagogical method he
warmly recommended to all subsequent tutors (Rutt, *Theological*, vol. I:1,
p. 54). Fiction, too, had very limited uses, namely to 'amuse the imagination, and give play to the passions' (Rutt, *Theological*, vol. XXIV, p. 27).
This denigration of the literary is also evident in his response to the style
of Barbauld's essay; for instance, to her claim that establishments are 'the
womb and grave' of sects he retorts: 'though this is very prettily said, it
is by no means true in fact' (Rutt, *Theological*, vol. I:1, p. 283).

For Barbauld, as a woman writer dedicated to expanding and enhancing the discursive space allowed to literature and its sociable contexts,
Priestley's philistinism posed a threat to the principal sphere in which she
felt able to make her mark. Thus, where Priestley drove a wedge between
the love of God and what he described as the 'lower appetites' – 'sensual
pleasure, the pleasures of imagination and ambition' (Rutt, *Theological*,
vol. XV, p. 134) – Barbauld strove to bring these into close alignment. The
chief problem with Priestley's grand and stupendous ideas of the Deity
was the threat these ideas posed to the integrity of the self. While careful
to point out that she is no enemy to philosophy and reason, Barbauld
nevertheless believed that enlarged and abstract ideas of the Deity raised
God 'too high for our imaginations to take hold of', and that growing
'giddy with the prospect the mind is astonished, confounded at its own
insignificance . . . and the only feeling the soul is capable of in such a
moment is a deep and painful sense of its own abasement' (*Works*, vol. II,
pp. 237–8).

When Barbauld wrote to Mary Priestley, indirectly asking for
Priestley's estimate of the essay, he responded candidly and forcefully,
beginning his letter of December 1775: 'As my wife informs me that you
wish to know what I think of your late publication, I shall very freely tell
you' (Rutt, *Theological*, vol. I:1, p. 278). Given his pre-eminence as a theological controversialist,[16] Priestley was anxious to reinstate the profound
connection between philosophy and piety. But what disturbed him most
was Barbauld's desire to shift devotion away from a hierarchical/filial
model to a more egalitarian/Romantic model. Instead of devotion re-
sembling, as Priestley thought it should, the 'mixture of love and rever-
ence that a child bears towards his parent', Barbauld modelled devotion

upon the passion of heterosexual love. To Priestley, this was impious, even profane.

When the essay was republished in 1792, Barbauld omitted one of the sections most objectionable to Priestley,[17] but for the moment she held to her views. Indeed, a year later, in 1776, in private correspondence, she put her views even more strongly, arguing that magnificent conceptions of God went beyond inducing a worm-like 'abasement' to 'such an annihilation of ourselves as is nearly painful'. Following Burke, who offset the sublime with the beautiful in *A Philosophical Enquiry* (1757), she warned that, while such grand views

give some high pleasures & set religion upon a broad & firm basis ... we must correct what unfavorable tendency they may have, by often suffering our minds to dwell on those more affecting circumstances which arise in what we may call the more personal intercourse of a devout heart with its maker. The former is the *sublime*, the latter the *pathetic* of Religion.[18]

In 1775, Barbauld's view of Christian history was that she was living in a period of reasoning and examination. With religious persecution well behind them, sectarians had given themselves over to 'a critical and disputatious spirit' with the result that public worship consisted of argumentative sermons rather than the more desirable 'prayer' or 'praise'. Although she conceded that the oppositional energies of sectarianism were vital to the health of a nation's religious culture, Barbauld came to the rather negative conclusion that, while sects 'communicate a kind of spirit and elasticity necessary to the vigour and health of the soul' – just as 'the process of vegetation restores and purifies vitiated air' – this revivifying effect is 'soon lost amidst the corrupted breath of an indiscriminate multitude' (*Works*, vol. II, pp. 258–9). The other analogy, taken from the natural world, concerns the relation of rivers to ocean:

So the purer part of the element, continually drawn off from the mighty mass of waters, forms rivers, which, running in various directions, fertilize large countries; yet, always tending towards the ocean, every accession to their bulk or grandeur but precipitates their course, and hastens their reunion with the common reservoir from which they were separated. (*Works*, vol. II, p. 258)

The language of this second analogy is very close to her 'Character' of Priestley, a poem of uncertain date,[19] written after his time at Warrington – probably during the divisive climate of the later 1760s and early 1770s, when there were renewed accusations that Dissenters were disloyal.[20] Whilst celebrating the sublimity of Priestley's arduous genius – his 'eccentric, piercing, bold' work in theology and natural philosophy – and urging him to pursue the track revealed by his 'ardent genius', Barbauld is nostalgic for the lost world of Warrington sociability, before the turbulent years of Priestley's mature, public life. The contrast of past and present is a contrast between the beautiful stream and the sublime river, with a preference for a return to her poetic beginnings, which she owes to the 'wild cascade' of Priestleyan inspiration:

> So, where the' impetuous river sweeps the plain[,]
> Itself a sea, and rushes to the main,
> While it's firm banks repel conflicting tides
> And stately on its breast the vessel rides;
> Admiring much, the shepherd stands to gaze
> Awe-struck, and mingling wonder with his praise;
> Yet more he loves its winding path to trace
> Thro beds of flowers, and Nature's rural face,
> While, yet a stream, the silent vale it chear'd
> By many a recollected scene endear'd,
> Where, trembling, first, beneath the poplar shade
> He tun'd his pipe to suit the wild cascade.
>
> (*Poems*, p. 38)

The poem stops short of the essay's dispiriting conclusion that it is the destiny of sectarianism's sublime energy to be obliterated in the nonde-script ocean of Establishment, but it is still assimilationist in its overall drift. The concern is to emphasize Priestley's loyalty to church and state: for all the turbulence of this 'impetuous river', the vessel of state rides safely on his breast. Despite this assurance, however, the poet is still more comfortable attuning her poetic art to the softer 'social hours' of their earlier intimacy:

> But, O forgive, if touch'd with fond regret
> Fancy recalls the scenes she can't forget,
> Recalls the vacant smile, the social hours
> Which charm'd us once, for once those scenes were ours!
> And while thy praises thro wide realms extend
> We, sit in shades, and mourn the absent Friend[.]
>
> (*Poems*, pp. 37–8)

MARY PRIESTLEY AND MRS BARBAULD

Blessed with 'So cool a judgment, and a heart so warm' (*Poems*, p. 1), Mary Priestley represented for Barbauld the harmoniously orga-nized temperament so central to definitions of sociability,[21] unlike her philosopher-husband whose rough and unamiable rationality sometimes seemed at odds with the habits of social existence.[22] The early poems of the Warrington period which Barbauld addressed to Mary Priestley involve a number of shifting and complex languages, so much so that, in 1792, Mary Wollstonecraft used one of these poems to praise Barbauld, another (famously) to attack her. The poem which Wollstonecraft attacked in her *Vindication of the Rights of Woman* (1792), entitled 'To a Lady, with some painted flowers', dates from the Warrington period, with Mary Priestley ('Amanda') a likely candidate for the 'Lady'. Wollstonecraft's attack is a surprising one, for in the late 1780s both she and Barbauld had moved in the same radical circles associated with the publisher, Joseph Johnson.[23] Wollstonecraft was also an admirer of Barbauld, anthologizing her writings extensively in her educational works, and, even at the moment of attack, praising Barbauld for two lines from the poem, 'To Mrs P[riestley], with some Drawings of Birds and Insects': 'Pleasure's the portion of th'inferior kind;/But glory, virtue, Heaven for Man design'd' (*Poems*, p. 8). Whereas these lines qualify as the language of truth and soberness, the language of 'To a Lady, with some painted flowers' epitomizes for Wollstonecraft the artful flattery and the sexual compliments of a debased language of male sentimentality. Without taking much stock of the fact that the poem is an intimate poetic epistle from one woman to another, Wollstonecraft accuses Barbauld of an 'ignoble comparison', the traditional metaphoric association of women with flowers. Wollstonecraft argues: 'This has ever been the language of men, and the fear of departing from a supposed sexual character, has made even women of superior sense adopt the same sentiments.'[24]

As many critics have noted, Wollstonecraft's own rhetorical practice involved a pointed deflowering of language, an emphasis on utility rather than beauty: 'I shall disdain to cull my phrases or polish my style; – I aim at being useful, and sincerity will render me unaffected; for, wishing rather to persuade by the force of my arguments, than dazzle by the elegance of my language, I shall not waste my time in rounding periods, or in fabricating the turgid bombast of artificial feelings . . . I shall try to avoid that flowery diction which has slided from essays into novels, and from novels into familiar letters and conversations.'[25] She quotes the following passage from Barbauld's poem, with the most offensive words capitalized:

> Flowers to the fair: to you these flowers I bring,
> And strive to greet you with an earlier spring.
> Flowers, SWEET, and gay, and DELICATE LIKE YOU;

Emblems of innocence, and beauty too.
With flowers the Graces bind their yellow hair,
And flowery wreaths consenting lovers wear.
Flowers, the sole luxury which nature knew,
In Eden's pure and guiltless garden grew.
To loftier forms are rougher tasks assign'd;
The sheltering oak resists the stormy wind,
The tougher yew repels invading foes,
And the tall pine for future navies grows;
But this soft family, to cares unknown,
Were born for pleasure and delight ALONE.
Gay without toil, and lovely without art,
They spring to CHEER the sense, and GLAD the heart,
Nor blush, my fair, to own you copy these;
Your BEST, your SWEETEST empire is – to PLEASE.[26]

Here and elsewhere in her text Wollstonecraft's horror of female homosociality is evident.[27] Unlike Barbauld, who praised nunneries as refuges
for women (*Works*, vol. II, p. 212), Wollstonecraft disliked exclusively
female societies, and had a horror of female intimacy: 'To say the truth
women are, in general, too familiar with each other, which leads to that
gross degree of familiarity that so frequently renders the marriage state
unhappy.'[28] Furthermore, the 'language of passion' which they use towards each other 'slips ... from their glib tongues', and is a language
composed entirely of 'phosphoric bursts which only mimick in the dark
the flame of passion'.[29] Whereas Barbauld would have agreed about the
'gross material fire' of masculine desire, her evaluation of the differences
between men and women ran directly counter to Wollstonecraft's denigration of the feminine. Women's love, for each other and for the opposite
sex, was intrinsically social, characterized by a friendship rooted in 'those
endearing intercourses of life which to a woman are become habitual'.
Men, on the other hand, 'are hardly social creatures till [their] minds are
humanized and subdued by that passion which alone can tame [them]
to '"all the soft civilities of life"' (*Works*, vol. II, pp. 3–4).

Barbauld wanted to 'burn' Dr Fordyce's *Sermons to Young Women* (1765)
for its aspersions on female friendship (*Works*, vol. II, p. 59). Another noxious conduct book, published in the same year, was the popular *A Picture
of True Conjugal Felicity* (1765), in which the mild and docile 'Amanda' en-
joys 'the amiable female privileges of ruling by obeying, of commanding
by submitting, and of being perfectly happy from consulting another's
happiness'. Her harmonious marriage to Manley represents, needless
to say, 'strength and softness blended together'.[30] Barbauld's poetical
name of 'Amanda' for the recently married Mary Priestley may have

been something of a shared joke between the two young women, each of whom had been too rationally educated to indulge in the prospect of what Wollstonecraft would later denounce as woman's 'illicit sway'. But even if 'To a Lady, with some painted flowers' does not emerge out of some shared private understanding of the limitations of conduct book discourse, its oppositions of masculine and feminine reflect Barbauld's un-Wollstonecraftian desire to maintain the distinction of the sexes. Over twenty years later, however, in the era of the rights of man, Barbauld's feminist language of sensibility had become a liability.[31]

THE BIRMINGHAM RIOTS

During the summer of 1791, there was to be no protection for Britain's 'naturalized' Dissenting subjects. On the second anniversary of the Fall of the Bastille, a group of about eighty Birmingham citizens 'of various denominations' attended a celebratory dinner at a local hotel.[32] This anniversary event provoked several days of horrific rioting and looting by church and state mobs. In her unpublished eye-witness account of these events, Martha Russell, a pupil of Priestley then in her mid-twenties, tells a remarkable story of Mary Priestley's spirited response to her female friends' fears of trouble brewing over the Bastille anniversary dinner. Mrs Humphries and other Dissenting women were 'very much alarmed & wished the dinner might be put off', an alarm increased by the appearance of an anonymous and inflammatory handbill, supposedly written by a Dissenter. Mrs Priestley, was 'quite of a different mind [from Mrs Humphries] ... she said she sd have no objection to stand in the shoes of him that wrote the handbill & that she had no idea that any ill consequences cou'd arise from having the dinner'.[33] In the end, the Old and New Meeting Houses of the Unitarians were destroyed, and twenty-seven private houses burned or pulled down. The first object of the mob's rage was Joseph Priestley, who lost not just his house and his library, but his laboratory as well, reputedly one of the finest in Europe. By all accounts, he was lucky to escape with his life. Burning him alive was the chant of the mob,[34] although they had to be satisfied with burning him in effigy.[35]

The victims' accounts of these riots, particularly those by the Russell and Hutton families, close friends of the Priestleys, powerfully convey the terror of that time, when the principles of open association and friendship underpinning Dissenting sociability broke down. William Hutton, between the burning and looting of his town and country houses, was obliged to 'run away like a thief' (he wrote) and 'skulk behind hedges ... avoided as a pestilence'.[36] Martha Russell wrote vividly of the great danger they were in, even after they had fled to London. While her father William Russell made repeated calls on Pitt, urging him to send reinforcements to Birmingham, Priestley (she wrote) 'never stird out of the house and only was visible to his intimate frds – he told my Father we must come & see him for that he was like a wild Beast he did not show himself in the streets & when he did it was only at night with his keepers'.[37]

Whilst admiring Priestley, and acknowledging the extent to which he was goaded into controversy by his opponents,[38] William Hutton had no doubt that his friend's 'warm expressions' and his passion for proselytism had contributed to the ferocity unleashed against his own and other prominent Dissenting families in Birmingham. In his *Narrative of the Riots*, Hutton wrote: 'If the Doctor chooses to furnish the world with candles, it reflects a lustre upon himself, but there is no necessity to oblige every man to carry one. It is the privilege of an Englishman to walk in darkness if he chooses.' Hutton's ambivalence about Priestley is pervasive. Within a few pages the candle of Enlightenment transforms itself into a dangerous spark, unleashed by the Unitarians' enemies: the 'many-headed monster' of an enraged mob had escaped the control of its masters, Hutton wrote, for 'what man could play with a candle amidst gun-powder, because he thinks he is master of the blaze?'.[39]

Catherine Hutton shared her father's view of Priestley. Although a 'good man, attached to his King and country, and meaning well to every creature', he was (she wrote) 'one of the primary causes of the riots ... by rousing the spirit of bigotry'.[40] Martha Russell may have claimed, immediately after the riots, that 'we found all our friends very sociable our common trou[ble] seemed to have unitd us & the dissenters never were so united one amongst another & so sociable & friendly', but the truth was that very few Dissenters wanted to see the Priestleys again in Birmingham. '[W]e have been driven off the Birmingham stage by the audience and our fellow-actors', Mrs Priestley wrote to Barbauld, adding bitterly that she hoped she had learned 'to bear other people's misfortunes ... as well as many under the mask of friends have borne ours in this place' (Rutt, *Theological*, vol. 1:2, p. 366). Hutton confirmed the ostracism, writing to his daughter that Priestley's own congregation at the New Meeting House had voted that he 'should not return' adding that 'the Doctor has said this hurts him more than all his sufferings'.[41]

Despite Mary Priestley's confidence on the day of the riots that there was nothing to fear, she had actually been burning all her correspondence a few days before. A few weeks after the riots she wrote to Barbauld:

Our property may be said to be entirely destroyed; the few remains that have been picked up so demolished as to be of little value ... A few days before the riot, I burnt all my letters. I had often taken them out, and burnt part before; but that morning I determined to burn all. I consumed every parcel. The last bag was full of yours. I put a handful into the fire, when casting my eye upon a letter with some verses, I thought I would save them a little longer, and read them over before I burnt them. These went with every thing else; but whether destroyed, or kept for private amusement, I cannot say. (Rutt, *Theological*, vol. I:2, pp. 366–7; 26 August 1791).

With so many government spies and informers surrounding them, as well as malicious neighbours, there was a worse fate for letters than destruction by fire. 'One of the most mortifying circumstances in this calamity', Priestley informed the public, was 'the dispersion of a great number of letters from my private friends ... into the hands of persons wholly destitute of generosity or honour' (Rutt, *Theological*, vol. XIX, p. 382).

In the same month that Mrs Priestley composed this letter, Priestley was penning a remarkable passage on the loss of his house, his library and his laboratory. Suffering terribly at the thought of the pleasure many took in his losses,[42] he imagined to himself the outrage which would have greeted the reverse situation – a clergyman of the Church of England attacked by Dissenters:

I was forcibly struck with this idea on seeing a most ingenious imitation of plants in paper, cut and painted so like to nature, that, at a very small distance, no eye could have perceived the difference; and by this means they were capable of being preserved from the attacks of insects, so as to be greatly preferable to any *hortus siccus*. It appeared to me that weeks, and in some cases months, must have been employed on some single plants, so exquisitely were they finished.

What would this ingenious and deserving young lady have felt, how would her family and friends, how would all botanists, though they should only have heard of the ingenious contrivance and the labour and time she had spent upon her plants; nay, how would the country in general have been filled with indignation, had any envious female neighbour come by force, or stealth, and thrown all her flowers into the fire, and thus destroyed all the fruits of her ingenuity, and patient working for years, in a single moment ...

If the same malicious female should not only have thrown this lady's flowers into the fire, but ransacked her apartments, and, getting possession of all her private letters, have amused herself with reading them, and published them in all the neighbourhood, in order to do her all the injury in her power, would not the crime be thought worthy of the severest punishment, as a violent breach of all the bonds of society?[43]

In *Mansfield Park* the unpleasant Bertram sisters, having summarily looked over and dismissed their mouse-like cousin Fanny, return to their 'favourite holiday sport of the moment, making artificial flowers or wasting gold paper'. There is, however, nothing trivial, wasteful or decorative about Priestley's artificial flowers. Indeed, he seems almost in awe of these flowers; they are the miraculous creations of female labour and ingenuity, a complete triumph of artifice over nature. If flowers have a tendency to unsettle oppositions between natural and artificial realms, they also unsettle public/private realms. Priestley's imagined creator of paper flowers epitomizes the privileges of private, domestic space, and yet those flowers have an important public/scientific role to play. In the mid to late eighteenth century, botany was generally regarded as women's favourite science, with women taking the lead in promulgating botanical knowledge through the collection, drying, painting and engraving of flowers. Dissenting women were particularly prominent in botany, but there were others too, such as the likely source for Priestley's young lady, namely Mary Delany, whose *'hortus siccus'*, her exquisite art of paper mosaic, was celebrated for its scientific accuracy and elegant taste in Erasmus Darwin's *The Loves of the Plants*, first published in 1789 and reprinted by Joseph Johnson in 1790 and 1791.[44] In focussing upon the 'delightful science' of botany, Darwin's aim was a reconciliatory one: to 'inlist Imagination under the banner of Science, and to lead her votaries from the looser analogies, which dress out the imagery of poetry, to the stricter ones, which form the ratiocination of philosophy' (Advertisement, *The Botanic Garden*).

Darwin's poem enables Priestley to stare down Burke's taunt about the *'hortus siccus'* of Dissent by celebrating a new, feminized scientific garden: this young woman's painted paper flowers are superior to dried specimens because less perishable, less vulnerable to the attacks of insects. Their beauty resides, in effect, in their supreme scientific utility. We might even say that they exemplify a manly rather than feminine beauty, in so far as they have been achieved, like the sublime, through supreme exertion. The analogy Priestley draws between these paper flowers and his exquisite, irreplaceable laboratory instruments works to achieve a number of different aims. Most obviously, the analogy makes intimate and personal the public violence and violation of the Birmingham riots. More subtly, the analogy draws the teeth of Priestley's scientific radicalism. Even the radical socio-sexual implications of Darwin's poem are annulled by the assertion that these flowers escape fertilization by insects, transforming the *'hortus siccus'* into the *'hortus conclusus'* of virginal enclosure; there will be no polygamous marriages and other scandalous practices taking place here.[45] Poignantly, despite these advantages, the paper flowers are exquisitely vulnerable to fire.

Priestley's substitution of a female victim for himself is a brilliant stroke, sensationalizing the violence whilst also working to contain acute feelings of outrage and grief. But why does he also represent the destructive, anti-social force of the riots as feminine? Only a year before, Burke had represented the uncontrollable revolutionary violence of France 'in the abused shape of the vilest of women' (*Reflections*, p. 165). Given Priestley's careful concern to lay the blame for the riots on those directing the mob, he would not have stooped to Burke's scapegoating of the lower classes. His analysis is in fact closer to the one Wollstonecraft was to devise a year later in refutation of Rousseau's strictures that young women should be subject to the 'most constant and severe restraint' of decorum, and that they should have 'but little liberty' for 'they are apt to indulge themselves excessively in what is allowed them'. Wollstonecraft responded by aligning middle-class women with violent insurrection from the most oppressed groups: 'Slaves and mobs have always indulged themselves in the same excesses, when once they broke loose from authority. The bent bow recoils with violence, when the hand is suddenly relaxed that forcibly held it.'[46] Whereas Wollstonecraft argues against restraints for women, Priestley is more ambivalent. Indeed, that the polarities of extreme civility and extreme savagery should meet in the figure of the middle-class woman and her neighbour suggests some conflict on his part concerning the important role of sociability underpinning polite culture. *In extremis*, Priestley recognized that sociability as feminine, but (as Montagu so well understood) granting this recognition any enduring meaning, would undermine the male homosociality on which his authority was based.

When Mary Priestley died in America, three years into their exile, Priestley's grieving correspondence aligns his new personal loss with the losses of the riots, particularly the loss of those intimate poems through which Barbauld had memorialized their early years at Warrington. To Barbauld he wrote:

Though for many years she wrote but few letters, there were not many persons who were more frequently the subject of our conversation, or whom she spoke of with so much pleasure as yourself. Indeed, pleasing impressions of so early a date, are not soon effaced ... If my diaries had not been destroyed in the riots, I should have been able to retrace some of them better than I can do now.

She often lamented the loss of a folio book, into which she had copied all your unpublished poems, and other small pieces, especially the first poem we ever saw of yours, on taking leave of her, when we left Warrington. The perusal of it would give me more pleasure now than it did at first. (Rutt, *Theological*, vol. I:2, p. 364)

The following year we see him writing again to Barbauld: 'You had no copy of your first poem to my wife, or I should value that above any other; and also the little poem you wrote on the birth of Joseph' (Rutt, *Theological*, vol. I:2, p. 411). The poetry he seeks to retrieve through corre- spondence with Barbauld commemorates important moments of domes- tic, familial life in the context of female friendship: leave-taking, the birth of a child – records of moments which perished with his diaries, and with his wife's folio book, but which might just have been preserved by their au- thor. The phantasmatic relationship Priestley creates here between letters and bodies – letters and poems standing in for bodies – suggests a new ap- praisal of the value of Warrington's vanished 'social hours' (*Poems*, p. 37).

SOLIDARITY IN ADVERSITY

Shortly after the Birmingham riots, Barbauld produced her *Civic Sermons to the People*, a sixpenny pamphlet published anonymously by Joseph Johnson in 1792. The title, while unique,[47] reconfirms the central role of religion and theology in eighteenth-century political discourse and practice. More pointedly, but without ever naming her opponent, it cocks a snook at Burke, who, at the same time as he was characterizing Dissent as a '*hortus siccus*', had villified the 'political sermon' as one of the 'nondescripts' beautifying it (*Reflections*, p. 94). For Barbauld radical politics were an extension of her religious and moral principles. As she put it so succinctly in her 1792 dispute with Gilbert Wakefield, 'Public Worship is a civic meeting . . . a virtual declaration of the rights of man' (*Works*, vol. II, pp. 446–8).

Barbauld opens her first *Civic Sermon* by wittily stepping around Burke's notorious description of the people as the 'swinish multitude'. Instead, she reflects upon the sociability of cattle:

I have called these Sermons. A Sermon is a discourse. Your cattle cannot dis- course; they like each other's company, they herd together, they have a variety of tones by which they can make each other sensible when they are pleased, angry, or in pain, but they cannot discourse. To discourse is to communicate ideas, that is thoughts, to compare – to reason upon them. This is the privilege of man. It is by this faculty that he is above the brutes, and it is to persuade you to use this faculty that these discourses are chiefly written. Many seem to think that poor people, or those who work to maintain themselves, have not this faculty and

that you ought to be led and governed like the brutes, without knowing why or
how. But this is worse than sinking you from your station, it is degrading you
from your species. (*Civic Sermons*, pp. 4–5)

Barbauld is emphatic that government is the concern of everyone. It is
'proper to enquire *why* some men are set over and govern other men' –
why three million should be 'allowed to manage as they please' the
affairs of nine million men and women of the lower classes. In order
to demystify the operations of government, and thereby minimize the
distance between the idly sauntering fashionable world and the world of
the industrious poor, she wittily reveals the 'mystery' of every realm in
which one is not a participant:

You can all of you get information enough concerning your respective trades
and handicrafts, and yet many of them are very difficult and full of mystery
to those who have never taken the pains to enquire into their principles. The
clay that is wrought into shape under the hands of the potter, seems to the
stander-by to be swelled, and rounded, and touched into form, as it were by
enchantment. The dextrous throwing of the shuttle, and the web of cloth that
grows beneath the fingers of the weaver, is gazed at with admiration by the
fine gentleman or fine lady, who saunter through your busy manufactories, and
they see colours mingle, and flowers and figures start into the work, without
being able to comprehend how they are produced there . . . The principles of
Government . . . are not more difficult than the principles of the arts by which
you get your bread. (*Civic Sermons*, pp. 6–7)

If the 'enchanted ground' of Barbauld's 1775 essay on 'Devotional Taste'
had been sexual love, in 1792, swept along by the French Revolution's
momentum, the enchanted ground becomes the factory floor, with pots
magically 'touched into form', and coloured 'flowers and figures' springing to life within woven fabric. The miracle of Priestley's paper mosaic
garden has shifted from the drawing room to the manufactory.

Almost twenty years after the publication of Barbauld's *Civic Sermons*,
the secret of their authorship was still a well-kept one.[48] The radical
open invitation to the people to participate in government is, however, suddenly abrogated towards the end of the first sermon, when
Barbauld mentions the Birmingham riots. To the rioters she makes it
clear that they are not called 'to the assemblies of Citizens', for they are
brutes and '*must* be governed like brutes'. The exclusions are graphically
announced:

You who own no law, cannot judge of laws. You *must* be slaves, not thro' the
appointment of men, but by the eternal law of nature. A King, with such dispositions, cannot govern; he may prowl about for a time, and tear in pieces and

destroy; but he cannot govern ... To you Government is known by its restraints, and Religion by its terrors ... for you ... it builds hospitals, workhouses, and prisons. (*Civic Sermons*, pp. 17–19)

In breaking loose and attacking the persons and properties of Dissenting families, the rioters had forfeited their rights to be addressed within Barbauld's rubric of universal brotherhood, defined according to principles associated with sociability. Nor is she less hostile to the King and his minions, believing them responsible for letting loose the mob which they could not, in the end, control. Instead of governing the people by means of the proper exercise of his reason, which includes respect for the social dispositions and habits of his people, the King rules by terror like a wild beast, emerging sporadically and unpredictably to inflict arbitrary injury.

Two months after the riots, the terror was still such that Priestley's friends in the north were too frightened to offer hospitality to him, leaving him to remark to his wife's brother: 'Thus the chased deer is avoided by all the herd.'[49] Barbauld's 'To Dr Priestley, Dec. 29, 1792', published in January 1793, harnesses the pathos of her friend's intense isolation and vulnerability, positioning it as the climax of the first half of her poem, in which she urges Priestley to participate in her own indignation at the abuse and persecution he has suffered:

> Burns not thy cheek indignant, when thy name,
> On which delighted science lov'd to dwell,
> Becomes the bandied theme of hooting crowds?
> With timid caution, or with cool reserve,
> When e'en each reverend Brother keeps aloof,
> Eyes the struck deer, and leaves thy naked side
> A mark for power to shoot at? ...   (*Poems*, p, 125)

In the wake of the Birmingham riots, the protection society owes to Priestley as a 'naturalized subject' has evaporated, together with the protection and support he might reasonably have expected from his fellow Dissenters. The pathos of the failed brotherhood of Dissenters is counter-balanced, however, by the second half of the poem, which shifts register to celebrate the singularity and sublimity of Priestley's prophetic mind. Inspired by Milton's own resignation and stoicism ('On evil days though fallen and evil tongues'), the poet transmutes her narrow indignation into a wide and elevated prospect, from which she and Priestley together gaze on futurity:

To thee, the slander of a passing age
Imports not. Scenes like these hold little space
In his large mind, whose ample stretch of thought
Grasps future periods. – Well can'st thou afford
To give large *credit* for that debt of fame
Thy country owes thee. Calm thou can'st consign it
To the slow payment of that distant day,
If distant, when thy name, to freedom's join'd,
Shall meet the thanks of a regenerate land.

(Poems, p, 125)

The poem is a powerful statement of Barbauld's solidarity with her old friend. Gone are her reservations concerning an abstract and unsociable pursuit of knowledge at the expense of imagination and feeling: a feminized 'delighted science' now dotes on Priestley's name. Gone too is the 'fond regret' for the past which had so muted her earlier celebration of Priestley's public life and fame; the genius which, once upon a time, had made him an 'absent Friend' to his social circle is now mobilized for the benefit of the nation as a whole. In the end, the violence of the riots vindicated Barbauld's 'pretty' paradox about establishments as the 'womb and grave' of sects. At this point in time, with friends falling off on all sides, the past is sealed off, the future beckons. From the ashes of the riots and 'Priestley's injured name' will rise the epic prospect of Barbauld's *Eighteen Hundred and Eleven*.

NOTES

I would like to thank Carol Willock for her imaginative research assistance on this topic, and for her perceptive comments on drafts of this chapter. For full citations see Bibliography.

1 Le Breton, *Memoir*, pp. 38–9.
2 Montagu's formulation fits the description of 'double dissent' recently ascribed to the writings of Dissenting women; see Ross, 'Configurations', p. 93.
3 White, 'The "Joineriana"', pp. 513, 515.
4 Barbauld, *Poems*, pp. 17–19.
5 Even the most sympathetic reviewers found Barbauld's dystopic *Eighteen Hundred and Eleven* (1812) unpalatable, with one commenting: 'The whole tone of it is in a most extraordinary degree unkindly and unpatriotic – we had almost said unfilial' (*Eclectic Review*, 8 (1812), p. 474; quoted Barbauld, *Poems*, p. 310).
6 Robinson, *Henry Crabb Robinson on Books*, vol. 1, p. 64.
7 'Women are naturally inclined not only to love, but to all the soft and gentle affections; all the tender attentions and kind sympathies of nature', she wrote

in a letter of 1774. See Aikin, *Works*. Hereafter abbreviated in text as *Works*; this reference, *Works*, vol. II, p. 2.

8 Burke, *Reflections*, ed. O'Brien, pp. 95–6.

9 Wollstonecraft, *Vindication of the Rights of Men*, in *Works*, vol. V, p. 9.

10 See Rutt, *Theological and Miscellaneous Works*, vol. 1:1, pp. 282, 285; hereafter abbreviated in text and notes as Rutt, *Theological*.

11 On this topic, see Wykes, '"The Spirit"'.

12 For a refutation of the image of Priestley as innocent victim and martyr, see Ditchfield, 'Priestley Riots'.

13 William Turner of Newcastle (1761–1859) includes this detail in his memoir of Mrs Barbauld, in the *Newcastle Magazine* in 1825; see Barbauld, *Poems*, pp. 219–20.

14 Burke, *A Letter*, p. 62. For readings of 'The Mouse's Petition' and its controversy, see Keach, 'Barbauld', and Saunders, '"Mouse's Petition"'.

15 Remonstrating with Barbauld, Priestley made direct application of her words to himself: 'but I, whose religious sentiments have undergone what you call (p. 9) "a total revolution . . . "' (Rutt, *Theological*, vol. 1:1, p. 279).

16 Priestley admitted to Barbauld: 'few persons now living have had more to do with religious controversy than myself' (*ibid.*, vol. 1:1, p. 284).

17 Rutt annotates the revisions in footnotes to Priestley's letter to Barbauld; see *ibid.*, vol. 1:1, pp. 278–86.

18 Barbauld to Nicholas Clayton, 1776, quoted in Webb, 'Rational Piety', p. 299.

19 Two dates have been suggested, 1771 and 1800; see Barbauld, *Poems*, p. 246.

20 See Miller (ed.), *Priestley*, p. xxii. For Priestley's conversion to Socinianism and his attack on monarchical politics in 1768, see Clark, *English Society*, pp. 396–406.

21 See Mullan, *Sentiment and Sociability*.

22 For a brief commentary on their marriage, see Schofield, *Enlightenment*, pp. 91–3. See also McLachlan, 'Mary Priestley'.

23 See Tomalin, *Life* and Anne Janowitz's chapter in this volume.

24 Wollstonecraft, *Works*, vol. V, p. 122.

25 *Ibid.*, vol. V, pp. 75–6. One of the best articles on Wollstonecraft's rhetoric is Furniss's '"Nasty Tricks"'.

26 Wollstonecraft, *Works*, vol. V, pp. 122–3.

27 For an excellent discussion of this topic, see Johnson, *Equivocal Beings*.

28 Wollstonecraft, *Works*, vol. V, p. 197. The passage continues: 'Why in the name of decency are sisters, female intimates, or ladies and their waiting-women, to be so grossly familiar as to forget the respect which one human creature owes to another?'

29 *Ibid.*, vol. V, p. 258.

30 Quoted in Vickery, *Gentleman's Daughter*, p. 84.

31 For an astute account of the differences between Wollstonecraft and Barbauld, including a timely rebuttal of the usual readings of Barbauld's 'The Rights of Woman' (c. 1793), see Newlyn, *Reading, Writing*, pp. 155–60.

32 *Life of William Hutton*, pp. 238–9; hereafter abbreviated to Hutton, *Life*. The dinner was chaired by a member of the Church of England, Mr Keir (Rutt, *Theological*, vol. XIX, p. 374).

33 Russell, 'Birmingham Riots'.

34 'the mob . . . said if they cou'd find docr Priestley they wou'd burn him alive', *ibid.*

35 Rev. W. Jesse to the Earl of Dartmouth: Dartmouth, *Manuscripts*, vol. III, p. 273.

36 Hutton, *Life*, p. 270.

37 Russell, 'Birmingham Riots'.

38 'To dispute with the Doctor was deemed the road to preferment. He had already made two bishops, and there were still several heads which wanted mitres' (Hutton, *Life*, p. 231).

39 *Ibid.*, p. 243.

40 Hutton, *Reminiscences*, p. 88.

41 *Ibid.*, p. 99.

42 The King's pleasure was widely reported, and apparently Edmund Burke 'could not contain his joy' (Rutt, *Theological*, vol. XXV, p. 398).

43 Priestley originally composed the passage as Preface to his *Letters*; and later included it in *An Appeal to the Public, on the Subject of the Riots in Birmingham* (1792), in Rutt, *Theological*, vol. XIX, pp. 385–6. The *Letters* is accessibly reprinted as Priestley, *Farewell Sermon*.

44 For Mrs Delany's 'mimic bowers,' made of 'paper foliage' and 'silken flowers,' see Darwin, *The Botanic Garden*, Canto II, lines 155–64, pp. 69–70. Its publisher Joseph Johnson brought out Part II a second time in 1791, together with Part I. For a fascinating discussion of the overlap between scientific botanical illustration and decorative flower painting, see chapter 4 of Pointon, *Strategies*.

45 For an incisive and entertaining essay on the scandalousness of Darwin's project, see Bewell, '"Jacobin Plants"'.

46 Wollstonecraft, *Works*, vol. V, p. 152.

47 A title-search for the period does not yield any other 'Civic Sermons'. Coleridge translated his learned title, *Conciones ad Populum* (1795), as 'Addresses' rather than 'Sermons' to the people.

48 In 1811, Henry Crabb Robinson noted, in scandalized terms, that Barbauld 'confessed' to him that she had written them; see Robinson, *Henry Crabb Robinson on Books*, vol. I, p. 23.

49 Joseph Priestley to his brother-in-law, 8 September 1791, from typescript of Priestley's letters held in Warrington Library (British Library, 10902. i. 8).

6

'Reciprocal expressions of kindness': Robert Merry, Della Cruscanism and the limits of sociability

Jon Mee

The Della Cruscans have recently been rediscovered for literary history by Jerome McGann.[1] McGann's view is that Robert Merry or 'Della Crusca' and his followers were the immediate targets of Wordsworth's attack on the 'degrading thirst after outrageous stimulation' in the 1800 'Preface' to the *Lyrical Ballads*.[2] He wants to recuperate Della Cruscanism as a pervasive and popular influence on the poetry of the Romantic period which has been obscured by the twin peaks of Wordsworth and Coleridge. In this chapter I shall be building on the foundations provided by McGann's work, but concentrating in much more detail on the career of Robert Merry himself as a whole, looking beyond the years of his most intense Della Cruscan popularity between 1787 and 1789. I believe that Merry's poetry of the late 1780s and early 1790s seriously and consistently pursues the idea of an expanded and potentially unlimited version of the public sphere. In the process he seemed to abolish the distinction, strenuously maintained in much of the eighteenth-century literature on the subject, between polite sociability and the anarchy of the crowd. By 1792 Merry had come to be regarded as one of the most effective figures in the opposition press, according to the newspaper historian Lucyle Werkmeister.[3] Some of his former friends did not view the extended sociability which came with this political activity as a positive development. Their memoirs present Merry – educated at Harrow and Cambridge, the son of a Governor of the Hudson's Bay Company – as a paragon of sensitive sociability who unfortunately dissolved himself into the uncouth passions of the crowd. James Boaden, for instance, claimed that Merry 'became perfectly *rabid* with the French revolution; associated himself with the radical press, and spoke its furious and disgusting language'.[4] By 1796 Merry, along with many other radical writers, had effectively become an internal exile within Britain, and decided to flee to the United States with his wife, the actor Anne Brunton. He died there in 1798.

Although Boaden and others represented Merry as someone who after 1789 was almost possessed by the vulgar mania for the French Revolution, the poet of sensibility had always been interested in extending the boundaries that regulated notions of polite sociability. The logic of this career was apparent in Merry's earliest poetic writings, anthologies of expatriate poetry published in Florence in the early 1780s (from whence the name Della Crusca). It was a logic identified and attacked by the Tory critic William Gifford in *The Baviad* (1791) and *The Maeviad* (1793), satirical poems in which a concern about literary standards masks a deeper desire to reinforce cultural boundaries, that is, in Gifford's own words, 'to correct the growing depravity of the public taste, and check the inundation of absurdity now bursting upon us from a thousand springs'.[5] The worst fears of Gifford and his ilk about the consequences of such cultural depravity had been confirmed when Merry the poet of feeling turned into a radical politician in the 1790s: 'The change in his political opinions gave a sullen gloom to his character which made him relinquish all his former connexions, and unite with people far beneath his talents, and quite unsuitable to his habits.'[6] What is striking about this judgement, taken from the obituary in the *Gentleman's Magazine*, is that it is formulated as a scandal of sociability. Merry, the brilliant conversationalist recorded in several literary and theatrical memoirs of the period, oversteps the boundaries of polite sociability to become the gloomy politician. In fact the obituary implicitly admits that Merry remained a sociable animal, but makes it clear that his orbit was now beyond polite definitions of what sociability could be. The Romantic reaction which McGann recognizes in the writing of Wordsworth entailed a much more restricted notion of sociability, rolling back many of the developments of the previous century that the writings and career of Merry took to the limit.

In outlining the differences between the poetry of Wordsworth and the poetry of Della Cruscanism, McGann suggests that the latter is 'conversational', where the former is 'meditative'.[7] This opposition is in danger of obscuring the fact that the idea of culture as a 'conversation' was a ubiquitous and much-contested one in the eighteenth century. Wordsworth's conception of culture was no less predicated on the idea of conversation than Merry's. The questions which McGann ought really to address are 'what were the limits of that conversation?' and 'who had the right to impose them?' Before turning to the very different answers to these questions which are offered by Merry and Wordsworth, however, I would like to contextualize this by saying a little more about the development of the idea of culture as conversation.

A crucial and influential early statement of this idea can be found in Shaftesbury's *Characteristicks* (1711),[8] written in the wake of the settlement of 1688 by the grandson of one of its great Whig architects. Lawrence Klein has suggested that the *Characteristicks* should be regarded as an attempt to think of what a new Whig culture could look like. *Characteristicks* offers the idea of culture as conversation, that is, as a polite and open exchange between equals, which contributed to the development of the bourgeois public sphere familiar from Jürgen Habermas's work.[9] Privileging the society of gentlemen over the authority of church and court, Shaftesbury offered a philosophy for a sociable century. Shaftesbury conceived of sociability as 'an absolutely natural propensity',[10] an innate human 'enthusiasm', but true sociability was not a rude or primitive state. The culture of sociability was above all a culture of politeness, perhaps the key word in Shaftesbury's lexicon. Politeness meant that a certain amount of work had to be done on the self in order, paradoxically, to make oneself natural. Prejudice and opinion can mislead one, for instance, into believing that one should be motivated by egoism. One has to know oneself in order to perceive where one's real interests lie. In his 'Advice to Authors', Shaftesbury discusses this process in terms of a division of the self which will allow us to produce a dialogue through which the passions can be shaped into a polite form. Indeed he suggests that the maxim 'RECOGNIZE YOUR-SELF' should be understood as '*Divide your-self*'. He recommends authors to retire into the 'Woods and River-Banks' so that the 'vehemence' of 'Fancy' may cool and be recuperated into ART.[11] The inner promptings of 'Fancy' or 'enthusiasm' were essential for social being no less than poetry, but they had to be regulated if they were not to overwhelm the very subjectivity for which they provided the raw materials. Shaftesbury's preparation for authorship sounds much like Wordsworth's 'emotion recollected in tranquility'. Meditation has a role in sociability for both Shaftesbury and Wordsworth, who in 1815 described his Whig predecessor as 'unjustly depreciated'; it is a preparation of the self for coming before the public.[12]

The dialogue that takes place within the self was also Shaftesbury's model for culture. In place of the authoritarianism of the court or the church, Shaftesbury imagined a society in which truth would be discovered by the exchange of views in conversation. In Shaftesbury's view, art flourished in a free society. 'All Politeness', he says in the first volume of *Characteristicks*, 'is owing to Liberty.'[13] Tyranny, he argued, restricted the kind of free exchange that was necessary to the arts. Alternatively he seems to suggest that freedom is impossible without the development of the arts as a model for polite interaction. The aesthetic offers a model of the kind of shaping that is necessary for polite social interaction in public. If this noble 'enthusiasm' was opposed to the artificiality of courtly politeness, it was equally to be contrasted with the vulgar 'enthusiasm' of the mob, that '*Panick* ... rais'd in a Multitude, and convey'd by Aspect, or as it were by Contact or Sympathy'.[14] A tolerationist by nature, Shaftesbury believed these panics had to be regulated by an enlightened magistracy rather than suppressed, but his vision of vulgar enthusiasm should alert us to the limits of his philosophy of sociability. Sensitive management of the self was his model for polite sociability, but only certain kinds of people, he assumed, were able to carry out this process themselves. The enthusiasm of the crowd ought not to be persecuted perhaps, but it could not be relied upon to manage itself.

Later philosophers of commercial society such as Adam Smith wanted to make the distinction between sociability and enthusiasm a more secure one than Shaftesbury had done. Defining sociability and benevolence in terms of 'enthusiasm', as Shaftesbury did, was to place it in uneasy proximity to the passions of the crowd and ranting fanatics associated with that word. Not that Shaftesbury himself was unconcerned about this issue. 'The ambiguity of sympathy in Shaftesbury's account', as John Mullan has noted, 'proceeds from an uneasy sensitivity to the limitations of such "Company" and "mutual Converse", from an awareness of the necessary separation of polite society from society at large.'[15] Robert Merry deserves to be included among the poetic heirs of Shaftesbury nominated by Michael Meehan (who presents Wordsworth as his culminating example).[16] For Merry, literature was, as an intrinsically sociable activity, an aspect of 'mutual Converse', but compared to Shaftesbury and many of his followers, Wordsworth included, Della Crusca paid scandalously little regard to the question of regulation, defining his muse in terms of an 'enthusiasm' seemingly oblivious to the boundaries of politeness, and ultimately inviting the participation of the crowd in the public sphere.

I have already pointed out that Merry's first poems were published at Florence. *The Arno Miscellany* (1784) and *The Florence Miscellany* (1785) were both anthologies put together by British exiles, the latter especially making great play of what Hester Piozzi, one of the contributors, called 'reciprocal expressions of kindness'. Not only did the poems stress the beauty of the 'mutual benevolence' that flourished between friends, but also even at this early stage (although Piozzi was not so keen on this aspect) extended its doctrine of benevolence to encompass politics.[17] Merry took the name Della Crusca from the Florentine academy, which

had been disbanded by Grand Duke Leopold, the Austrian ruler of
Tuscany, in 1783. The name was an expression of his sympathy for Italian
hopes of being liberated from the Austrian yoke. Merry first came to
public notice in Britain when poems from *The Florence Miscellany* began
to be picked up in the periodical press in 1786, but he only became well
known in the following year when he started providing poetry for a new
London newspaper, *The World*. Its editor, Edward Topham, was an old
friend of Merry, who placed him on a retainer to provide verse for the
paper.[18] *The World* had already been proving a success with its mixture of
what Hannah More disapprovingly described as 'elopements, divorces,
and suicides, tricked out in all the elegancies of Topham's phraseology'.
Merry's poetry further secured the initial success of Topham's paper,
and its reputation for raciness. Merry was already participating in a less
regulated notion of sociability than that implied by what has been called
the 'graceful conviviality' of the Florentine collections.[19]

It was with the publication of 'Adieu and Recall to Love', under the
pseudonym 'Della Crusca', on 29 June 1787, that Merry literally made
a name for himself in literary London.[20] 'Adieu and Recall to Love' teas-
ingly implied a story of romantic disillusionment and desperate hope that
would have appealed to a readership eager to read about the intrigues
of the fashionable world. Its conclusion,

> O rend my heart with ev'ry pain!
> But let me, let me love again,

invited a reply, and Topham was quick to arrange one. 'The Pen' by
Anna Matilda appeared in the paper soon afterwards.[21] The story of the
fitful correspondence which followed, and the way Topham recruited
others to keep the phenomenon going, is perhaps familiar enough not
to need repeating here in detail. Nor is there any need to repeat the
tale of Merry's disappointment when he finally met Anna Matilda in
March 1789 – a meeting which, by revealing her to be no other than the
middle-aged and married dramatist Hannah Cowley, finally brought his
participation to an end.[22] What is of primary interest is how the phenomenon of Della Cruscanism, which dragged on without Merry in
the pages of *The World* into the early years of the 1790s, represented a
commercial democratization and eroticization of the ideal of sociability,
recasting Shaftesbury's ideal of a dialogue between landed gentlemen in
terms of the amours of a feminized 'Bon Ton'. The flirtatious display
of feelings on the page, including displays of female desire with multiple correspondents, looked like an orgy of unregulated sensibility rather

than polite sociability. Instead of the regulated sympathies imagined by Shaftesbury as the basis of Whiggish sociability, always gendered as masculine in its self-control, here were men and women theatricalizing their feelings in the interests of a commercial venture and suggesting 'that there is nothing to stop anyone who can feel from springing into verse'.[23]

Although Merry himself seems to have tired rather quickly of being Topham's resident poet, the same unregulated enthusiasm distinguishes his other poetry of this period. Merry told Piozzi that his long poem *Diversity* (1788) was written under a 'poetical mania'.[24] Contradicting William Mason's opinions on 'the *regularity* of lyric poetry', Merry's Preface announces his preference for the 'irregular ode' and implies that his 'Extatic POETRY' will be closer to what Shaftesbury considered the disordered passions of the crowd than the buttoned-in subjectivity of polite sociability. Whereas the fear that sociability might abandon itself to mere sensation structures Shaftesbury's definitions of enthusiasm, Merry's poem flaunts his emotional vicissitudes as proof of his sensibility. The world of the poem is one in motion; its universe is fluxile and in-perception. Genius 'on each bonding billow threw/A quiv'ring shade of deeper blue'.[25] Such poetry seems untroubled by the Humean nightmare of a subjectivity simply made up of sensation without a governing free will, a fear reflected perhaps in Piozzi's judgement that the poem was 'fine' but 'all so about nothing'.[26] David Riede has narrated Coleridge's journey away from the materialism of Joseph Priestley precisely in terms of his concern to preserve the unity of self against the 'delirium' of mere sensation.[27] When Coleridge made his distinction between imagination and fancy in the *Biographia*, he stressed the role of the controlling will in the former. Coleridge believed that associationism denied free will and left the individual 'divided between the despotism of outward impressions, and that of senseless and passive memory'. 'Fancy', as Riede puts it, 'is, in effect, imagination as conceived in an empiricist epistemology.' The primary imagination is the expression of the divine in the human. It is echoed in the secondary imagination, a power that is a product of 'the conscious will': that is, it affirms the notion of a determinate and unified subjectivity.[28]

From the Coleridgean perspective Merry is a poet of fancy. For Merry, however, the delirium of sensation seems to have been the very essence of 'the Freedom of the Mind'.[29] Like John Thelwall, whose poetry and politics in the mid 1790s were similarly established on the basis of the 'free-born energies of the soul', Merry seems to imagine human identity as enriched rather than threatened by a conception of the poetic self

as infinitely open to sensation.[30] For Thelwall and Merry, this kind of
open-ended imaginative sympathy was associated with 'universal benevolence', an idea which both Hume and Smith had perceived as a threat
to the genuine sociability founded on concrete social relationships. For
the latter pair, such over-extended benevolence was inflationary, stretching the possibilities of sympathy till it was devalued. This perspective,
of course, was to be given a powerful counter-revolutionary articulation
in Burke's *Reflections on the Revolution in France* (1790).[31] For Burke, universal
benevolence was simply a dangerous and destructive enthusiasm. Only
the more immediate relations of 'the little platoon' could be trusted.
In 1788, when *Diversity* was published, attitudes were less polarized. The
Critical Review could praise the warmth of the poem, but it was still discom-
fited by the extent of its 'maniac RAPTURE'; 'the fire sometimes scorches,
instead of warming; and our sight is dazzled not enlightened'.[32] Merry's
enthusiasm threatened to melt not cement the social bond. 'The point
is not to bring order to variety', McGann says of Della Cruscanism
more generally, 'but to stimulate and provoke.' Merry's version of patriot eloquence, its celebration 'in Diversity' of Genius's 'wild propensity
of change', had moved far beyond the regulatory tradition of sociability
associated with Shaftesbury's Whiggism.[33]

The French Revolution was to provide the real turning point in
Merry's career, and provide an urgent reference point for his faith in universal benevolence. In the course of a few short years, Merry's position
became progressively radicalized: making the transition from the sociable Whig gentleman to the radical writer disparaged by the *Gentleman's
Magazine* in its obituary. In 1789, like many other young men and women,
he rushed to the site of the Bastille, but his revolutionary tourism was
to be combined with a deep and transforming commitment to radical
politics both in Britain and France. In the process he extended his circle
of sociability, and began to address an entirely different kind of public, all
the time with the theatrical self-consciousness which had been a hallmark
of the Della Cruscan years. In autumn 1791, according to the biographer
of Della Cruscanism, Merry was living 'at the extreme of sociability'.[34]
He was a member of the boisterous and theatrical 'Keep the Line Club'
(founded by Merry with Topham, Miles Peter Andrews and Reynolds in
October 1791), and already belonged to the 'Beefsteak Club'. Both groups
were closely involved with the theatre world, and had strong associations
with Foxite Whigs such as Richard Brinsley Sheridan, with whom Merry
had been connected at least since his time at *The World*. Yet these Whig

circles were themselves being thrown into an identity crisis by the French Revolution. Aristocratic magnates, such as Fitzwilliam and Portland, whose money helped to subsidize the Opposition press, were suspicious of Sheridan, whom they believed to be leading the party in a dangerously reformist direction; as a consequence, they withdrew their financial support from the party's newspapers some time in 1791. But concerns on this front were not only expressed by those Portland Whigs who eventually joined Pitt's government in 1794: Fox himself was not entirely confident that Sheridan was taking a prudent line in his management of newspaper opinion. Merry was someone who, even as early as 1791, Fox regarded as beyond the fringe of political propriety: 'I wish something could be done about our newspapers they seem to try & outdo the Ministerial papers, in abuse of the Princes, the Morning Chronicle is grown a little better lately, but the others are intolerable, the Gazeteer particularly. Mr Merry has got that I am told.'[35] Not suprisingly Merry was among those Whigs, along with Sheridan, involved with the formation of the 'Society of the Friends of the People, Associated for the Purpose of Obtaining a Parliamentary Reform' on 11 April of the following year. Fox had not entirely approved of this initiative, but soon afterwards Merry had moved not only further outside Fox's orbit, but also beyond the Friends of the People.[36] By this stage Merry had started to associate with the *Monthly Review*, which generally supported his poetry throughout the rest of his career, and to mix with figures such as Joseph Priestley, John Horne Tooke and Thomas Holcroft. Here was a move beyond the circles of Whig gentlemen towards the Dissenters and radicals of the Society for Constitutional Information, a move which to Gifford seemed like a political fulfilment of the social promiscuity foreshadowed in his Della Cruscan poetry.[37] Gifford specifically linked 'Holcroft's Shug-lane cant' with 'Merry's Moorfields whine', placing both in the East End, away from the polite literary culture of the West End, and on the fringes of cultural bedlam.[38]

Jon Klancher has drawn a distinction between ideas of 'circulation' and 'dissemination' in the press at the time. The rational circulation of knowledge, on which the Britons' image of themselves as a polite and commercial people depended, was threatened in the eyes of conservative commentators by the spectre of an unregulated spread of information, 'a dissemination which constitutes the writing and reading of the "lower orders", associated in the 1790s above all with the activities of the London Corresponding Society'.[39] Merry's *Laurel of Liberty* (1790) signalled his readiness to align himself with this unregulated flow, 'the progress of

Opinion [he wrote in the Preface], like a rapid stream, though it may be checked, cannot be controuled'. The poem describes itself as 'enthusiastic verse'. It celebrates the 'extatic fervour in the soul' and 'dear delirium' which drew Merry to France, using the language of enthusiasm to suggest that he has been possessed by a spirit of liberty abroad in the world. This idea may have owed something to Priestley's necessitarianism, as Horace Walpole suggested when he traced the *Laurel of Liberty* back to 'the new Birmingham warehouse of the original Maker'. But what is clear is that the poem celebrates 'the Rise of Reason and the Fall of Kings' in a language which deliberately disavows regulation and throws the stability of subjectivity into hazard.[40] *The Laurel of Liberty* in fact produced an explicitly politicized extension of the flirtations of Della Cruscanism when it was answered by Mary Robinson's 'Ainsi va Le Monde' (1791).[41] Mixing eroticism with political radicalism, it was this extended exchange, rather than the high period of Della Cruscanism proper, which brought forward the angry Tory satire of Gifford's *The Baviad* in 1791.[42]

By this stage Merry, always 'a most entertaining character', according to the playwright Frederic Reynolds, was a literary celebrity who was cutting a figure in circles of radical intellectuals both in London and in Paris.[43] The page of poetry for Merry always seems to have been an extension of his sociable nature. In April 1791, for instance, he met Samuel Rogers, soon to become his patron, at a party given by Helen Maria Williams (herself back from Paris, where she had met Merry).[44] Memoirs of the period recall his praise of Paine at various social gatherings, but the apotheosis of this phase of his radical sociability came with the performance of his anniversary ode at the meeting of the 'Friends of Liberty' at the Crown and Anchor.[45] The chorus of the ode is typical of Merry in its enthusiasm for the idea of rapidly communicated sympathy:

> Fill high the animating glass,
> And let the electric ruby pass
> From hand to hand, from soul to soul;
> Who shall the energy controul.
> Exalted, pure, refin'd,
> The Health of Humankind![46]

Like a kind of animal magnetism, universal benevolence is imagined as an 'energy' that can communicate itself beyond all barriers. Merry's metaphor instantiates the revolutionary enthusiasm that Burke feared as a virus capable of making 'a kind of electrick communication everywhere'.[47] Indeed Burke had specifically warned against the influence of men of letters such as Merry, who threw off their ideas in the heat of inspiration, avoided the kind of cooling-off period advised by Shaftesbury, and invited the sympathetic identification of their social inferiors in which they might lose their own sense of a properly bounded subjectivity. While Burke's revolutionaries are capable of cold calculation, they also lose themselves in their fantasies of benevolence: 'Confounded by the complication of distempered passions, their reason is disturbed; their views become vast and perplexed; to others inexplicable; to themselves uncertain.'[48] To his former friends in polite society, Merry was undergoing precisely this kind of loss of identity. Significantly, Merry did not go to the Crown and Anchor meeting, from which those who did attend dispersed before nine o'clock to avoid trouble, but according to a disapproving report in *The Times*, was dining in a tavern with John Horne Tooke, William Seward and James Boswell. The same report claimed that Thomas Paine joined them after dinner. Paine's radicalism had been judged too extreme for the constitutionalist temper of the Crown and Anchor meeting. This more free-and-easy meeting in a tavern is a useful symbol of the rapid change in Merry's own circulation.[49] Soon he was composing odes not for genteel meetings, but for the more extensively circulated cheap radical press. His 'Ode to Freedom' was published in the *Argus* in March 1792 and thereafter he regularly contributed anonymous political squibs to the paper. The figure of Della Crusca, unregulated enough in itself to many commentators, was now being disseminated even further, between newspapers such as the *Argus*, the *Oracle* and the *Telegraph*. In the eyes of James Boaden, who had once consorted with Merry in the 'Keep the Line Club', 'the poet and the gentleman vanished together'.[50] Merry's squibs, such as the memorable parody of Pitt as 'Signor Pittachio', were regularly picked up and disseminated further in the popular radical press, issued as broadsides, and reprinted in journals such as Spence's *Pig's Meat* and Eaton's *Politics for the People*.[51] If Merry was not actually a member of the London Corresponding Society, it certainly made full use of his writing.[52] He had surrendered himself to the dissemination of opinion in a very radical sense. His poem *The Wounded Soldier* (1795), for instance, was printed not by the respectable publishers that previously produced most of his poetry, but by T. G. Ballard, one of the London Corresponding Society's regular printers (and an LCS member himself).[53] J. Hargreaves-Mawdsley, in a discussion of what he takes to be Merry's decline, notes the obvious parallels between the content of *The Wounded Soldier* and Wordsworth's *Guilt and Sorrow, or Incidents upon Salisbury Plain*, written just a year earlier, but

comments with disappointment that Merry's language 'is like that of a
tract ... intended for the simplest reader'.[54] Although it may be difficult
for the modern reader to see beyond our sense of the literary superiority
of Wordsworth's unpublished poem, the very different orientation of *The
Wounded Soldier* has to be recognized. Merry's poem may be like a tract
precisely because he was trying to find a way to write poetry for a popular readership in a way Wordsworth never really did. The title page of
The Wounded Soldier advertises Thelwall's *Tribune*, Spence's *Pig's Meat*, and
Eaton's *Politics for the People* 'and a great Variety of Patriotic Publications'.
If he failed as a poet with *The Wounded Soldier*, it was in the interests of
trying to reconstitute the social boundaries of literature.

By 1795 Merry was cut off from the resources of polite sociability on
which he had previously thrived. He had spent much of 1792–3 in Paris,
mixing with pro-revolutionary British residents there such as Edward
Fitzgerald, John Oswald, Thomas Paine, Sampson Perry and Helen
Maria Williams. This group celebrated news of Dumouriez's victory at
Jemappes with songs, dancing and toasts. They also wrote and signed a
manifesto of solidarity with the National Convention, which appeared
to be welcoming its offers of brotherhood and liberty to all peoples seeking assistance. This declaration looked treasonous when combined with
its opinion that the people of Great Britain ought to be consulted in
their own 'national convention'. One of Merry's speeches to this club
was forwarded to the Foreign Office by the spy Monro, and the French
put the poet's name on a list of 'British citizens of tested civism' who
could be trusted 'to purge the city as well as possible of all Pitt's spies',
but once war broke out Paris was a difficult place to be even for such
civic-minded Englishmen. Only a passport signed by the painter J-L.
David, whom he had met in Italy a decade before, saved him from being
rounded up as an enemy alien.[55] Merry found Britain on his return an
inhospitable place, the government-funded press rejoicing in the story
of this friend of liberty having to escape from the Jacobins. Although
in the period after his return, he made new friends, such as William
Godwin, who listed Merry among the many 'excellent persons' he had
met in 1793, the possibilities for an ever-expanding circle of social relations seemed unfavourable.[56] He considered fleeing for the Continent in
September 1793 with Charles Pigott, the radical pamphleteer, another
déclassé gentleman and pensioner of Samuel Rogers. They turned back
at Harwich, however, due to reports of the difficulties met by travellers
on the Continent, and Merry chose an internal exile, retiring to the
provinces, convinced that his correspondence was being opened by the

government.[57] Given that Pigott was to die the following year after con-
tracting gaol fever in Newgate, Merry's fears for his own safety may not
have been exaggerated. Debtors were also circling this floundering figure, and only Godwin's generosity saved Merry from being arrested for
debt in the early summer of 1796.[58] Merry's sources of income were being
squeezed. Writing for the theatre at Covent Garden, for which he had
produced several plays in the past few years, was made impossible. He
was now estranged from his former theatrical friends, and Harris, the
manager of Covent Garden, made it clear that he would not accept his
work. Merry told Samuel Rogers that 'the name of a Republican would
damn any performance at this time'.[59] The government may have been
behind these problems too. After the treason trials of 1794, bankruptcy
was a favoured means of quietly dealing with political opponents, especially celebrities, without the uncertainties of a trial by jury.[60]

By 1796 Merry had come to the end of his tether and decided to
move to the United States where his wife could find work again as an
actor. He bid farewell with a long poem, *The Pains of Memory* (1796), a sad
rejoinder to *The Pleasures of Memory*, which had made his patron Rogers
famous in 1792. The poem has the kind of episodic structure familiar
from *Diversity*. John Aikin's positive response in the friendly *Monthly Review*
pointed out that it took the form of 'a succession of detached pieces, but
little connected by any methodical train of thinking'.[61] In fact it once
again is structured by the materialist logic of association, but now these
are the associations of painful memories. The poem presents another
striking contrast with Wordsworth, for whom in 'Tintern Abbey' and
The Prelude the memory comes to be the means of access to a deeper
sense of self beyond the vicissitudes of mere association. Wordsworthian
memory uncovers in the natural world the 'workings of one mind'.[62]
Merry's poem opens, however, with 'nature dead, divested of her green'.
Nature offers no sphere of consolation beyond human society, and by
recalling happier days only 'adds to the immediate evil he endures'. Even
in defeat, however, Merry trusts to the promptings of 'Fancy', the faculty
that allows a vision of a different kind of world:

> And from the faded promises of youth
> Retain the love of liberty and truth.

These visions of 'liberty and truth' could perhaps have been fulfilled
in the new republic for which he left in 1796; apparently Merry even
planned a book on American social life, but he died two years later,

widely admired in the United States as the patriot poet Della Crusca.[63] In London a proposal for publishing the complete poetry and prose by subscription in two volumes for a guinea had come to naught.[64] A literary public that could both afford such a price and still subscribe to a vision of unlimited circulation could no longer be found in 1796. The limits of sociability were now being strictly enforced.

Comparing Wordsworth and Coleridge with Merry allows us to see what we might think of as two models of Romanticism, both of which might be defined in relation to sociability. Merry was committed to the idea of an ever-expanding public sphere based on reciprocity of feeling. The origins of his commitment might be found in the literature of sociability influenced by Shaftesbury, not to mention the societies and clubs in which Merry was so involved in the 1780s and early 1790s. However, eighteenth-century sociability was always haunted by a concern about limits and the regulation of feeling. The French Revolution was welcomed by Merry as a fulfilment of his dreams of universal benevolence, but for most commentators after Burke it supplied ultimate proof that the people could not be trusted to regulate themselves into politeness. Under pressure from events in France, the tolerance which had sometimes been extended in previous decades was rapidly withdrawn. For Burke, the enthusiasm for universal benevolence among literary men was threatening to encourage the unruly passions of the mob and the destruction of polite sociability. Critics such as James Chandler have argued that Wordsworth had already been heavily influenced by Burke by the time he came to write the 1800 Preface.[65] Certainly Wordsworth's poetry increasingly offered a constricted version of the conversation of culture in terms of the more restricted intimacy of 'friendship'. Only a few years earlier Merry had been pushing his idea of sociability to new horizons, suggestive of a limitless circle of benevolence. Perhaps in reaction to the phenomenon of Della Cruscanism, Wordsworth and Coleridge came to represent their writing in terms of the interactions of a close and even closed circle of friends in retirement. Human solidarity beyond these local encounters is a transcendent, mystified phenomenon. Shaftesbury had considered retreat and meditation a necessary preparatory to the conversation of culture; it was a stage in the regulation of the unrulier passions. Transforming Shaftesbury, many of the Romantic poets who came after Merry exaggerated this stage in the process, stressing retirement over the subsequent entry into the conversation of culture, and offering a narrower and more personal idea of that conversation for an age it feared was becoming, as Coleridge put it, '*sore* from excess of stimulation'.[66]

Critics such as Kelvin Everest have read this aspect of Coleridge's conversation poems as a creative response to the repressive government policies that forced Merry into exile. More specifically, Everest reads the trope of the reclusive rural idyll in these poems as a metonym for a broader and still fundamentally political sense of sociability and community. Yet I am not so sure that the 'persistent desire for the small community of kindred souls in nature' that emerges from the poetry of Wordsworth and Coleridge in this period can be so easily translated into a broader notion of 'sociability'. Everest is surely right to connect Coleridge to an eighteenth-century poetic tradition – very much influenced by Shaftesbury, though Everest does not name him – in which 'retirement quite conventionally pointed back to society'.[67] Yet placing Coleridge in this tradition only serves, I believe, to reveal the extent to which Shaftesbury's dialectic of retirement and sociability becomes stalled in his poetry (and perhaps sometimes in the poetic tradition that preceded it). Nor is this stalling, I would suggest, registered in Coleridge's poetry as the negative effect of external political conditions. More often regret is associated with the need to leave the retired life in the first place. Even in poems such as 'Reflections on Having Left a Place of Retirement', wherein the classic Shaftesburian 'ascent' to a higher vision in a secluded natural scene seems to function structurally as a prelude to a return to a life of active benevolence (here after the example of the prison reformer John Howard), the weight of the poem eventually falls on the sad necessity of leaving the place of seclusion. The penultimate paragraph's vision of the active life is capped in the final stanza by a nostalgia for the private and domestic security left behind:

> Yet oft when after honourable toil
> Rests the tir'd mind, and waking loves to dream,
> My spirit shall revisit thee dear Cot!
> Thy Jasmin and thy window-peeping Rose,
> And myrtles fearless of the mild sea-air.
> And I shall sigh fond wishes – sweet abode!
> Ah! – had none greater! And that all had such!
> It might be so – but the time is not yet.
> Speed it, O Father! Let thy kingdom come!
>   (lines 63–71)[68]

Originally the poem was published in the *Monthly Magazine* as 'Reflections on Entering into an Active Life'.[69] The title suggests the kind of poem we might expect from a public lecturer on civic and religious matters – as Coleridge had recently been – in a journal strongly

associated with Dissent. The more familiar title first used in Coleridge's
1797 collection lays greater stress on the ambivalence with regard to the
active life. The conventional signpost back to society, which the penultimate paragraph rehearses, seems to swing round in the other direction. Contrast this impulse with Thelwall's conversation poems of the
period 1795–8, as Judith Thompson has recently done to excellent effect,
and one sees the latter's much stronger sense of 'the despair, isolation and
persecution suffered by the reformer who refused to lie low'.[70] Where
Coleridge and Wordsworth go on to construct a new poetic from the
stalling of the dialectic of retirement and the active life, Thelwall registers
frustration and regret of the sort one finds in Merry's *Pains of Memory*. It is
not clear to me that the former is the 'advance' it is so often taken to be.

Two different ideas of Romantic sociability can be identified here. We
might even adapt Coleridge's terms in order to contrast the sociability of
Fancy with that of the Imagination. Coleridge and Wordsworth increasingly theorized the deep imagination, which uncovered layers of self to
be regulated, far beyond Shaftesbury's relatively simple model of self-
command. Clifford Siskin's work has recently stressed the importance of
figurations of identity as narrow and deep in their work.[71] The delight
of literature was to be found in this unpeeling of subjectivity towards a
core identity which could never be fully expressed. Only intimation and
unspoken sympathy could hint at it. Merry's model of poetic communication was based around throwing out to the public the vicissitudes of
fancy in the expectation of being enriched by sympathetic echoes. There
is an almost Shelleyan universe-in-process in his poetry. Subjectivity here,
like much of Merry's poetry, is episodic. It finds itself in reciprocity no
less than Wordsworth's 'Tintern Abbey' or Coleridge's conversation poems, but Merry's idea of reciprocity is much more diverse, open and
unstable. Predicated on what McGann calls a 'materialist tradition of
sensibility', oriented to an expanding market of print culture, it produces
a subjectivity that is both theatrical and libertarian, a much more sociable
self than the one projected by either Wordsworth or Coleridge, a version
of Romantic subjectivity aligned to what Paine called 'the open theatre
of the world'.[72]

NOTES

For full citations see Bibliography.
1 See McGann, *Poetics of Sensibility*, pp. 74–93. For an earlier rediscovery, see
 also Adams, 'Robert Merry'.
2 Wordsworth, 'Preface' to the *Lyrical Ballads* in *The Prose Works*, vol. 1, p. 130.

3 Werkmeister, *Newspaper History*, p. 39. Werkmeister lists the four most prominent Opposition journalists operating in 1792 as Merry, James Mackintosh, and the brothers Daniel and Charles Stuart.

4 Boaden, *Memoirs*, vol. II, p. 47.

5 Gifford, *The Baviad and the Maeviad*, p. xv.

6 *Gentleman's Magazine* 69 (March 1799), p. 254.

7 McGann, *Poetics of Sensibility*, p. 79.

8 On Shaftesbury and the trope of conversation, see Klein, *Shaftesbury*, pp. 8–10, 96–100 and 196–7.

9 *Ibid.*, p. 8. See Habermas, *Structural Transformation*.

10 Mullan, *Sentiment and Sociability*, p. 23.

11 Shaftesbury, *Characteristicks*, vol. I, pp. 170, 160.

12 Wordsworth, 'Preface' to the *Lyrical Ballads* and 'Essay, Supplementary to the Preface' to *Poems* (1815), *Prose Works* vol. I, p. 148 and vol. III, p. 72.

13 Shaftesbury, *Characteristicks*, vol. I, p. 64.

14 *Ibid.*, p. 15.

15 Mullan, *Sentiment and Sociability*, p. 29.

16 See Meehan, *Liberty and Poetics*, especially Part V on Wordsworth.

17 *The Florence Miscellany*, pp. 5–6.

18 *The World* first appeared on 1 January 1787. Charles Este and Miles Peter Andrews assisted Edward Topham and John Bell printed the paper. For details of the relationship between the proprietors and Merry, see Hargreaves-Mawdsley, *English Della Cruscans*, pp. 157–8, and Werkmeister, *London Daily Press*, pp. 92, 156–8.

19 For More's comments on *The World*, see Roberts, *Memoirs*, vol. II, p. 77; see also Pascoe, *Romantic Theatricality*, p. 68.

20 Hargreaves-Mawdsley, *English Della Cruscans*, p. 158.

21 See *The Poetry of the World*, vol. I, pp. 1–2: 2. For Anna Matilda's reply, see pp. 3–4.

22 See Hargreaves-Mawdsley, *English Della Cruscans*, pp. 171–2, 194 and 200–1.

23 Pascoe, *Romantic Theatricality*, p. 79. For Shaftesbury's views on manliness, see the discussion in Barker-Benfield, *Culture of Sensibility*, pp. 111–16.

24 See Hargreaves-Mawdsley, *English Della Cruscans*, p. 188.

25 See 'Preface' to Merry, *Diversity*, p. viii, pp. 13 and 11.

26 See Hargreaves-Mawdsley, *English Della Cruscans* , p. 52.

27 See Riede, *Oracles and Hierophants*, pp. 175–91. Coleridge asked in his notebook: 'What is the height, & ideal of mere association? – Delirium' see *Notebooks*, vol. I, p. 1770. While I agree with Riede's account of Coleridge's retreat from Priestley's materialism, I would make sense of it in terms of a larger reaction against enthusiasm, as redefined by Burke, which comprises a reaction against the delirium of the crowd both as popular materialism and religious fanaticism. Both forms of enthusiasm were regarded by Burke and Coleridge as destroying a properly regulated sociability based on the notion of a unified self in a hierarchy before God. Both were also associated with the kind of electric communication that Burke and Coleridge each identified with the expansion of print culture. See the discussion of

the discourse of enthusiasm in my forthcoming *Enthusiasm, Romanticism, and Regulation.*

28 Coleridge, *Biographia Literaria*, vol. I, pp. III and 304–5 and Riede, *Oracles and Hierophants*, p. 196.

29 This phrase occurs in Merry's 'Inscription written at La Grande Chartreuse', first published in the *European Magazine* 18 (November 1790), p. 388.

30 Thelwall, *Peripatetic*, vol. I, p. 123. Despite their differences Hume, Smith and Coleridge all shared a concern about the kind of enthusiasm which could create a kind of delirium in the individual and threaten social conformity.

31 See Burke, *Reflections*, in *The French Revolution 1790–1794*, ed. Mitchell, p. 97. For Burke's polarization of attitudes towards universal benevolence and his treatment of the Revolution in terms of enthusiasm, see Radcliffe, 'Revolutionary Writing', and Pocock, 'Edmund Burke'.

32 Merry, *Diversity*, p. 12 and *Critical Review* 67 (1789), pp. 129–30.

33 McGann, *Poetics of Sensibility*, p. 90 and Merry, *Diversity*, p. 34.

34 Hargeaves-Mawdsley, *English Della Cruscans*, p. 206.

35 Fox's opinion of Merry is quoted in Ginter, 'The Financing of the Whig Party Organization'. For further details of suspicions of Sheridan and his management of opinion for the party from both the Portland Whigs and Fox, see Clayton, 'Political Career', especially, pp. 57–75. I am grateful to Dr L. G. Mitchell for directing me to these references.

36 See Werkmeister, *Newspaper History*, pp. 72–9. Merry had joined the Society of the Friends of the Liberty of the Press in June 1791, another group populated by friends of Sheridan. Werkmeister describes both societies as 'equally conservative', p. 355. Merry seems to have been helping Sheridan on the *Morning Post* from earlier in the same year. See Werkmeister, *London Daily Press*, pp. 207, 343–4.

37 See Hargreaves-Mawdsley, *English Della Cruscans*, p. 217. Merry was ousted from the Beefsteak Club in the middle of 1792, a move which may also reflect his changing social and political affiliations at this time. See Werkmeister, *Newspaper History*, pp. 92–3.

38 See Gifford, *The Baviad and the Maeviad*, p. 25. Needless to say, Merry was also fulfilling the worst fears of the Portland Whigs about Sheridan's newspaper policies.

39 Klancher, *Making*, p. 36.

40 See Merry, *Laurel of Liberty*, pp. vi, 7, 23 and 37 and Walpole's letter (10 November 1790) to Edward Jerningham, who ironically was associated both with the Della Cruscanism of the *World* and the early enthusiasm for the French Revolution, Jerningham, *Letters*, p. 50.

41 See Robinson, *Poems*, pp. 198–209.

42 He was preceded by the satire [Anon.], *Modern Poets* (1791) and the *Analytical Review* 9 (February 1791), pp. 193–5. Gifford wrote of the exchange between Merry and Robinson that 'Merry had given an example of impious temerity, which this wretched woman was but too eager to imitate', *The Baviad and the Maeviad*, p. xvii.

43 Reynolds, *Life and Times*, vol. II, p. 45.

44 Hargreaves-Mawdsley, *English Della Cruscans*, p. 236.

45 For the praise of Paine, see Clayden, *Early Life*, p. 174, and for the Crown and Anchor meeting, see Goodwin, *Friends of Liberty*, p. 179, and Hargreaves-Mawdsley, *English Della Cruscans*, p. 238. There are descriptions of the meeting in the *Gentleman's Magazine* 61 (1791), pp. 673–5 and the *European Magazine* 20 (1791), pp. 78–9. The former claims, p. 673, that 'about fifteen hundred gentlemen' attended and that Merry's 'Ode' was sung by Sedgwick to music composed by Storace. The latter affirmed this view of the meeting itself, but went on to report that 'a number of idle people' assembled at Newgate and called for the release of their hero Lord George Gordon, p. 79. The contrast nicely illustrates the difference between ideas of regulated sociability and the unruliness of the mob. Gordon's name above all others was associated with the enthusiasm of the latter. See also Anne Janowitz's chapter in this volume for the significance of this occasion for Anna Letitia Barbauld.

46 Merry, *Ode*, pp. 6–7.

47 *Ibid.*

48 See Burke, *Letter to a Noble Lord* in *The French Revolution*, ed. Mitchell, p. 98.

49 See Goodwin, *Friends of Liberty*, p. 179, and *The Times* July 16 (1791).

50 Boaden, *Memoirs*, vol. II, p. 47.

51 For further details on the Pittachio broadsides, see my 'Political Showman' and Barrell's *Imagining*. Merry is also quoted with approval in Richard 'Citizen' Lee's *Songs*.

52 A Merry was listed among those present at one of the very earliest LCS meetings in 1792, according to evidence given at Hardy's trial for treason, but there is no reason to think this was Robert Merry. See Thale (ed.), *Selections*, p. 7n.

53 For Ballard's activities in the LCS, see *Ibid.*, pp. 252n, 256n, 285, 325n, 330, 340n, 351n and 393.

54 Hargreaves-Mawdsley, *English Della Cruscans*, p. 275.

55 For Merry in Paris and his escape, see Erdman, *Commerce*, pp. 229–30, 230, 234, 265, and Hargreaves-Mawdsley, *English Della Cruscans*, p. 258. Monro wrote to the Foreign Office that 'the party of conspirators' had 'formed themselves into a society' on 17 December, but formal notice of their intent did not appear in the Paris papers till early January. See Alger, *Paris*, p. 330. Alger says that Merry left for Britain in May 1793, p. 346.

56 Hargreaves-Mawdsley, *English Della Cruscans*, p. 260.

57 *Ibid.*, p. 263.

58 *Ibid.*, p. 290.

59 On Harris and Merry, see Werkmeister, *Newspaper History*, p. 93. Merry had written the following plays, *The Picture of Paris* (1790) with C. Bonnor, *Lorenzo, A Tragedy* (1791), *The Magician No Conjurer* (1792). All of these were performed at Covent Garden, although the last, which included a satirical attack on Pitt, lasted only until its fourth night, but he could find no one to perform his *Fénelon* (1795), which was published by Parsons, another LCS publisher.

For his comments to Rogers, see Clayden, *Early Life*, p. 284. Merry's play *The Abbey of St Augustine* was produced in New York shortly before his death. See Hargreaves-Mawdsley, *English Della Cruscans*, p. 291.

60 On the government's use of bankruptcy for political ends, see Werkmeister, *Newspaper History*, pp. 231, 344–5 and 434–5.

61 *Monthly Review* 21 (1796), pp. 149–51 (p. 150). Aikin claimed that much of 'the false glitter of language and tinsel of imagery' of Merry's earlier poetry had been removed from *The Pains of Memory* (p. 151).

62 See William Wordsworth, *The Prelude*, ed. Wordsworth *et al.*, Book 6, line 636.

63 Merry, *Pains*, pp. 2, 4 and 36. On Merry's plans in America, see Hargreaves-Mawdsley, *English Della Cruscans*, p. 292.

64 See Merry, *Proposals*. A collection of his poetry – possibly the same one – advertised in the *American Universal Magazine* 1 (January 1797), p. 31 also seems never to have been published. The same journal also published an 'Ode to Mr R. Merry, On his arrival in America' by G. L. G. of Baltimore in its May issue 1 (1797), pp. 189–91. The editor of the magazine was Richard 'Citizen' Lee, who had published some of Merry's squibs as broadsides in London, and was now a fellow exile from Pitt's terror.

65 Chandler, *Wordsworth's Second Nature*, pp. 82–3.

66 Coleridge to Thomas Allsop, 30 March 1820, *Collected Letters*, vol. V, p. 24.

67 See Everest, *Coleridge's Secret Ministry*, pp. 91 and 192.

68 Coleridge, *Complete Poetical Works*, pp. 106–7.

69 The poem was originally published in the *Monthly Magazine*, 2 (October 1796), p. 712.

70 Thompson, 'An Autumnal Blast', p. 435. Everest himself notes these differences with Thelwall, *Coleridge's Secret Ministry*, p. 129.

71 See Siskin's *Historicity of Romantic Discourse* and *Work of Writing*.

72 McGann, *Poetics of Sensibility*, p. 80 and Paine, *Rights of Man*, p. 25.

7

Spouters or washerwomen: the sociability of Romantic lecturing

Gillian Russell

The founding of the Royal Institution in 1799 and the tremendous success of Humphry Davy's lectures in chemistry there between 1802 and 1812 led to an expansion in lecturing in the metropolis and across Britain in the early nineteenth century.[1] The subjects of these lectures ranged widely, from astronomy, natural philosophy, *belles lettres*, music, engineering to the medical sciences. In the manner of voluntary societies throughout the eighteenth century, lecturing institutions expressed social affiliations, particularly by emerging professional groups such as men of science and literati, as well as asserting a claim to broader social recognition.[2] This had a material manifestation in the construction and adaptation of buildings for a particular role as lecturing institutions. Furnished with auditoriums, libraries, conversation rooms and laboratories, places such as the Royal, the London, the Surrey and Russell institutions represented an institutionalization of knowledge in both a material and social sense which anticipated the development of the modern university. The most substantial discussion of the contribution of lecturing to late Georgian public culture has been that of historians of science.[3] Relevant work in Romantic literary studies has tended to discuss the lectures of Coleridge and Hazlitt in the context of these writers' biographies or in analyses of their literary criticism, in which case the focus has been on the content of the lectures rather than their broader social and cultural significance.[4] While lectures were undoubtedly of historic importance in cementing the cultural authority of imaginative literature, the focus in this chapter will be oriented differently towards an analysis of the significance of the lecture as a sociable event: indeed, my argument will be that post-1800 lecturing is largely a response to the crisis in sociable relations that characterizes the 1790s and that it needs to be regarded within the context of, and as a response to, other forms of sociable behaviour in the early nineteenth century.

In 1808 Coleridge reported in a letter how his servant Mrs Brainbridge had described a visitor as 'a sort of a *Methody Preacher* at that Unstintution, where you goes to *spout*, Sir'.[5] Mrs Brainbridge's comment is interesting in a number of respects, not the least for how it indicates lecturing's identification with a material structure, its 'unstintutionalization' in her terms. Her association of lecturing with the enthusiasm of a Methodist preacher and the effusions of the amateur actor also reflects the lecture-room's uncertain position in late Georgian culture, somewhere between the church and the theatre. Lecturing can be regarded as a form of secular sermonizing which exploited the idea of enunciation as expressive of direct access to the divine at the same time as channelling such enthusiasm towards the ideals of Enlightenment science. Similarly, in his use of the arts of performance, the capacity to attract an audience through manipulation of speech and gesture, the lecturer could harness the power of the actor while importantly remaining in his own character, not subjecting himself or his audience to the uncertainties of impersonation. The 'Methody' preacher and the spouter, both of which were regarded as dubious, marginal versions of the priest and the actor, therefore shadow the identity of the lecturer as well as complicating the significance of lecture-going for the late Georgian public.

If he was preacher and performer, the lecturer also resembled the politician in that public oratory was a time-honoured civic art, crucial to the life of the polis. Training in public speaking in schools and by tutors and the vast number of treatises and manuals on the subject also indicate the importance of the arts of speaking in the construction of masculine subjectivity.[6] In entering the lecture-box, the lecturer was therefore asserting a speaking position (in figurative and material terms) that was implicitly political and 'manly'. Because of its independence from institutions such as parliament, the law and the church, lecturing, like debating, was one of the crucial sites of the Enlightenment public sphere in a Habermasian sense. It was a 'rational entertainment', whose more earnest political or scientific dimensions were bound up with its status as a sociable event. In other words, in analyzing lectures it is important not to overestimate the 'rational' at the expense of the 'entertainment'. The success throughout the English-speaking world of George Alexander Stevens's 'Lecture on Heads' was a constant reminder to the late Georgian public of the theatricality of the lecturing mode and the lecturer's identity as Enlightenment showman.[7] Adam Walker, for example, protégé of Joseph Priestley, lectured on his transparent orrery, the Eidouranion, at the Haymarket and Royalty theatres and in rooms in George Street, Hanover Square, the home of fashionable music concerts.[8] Hester Piozzi attended what she described as Walker's 'Astronomical Lecture and Show' at the Haymarket in the crisis year of 1798, commenting that it was 'well calculated to keep Men's Minds from heat of Party at the present Moments'.[9] For Piozzi, Walker's 'show' was a diversion from the more pressing anxieties of the times, an interpretation reinforced for her by the fact that the lecture took place in the metropolis's leading summer theatre. What then are we to make of Piozzi's attendance three years earlier at one of the political lectures of the radical John Thelwall? Piozzi was strongly opposed to Thelwall's politics, describing him in 1795 as someone who 'figured away among the seditious Fools' in the London Corresponding Society, so her attendance at the lecture seems to have been motivated by curiosity and also by some of the same reasons that attracted her to Walker in 1798.[10] In spite of her revulsion from his politics, Piozzi found Thelwall impressive as a political performer: 'he is a very fluent orator', she remarked, 'and among much trash produces some very good hits'.[11] ('Hits' was a term often used to describe particularly effective moments in an actor's performance.) Piozzi's presence at Thelwall's lecture, for which she paid an admission fee of one shilling, is an indication that his lectures belonged in the same spectrum of Enlightenment public culture, in which knowledge was commercialized and theatricalized, as Walker's Eidouranion. In other words, Thelwall's lectures represented a very different political and sociable space from that of the mass gatherings at Copenhagen Fields, which Piozzi would not have attended and at which Thelwall gave an oratorical performance as demagogue rather than lecturer.[12] The problem of Thelwall's lectures was not only that they attracted an artisanal class caricatured by Isaac D'Israeli as 'wild apprentices . . . tiny taylors' sitting among 'the bloody offals of butchers stalls' but that people of gentility such as Piozzi and Joseph Farington mixed in such company.[13] In this respect Thelwall's lectures approximated the Habermasian ideal of the public sphere as 'social intercourse' which in the process of converting culture into a commodity 'established the public as in principle inclusive'.[14] In the context of the Revolution controversy, however, such inclusivity could not be tolerated by Pitt's government, with far-reaching consequences not just for Thelwall but for lecturing and Enlightenment public culture in general.

When Piozzi witnessed Thelwall in late 1795 his lecture-room was about to be closed down as a result of the Two Acts which specifically banned lectures 'on the Laws, Constitution, Government and Polity

of these kingdoms'.[15] As the most celebrated 'political lecturer' in
the metropolis, Thelwall was undoubtedly the principal target of this
legislation.[16] He had made his name as an orator at the Coachmakers'
Hall Society for Free Debate in the 1780s and became a key figure in
the struggle over rights of free speech in the aftermath of the French
Revolution. After the government suppressed the Society for Free Debate
in November 1792, he struggled to establish debating societies in a number of venues across London before turning to lecturing. Beginning with
'an obscure little newspaper-room' in Compton Street, Soho, Thelwall
eventually established himself in Beaufort Buildings in the Strand, which
functioned not only as a lecturing venue but also as a place where the
texts of his lectures and other material were printed and sold, a meeting place for the LCS and lodgings for the lecturer and his family.[17]
Thelwall's identification with the venue of his lectures is a particularly
striking aspect of attacks against him and his own self-representation.
Thelwall represented the threat to his lecturing as a threat not simply to
rights of public assembly but to any kind of social gathering of individuals
for the purposes of free discussion: intrinsic to his argument is an emphasis on Beaufort Buildings as a space which blurs the distinction between
the public and the private. He argued that provisions in the Two Acts
enabling authorities to enter a house in which a lecture was suspected
to be taking place meant that 'the power of the magistrates will . . . be
no greater over my lecture-room, than it is, at this moment, over every
room, house, or tenement throughout the nation'.[18] There was no social
space free from the corrosive intrusion of government. The violation of
the social intercourse of the coffee-house, where every word was being
listened to by 'party hirelings and venal associaters', and the readiness
of spying servants 'to catch and betray the idle conversation of your un-
guarded moments', made it 'more than ever requisite' to acquire 'every
species of political and constitutional knowledge'.[19] Sociability was here
being constructed as a key site of political struggle for the 1790s. Thelwall
represented what he described as 'the free incense of friendly communication' as a natural right which preceded political knowledge and which
that knowledge was compelled to defend.[20]

Thelwall mounted similar arguments in defence of his lecture tour
to the provinces in 1796 after the failure of his journal *The Tribune*, the
mouthpiece for his lectures, left him in financial ruin and London was
made impossible for him by the Two Acts. He travelled to Yarmouth,
Wisbech, Lynn, Derby and Norwich, where he lectured to between

4,000 and 5,000 people, one contemporary's comment – 'We have got Thelwall' – indicating the orator's celebrity status in radicalism and in public culture in general.[21] Throughout his provincial tour, Thelwall was hunted, in E. P. Thompson's memorable terms, by the forces of counter-revolution. His lectures were broken up by mobs and Thelwall physically assaulted; at Yarmouth he was nearly kidnapped. What has not been noted in accounts of Thelwall's ordeal in this period is the extent to which the struggles over his lectures were struggles over provincial sociability in a broader sense. His lectures at Lynn, for example, were delivered at the Globe tavern, where Thelwall was engaged to have dinner afterwards 'with a party of respectable farmers of Lynn and the surrounding villages'.[22] This was a gesture of political solidarity, demonstrating also to Thelwall the civic virtues of a network of radically inclined gentlemen through the observation of hospitality to an outsider. The subsequent besieging of the tavern by a crowd, and the firing of shots, indicate that more than Thelwall's right to lecture was at stake: his opponents were attacking rights to sociable association in general. Thelwall had a similar experience at Wisbech, where he was firstly prevented from lecturing in the local theatre, then denied the bowling green as a venue: he finally retreated to the castle of a sympathetic local magnate under whose protection he lectured in the drawing-room to about one hundred people.[23] The theatre and the bowling green, prime examples of the commercialization of leisure in the provinces which Peter Borsay has characterized as the 'English urban renaissance', were therefore the venues for a struggle between Thelwall and his opponents over the fundamental meanings of the values associated with Enlightenment sociability.[24]

Thelwall experienced a similar pattern of legal harassment and physical violence when he tried to lecture in Yarmouth. His account of events there emphasizes that prior to his lectures he had spent some time with sympathetic local inhabitants in 'private manner', during which he attempted to prove, by means of 'the sentiments and feelings evinced in my conversation', that he was not the ranting villain of Beaufort Buildings.[25] Such a strategy appropriated the discourse of Shaftesburian politeness for the purposes of 1790s radicalism, and in the process intensified the political meanings of sociability. Hence Thelwall emphasized the importance of his lecture not primarily for its content but as a sociable event, a rational entertainment. The people assembled to hear him, he claimed, were 'of both sexes, and of all ages, mostly very genteel people', exhibiting 'firmness, general concord, and discreet good-humour'. He even went so far as to describe the occasion as 'a scene of fashion, gaiety, and pleasure' which had been 'metamorphosed into one of carnage and horror, of fractured heads, and garments covered over with blood', a description recalling Burke's juxtaposition of a feminized *ancien régime* and revolutionary barbarity in *Reflections on the Revolution in France*.[26] In Yarmouth, however, it was the anti-Jacobins who were the barbarian marauders threatening feminized social intercourse.

Thelwall's defence in 1796 of the sociability of his lecturing was addressed not only to the forces of counter-revolution but to his political ally and 'father', William Godwin, who had attacked his lectures in *Considerations on Lord Grenville's and Mr Pitt's Bills*, published in November 1795. Referring to Thelwall not by name but as 'the political lecturer of Beaufort Buildings', Godwin had mounted a critique of lecturing and debating based on their dangerous theatricality. Godwin conceded that Thelwall's motives were 'pure' ones but argued that they had been corrupted by the very mode of public oratory which appealed to the 'passions' of the audience and the gratification of the lecturer's self-regard.[27] Both lecturer and his auditors could become carried away by the power of his performance, in ways that led them to express their politics in physical violence against persons rather than a philosophical dismantling of the current system of government. In a crucial statement, Godwin argued against the validity of Beaufort Buildings or the debating clubs as forums of political expression: 'Sober inquiry may pass well enough with a man in his closet, or in the domestic tranquillity of his own fire-side: but it will not suffice in theatres and halls of assembly'.[28] Such an argument, consistent with Godwin's emphasis in *Political Justice* on the utility of 'small and friendly societies' as opposed to the dangerous tendencies of public assemblies or systematically organized networks of clubs such as the London Corresponding Society, proposed a dissociation of the link between the public and private spheres which Thelwall's lectures, in their performative context, exemplified.[29] Godwin was reconfiguring radical politics away from the scene of speaking, represented by Beaufort Buildings, to a scene of reading that isolated and privileged the masculine subject.

Thelwall's lectures were undoubtedly theatrical, as Hester Piozzi's response suggests, but his performances were more sophisticated than Godwin allowed. An example is Thelwall's 'staging' in a lecture of his last encounter with Joseph Gerrald, who had been condemned to transportation to Australia: 'I would not then disgrace the manly scene before me with a tear; but now it is no shame, it is no reproach to let them flow down my cheek, while I conjure you ... forget not, Britons, forget not . . . that Joseph Gerrald is an exile for his zeal in the cause of liberty'.[30] Thelwall's distinction here between his farewell to Gerrald as it actually happened – 'manly', without tears – and his performance of it in the context of the lecture as regulated feeling, tears that should be the spur to political action, suggests that he had some awareness of the need to discipline the theatricality of his lecturing style. Thelwall argued that lecturing was in fact a superior art to acting because the lecturer was not subject to a script written by others but could 'appear in his own character' giving 'utterance to the genuine sentiments of his own mind, and the real passions of his soul'.[31] Rather than being the ranting demagogue or the self-regarding spouter, the lecturer was capable of standing for an essentially performative ideal of transparency or openness. He could be the ultimate actor in Thomas Paine's 'open theatre of the world'.[32] As a form of political theatre in which the rational, manly subject of radicalism could appear as himself, Beaufort Buildings was therefore a potent space in the mid 1790s. It radicalized the public sphere not by offering a counter public but by extending the limits of the inclusivity encoded in notions of the commercialized public sphere in its classic Habermasian formulation. It was a place where Hester Piozzi could rub shoulders, however disdainfully, with the LCS. Its status as a place of assembly and Thelwall's domicile confused boundaries between the public and the private; it was both homosocial, adapting the rituals and conviviality of the debating club and tavern, and a feminized 'scene of gaiety and fashion'; it housed oral and print culture, like Thelwall himself, who was as adept in the gestural politics of tavern sociability (he once knocked off the head of a pot of porter as a sign of killing the king) as he was in the realms of poetry, philosophy and political theory.[33] The closing down of Thelwall's lectures and the subsequent hounding of him throughout Britain in 1796 and 1797 are a measure of how threatening Beaufort Buildings was as a forum for political knowledge and a particular model of the radical public sphere.

The 'political theatre' of Beaufort Buildings and the debating clubs cast a long shadow over public lecturing in the early nineteenth century, influencing its development and the institutions in which it took place.[34] Thelwall's impact can be gauged by a comparison between Isaac Cruikshank's 'Debating Society' of 1795 and Thomas Rowlandson's 'Surrey Institution', an illustration for Ackermann's *Microcosm of London* (1809). Cruikshank satirizes the debating clubs as sites of unregulated speech in which there is no community, only a cacophony of competing

1. Isaac Cruikshank, 'Debating Society', 1795.

2. Thomas Rowlandson, 'Surrey Institution' from *The Microcosm of London*, *1809*.

voices: Thelwall stands in the middle in full Mr 'Bawlwell' mode, while a manager desperately tries to control the debate. Rowlandson's Surrey Institution represents a much more disciplined theatre: he depicts a genteel company whose orderly and relaxed dispositions and smiling expressions suggest pleasurable sociability being refined by science and vice versa. Significantly, this is a 'mixed auditory' of men and women in contrast to Cruikshank's male gathering. Gender was to play a crucial role in the cultural and political configurations of lecturing after 1800. From the 1750s women had been involved in lecturing and debating clubs as participants and members of the audience in ways that paralleled their dominance of the feminized arena of theatre.[35] The didactic aims of lectures, however, legitimated female sociability to a greater degree than the morally suspect attractions of playgoing. Thelwall's activities in the 1790s complicated the gender politics of lecturing, firstly by the way that he had invoked the Humean ideal of mixed sociability (the 'scene of gaiety and fashion') in defending his lectures and, secondly, because of the way that he had deliberately conflated the space of his lectures with his own domestic space, constructing a speaking position that merged his identity as a professional and a man. These issues were further complicated by Godwin's dissociation of the public and private spheres in his response to Thelwall and his politicization of the scene of reading, embodied by a man by his fireside.

The lecturing institutions constructed or adapted after 1799 regulated the inclusive sociability of the Beaufort Buildings, by making the lecturer the servant or employee of a group of men constituting themselves as a formal institution, thereby ensuring that a particular individual or voice would never be identified with a space in the way that Thelwall had. These institutions also strictly monitored membership and constructed a built environment which clearly defined the institution's functions, unlike Beaufort Buildings, which could accommodate political activity, lecturing, the dissemination of printed texts, as well as Thelwall's household. The description of the Surrey Institution in the *Microcosm of London* conducts the reader on a tour through its 'elegant portico ... crowned with the appropriate statue of Contemplation', through the vestibule and 'anti-room', then on to a 'very elegant apartment' connected to the reading and pamphlet-rooms. 'Contiguous to these apartments' were the 'conversation-rooms', one of which led to the lecture theatre itself, adjoining which was the chemical laboratory and the committee room. The *Microcosm*'s tour concluded with the library 'sixty feet in length, with a gallery on three sides': 'This room is rendered particularly pleasant by the garden in its front, which is calculated to convey an idea of rural retirement'.[36] The material structure of the Surrey Institution therefore implied a great deal about the kind of sociability that went on within it, the links between the lecture and conversation rooms, the promotion of reading rather than the production of literature, even the cultivation of a garden on the Blackfriars Road, all suggesting an orientation away from the 'open theatre of the world' that was Beaufort Buildings. Within the walls of the Surrey male members could conduct themselves in a pseudo-domestic manner, much in the style of the gentleman's clubs of the period, except that the Surrey did not tolerate vices such as gambling nor did it have obvious political affiliations. Indeed, politics is significant by its absence from the *Microcosm*'s account of the Institution, the emphasis being on the utility of the 'intercourse' there between men of commerce and men of literature: 'by ready access to well-selected libraries, knowledge becomes more correct, taste more refined, and sentiments more liberal'.[37] Henry Crabb Robinson describes himself on five occasions as 'lounging' at the Surrey Institution, reading its books and magazines, a more public and performative version of Godwin's man by his fireside insofar as Crabb Robinson could be observed by his fellow members.[38] In 'lounging' at the Surrey, Crabb Robinson was staging a particular construction of himself in a public mode that was performative without being excessively theatrical, protected by the walls and garden of the Surrey's regulated sociability.

The presence of women at the core activity of these institutions – lecturing – was essential to the legitimation of their claims to politeness and civility as well as to their financial survival. Female involvement was encouraged in ways that emphasized women's roles as wives and daughters, thereby constructing the lecture theatre as a space of regulated heterosexual sociability (in contrast to the theatre). In the case of the Surrey, for example, wives and unmarried daughters of proprietors could pay an annual subscription in order to have access to the lectures and the circulating library: women recommended by the wives of proprietors could have the same privilege. Women seem to have been excluded by these rules from the news room, the reading room, the laboratory and the reference library.[39] For some men, attendance at lectures was an aspect of their homosociality. John Keats, for example, describes how he was 'pounced upon' by a number of male friends as he arrived late for one of Hazlitt's lectures at the Surrey.[40] The prospect of meeting these friends – perhaps there was a prior arrangement – is likely to have been one reason why Keats went to the lecture in the first place. For Crabb

Robinson lecture attendance was a matter of heterosexual sociability that complemented his homosocial 'lounging' in the reading rooms of places like the Surrey. He escorted a number of women, both married and unmarried, to lectures, the pedagogic purpose of which legitimated his role as chaperone.[41] For the lecturers themselves the lecture-room functioned as a distinctive form of social intercourse in which the lecturer was not only entertaining and educating his audience but also making himself socially available. Crabb Robinson made his first personal encounter with Coleridge through the latter's invitation to find him in 'the apparatus room close by the Lecture Room' where he would give him tickets of admission to that course of lectures as a whole. Crabb Robinson's comment – 'I am happy that I have thus formed Coleridge's acquaintance, for tho' we have not yet met, I feel we can meet' – suggests that such lecture-room encounters could function as points of transition to more intimate relationships, ante-rooms to friendship, rather like the relationship between the apparatus and the lecture-room itself.[42] A striking instance of the significance of lecturing as a kind of public exposure on the part of the lecturer was the approach made to Coleridge by a former love, Mary Todd, née Evans: 'Having heard his "name announced at the Royal Institution" and after attending a lecture and introducing herself to him, she wrote to [Coleridge] on 6 Apr 1808.'[43] It is not clear if Mary Todd had been chaperoned to the lecture or how indeed she had obtained a ticket. It is possible that she was using heterosexual sociability, if only the discursive legitimation of public lecturing in such terms, as a pretext to renew a previously intimate connection with Coleridge. Mary Todd's initiative, like the fashionable ladies at Humphry Davy's lectures 'busily noting down what they heard, as topics for the next conversation party', or Anne Lister's attendance at John Dalton's lectures in Halifax in order to pursue a current (female) love interest, are indications that women lecture-goers were not easily chaperoned by a regulated heterosexual sociability.[44] Like Hester Piozzi going to see Thelwall, the status of lectures as commercial entertainments, however regulated, could allow some women to determine their own version of 'liberal' social intercourse.

The interpenetration of gender and cultural politics that characterizes lecturing forms the basis of Byron's poem *The Blues*, written in 1821 and published in *The Liberal* in 1823. It takes the form of a two-part 'literary eclogue' which, as McGann and Weller note, shows the influence of Thomas Love Peacock and Christopher Anstey.[45] The structure of the poem and dialogic form also suggest comparisons with the two-act comic afterpiece in the theatre, particularly texts such as Richard Brinsley Sheridan's *The Critic* (1779). Byron's gesturing in this way towards Anstey and Sheridan indicates a continuity between his representation of lecturing in this poem as amusement for bluestockings and preoccupations with female sociability in eighteenth-century texts such as *The Bath Guide* and *The School for Scandal*. There was a material equivalence to this in the way that some lecturing venues such as the Willis Rooms, and the Russell and Surrey Institutions, were either adaptations of or built on the site of assembly rooms, dancing academies and museums that had been established in the expansionist phase of metropolitan public culture that began in the 1760s and 1770s. The earnest young ladies taking notes at Davy's lecture were therefore the daughters of Burney's Evelina and Georgiana, Duchess of Devonshire.

The setting of the first eclogue is 'London. – *Before the Door of a Lecture Room*'.[46] Like Keats in 1818, Inkel (Byron) is late and must rendezvous outside the lecture-room with his fellow poet Tracy (Thomas Moore). Scamp (Coleridge) is lecturing inside to a group comprised predominantly of women, 'Belles', who have made learning 'the fashion'. The location of the encounter between Inkel and Tracy on the threshold of the lecture-room is indicative of the poem's fundamental concern with cultural 'situatedness' expressed through sociability. In December 1811 and January 1812 Byron had gone inside the lecture-room at Fleur de Luce Court to hear Coleridge. In a characteristic act of performative concealment he was 'wrapped up', according to Crabb Robinson, 'but I recognised his club foot'.[47] Writing ten years later in a way that telescopes the middle phase of Coleridge's lecturing career between 1808 and 1811 and the very different political climate post-1819, Byron figuratively refuses to enter the lecture-room. He represents lecturing as the sphere of fashionable bluestockings such as Lady Bluebottle (Lady Holland), the patron of Scamp. In such a context poetry is debased as a form of currency in the marriage market: Tracy wants Inkel to write him a poem in order to attract the attention of Miss Lilac (Annabella Milbanke), 'a poet, a chemist, a mathematician'. The 'Eclogue Second', which concerns Lady Bluebottle's post-lecture collation, begins with Sir Richard Bluebottle complaining that his house has been taken over by 'the numerous, humourous, back-biting crew / Of scribblers, wits, lecturers, white, black, and blue'.[48] The links established here between the lecture-room and the dining-room highlight the fact that lecturing was not a discrete social activity but took place in the context of other forms of domestic

sociability. However, Sir Richard Bluebottle's alarm draws attention to
the blurring of boundaries between the public space of the lecture-room
and his own domestic space as a challenge to patriarchal and class authority. In 'Eclogue Second' there is a discussion about Scamp's friend
Wordswords – 'Does he stick to his lakes, like the leeches he sings, / And
their gatherers, as Homer sung warriors and kings?' – and about his
finding a place (Inkel quips 'As a footman?').[49] It seems that in this context Sir Richard's traditional 'private' role as patron of the arts has been
usurped by government, by the literary marketplace, but especially by
his wife, who has made literature the substance of her social life and
vice versa. The integrity of Sir Richard's private sphere, signifying his
substance as a man of property, has been subsumed by the space created
by his wife, a space of sociable activity organized around the pursuit
of literature which merges the lecture-room and the dining-room. The
category of author in *The Blues* is clearly one which has become unfixed
from the moorings of class and gender with the effect of destabilizing
those very moorings themselves. Inkel asks Tracy, 'Do you dine with Sir
Humphrey to day?', a reference to Sir Humphry Davy, who had fash-
ioned a place and a title for himself through his skills as a lecturer.
'I should think with Duke Humphrey was more in your way', Tracy
responds, to which Inkel replies: 'It might be of yore; but we authors
now look / To the knight, as a landlord, much more than the Duke. /
The truth is – each writer now quite at his ease is, / And (except with his
publisher) dines where he pleases.'[50] Some authors, however, are more
free than others. Inkel proposes, as it is 'now nearly five', that he takes
a turn in 'the Park', and Tracy offers to join him there. The royal parks
of St James's and Hyde Park had long been established as venues for
elite male sociability; they were theatres of display, of sexual encounter
and occasional violence. Inkel's resort to 'the Park', therefore, signifies
a rejection of the confinement of Lady Bluebottle's salon and the domination of the cultural sphere by women which it represents. Inkel and
Tracy ask Scamp to accompany them but he is unable to do so because
of the need to prepare for his next lecture. Inkel's noting of the time
introduces another dimension to the poem in that it denotes his hours as
being those of the fashionable elite. By thereby making Scamp's lecture
an afternoon occasion Byron was making a subtle point. The lectures
of Coleridge that he had attended in 1811 took place in the evening,
at 7 o'clock, unlike his lectures at the Royal Institution in 1808, which
started in the afternoon in order to appeal to a fashionable clientele.

Both the time and location of Coleridge's lectures at Fleur de Luce Court in Fleet Street, off Fetter Lane, represented a social and cultural migration 'down-market' for Coleridge, and the markers of time in Byron's poem would have reminded readers and Coleridge of this fact.[51] In *The Blues*, lecturing enables Byron to articulate his mobility within the Romantic cultural landscape – he is outside the lecture-room door, moving from fashionable salon to the park, participating in the literary sociability of women and the marketplace but still able to escape to the elite sociability signified by place and time. As Lady Bluebottle says of Inkel, Byron is a 'fugitive' writer, unlike Coleridge and Wordsworth, who are fixed in the lecture-room and by the dual meaning of 'place' in the Lakes.

Byron's representation of Coleridge the lecturer being entrapped by the company of women indicates how crucial gender was to the cultural politics of lecturing after 1800. The orientation of lecturing away from the 'open theatre of the world' of Beaufort Buildings, in spaces such as the Surrey Institution, was in effect a turning towards a version of domesticity and the private sphere. Coleridge's 'Prospectus' of his 1818 lectures promotes them as complementing the discussion of literature in the domestic context, as part of 'the entertainment of the social board, and the amusement of the circle at the fire-side' (significantly the latter is a place of 'amusement', not Godwinian sober enquiry).[52] The aim of the lectures, according to the 'Prospectus', is to offer a kind of curriculum of useful literature that would counteract the '*mischief* of unconnected and promiscuous reading', fitting the (male) auditor to take 'an intelligent interest in any general conversation likely to occur in mixed society'.[53] Coleridge's 'general conversation' is a mode of discourse but also a particular kind of cultural space that subsumes the lecture-room and the 'social table'. It proposes imaginative literature as a means of self-regulation, of cordoning off 'promiscuous books', enabling access to the universal values of 'good sense, taste, and feeling' that transcend the 'accidents of fashion, place, or age, or the events or the customs of the day'.[54] Whereas Thelwall invokes 'fashion' as a defence of his lecturing, Coleridge is careful to mark his lecture-room as distinct from the world of commercialized public culture, of 'rational entertainment', for which terms such as 'fashion' stood in late Georgian discourse. Such a distinction has a political significance too: for Thelwall the lecture-room represented a particular kind of sociable value that was a prerequisite of political knowledge and which that political knowledge had to defend;

for Coleridge in 1818 the value of general conversation about imaginative literature lay in the way that it created a space outside the political
(and also a different configuration of 'knowledge').

The many comments about Coleridge's lecturing style being like
his conversation and vice versa were therefore not just a reflection of
Coleridge's idiosyncrasies but a manifestation of the ideal of general
conversation that merged the lecture-room and the 'social board'.[55] At
times Coleridge deliberately cultivated a sense of his lectures as being
extensions of conversation elsewhere, as when he supported an attack
on Anna Letitia Barbauld's poetry by saying that Wordsworth had made
the same criticisms to him 'at Charles Lamb's two years ago'.[56] However,
the idea of lecturing as an extension of domestic sociability risked the
possibility of an absorption of the masculine subject into the private
sphere and consequent effeminization. This is what Byron suggests is
the danger that faces Scamp/Coleridge in *The Blues*; the risk of effeminization, as well as class transgression, is also apparent in the *Quarterly
Review*'s castigation of Hazlitt's lecturing as 'the style of eloquence which
is in use among washerwomen'.[57] Closely associated with and even syn-
onymous with the fear of effeminization was the view that the theatricality of lecturing might lead to an enthusiastic loss of self, or in Godwin's
terms a subordination of the identity of the speaker in the indeterminate
will of the inspired mob. The power of theatre as an enactment of the
possibility of self-transformation had always had a political meaning in
eighteenth-century culture, explaining in part the suspicion of amateur
acting, especially that of the male lower orders. Spouting clubs, venues
in which apprentices, soldiers and sailors, clerks and tradesmen, could
emulate Garrick or Kean by essaying speeches from Shakespeare, had
been linked with debating clubs as sites of promiscuous speech that were
a threat to the social order.[58] In 1771 the *Oxford Magazine* had asserted:
'The great number of meetings held in this metropolis, under the de-
nomination of Spouting Clubs, calls loudly for the interposition of the
legislature ... The youths who meet at these places are, for the most
part, apprentices of the lower classes, whose ignorance and want of education can only be equalled by the mad ambition they have to become
actors'.[59] Such activities were as popular fifty years later: in the same
letter recounting how he arrived late at Hazlitt's lecture, John Keats
describes attending a private theatre or spouting club 'of the lowest order,
all greasy & oily'. Rather than spending the whole evening in 'one dirty
hole', Keats went to see Edmund Kean as Richard III in Drury Lane
before returning to the private theatre where he went backstage to

socialize with the actors and actresses.[60] Keats's letter is a reminder that as a kind of public performer Hazlitt was competing with other forms of histrionic utterance and with other theatres of speech: geographically, culturally and politically the public lecturer existed in close proximity to the greasy spouter and the star actor, as well as to demagogues such as 'Orator' Hunt.[61]

Coleridge's awareness of the connotations of spouting and the cultural geography of public speaking in London was apparent in his rejection in 1811 of Coachmakers' Hall (Thelwall's 'seminary') as a possible venue for his lectures: it had 'no literary or philosophical Redolence ... partly from past political spouting clubs, and partly from it's [*sic*] present assignment to Hops & the Instruction of Grown Gentlemen in Dancing' (interestingly equating 'political spouting' and dancing as 'unmanly' activities.)[62] Coleridge's attempt to consign Thelwall to history was complicated by the latter's re-emergence in the 1810s as a radical journalist and lecturer on elocution and literature, including Shakespeare. Although his work in these fields has been described as 'apolitical' – 'Nothing survived of the Patriot except his fading notoriety' according to E. P. Thompson – his views on elocution were continuous with the Enlightenment principles that had informed his lecturing in the 1790s.[63] In 1806 he described 'tone and look and gesture' as 'essential parts of the original language of Nature' which were capable of effecting change in its broadest sense: 'what is Oratory if it does not awaken and influence and impel?'[64] In 1818 Thelwall competed directly with Coleridge as a lecturer in Shakespeare, suggesting the importance of imaginative literature and Shakespeare in particular as domains in which politics and old notorieties could be recast.[65]

Aware of Thelwall's continuing presence in the metropolitan lecturing scene, both Coleridge and Hazlitt cultivated a performative style as lecturers, a conversational mode, which disciplined the possibility of an excessive theatricality that would have made them suspect in both political and gender terms. For example, at the Royal Institution in 1808 Coleridge famously introduced the theme of one of his lectures in the following way:

there were several books laying. He opened two or three of them silently & shut them again after a short inspection. He then paused, & leaned His head on his hand, and at last said, He had been thinking for a word to express the distinct Character of Milton as a Poet, but not finding one that wd. express it, He should make one "*Ideality*".[66]

Coleridge used silence, restraint, the kind of understated physical gesture that would be typical of more intimate contexts such as the dinner
table or the conversation room, in order to gain the attention of his
audience, in the process also establishing his credentials as a man to
be trusted, speaking in his own character, not an assumed one. Mary
Russell Mitford's comments on Hazlitt's lecturing style suggest that he
too avoided the histrionic: the 'superior effect' of his lecturing was owing
to his 'fine delivery – to certain slight inflections in his very calm and
gentlemanly voice – to certain almost imperceptible motions of his graceful person and above all to a certain momentary upward look full of
malice French and not quite free from malice English by which he con-
trives to turn the grandest compliment into the bitterest sarcasm'. The
adjectives 'slight', 'almost imperceptible', 'very calm' and 'momentary'
suggest a lecturing performance that was very much under control. Such
self-discipline enabled Hazlitt to avoid accusations of ranting excess that
had silenced Thelwall's lecturing career in the 1790s but it also allowed
him to exploit the lecture-room as a place of viewing pleasure for women
without compromising his masculinity. Mitford's comment – 'In short
the man, mind and body, has a genius for contempt and I am afraid, very
much afraid, that I like him the better for it' – suggests a guilty enjoyment
of not only Hazlitt's capacity for malice but also his performative style,
its fusion of mind *and* body.[67]

If there was a danger that the lecturer might become the spouter,
there was also a possibility that the lecture-room itself might revert to
a 'licentious theatre'. Audiences brought with them some of the interventionist forms of behaviour such as interjections and hissing that were
customary at Covent Garden and Drury Lane. A letter to *The Times* in
November 1818 noted that one of Hazlitt's lectures had factionalized the
audience, who responded with hissing and applause when he made 'an
unfortunate and irrelevant political allusion'. The lecture had to be 'suspended for some minutes' due to the disturbance. The writer went on:
'Now, whatever a lecturer's private political notions may be, he is wrong
in venting them before a mixed auditory, assembled for amusement and
instruction in science and literature ... I ... was not a little shocked at
seeing so well dressed and (to my own knowledge) generally respectable
an audience emulating the uproar of a one-shilling gallery.'[68] Such a
comment, which intertextually relates to Burke's representation in the
Reflections of the National Convention as a theatre in which the gallery
dominated, highlights the extent to which the sociability of theatre –
socially inclusive and intrinsically political – shadows the sociability of

public lecturing. As a space mediating between the playhouse and the performative 'social board' of the domestic sphere, the lecture-room was therefore one of the key sites of Romantic culture in which a distinctive literary public – a depoliticized 'mixed auditory' with a particular class identification – came into being. This chapter has been an attempt to suggest that the reconfiguration of sociability was not an effect of the emergence of this public, but a crucial factor in its making.

NOTES

For full citations see Bibliography.

1 Hadley, 'Public Lectures'. (I am grateful to Deirdre Coleman for drawing my attention to this essay.) Also: Klancher, ' Lecturing' in McCalman (ed.), *Oxford Companion*, p. 581.
2 See Clark, *British Clubs*, Wilson, *Sense of the People*, esp. chapter one.
3 Esp. Golinski, *Science*. See Knight, *Davy*; Foote, 'Sir Humphry Davy'.
4 E.g. Howe, *Life*, pp. 241–89; Armour and Howes, *Coleridge*, pp. 49–64; Baker, *Hazlitt*, pp. 184–90, 60–3; Lefebure, *Coleridge*; Jones, *Hazlitt*. R. A. Foakes's edition of Coleridge's lectures 1808–19 is an invaluable resource upon which I have relied significantly for this essay: Coleridge, *Collected Works*, (*Vol. V Lectures 1808–1819 on Literature*), ed. Foakes, hereafter referred to as *Lectures 1808–1819*.
5 Coleridge, *Collected Letters*, vol. III, p. 51.
6 See De Bolla, *Discourse*, also Fliegelman, *Declaring Independence*, Cohen, *Fashioning Masculinity*.
7 See Kahan, *Stevens*, Altick, *Shows*, pp. 366–8. See also Money, *Experience and Identity*, pp. 131–2 for the links between 'serious instruction and popular entertainment' (p. 131).
8 For Walker see entry in Highfill Jr *et al.*, *Biographical Dictionary*, vol. XV, pp. 210–12.
9 Piozzi, *Piozzi Letters*, vol. II, p. 483.
10 *Ibid.*, vol. II, p. 256.
11 *Ibid.*, vol. II, p. 306. Joseph Farington also attended one of Thelwall's lectures in December 1795. He claimed that 'Many Ladies were in the room: many Gentlemen: and the generality seemed poeple [*sic*] of the middle rank – The Plaudits came from a third or 4th. of the whole, the great majority appearing to be merely visitors out of curiosity': Farington, *Diary*, vol. II, p. 443.
12 Thelwall, *Politics of English Jacobinism*, pp. xxv–vi; Goodwin, *Friends of Liberty*, p. 385.
13 D'Israeli, *Vaurien*, vol. I, p. 51.
14 Habermas, *Structural Transformation*, pp. 36, 37.
15 Thelwall, *Politics of English Jacobinism*, p. xxvi. For subsequent regulation of lecturing see Weindling, 'Science and Sedition'.

16 My account of Thelwall's career is derived from the following: *The Life of John Thelwall*; Cestre, *Thelwall*; Thelwall, 'Prefatory Memoir'; Thompson, 'Hunting the Jacobin Fox'; Thale, 'London Debating Societies'; Scrivener, 'Rhetoric and Context'.

17 Thelwall, 'Prefatory Memoir', p. xxvi; Thale (ed.), *Selections*, pp. 103n, 133n, 135, 145.

18 Thelwall, *Prospectus*, p. 21.

19 'On the moral tendency of a System of Spies and Informers', quoted in *The Life of John Thelwall*, p. 127. A boy who lived with Thelwall in Beaufort Buildings, helping out in the lecture-room, gave evidence at his trial for treason in 1794: *The Life of John Thelwall*, p.173.

20 *Ibid.*, p. 127.

21 Jewson, *Jacobin City*, p. 72.

22 *Morning Post*, 20 September 1796.

23 *Ibid.*

24 For bowling greens and provincial sociability in general see Borsay, *English Urban Renaissance*, pp. 173–5.

25 Thelwall, *Appeal*, p. 15.

26 *Ibid.*, pp. 22, 23.

27 Godwin, *Political and Philosophical Writings*, vol. II, p. 132.

28 *Ibid.*, vol. II, p. 133.

29 *Ibid.*, vol. III, p. 121.

30 Quoted *The Life of John Thelwall*, p. 342.

31 Thelwall, *Prospectus*, p. 4.

32 Paine, *Writings*, vol. II, p. 426.

33 For the porter incident see Thelwall, *Politics of English Jacobinism*, p. xxiii.

34 George Hardinge, M. P. described Beaufort Buildings as Thelwall's 'political theatre' in a speech to parliament, quoted in Coleridge, *Collected Works*, (*Vol. II Lectures 1795 on Politics and Religion*), p. 297n. See also reference to the debating societies of the 1790s as 'a theatre of licentious discussion' in Pyne and Combe, *Microcosm*, vol. I, p. 224.

35 Thale, 'Case of the British Inquisition', p.32.

36 Pyne and Combe, *Microcosm*, vol. III, pp. 157–8. See also Carnall, 'Surrey Institution'. The institution had formerly housed the Leverian Museum and after 1830 became a theatre for radical speeches and sermons under the auspices of Richard Carlile, suggesting a reorientation towards the kind of space represented by Beaufort Buildings: Hadley, 'Public Lectures', p. 56.

37 Pyne and Combe, *Microcosm*, vol. III, p. 156.

38 Robinson, *Henry Crabb Robinson on Books*, vol. I, pp. 180, 217, 223. See also Charles Lamb's comment: 'I think public reading-rooms the best mode of educating young men. Solitary reading is apt to give the headache. Besides, who knows that you *do* read?', quoted in Hadley, 'Public Lectures,' p. 43.

39 Surrey Institution, (Various circular letters, cards of admission etc. relating to the Surrey Institution) London, 1808–23. British Library 822.1.9.

40 Keats, *Letters*, vol. I, p. 214. The friends were 'Hazlitt, John Hunt & son, Wells, Bewick, all the Landseers, Bob Harris, Rox of the Burrough Aye & more'.

41 These women included Elizabeth Ogilvy Benger, Mrs Flaxman, Mrs C. Aikin, Mrs Pattison, her mother and sister, Mrs Gurney. See Coleridge, *Lectures 1808–1819*, vol. I, pp. 324, 374, 396, 425; vol. II, p. 186.

42 See *ibid.*, vol. I, pp. 113, 114. Edward Jerningham approached Coleridge in a similar manner: 'I formed an acquaintance with Him: that is, I generally spoke to Him at the End of the Lecture – with which He appeared much pleased': *ibid.*, vol. I, p. 143.

43 *Ibid.*, vol. I, p. 91.

44 Southey, *Letters from England*, quoted Foote, 'Sir Humphry Davy', p. 11; Lister, *Own Heart*, p. 82. See Clara Tuite's chapter in this volume.

45 Byron, *Poetical Works*, vol. VI, p. 665.

46 *Ibid.*, vol. VI, p. 378.

47 Coleridge, *Lectures 1808–1819*, vol. I, p. 411. See also Byron, *'Famous in My Time'*, pp. 147, 149.

48 Byron, *Poetical Works*, vol. VI, pp. 298, 302.

49 *Ibid.*, vol. VI, p. 303.

50 *Ibid.*, vol. VI, p. 307.

51 See Hadley, 'Public Lectures', p. 45.

52 Coleridge, *Lectures 1808–1819*, vol. II, p. 39.

53 *Ibid.*, vol. I, p. 40.

54 *Ibid.*

55 E.g. Crabb Robinson: 'his conversation which was a sort of lecturing & soliloquizing and his lectures which were colloquial,' quoted in *ibid.*, vol. I, p. xlvii.

56 Robinson, *Diary*, p. 14. Coleridge invoked the circle of Wordsworth and Lamb as a form of authorization but also in order to soften the impact of the critique by making it less public, i. e. the subject of a private conversation which he is merely reporting in public. Crabb Robinson commented that Barbauld's friends were present and would certainly communicate to her what Coleridge had said, thereby making the lecture-room a mediating space between two circles of friendship.

57 *Quarterly Review* (1817/18), p. 459.

58 For spouting clubs see Thieme, 'Spouting'. Also Russell, *Theatres*, pp. 132–3.

59 'Fatal tendency of frequenting Spouting Clubs,' *Oxford Magazine* 6 (1771), pp. 215–17 (p. 215).

60 Keats, *Letters*, vol. I, pp. 215–16. He went to Hazlitt's lecture on 20 January 1818 and to the private theatre on 12 January. For private theatres frequented by Keats see Beaudry, *English Theatre*, pp. 26–7.

61 Robinson, *Diary*, p. 54: 'We then passed Palace Yard and heard Mr Hunt, the demagogue of the day. He speaks in a gentlemanly manner, though the substance of his speeches is as low as the people he addresses them to' (1817).

62 Coleridge, *Lectures 1808–1819*, vol. I, p. 156.

63 Scrivener, 'Rhetoric and Context', p. 126, Thompson, 'Hunting the Jacobin Fox', p. 123.
64 Thelwall, *Selections*, p. 11.
65 See, for example, *Morning Chronicle*, 30 January, 6 February, 13 February, 27 February 1818.
66 Farington, *Diary*, vol. IX, p. 3278.
67 Mary Russell Mitford, holograph letter in Reading Public Library, quoted in Jones, *Hazlitt*, p. 285.
68 *The Times*, 12 November 1818.

8

Hazlitt and the sociability of theatre

Julie A. Carlson

Whoever sees a play ought to be better and more sociable for it.[1]

This assertion by William Hazlitt forms the subject of the present chapter
that considers theatre in the Romantic period as a forum for sociability
and a model of sociality. Hazlitt's statement links the moral utility of the
stage to its capacity to render persons more sociable and then associates
both functions with the viewing, not merely reading, of plays. Claims
for the moral value of theatre are more familiar to us because they have
been more controversial. A long history of anti-theatrical prejudice has
necessitated reiterated counter-assertions of the ethical value of stage
representation.[2] Claims for its sociability are arguably banal, theatre
being a public forum that brings people together and thus by definition
has a social and socializing function. Yet assertions regarding the sociability of theatre in the Romantic period have been impeded from two
sides, namely, the period's alleged bias against theatre and its tendency
as a revolutionary and post-revolutionary culture to conceptualize social formations in more politicized terms (i.e. nation, people, democracy,
public sphere). The former closets everything that relates to the collective
and material aspects of theatre, the latter underestimates quotidian and
psychic reactions to being a group. This chapter works against both biases to consider how playgoing makes viewers more sociable individuals,
why Romantic theatre critics foreground the attainment of sociability as
one of the chief advantages of theatre, and what sociability gains and
loses from its connection to theatre. It turns out that if we take seriously
the connection of sociability to theatre, as writers of the time apparently
did, we modify the alleged irrationality of theatre and the rationality of
the political public sphere. Ascribing the connection to Hazlitt makes
the ideality and reality of theatre essential to preserving 'old friends'.

My point is not that Hazlitt is singular in asserting the sociability of
theatre in this period. In fact, his claim is preceded by several writers

who similarly support theatre for its capacity to consolidate individuals once their going to theatre has brought them together. Some, especially Thomas Holcroft and Joanna Baillie, conceive theatre's sociability primarily as a consequence of its moral efficacy, the dimension that their writings foreground. For Holcroft, moral efficacy resides in the accuracy and breadth of theatre's study of man and thus its coordination of rationalist benevolent aims.[3]   For Baillie, it exists in theatre's capacity to analyze and consequently avert passions that overwhelm the mind, the accurate staging of which levels social distinctions on stage and off.[4] Others, like Leigh Hunt and Charles Lamb, join Hazlitt in celebrating the sociability of theatre, actually preferring theatre's capacity to socialize individuals over its tendency to moralize. That these three writers have long been viewed as the best Romantic theatre critics suggests that the primacy of sociability to their promotion of theatre is one source of the high esteem in which their writings are held, even if we have somewhere along the way lost sight of this connection. Hunt values playhouses because they 'scatter egotism and collect sociality' by assembling 'people together smilingly and in contact, not cut off from each other by hard pews and harder abstractions'.[5] Hazlitt similarly situates playgoing between the 'pride and remoteness of abstract science' and the 'petty egotism of vulgar life' and delineates the social serviceability of theatres especially in large cities, where they alleviate 'the dissatisfaction and *ennui* that creep over our own pursuits from the indifference or contempt thrown upon them by others', and 'reconcile our numberless discordant, incommensurable feelings and interests together, by giving us an immediate and common topic to engage our attention, and to rally us round the standard of our common humanity'.[6] Lamb specifies the advantage of these ends over theatre's capacity to render viewers virtuous by confessing 'that (with no great delinquencies to answer for) I am glad for a season to take an airing beyond the diocese of the strict conscience, – not to live always in the precincts of the law-courts, – but now and then, for a dream-while or so, to imagine a world with no meddling restrictions'.[7] In other words, the three most recognized Romantic theatre critics evince a sea-change in cultural defences of theatre, valuing it explicitly not on moral grounds but for its capacity to unite people, humanize them, reconcile their conflicting interests and give them something to talk about. They thereby imply that collective diversion is central to a social body's coherence and healthy functioning.

Hazlitt is crucial to illustrating this change for several reasons. His own writings on theatre, which reflect the larger shift in conceptions of theatre

that this chapter traces, emphasize the sociability of theatre as well as
the force of the 'ought' of this chapter's epigraph: sociability can be
achieved, but is not guaranteed, by seeing plays. Discerning the larger
shift in defences of theatre involves first determining the situation of
theatre and sociability within discussions of the eighteenth-century public sphere. Increasing discussion during the 1790s of the insufficiencies of
reason for attaining social coherence, I wish to argue, influences emerging descriptions of theatre as a prime site of humanity, sociability and
collective dreams. Jürgen Habermas gives little attention to theatre in
delineations of the political or literary eighteenth-century public sphere
for some good reasons. It is clearly counter-productive to foreground
an avowedly arational sphere when the primary goal of the political
public sphere is to 'rationaliz[e] public authority under the institution-
alized influence of informed discussion and reasoned agreement'.[8] It is
also counter-intuitive to make of spectacle a chief arena of reading, or
of the interiorizing processes Habermas associates with it and the intimate sphere of the family.[9] Yet this downplaying of theatre has facilitated
some of the conceptual limitations, especially regarding delineations of
private and public, private and intimate, that have troubled critics of
Habermas and that, in my view, arise in part from his overemphasis on
the novel. As the genre and staging of domestic tragedy make clear, interiority needs theatricality to make its presence known. Moreover, as the
aesthetic form that exacerbates tensions between reading and viewing,
theatre is instrumental in negotiating changes in forms of representation
and representability.

This latter claim touches as well on the least controversial grounds
for theatre's inclusion in the public sphere – the emergence around 1800
of theatre criticism as a 'new' genre of print culture.[10] Even allowing
for its puffs, biases and collusions with management, theatre criticism
joins other forms of rational commentary in shaping consensus, public
opinion and taste. It starts by evaluating the actors' parts but in order to
make spectators cohere in themselves and in society. Like literary criticism generally, theatre criticism links imaginative to rational processes
by discussing and evaluating characters in relation to how well they
manifest a balance between these mental processes. Exemplary here
are Shakespeare's character and his characters in their reconciliation of
observation and meditation. But at the same time, writings on theatre
foreground the interaction of vision, conformity and repetition in their
production and apprehension of character more than do evaluations of
characters in novels or poetry. The actor's proximity to life, on the one

hand, and supplementary relation to reading, on the other, highlight the vitality *and* unoriginality that attend any living person's manifestation of character. This latter reality helps to explain the extremes in tone of theatre reviewing, at once more affable and more vindictive, more humane and more lethal, than other forms of literary reviewing. It thereby complicates the sociability that theatre criticism at the same time is advocating as its most worthy contribution to the public sphere.

This challenge to sociability comes not only through theatre's special insight into the priority of image over identity and thus its implicit subversion of humanity. It must be situated in the broader context of cultural redefinitions of human attachment issuing from revolutionary discourse. In the early 1790s, allegiance to radical politics entails conceiving friendship as interchangeable with universal benevolence, which means construing affective bonds as rational, transferable, replaceable and common. True friends of man are now friend to no particular man (not to speak of woman) because according to new philosophical principles 'every man would be a brother'. Affections no longer need to be confined 'to a particular channel, when they would be continually refreshed, invigorated, and would overflow with the diffusive soul of mutual philanthropy, and generous, undivided sympathy with all men'.[11] This redefinition of friend and the fall-out intensified by the falling-out of friends that it occasions lie beyond the scope of this chapter. One could say that much of the pathos of first-generation Romantic writing is fuelled by the struggle to locate one's friends after having dissolved the category in one's youth – the anguished 'have I one friend?' of the final chapter of *Biographia Literaria* speaking at a minimum for Coleridge, Holcroft, Godwin, Lamb and (later) Hazlitt. One might also contend that achieving reconciliation among former friends becomes one of the central functions of the literary public sphere in this period. One general and one specific ramification of this redefinition of friend overlap with our interests in the sociability of theatre. Efforts to locate one's friends frequently intersect with new definitions of kinds of writing – Godwin describing the function of history as the reanimation of dead friends, Coleridge periodically issuing a *Friend* (with principles) during the period of his public estrangement from Wordsworth, and Hazlitt visiting theatre as the site (and for the sight) of old friends.[12] Hazlitt comes to ascribe sociability to the operations of theatre through his captivation by the theatricality of new philosophical friends.

Supporting this latter claim requires that we add a third phase to the usual two-part division of Hazlitt's theatre criticism. The standard view divides his career into two phases, the first when he writes as a regular critic of either a daily or weekly paper and concentrates on individual productions and performances, that period beginning in November 1813, when Hazlitt takes over theatre criticism in the *Morning Chronicle*, and continuing until around April 1818. The second phase involves his monthly essays to the *London Magazine* (beginning in January 1820), when the drama in general is his topic.[13] This chapter proposes a third phase that comes first and that serves as the precondition to the priority he ascribes in both ensuing phases to the sociability over the morality of theatre: Hazlitt's completion of the memoirs of his friend, Thomas Holcroft, the actor, playwright and New Philosophical radical who dies in 1809. Published in 1816 as *Memoirs of the Late Thomas Holcroft, written by Himself, and continued to the Time of his Death, from his Diary, Notes, and other Papers*, Hazlitt's activity of completing his friend's *Life* occurs in the latter part of 1809 and recounts the important years of Holcroft's acting, playwriting and political activities – the part 'written by Himself' only covering up to Holcroft's fifteenth year. In transcribing the events of this life, Hazlitt encounters not only a successful intersection of revolutionary with theatrical interests but the last defence of the revolutionary effectiveness of theatre on rationalist grounds. In reanimating the two most famous scenes of Holcroft's life, Hazlitt experiences the theatricality of rationalist friendship and the in/substantiality of old friends to theatre.

Both scenes involve Holcroft's best friend, William Godwin, and comprise the high and low points of their twenty-year relationship. The most famous scene links friends, theatricality and the political public sphere, that being the Treason Trials of October and November 1794, in which Holcroft is charged along with eleven other men with seditious activities pertaining to involvement in the London Corresponding Society. Godwin, as is well known, rises to his friend's defence, publishing his 'Cursory Strictures on the Charge Delivered by Lord Chief Justice Eyre to the Grand Jury' in *The Morning Chronicle* on 21 October. He wins the day in advance of a trial then and now viewed as a high point of London radical culture and urban theatricality and in a gesture viewed as a monument to disinterested friendship.[14] The second scene ends the lowest point in Holcroft's and Godwin's relations, a dying Holcroft desiring to see Godwin, from whom he has been estranged for the past four years. 'On Sunday [Holcroft] expressed a wish to see Mr Godwin, but when he came, his feelings were overpowered. He could not converse, and only pressed his hand to his bosom, and said, "My dear, dear friend!"' (*MTH*, p. 237). Captured in these scenes are two crucial constituents of

Romantic friendship: the special urgency of having a friend when one's
principles, especially regarding affective and domestic relations, place
one outside the boundaries of conventional sociality; and the lethal consequences of such friends 'having words'. Holcroft's diary entry of 13
January 1799 already casts the fault lines in their friendship as literary–
critical, and, in particular, dramatic:

H. When you brought your tragedy [*Antonio*] to me, you gave a minute detail of
the rules I was to observe in criticising your work . . . One of the first of them was,
not to find fault in such an absolute and wholesale style, as might at once kill your
ardour . . . Yet, having read mine [*The Lawyer*], you come with a sledge hammer
of criticism, describe it as absolutely contemptible, tell me it must be damned,
or, if it should escape, that it cannot survive five nights, that the characters and
plot are but transcripts of myself, and that everybody will say it is the garrulity
of an old man . . .
G. I thought it my duty to speak my thoughts plainly . . . There is another difference between us . . . I am so cowed and cast down by rude and unqualified
assault, that for a time I am unable to recover. You, on the contrary, I consider
as a man of iron. (*MTH*, pp. 219–20)

The final break in their friendship comes as a result of Godwin's fury
over Holcroft's 'radical revision' of Godwin's third play, *Faulkener* and of
Holcroft's mortification over viewing the character of Mr Scarborough
in Godwin's *Fleetwood* as patterned after him.[15] It is little surprise that
men whose livings depend on words conceive of words as having
death- and life-defying properties. More instructive are the publicity
and theatricality that surround their last intimacy – this being a favourite
scene of every biography of Holcroft and Godwin – and the scene's establishment of a beyond-words that comes to signify 'true' friendship as
undying because unconditional, and therefore uncritical. Hazlitt is not
alone in feeling moved by this scene or being moved by it to devise a new
genre of friend. What distinguishes him is seeing through the theatrical dimensions of death-bed reunions to the stage properties that keep
friendship and sociability alive.

HOLCROFT'S AND HAZLITT'S HOLCROFT

The relation of Hazlitt's *Memoirs of the Late Thomas Holcroft* to his career as
a critic of drama itself enacts the aesthetic logic that comes to characterize
his notion of dramatic character: accounting for the species through the
individual. As I hope to show, this phrase describes both what Hazlitt
does in composing Holcroft's *Life* and what he learns through doing it. By

focussing on the individual, Thomas Holcroft, Hazlitt comes to reflect on the species of the playwright and political visionary, the interaction between the two species, and the special pressures that contingencies of history place on *this* playwright and visionary. The latter discussion prompts a thoroughgoing defence of Holcroft's character, in this regard only contradicting the new philosophical principles that otherwise undergird Holcroft's and Hazlitt's depictions of Holcroft. Holcroft justifies his inclusion of even the most 'insignificant circumstances' of his life for their relevance to the comprehension of his character, which he is detailing in the hopes of inspiring 'ardent emulation in the breasts of youthful readers' (*MTH*, pp. 12, 18). Hazlitt at various times finds himself on the defensive, 'deviating from my [i.e. Holcroft's] plan, which was not to write a panegyric, but a history' (*MTH*, p. 128). Two spots in the *Memoirs* where Hazlitt mobilizes his defences indicate what he gains from composing the life of his friend. Both take their distance from Holcroftian abstraction and thus prepare the way for more sociable notions of theatre.[16]

One comes near the end of the *Memoirs*, when Hazlitt mentions but neither describes nor evaluates the *Theatrical Recorder* of 1805, Holcroft's two-volume collection of critical writings on theatre, the 'plan' of which is to cover 'every thing passing in the theatrical world, which is of a nature to be at all times interesting' (*TR* I: iii). In itself, the absence of commentary is unremarkable and more or less in line with the scholarly treatment of this text, in its day and thereafter. But in our context, it suggests not only Hazlitt's exclusion of Holcroft from the circle of Romantic theatre critics but what separates Romantic theatre from rational entertainment and Romantic sociability from New Philosophical friendship. The date of composition of *Theatrical Recorder* coincides with the period of fall-out from New Philosophical attempts to redefine friendship as benevolence, written as a consequence of what Holcroft terms his 'exile' from England from 1799 until 1802 – an exile stemming from his inability to get out from under the stigma of being an 'acquitted felon' and thus to make a living from his writings for the stage. In letters of this period Holcroft characterizes residence abroad as not only perpetuating his lifelong effort to 'inform, with the hopes of benefiting, mankind' but as fulfilling his self-description as 'the friend of man', for benevolence 'cannot be attained by making [my compatriots] angry' (*MTH*, p. 240). The dramatic principles set out in *Theatrical Recorder* likewise serve benevolent ends. They internationalize the content, characters and scope of British drama and describe theatre as the best site for disseminating truth through its 'study of man'.

In contrast to Godwin, whose 'discovery' of poetry, imagination and erotic love between 1796 and 1799 prompts him to qualify in subsequent editions the severe rationalism of the first edition of *Enquiry concerning Political Justice* (he even turns to writing tragedy in 1800), Holcroft undergoes no major conversion regarding the suitability of theatre or illusion to the New Philosophy.[17] Though stage censorship limits what characters in his plays can say directly about political reform, Holcroft deems his New Philosophical principles fully compatible with the content and effect of his plays and his commentary on theatre theory and practice. Those principles advocate the study of man as promoting human welfare through the dissemination of truth. And both the analysis of human character and widest dissemination of the links among action, consequence and character are best achieved through theatre. '[O]f all the human efforts and known means, by which the most useful, essential, and dignified moral effects may be produced, the drama affords the best and least doubtful' (*TR* I: 275). It provides the 'best' means because 'moral conduct depends upon the consequences of human actions being well understood'; it provides the 'least doubtful' because the 'thoughtless multitude', for whom reading is a 'task', 'will always resort to the playhouse as to a place of supreme pleasure' (*TR* I: 270, 214).

Holcroft's conviction that theatre is indispensable to the goals of the New Philosophy in turn influences his critical writings on drama and the proper conduct of criticism. In general, these remarks work to secure the moral operations of theatre by making stage production, reception and criticism more rational and more conducive to benevolence. These aims are reflected in the various 'departments' into which each issue of *Theatrical Recorder* is divided ('The Art of Acting', 'The History of the German Stage', a translation of a play either from France or Germany with accompanying 'Remarks' regarding the conformity of the play's sentiments to English character, and 'Costume'). All seek to facilitate the accuracy and international breadth of theatre's depictions of human character, and none so epitomizes these goals as 'Costume', dedicated to diffusing 'accurate knowledge' of the 'manners and customs' of 'Eastern nations', those being the ones 'too much transgressed against upon the stage' (*TR* I: 77–8).

A corollary to the expansion of mind and kinds of person represented in and by theatre is the attention that *Theatrical Recorder* directs to the proper conduct of criticism. Accentuating the critic's grave responsibility, Holcroft deems New Philosophical principles necessary and sufficient for artistic public health (*TR* I: 122). If critics take the 'honourable road of sincerity, candour, and justice', both artists and critics will find their professions more highly regarded and their service to society better secured (*TR* 1: 55). It is tempting to construe Hazlitt's silence regarding *Theatrical Recorder* as an attempt to protect Godwin from its characterization as 'cynical' Godwin's sledge-hammer approach to evaluating Holcroft's *The Lawyers* (*TR* 1: 136). Other facts speak against this implication. For one thing, Hazlitt publishes in the *Memoirs* Holcroft's letters and journal entries that incriminate Godwin, the publication of which Godwin fought so vigorously that he delayed publication of the *Memoirs* for years.[18] For another, the terms and reasons that Hazlitt gives in the *Memoirs* for championing Holcroft he uses again, sometimes verbatim, in descriptions of Godwin.[19] This congruence strengthens my initial suggestion that Hazlitt's silence has more to do with romanticizing by socializing theatre than siding with Holcroft against Godwin. Indeed, the second spot of defensiveness in the *Memoirs*, where Hazlitt's history veers into 'panegyric' by praising and blaming Holcroft's 'philosophical' heroes, is applied elsewhere to Godwin (*MTH*, pp. 128, 129).

Hazlitt's defence of Holcroft's character requires that he overturn prejudices against his two chief career activities – actor and political visionary. To the usual allegations that both activities place him outside the bounds of conventionality, the former by lacking respectability, the latter by challenging what counts as it, are added specific charges against Holcroft's rendition of both roles. His start as a strolling player is embarrassing, his end as a political visionary is treasonous. Countering both sets of charge highlights what the two activities share, that people who pursue either path live in a more ideal world than the rest of humankind. To those 'persons of nice tastes' who deem Holcroft's years as a strolling player 'unworthy of a man of genius', Hazlitt avers that 'the player as well as the poet lives in an ideal world' for 'the business of his life is to dream' (*MTH*, pp. 81, 82.). The business of dreaming, moreover, is pursued more profitably in provincial barns than metropolitan theatres (*HoT*, pp. 161–4). This commitment to vision separates him from 'every one else', but it also augments the psychic reality of everyone else as well as the material conditions of the actor who, by dwelling in possibility, transcends the constraints of his circumstances (*MTH*, p. 82). To the party of patriots who construes his New Philosophical principles as treasonous, Hazlitt characterizes Holcroft's only 'crime' as having thought too highly of humanity. What is 'singular' is not the principles themselves, which are as old as the Scripture that enjoins us to 'love thy neighbour as thyself', but the view of humankind that their rejection projects

(*MTH*, pp. 132, 134). To construe as the 'worst enemies of society' those who have 'augured most highly of the powers of our nature' is to see that 'self-love' lives in the moment and is therefore 'offended' rather than 'flattered' by notions that persons, and thus times, could be better (*MTH*, p. 132).

The simple fact of accounting for the facts of Holcroft's life causes Hazlitt to link actor to political visionary, a connection that becomes generalized in his subsequent writings on theatre and revolution. More crucial is how the times during which Holcroft acts extend the singularity ascribed to the idealism of these two domains to *all* 'good' and 'thinking men' (*MTH*, p. 133). In the heyday of French Revolutionary enthusiasm, 'it seemed as if the present was the era of moral and political improvement', that 'nothing was too mighty for this new-begotten hope' and that the ideal state of society was to be realized very shortly (*MTH*, pp. 133, 155). The imminence of perfection means that friends of liberty should forgo dreaming and exercise their rational faculties to devise concrete plans that remove the 'curb of prudence' normally needed to keep unperfected humans in line (*MTH*, p. 156). Hazlitt questions the wisdom of this assessment but not the disposition that underlies it. Such character approaches human nature from the golden side and grants to all persons the dream-world normally occupied only by actors and visionaries.

From the vantage of 1809, then, a vast chasm looms between Holcroft and Hazlitt that separates less the dead from the living than political dreamers from political realists. The 'hope, that such [kind] feelings and such [generous] actions might become universal, rose and set with the French Revolution. That light seems to have been extinguished for ever in this respect. The French Revolution was the only match that ever took place between philosophy and experience' (*MTH*, p. 156). Perception of this chasm affects everything that Hazlitt writes and influences his sensitivity to the non-linearity and unpredictable pacing of time. A few years can make an eon of difference to the delineation of epochs, expectations, ideals; for the conjunction between dreams and their realization that in the 1790s seemed so imminent is seen as postponed indefinitely by 1809. Hazlitt's desire to bridge this chasm is discernible in his repeated efforts to restore the legitimacy of dreaming by taking a more realistic approach to the pursuit of benevolence. His characteristic means of doing so is already in evidence when he pins on Holcroft's treatment of fictional character the failure to attain his perfectible aims.

The problem with fictional characters like Frank Henley and Anna St Ives is that they are 'ideal beings' rather than 'natural' ones, 'not so properly characters (that is, distinct individuals) as the vehicles of certain general sentiments, or machines put into action, as an experiment to shew how these general principles would operate in particular situations' (*MTH*, pp. 128–9). 'They are the organs through which the voice of truth and reason is to breathe, and whose every action is to be inspired by the pure love of justice' (*MTH*, p. 129). Far from advancing truth and justice, however, such fictional depictions retard them. The concretization of such abstract principles actually turns virtue into its opposite. Rather than seek to emulate these characters, viewers revolt against them precisely because their perfection is inhuman and thus neither provokes nor fosters sympathy (*MTH*, p. 130). Unfortunate as these consequences are for the perfecting of society through art, even here Hazlitt lightens the indictment against Holcroft. The problem is generic, not individual. 'It was not for want of genius, but from the impossibility of the undertaking.' 'I have made these remarks to shew the difficulty of embodying a philosophic character in a dramatic form' (*MTH*, p. 130).

HAZLITT AND THE SOCIABILITY OF THEATRE

Hazlitt's writings on theatre proceed from this insight, that humans not only have difficulty envisioning but liking characters who embody philosophical abstractions. Ideally, we may want human passions to be 'under the control of reason or virtue' (*MTH*, p. 130); in actuality, we do not wish to encounter such automatons on stage or in society. This recognition does not cause Hazlitt to eschew idealism in either art or politics but to stress the importance of realism in achieving it. This goal influences his notions and evaluations of dramatic character and the forms of sociability that theatre fosters and represents. For Hazlitt's writings on drama stress the life-like-ness and amiability of its characters to ensure that theatre fosters the humanity of its spectators by enhancing their sociable rather than moralistic qualities. Dramatic characters must be 'real beings of flesh and blood', who 'speak like men, not like authors' (*HoT*, p. 9). This closeness to life distinguishes Shakespeare's characters, each of whom 'is as much itself, and as absolutely independent of the rest, as if they were living persons, not fictions of the mind' (*HoT*, p. 9).[20] It underlies Hazlitt's praise for Shakespeare as the 'least moral of all writers; for morality (commonly so called) is made up of antipathies, and his talent consisted in sympathy with human nature' (*HoT*, p. 81; see also p. 11).

Realism about what features move individuals and bring people to-gether influences Hazlitt's descriptions of the sociability achieved by theatre. Even the anticipation of playgoing improves one's disposition and makes one 'rise with a pleasanter feeling in the morning'.[21] Regular attendance makes 'play-going people' 'among the most sociable, gossip-ing, good natured, and humane members of society' (*HoT*, p. 142). This is in part because playgoing is both 'a test and school of humanity' – a test because '[w]e do not much like any persons who do not like plays, [for] we imagine they cannot much like themselves or anyone else'; a school because 'the really humane man' is 'prone to the study of humanity', a study that is best exemplified on and disseminated by the stage (*HoT*, pp. 142–3). Even after audiences disperse, theatre perpetuates the so-ciability it occasions by giving otherwise discordant people 'ideas and subjects of conversation and interest in common' (*HoT*, p. 135). In bring-ing and keeping people together, both as a collectivity and as individuals, theatre enhances the biological, emotional and social 'circulation' of a people and keeps 'the world' from 'go[ing] amiss' (*HoT*, p. 133).

Hazlitt's descriptions of the public conversations that theatre inspires reflect changes in cultural assumptions about what unifies and solidifies the public sphere. His descriptions stress the importance of diversion over rational direction in two contradictory respects. Much of what theatre gives people to talk about are 'common-places' rather than involved or controversial positions that, in contrast to the latter, 'rally us round the standard of our common humanity' and foster the 'progress of civilisa-tion' (*HoT*, pp. 135, 143, 135). Alternatively, those discussions that employ New Philosophical procedures by tracing 'the distinct and complicated reaction of the character upon circumstances' require the fostering of indirection as the means of theatre representation (*HoT*, p. 35). Here is where Hazlitt distances himself from Holcroftian notions of representa-tion that propose a direct and didactic relation between the articulation of truth and the reformation of character. For Hazlitt, representation achieves its beneficial effects only after the event, if at all. In the moment, the best actors 'stagger' their audiences, thereby delaying but then inten-sifying an 'exercise of intellect' thereafter (*HoT*, pp. 121, 35). Sustaining indirection is so important to the proper reception of theatre that it be-comes a key criteria for evaluating actors and coordinating the timing of the mental faculties put into operation by theatre. Hazlitt devalues actors whose performances are 'correct, equable, and faultless' on the grounds that they neither provide 'the greatest enjoyment at the time' nor add to 'our stock of ideas' afterwards (*HoT*, pp. 135, 34). Truly great actors impress viewers through their preternaturality, unevenness and irregularity and thus prompt discussions that augment social coherence and a society's understanding of the relation between circumstance and character.

Such efforts to counter the alleged immediacy and reality of theatre representation coincide with Hazlitt's promotion of theatre for its association with dreams. The value of this association is performative in an ontological and political sense: 'Is it nothing to dream whenever we please, and *seem* whatever we desire? Is real greatness, is real prosperity, more than what it seems?' (*HoT*, p. 159). Theatre both educes the mental condition conducive to political reform by suspending normal patterns of thought and sustains the only living beings in the early 1800s who affirm without apology that they live in a world of dreams. Hazlitt's depiction of the dream-world of players is literally indebted to Holcroft, echoing his citation in the *Memoirs* of Holcroft's own defence of acting in *Hugh Trevor* for transforming 'the village barn' and transporting its inhabitants to sites and times of magic.[22] But it is also central to achieving the sociability of theatre. In granting access to former times both on stage and off, actors foster an 'air of romance', 'amiabi[lity]' and 'carelessness' that allows people to congregate with minimal conflict or controversy. In their suspension of the now, they scatter egotism and give playgoers passage to 'idler' times (*HoT*, pp. 136, 158, 160). This air of romance, which makes it 'pleasanter to see [actors,] even in their own persons, than any of the three learned professions', intensifies human affection for them. 'There is no class of society whom so many persons regard with affection as actors' because in them we view 'stately hieroglyphic[s] of humanity' and a culture's best and 'oldest' friends (*HoT*, p. 136).

Taking seriously Hazlitt's conviction that sociability is effected through the medium of theatre puts into a different light several peculiarities in his approach to theatre. First, the importance of its fostering of dreams occasions Hazlitt's counter-intuitive approach to stage representation, whereby 'the stage' works its magic more off the stage – certainly, the large metropolitan stage – than on. The romance of players is more palpable in provincial theatres than those in London, more evident when we see actors on the street than on stage. In this regard, actors themselves embody Hazlitt's description of Shakespeare's characters, whose virtual identity to human character makes representation both redundant to their aliveness and a serious reduction of it. Seeing actors on stage reduces the multiplicity of their times and parts to one.

Hazlitt's de-materializing of theatre dovetails with the usual Romantic approach to representation in the case of Shakespeare. As is well known, even the most enthusiastic theatre writers resist seeing Shakespeare's characters realized on stage. Hazlitt's bardolatry, however, does not express a mere preference for closet drama nor an indictment of theatre's generic assault on dreams. For him, theatre is one of the few remaining cultural arenas in which dreaming is a legitimate activity, the fostering of which is essential to reducing the chasm that separates the disillusionment of the 1800s from the idealism of the early 1790s. Hazlitt concerns himself, then, not with theatre's reduction of 'dreams' to 'flesh and blood' but theatre's reduction of 'flesh and blood' to flesh and blood. In Hazlitt's treatment, both the genius of Shakespeare and the genre of theatre force the question of whether, or in what respects, art makes people human, not to mention humane. Consideration of Shakespeare exposes the a- and inhuman implications of art's investment in image-making; the genre of theatre displays the undecidable aspects of the question.

Hazlitt's evaluations of stage representations of Shakespeare unveil some ongoing implications of the individual's prehistory in the mirror stage. This prehistory, by which the not-yet-self apprehends herself as a self through the image and then accrues aspects of her social and cultural identity in relation to classic fictions from childhood, makes theatre the most powerful aesthetic form of identity formation because of its dependence on images, both visual and popular-cultural. The case of Shakespeare in Romanticism displays a major tension between these two domains of image-making, for bardolators contend that making Shakespeare's characters visible, image-able, on stage is a reduction of, and assault on, his transcendent cultural image. What Hazlitt makes equally clear is that the viewing of Shakespeare's characters can comprise an assault on one's personal identity, when love for those characters has been constitutive of one's self-formation. For seeing them embodied by others destroys the sanctity of one's 'own conception' of them. Even the very best actors (Kean and Siddons) prove the rule that the 'representation of the character on the stage almost uniformly interferes with our conception of the character itself'. 'Mr Kean's Othello is his best character, and the highest effort of genius on the stage. We say this without any exception or reserve. Yet we wish it was better than it is ... [At times he] disturbs our idea of the character' (*HoT*, pp. 50–1, 69; see also p. 12). This recognition, that Shakespeare's characters are often a person's oldest and dearest friends, the characters on whom and in relation to whom one's character and models of attachment are formed, gives rise to the uncharacteristic vagueness of Hazlitt's descriptions of the proper effect of Shakespeare's characters when they are viewed. To remain formative (and thus relevant) throughout the stages of an individual's development, such characters must retain the 'great masses' and 'gigantic proportions' that initially 'stagger[ed]' us rather than attain 'the details' that are gained 'by custom and familiarity' (*HoT*, p. 122).

Such comments articulate the egocentrism that attends the ego-consolidation effected by Shakespeare's characters. Do not disturb my conceptions of Hamlet, Othello, Lear, for my self-conception is dependent on them. Remarks on other aspects of theatre analyze this reaction more directly. Hazlitt's answer to why 'we go to see tragedies in general' explores a formative tension between claims of morality and curiosity (*HoT*, p. 38). People attend tragedies because there is a 'natural tendency in the mind to strong excitement, a desire to have its faculties roused and stimulated to the utmost', by watching others react under duress and in situations of extremity (*HoT*, p. 38). Theatre satisfies this curiosity precisely by severing it from moral obligation, for in that dream-space humans are released from their duty to act and react humanely. Whereas writers like Baillie beg the question from the start by calling this 'instinct' 'sympathetic curiosity', Hazlitt depicts sympathy and curiosity as independent, often antagonistic, processes.[23] 'Whenever [the mind's tendency to strong excitement] is not under the restraint of humanity, or the sense of moral obligation, there are no excesses to which it will not of itself give rise' (*HoT*, p. 38). For this reason, too, Shakespeare is the least moral of all our writers because he recognizes that 'love of power' is 'natural to man' (*HoT*, pp. 114–15). Characters like Iago, Richard II, Macbeth, Coriolanus are 'objects of greater curiosity' than his more humane protagonists because, in their 'complete abstraction of the intellectual from the moral being', they speak to the inhumanity in us (*HoT*, pp. 52, 41). As spectators we 'halloo and encourage the strong to set upon the weak', even though we 'do not share in the spoil', because '[o]ur vanity, or some other feeling, makes us disposed to place ourselves in the situation of the strongest party' (*HoT*, pp. 117, 114). 'This is the logic of the imagination and the passions' that 'naturally falls in with the language of power' (*HoT*, pp. 116, 113). Much of the value of Hazlitt's writings on theatre is the straightforwardness with which he acknowledges the inhumanity of art. He recognizes not only that 'poetry is right-royal' and the imagination an 'aristocratic' faculty but that humankind's fascination with the image renders people a-human and inhumane.

Hazlitt's theatre criticism is divided over whether to enlist theatre to comprehend better the inhumanity of humankind or to change humankind into more amiable and sociable creatures. He employs both strategies at different times and, in fact, goes further than other Romantic theatre critics in pursuing each direction. On the one hand, theatre promotes sociability by bringing people together, making individuals coherent to themselves and cohere as a group, and restoring their carelessness and amiability by being placed in proximity to a 'happier, idler race of mortals' (*HoT*, p. 160). On the other, theatre displays what impedes sociability – on the simplest level, egoism, and, more fundamentally, human resistance to the non-congruence between image and living reality. What Hazlitt resists in seeing Shakespeare's characters realized is what people resist in encounters with their fellows: alterity, the fact that we cannot manage them. Paradoxically, as Jacques Lacan has shown, resistance to alterity arises in spaces of greatest similarity – in this case, theatre to life, Shakespeare's characters to living character, my friend to me.[24] This dynamic influences the form of sociability that Hazlitt comes to apprehend in theatre and the kind of vision that sustains it. Increasingly, Hazlitt values theatre as the site of old friends, actors as the most reliable friends, and both as preferable to dealing with the changeability, irritability and mortality of live friends. Preserving love for even theatrical friends requires a dimming of vision that, according to friends, characterizes Hazlitt's 'curious' habits as a playgoer. In 'almost every case', writes P. G. Patmore, his commentary is the result of 'a few hasty glances and a few half-heard phrases' from which 'he drew instant deductions'; his quotations from Shakespeare are loose and invariably inaccurate.[25] William Archer declares himself at a loss to 'even conjecture how these errors [in citation] arose', but given what Hazlitt seeks from theatre, this haphazardness makes perfect sense (*HoT*, p. xxx). For his aim is not accuracy in relation to Shakespeare but in relation to his earliest memories of him. Only the latter fosters Hazlitt's ongoing potential, unfolding the stages of his identity in accordance with the ideality of Shakespeare's characters. In this regard, theatre is a house less of representation than recollection, which we enter when we wish to recall our oldest friends.

SOCIABILITY, THEATRE

I began by conceding that there is something arguably banal about linking sociability with theatre. By design theatre is a social space that assembles disparate people for entertainment and cultural enlightenment, achieving in the process some semblance of group coherence. No one at any stage would claim that theatre is exclusively a moral institution nor would they situate their defence of its morality wholly in rational activity, for virtually every commentator prizes its capacity to amuse. What emerges from Hazlitt's writings is the weight that arguments for the sociability of theatre assume in post-revolutionary England – how this weight shapes Romantic conceptions of theatrical representation and of theatre's function in broadening social and political representation. What also becomes clear is that theatre's liminality is *social*, not simply aesthetic, that theatre is suspended between private and public dynamics of both cultural and individual identity. Coordinating these features accounts for many of the tensions evident in Romantic approaches to theatre. Perhaps more to the point, varying approaches to theatre reveal warring conceptions of human identity. At one extreme, closet drama works to maintain the individuality and interiority of identity; at the other, stage enthusiasts celebrate the mechanics of collective identity.

Viewed in the context of sociability, the period's alleged preference for closet drama expresses more than a refusal to materialize dreams, particularly dreams of socially marginal groups who are gaining prominence in plays and theatre audiences at this time.[26] Closet occupants also resist theatre's demand that individuals come together, even cohere, as a group. Solitary reading theoretically facilitates this refusal. It keeps the dream of individuality alive by ensuring that nobody questions the reality of totally private feelings or original ideas. Theatre critics depict this reality as fantasy and advocate playgoing as healthy for persons and peoples. As we have seen, they suspect persons who do not like plays of liking neither themselves nor others and of wanting to believe that one can be alone. So why do they all seek to preserve Shakespeare from the operations of theatre? And how do their discussions of theatre as a social institution reconfigure the reason of and for a public sphere?

The bardolatry of Hazlitt, Hunt and Lamb – indeed, of all the major Romantic writers – has been interpreted as manifesting various tensions between poetry (imaginative, ideal, interior) and theatre (sensational, real, exterior).[27] In our context, it suggests conflicts over conceptions of identity that the Romantic Shakespeare intensifies rather than dispels. For Shakespeare has a special relation to two warring tendencies that characterize literary criticism generally in this age and that are exacerbated in theatre criticism, the growing personalizing of literature and professionalizing of reading. At the same time that critics are characterizing Shakespeare as the most lifelike, amiable and representative of all England's writers, they feel that materializing and disseminating this characterization on stage represents a threat not just to Shakespeare's but their own genius and special powers of intuition. And at the same time that they perceive fostering love for Shakespeare as a cultural service and social imperative, they find that being subjected to other people's conceptions of Shakespeare is an infringement on their individuality. Housing a national icon like Shakespeare in theatre, then, diminishes the specialness of one's love for Shakespeare and of the patterns of attachment that any individual derives from it. Even theatre's status as a house of memory proves a mixed blessing to persons who view art as central to their interiority. The 'same' memories that consolidate a culture reduce the uniqueness of an individual's reality.

On the other hand, when the critic is not so concerned with manifesting his genius by detailing his unique apprehension of the transcendent power of Shakespeare, he sees theatrical representation as an asset because of its genial, commonsensical and collectivizing view of human identity. For Hunt and Lamb as well as Hazlitt, theatre is a comfortable and good-natured institution, one that gives people common topics to discuss and welcome reprieves from the monotony of urban reality. It socializes individuals and encourages them to affix their affections on professionals who assume multiple identities and live in several stages of time. One can interpret such reactions as politically reactionary in voicing nostalgia for less complicated, or more magical, social arrangements. But they also are up to the minute in cultivating public dreams without pursuing the 'harder abstractions' of universal benevolence.[28] In this light, sociability appears as a more humane, less rigorous and rationalist, form of human attachment, one geared towards building consensus, cohesion, and coherence through aesthetic forms of representation. Theatre attains these ends by eschewing rationalism and the social divisions that its modes of analysis occasion. It understands distraction, not abstraction, as more likely to move persons to become a people. Precisely its status as recreation allows theatre to function as a more reasonable, because less rationalist, public sphere.

In its humane guise, then, the sociability promoted in theatre writings by Hazlitt, Hunt and Lamb handles some of the fall-out from the failure of revolutionary friendship and its dream of disinterested relations between people. In their treatment, the sociability of theatre counters two general objections to New Philosophical notions of friend. It softens the abstractness of being a 'friend to man' without sanctioning the reduction of benevolent motives to sheer self interest. It re-particularizes affection without conflating feeling with privacy or longing for past times, for theatre is a past-time that makes possible better days and persons. Here, too, theatre's memorializing function is useful in pluralizing one's perception of time. More to the point, theatre strengthens by exercising memory more than do other aesthetic arenas and in so doing extends if not actual lifespans then certainly the depth and intensity of human life. For the ephemerality of the artistic medium of theatre – the actor – makes its durability dependent on memory. While actors 'teach us the shortness of human life', they teach us as well how to extend its value; our experiences of them are 'among our earliest recollections – among our last regrets. They are links that connect the beginning and the end of life together' (*HoT*, p. 123). While 'intellectual objects, in proportion as they are lasting, may be said to shorten life', the 'grand and ideal, that which appeals to the imagination . . . remains with us . . . from youth to age' (*HoT*, p. 123). *This* means of extending life, rather than the elimination of mortality that Godwin predicts as a long-term goal of perfectibility, is now applied to the post-revolutionary friend. By rendering the category theatrical, 'friend' transcends both death and words. 'He could not converse, and only pressed his hand to his bosom, and said, "My dear, dear friend!"' The prescience of Hazlitt's writings on theatre is in keeping open the question of whether such forms of expression bespeak either the human or the humane.

NOTES

I wish to thank the editors of this collection, Gillian Russell and Clara Tuite, and Kevin Gilmartin for very helpful responses to drafts of this chapter. For full citations see Bibliography.

1 'Our National Theatres', Hazlitt, *Selected Writings*, p. 157.
2 See Barish, *Antitheatrical Prejudice*.
3 Thomas Holcroft articulates this position most fully in his *Theatrical Recorder*. Subsequent references to this work will be abbreviated *TR* and included with volume and page number in parentheses in the text.
4 'Those strong passions that, with small assistance from outward circumstances, work their way in the heart till they become the tyrannical masters of it, carry on a similar operation in the breast of the monarch and the man of low degree' (Baillie, 'Introductory Discourse,' *A series of Plays on the Passions*, p. 11).
5 Hunt, *Dramatic Criticism*, p. 316.
6 'On Play-Going and on Some of our Old Actors', Hazlitt, *Hazlitt on Theatre*, p. 143. Subsequent references to this work will be abbreviated *HoT* and included with page numbers in parentheses in the text.

7 Lamb, 'On the Artificial Comedy of the Last Century', *Works and Letters*, p. 127.

8 Thomas McCarthy, 'Introduction' to Habermas, *Structural Transformation*, p. xii.

9 Habermas, *Structural Transformation*, pp. 43–51.

10 On this topic and dating generally, see Hayden, *Romantic Reviewers*.

11 Hazlitt, *Memoirs of the Late Thomas Holcroft*, *Works*, vol. III, p. 135. Subsequent references to this work will be abbreviated *MTH* and included with page numbers in parentheses in the text.

12 Godwin's revision of history as the reanimation of friends begins with his *Life of Chaucer* (1803) and culminates in his *Essay on Sepulchres* of 1809. Of interest is the convergence of these generic 'friends' around 1809, Coleridge's issuing *The Friend* as newspaper between 1809 and 1810, Godwin publishing *Essay on Sepulchres* in 1809 and Hazlitt composing the *Memoirs of the Late Thomas Holcroft* in late 1809 and 1810.

13 Archer, 'Introduction', *Hot*, pp. xiii–xiv.

14 Godwin, *Uncollected Writings*, pp. 145–76.

15 Scarborough's stern treatment is depicted as causing his son's suicide, a topic that hit too close to home for Holcroft. The less literary cause of friction is ascribed even by Holcroft to 'Mrs Godwin'. Marshall, *Godwin*, pp. 235, 260; also Brown, *Life*, p. 206.

16 On what Hazlitt means by abstraction and why readers should not overgeneralize his critique of the category, see Bromwich, *Hazlitt*, pp. 75–7.

17 On Godwin's discovery, see St Clair, *Godwins and the Shelleys*, pp. 221–37. For an alternate view of the motivations for Godwin's revisions that stands in an interesting relation to the larger concerns of this chapter, see Philp, *Godwin's Political Justice*, pp. 162–7. In his view, what occasions the changes in subsequent editions of the *Enquiry concerning Political Justice* is the loss of the forms of sociability that initially sustained his rationalist tenets – by which Philp means the loss both of the circle of radical Dissent as the chief audience for his writings and the tight social circle in which his initial ideas were generated. In other words, sociability occasioned Godwin's faith in a rationalist and rigorous view of friendship.

18 Godwin's objections to Hazlitt's publishing excerpts from Holcroft's diary, a 'violation of the terms originally settled with Mr Hazlitt', apparently delayed publication for some six years ('Notes', *MTH*, p. 285). On this topic, see also Grylls, *Godwin*, pp. 178–9.

19 See, for example, Hazlitt, 'William Godwin', in *Spirit of the Age*, pp. 22–5; 'Modern Tragedy', in *Selected Writings*, pp. 110–13, especially 'Falkland, St Leon, Mandeville, are studies for us to contemplate, not men that we can sympathise with' (p. 113).

20 See also '[Drama] is the most substantial and real of all things . . . Its business and its use is to express the thoughts and character in the most striking and instantaneous manner, in the manner most like reality' ('Modern Comedy', in *Selected Writings*, p. 108).

21 'Our National Theatres', in *Selected Writings*, p. 156. See also Hunt, 'But who becomes grave at the thought of issuing forth to the theatre?'; Hunt, *Dramatic Criticism*, p. 85.

22 There are striking similarities between 'Minor Theatres – Strolling Players' (*HoT*, pp. 155–64) and Hazlitt's description of Holcroft's beginning as an actor in *MTH*, p. 82.

23 Baillie, 'Introductory Discourse', pp. 1–3.

24 See especially Lacan's analysis of '*der Nächste*' (the neighbour) and why 'his harmful, malignant *jouissance*' poses a 'problem for my love', in Lacan, *Seminar*, pp. 186–8. See also Samuel Weber's commentary on the *semblable* in *Return to Freud*, p. 17.

25 Archer is drawing from Hazlitt's friend, P. G. Patmore's *My Friends and Acquaintance* and from Talfourd's *Hazlitt's Literary Remains*, 'Introduction', *HoT*, pp. xxvi, xvii, xxx.

26 Charles Lamb gives the classic statement against the stage's reduction of dreams in 'On the Tragedies of Shakespeare, Considered with Reference to Their Fitness for Stage Representation' (1811), *Works and Letters*, pp. 289–303. On the closet's refusal of visibility to socially marginal groups, see Burroughs, *Closet Stages;* Carlson, *In the Theatre*, pp. 134–75; Carlson, 'Forever Young', and Michael Simpson, *Closet Performances*.

27 See especially Bate, *Shakespearean Constitutions*.

28 Hunt explicitly links his theatre criticism with nostalgia and both with the attainment of liberty. 'Indeed there is scarcely any one thing which will strike us with a fresher sense of our return to liberty, than this particular subject. It was the first on which we commenced writing for the public; it is connected with our ideas of youth, of enthusiasm, almost of boyhood' ('On Resuming our Theatrical Criticism', in *Dramatic Criticism*, p. 84).

9

'Obliged to make this sort of deposit of our minds': William Godwin and the sociable contract of writing

Judith Barbour

This chapter investigates sociability, sexual attachment and textuality in the correspondence and journals of William Godwin.[1] These are the informal writings of a man whose life work in writing is exemplary of the rise of metropolitan literary culture in the English Enlightenment. Godwin's *oeuvre* is overtly inflected with class feeling and a value system drawn from Miltonic traditions of intellectual puritanism. Less obvious is its deployment of a powerful undercurrent of sex and gender expectations of the social order for and of women.

As Enlightenment documents, Godwin's formal texts tend to blank out material writing itself and its sociable contexts. Mastery of literacy in the English language is a precondition of mastery of the social; a male pedagogical imperative subsumes oral and written words under autonomous mind-to-mind communication. In 1793, in Godwin's major opus *Enquiry concerning Political Justice*, disciplines and professions in writing are declared and made exemplary of Godwin's chosen field of literary print culture. The gender liberality accorded to female 'genius' where it is found in singers and musicians, is retracted by the judgement that musical performance is a species of collaborative repetition and thus ruled out of philosophic parity with the written text. The worst aspect of 'cohabitation' between people of the same or opposite sex is its intrusion of an *other* contender into the hatching-place of literary inspiration. Godwin's keenest dread of being crowded into cohabiting, as Mark Philp suggests in *Godwin's Political Justice*,[2] is not sexual angst as such but the need to keep a patent 'sincerity' stretched over the gap between a writer and 'his' words. Later in this chapter, I shall try addressing the question to Godwin via Mark Philp, 'how sociable can sex ever be?' Philp's chapter 7 concerns itself with Godwin's revisions in 1795 to *Political Justice* for the second edition, that is, before Godwin and Mary Wollstonecraft formed an acquaintance that led eventually to their marriage. Coincidentally, as it seems, this chapter pictures Godwin at the peak of his intellectual form and engaged in a varied array of sociable activities involving women and men. The enmeshing of sociability, sexuality and gender in the period between 1795 and 1798, as textualized in Godwin's informal writing, will be the focus of what follows.

'THE CASE IS DIFFERENT'

When Mary Wollstonecraft died on 10 September 1797 her friend Mary Hays had been her widower William Godwin's correspondent for longer than Wollstonecraft had known him, and discretion was not Hays's long suit. William Dunlap's New York diary in 1798 records 'Read "Emma Courtney" & review', and continues with one of his chats with actor Tom Abthorpe Cooper about the Brits: 'Call on Cooper: he says he remembers Miss Hays (the author of Emma Courtney) that she wrote a letter to Godwin desiring to be acquainted with him; that he waited on her & they became intimate – this must be soon after publishing political Justice, she was then about 30 years of age.'[3] Cooper's recall is accurate and the Hays–Godwin correspondence in the New York Public Library's Pforzheimer collection verifies that it was she who wrote to Godwin first, as an admirer and aspiring fellow author, just as Dunlap himself had (unselfconsciously) done in October 1795.[4]

R. M. Wardle, the editor of Mary Wollstonecraft's letters, details a collection of 160 hand-delivered notes[5] that passed almost daily between Mary Wollstonecraft and William Godwin after he returned from a trip to Norfolk in mid-July 1796. The exchange continued until Wollstonecraft moved into 29 Polygon, Somers Town, in May 1797, six months pregnant and six weeks married. A selection of these notes was first published in 1876 by Charles Kegan Paul, Godwin's mid-Victorian official biographer, who complained that he found them almost unintelligible: and certainly he was content to leave them in the margins of his large picture of Godwin among his 'contemporaries'. They show that Wollstonecraft retailed to Godwin matters confided to her by Mary Hays, Mary Robinson and Amelia Alderson, including any uncomplimentary remarks about himself: and also solicited him to gossip with her about Elizabeth Inchbald.[6]

In her *Letters Written During a Short Residence in Sweden, Norway, and Denmark* (1796) Wollstonecraft had dramatized a triangular relation among a woman letter-writer, her male lover and a reader who is to judge between them. Composed and published within four months of her death, Godwin's *Memoirs of the Author* (1798) foster the impression that he himself was that reader whom Wollstonecraft 'calculated' upon for redress against the unhappy past, the defections of lovers like Henry Fuseli and Gilbert Imlay, the melancholy of texts like *Werter* and *The Fair Penitent*. But these notes also reveal that though Godwin adjudicated Wollstonecraft's relations with other women, he insisted that his circle of friends and network of acquaintances remain his alone and untethered to the conjugal arrangement.

After they married, Wollstonecraft tried to redraw the lines of this complicity, as it isolated her from other women's confidences yet gave her no access to Godwin's confidential relationships. Mary Hays's indiscretions became a bone of contention between the couple, not quite so sharp a bone as the visits of a certain Miss Pinkerton to Godwin's lodgings:

You give a softer name to folly and immorality when it flatters–yes, I must say it – your vanity, than to mistaken passion when it was extended to another – you termed Miss Hay's conduct insanity when only her own happiness was involved – I cannot forget the strength of your expressions. – and you treat with a mildness calculated to foster it, a romantic, selfishness, and pamper conceit, which will even lead the object to – I was going to say misery – but I believe her [Miss Pinkerton] incapable of feeling it.[7]

On 5 October 1797 William Godwin wrote to Mary Hays,[8] in response to her request for the return of her letters to him and to his recently dead wife:

With this note you will receive all the letters & notes of yours, addressed to my wife, that I have been able to find, & as uninspected as you desire. I do not however wish to deceive you, you have a very inaccurate notion of the confidences that, between minds of an affectionate cast, subsists in the tender relation from which I have been so deplorably cut off, if you can suppose that my wife did not show me so much of the inclosed letters as relates to myself. But you are still more ignorant of my character, if you imagine that I harbour the smallest displeasure or resentment, at any expressions that may have fallen from you in the moment of wounded pride.

I have not inclosed your letters to myself, & th[is] is because I think, upon more reflection, you will not desire that I should. I always entertain, I cannot help it, an ill opinion of the person who employs a precaution of that sort. In the course of human affairs we are obliged to make this sort of deposit of our minds with the persons with whom we have much intercourse. He that shrinks from this species of confidence must, as I should think, have a very bad heart. It was the first thing that fully decided my judgment of Miss Pinkerton.[9] I am sure it is a thought that could not harbour with a person of a generous soul. The case is different, when the individual to whom the letters were addressed is dead: & I do not blame you in that article.

Godwin gives Hays a lesson in the backstage confidentiality subsisting between sexual partners and its exclusion of third parties, despite the polite rule that a gentleman always returned a lady's letters at her request. As we saw, Hays had initiated the correspondence with Godwin, annulling her gender prerogative of waiting for him to 'make' the first 'deposit': and he lectures her on the systematic inferences. In that October Godwin wrote Hays another three letters,[10] to announce that their intimacy must cease, as she had ruined it by her behaviour when Wollstonecraft died and in the month that had elapsed since the fatal event.[11] Godwin's striking phrase 'obliged to make this sort of deposit of our minds', at first sight an odd juxtaposition of writing with banking, provides the title of this chapter.

A deposit is a mulct or tax, an organic portion taken out in earnest of a contract to implement, increment and eventually restore a whole. Samuel Johnson's 1775 pamphlet *Taxation No Tyranny* deployed the same figure of thought to lecture the rebellious colonists of Massachusetts in their duty to pay taxes for the upkeep of the Hessian regiments quartered in the ring of British forts across the north-east mainland of America. In Johnson's logic the sanction of military force was implied in the promise of military defence. The ultimate text of the deposit is Mosaic penile circumcision as a mulct signing JHWH up to the protection of the Jews. And this patriarchal figment loses little in Godwin's application of it, since he kept copies of all his own letters after 1795, when Tom Wedgwood made him a present of a wetpress copy-machine. So it is that a rich vein of deposits of his mind is laid open before us.

Godwin's letter legislates (his preceptorial tone with all-comers) a distinction between returning Hays's letters to his dead wife and holding on to her letters to himself: 'The case is different'. On the face of it, this draws the non-transactional distinction between the living body and the dead one,[12] while the distinction between a heterosexual exchange (Godwin–Wollstonecraft) and a woman-to-woman one (Hays–Wollstonecraft), is supernumary. The case of writing–reading between women, live ones, is settled out of hand as Godwin carries an exemplary heterosexual exchange. Godwin interdicts Hays's attempt to 'purloin' her letters, either by withdrawing them physically from his hands, or by pretending, in her ignorance of what passes between a husband and wife, to retract them from the oversight he enjoyed of them when Wollstonecraft showed them to him. The conventional use of the masculine personal pronoun 'he', governs the general 'intercourse' of 'persons' but 'confidences' between heterosexual partners is eroticized, and moreover, ratified by his sacrifice, a mulct of his affectionate mind in 'the tender relation from which I have been so deplorably cut off'.

In contradistinction to closed sexual confidences, open social intercourse develops into 'confidence' (or mutuality) only in 'a person of a generous soul,' he states, appealing to the law of genre and the general good that mandates exchanges between free and equal subjects. On this very question of the application of degendered generosity Carole Pateman[13] has argued that the Rousseauvian paradigm of the 'social contract' falls away from the gendered societal norms of sexual relations, that no parallel 'sexual contract' to the Rousseauvian 'social contract' informs equitable policies or partnerships across sex–gender.

How sociable, after all, can sex ever be? Eve K. Sedgwick's dialectic of sexual disruption of male homosocial orientation in space[14] might be recast into sociable interruption of sexual tempo. Interruption is the bane of male sexual performance, witness (and by witnessing make it worse) the ill-timed conception of Tristram Shandy. But curiosity is the spice of lust and the apprehended danger of an interruption that is also an arrest, exposure, abolition of private cover, keeps the game up. Sexuality is therefore sociable in that it can be conceived as a form of Habermasian audience-oriented privacy. Sedgwick's oracular phrase 'male homosociality' describes sociable relations between men that straddle the internal gender divisions in the principles of 'cooperation' and 'cohabitation' that characterize the Enlightenment ideal of open communication between free and 'generous' souls. The former two terms form part of Godwin's leading terms in *Enquiry concerning Political Justice* (1793).[15] Marriage, Godwin's third term, is posited to anneal them into synthesis. That is a conventional logic, and within a teleology of splitting and suturing, the double-phase of male–female heterosexual relations, 'courtship to conjugality', falls into step. But Godwin, however logically committed to the heterosexual project, actually harbours strenuous objections to all three conditions – affecting a man's independent life, moreover his work, and in essence, his independent life of the work of writing. As he examines each term Godwin defers and accumulates a growing debt of dependence and experiences a hardening subjective resistance to self-compromising acknowledgements of codependence and indebtedness. Where these have a sexual component, so much the worse.

Godwin's preachment of generosity to Mary Hays as guarantor of mutual confidence is a double bluff. Only what is un-pre-cautious, *counts with* him; disregarding the historical contingency of what (he) *counts as*. A suppressed term – gender – and a suppressed struggle for self-possession in one's own words, vitiate the contract that Godwin seeks to refine, then when he oversaw by the privilege of a husband the two women's correspondence, and now by ratifying the knowledge of Hays that that gave him as a condition of their continuing exchanges.

His letter of 5 October 1797 continues:

The other letters I detain for the present, not from any motive that respects myself, but to give you time to reconsider the subject.

This letter which ^now^ lies before me is not the only letter I have lately seen of yours, in which you trumpet forth the praises of disingenuousness. I am happy, when I see a person set up for a preacher of immorality, to find them doing it in terms that must be repugnant to the feelings of every uncorrupted heart. I can truly say that no confidence you ever placed in me, lowered you in my esteem. I feel for disappointment, & sympathise with distress. But I have been less pleased with you, since you became, in your own opinion, a considerable author, & a person 'not altogether insignificant'.[16] To speak frankly, I think you have forgotten a little of that simplicity & [*cancelled*: unass] unpresuming mildness, which so well becomes a woman or a human creature.

Godwin's retention of Hays's letters is now a matter of 'detention' of her written surrogates, and his position as reader takes priority over hers as writer. In 1796 Hays's novel, *Memoirs of Emma Courtney*, had trespassed on others' privacy, including Godwin's, by plagiarizing private letters lightly worked over and disguised as fictitious. Resentment of Hays's behaviour[17] bursts from Godwin in spite of his reiterated negatives: 'I can truly say that no confidence'. It is precisely Godwin's claim not to temper or shave 'sincerity' that flags his attacks. The justification for detaining Hays's letters is pedagogical, to penalize Hays for breaching the sociable contract of writing between 'persons of generous soul' in which the part that *becomes* her – generically as 'a woman' and generally as 'a human creature' – is one of 'unpresuming mildness', or as he started to write, 'unassuming'.

Godwin's second letter to Hays on 10 October deals with events on Tuesday 5 or Wednesday 6 September 1797, when Mary Wollstonecraft lay dying. In this dark letter Godwin temporarily vacates his post as arbiter of literary sociability. The letter becomes clearer if read across the final chapter 10 of *Memoirs of the Author*, where the twelve-day vigil at Wollstonecraft's deathbed is primarily constituted as a circle of devoted male friends. Besides the three doctors in attendance, Godwin writes, 'She had for nurses, or rather for friends, 'Mrs Fenwick', another unnamed 'very kind and judicious lady', and 'a favourite female servant'.[18] As I read the 10 October letter, Hays had come to the house and tried to gain admission in the final days and had been turned away by Godwin. Godwin employs the first person plural 'we' to isolate Hays and fix her to the moment of retort – hers to him *verbatim*; now his to her conclusive: 'Your passionate answer to my first observation on Tuesday, the fifth of September, "that we felt ourselves much obliged to you for your kindness, but that my wife had already every attendance necessary, & that therefore we should not find it requisite to trouble you"'. The on-the-spot decision of the stricken husband to exclude an importunate caller is sublated in *Memoirs of the Author* into an elegiac vision of true sociality – a circle of mourners into which only certain callers may enter.

For its element of intertextual affect, I propose reading this letter back into the 5 October letter. Wollstonecraft dying and Wollstonecraft dead both block the line of Hays's communication with her, in asymmetrical opposition to Godwin's privileged access. Godwin reading Hays's letters over his wife's shoulder, Godwin writing to Hays over his dying and dead wife's body, redounds to the empowerment of Godwin's writing and the cancellation of Hays's. This recursiveness does not stop short at gender difference or the privileging of heterosexual alliances, but invests Godwin's mourning narration in *Memoirs of the Author* of *Wollstonecraft's* life story with a specific *autobiographical* distinctiveness, instantiated by the veiling of himself for the period of marriage, birth and death, and his resurrection into the writer of her elegy.

The word 'unassuming' was cancelled by Godwin in the MS draft of his 5 October letter. I showed the cancellation above, for the sake of continuity, as Godwin returns to the theme (to criticize Hays's 'assuming manners') in his letter of 22 October, where he writes:

You tell me that the assuming manners of which I have accused you resulted from a spirit of resisting imposition. This is rather an unfortunate account of the matter, as there is, to the best of my re-collection, no one of our common friends from whom I have not lately heard repeated complaints against you of the same nature. Which is most probable, 'that they are all united' in the imposition you talk of, or that the spirit of imposition dwells in your own heart? I shall adhere to my former solution, & ascribe ^it^ to a newly hatched literary vanity.

By 22 October, not he alone, but 'our common friends' are drawing together to censure Hays with a (presumptively mild) form of ostracism and emotional blackmail, the double bind of a claimed connection and an avowed disapproval: 'there is, to the best of my recollection, no one of our common friends from whom I have not lately heard repeated complaints against you of the same nature'. The punishment is fit to the crime, being no more than a withdrawal of his sociable countenance from her and a sanction of detaining her at his pleasure in her surrogates, her letters to hand and 'ly[ing] before me'. Godwin as a 'human creature' had once been a human child and the habit of withdrawing love and approval from the unruly child is ubiquitous, if not quite universal law.

An irony of history sees Mary Shelley at last returning Hays's letters to Godwin to her after his death in 1836, accompanied by a note in which Shelley deplores the publication of private correspondence.[19] There was a *quid pro quo* in this gesture of compliance, since Mary Shelley's posthumous biography of Godwin carefully shields him from the claims of any woman other than Wollstonecraft. So Mary Hays is dropped out of account and her letters are not going to be missed.

'DESIDERATI'

According to his most recent editor, Mark Philp, Godwin started on 'a reasonably full autobiography' in 1796–7, the period of his relationship with Mary Wollstonecraft, and after her unexpected death in September 1797, and his publication in January 1798 of her *Memoirs and Posthumous Works*, he continued to parallel his writings for publication with a private autobiographical stream. This was further disseminated in psychological and social self-experimenting, through a male lineage of eponymous protagonists of novels, from *Caleb Williams* (1794) to *Mandeville* (1817), and into the largely unread fictions of the 1830s, *Cloudesley*, and *Deloraine*. According to Philp, Godwin composed autobiography as he did his novels, 'back-to-front',[20] consulting his daily journal entries in order to move *backward* in time. What Philp titles the 'Autobiographical fragments' covering the period 1772–96, were the earliest written, and narrated very recent events. This pre-posterous compositional practice crystallized in the critical period for which we have no autobiography extant save what is implicit in the *Memoirs of the Author* and his edition of her *Posthumous Works*, the former manifesting his coming-of-age as a sexual being, the latter his only major editorial achievement. Together, the six volumes bear out Clifford Siskin's claim that forms of writing in the late eighteenth century generated 'forms of visibility, but what they made visible was not themselves but the modern subject – a self whose subjectivity is constituted by all of the ways it knows itself to be visible'. And 'Literature [was] the discipline that took writing as its professional work.'[21]

The spring of 1796 is recalled shortly after it happened, lit in a sociable glow:

In my little deserted mansion I received, on the 22d of April, a party of twelve persons, the most of whom good-humouredly invited themselves to dine with me, and for whom I ordered provisions from a neighbouring Coffee-house – among this party were Dr Parr and his two daughters, Mr and Mrs Mackintosh, Mr Holcroft, Mrs Wollstonecraft, and Mrs Inchbald.

I was introduced at about this time by Merry, the poet to the most accomplished and delightful woman, the celebrated Mrs Robinson – in the course of this summer, I paid a second visit to Norfolk in the company of Merry, and had the happiness by my interference and importunity with my friends, to relive [sic] this admirable man from a debt of £200,[22] for which he was arrested while I was under his roof, and would otherwise have been thrown into jail.[23]

Godwin hides the sexual live wire of Wollstonecraft's name inside a bundle of married couples. The controversial poet, 'Revolution' Merry, visiting London from Brecon Ash in Norfolk, where he and his wife, formerly Covent Garden's leading actor Anne Brunton, had been rusticating since forced to flee the Paris Terror, introduces Godwin to Mary Robinson, then living in London as General Banastre Tarleton's mistress. Godwin does not recall any previous acquaintance with Robinson in the company of John 'Jew' King,[24] though he was in frequent contact with King at the time of the coffee-house take-away supper, and, if Philp's dating of the composition of the autobiography is correct, at the time of writing this anodyne resumé of that occasion. Godwin's repertoire of sociability expanded for that brief season in 1796, and then only in written retrospect. Not only did his small cheap London bachelor lodgings presuppose extramural socializing, but he was under the lash of a professional writer's career, at call to private patrons, a hostile press and publishers' contracts.

In the late eighteenth century 'Genius' was beginning to shake off its gender-exclusive application to males. 'Genial' also was loosening its birth ties to 'genius' and its classificatory applications in 'genre' and in Pope's famous one-line tribute to the publisher Jacob Tonson, 'In genial Jacob's upper room', represented the purely sociable collegiality (Oxford English Dictionary: *lego*, I choose) of professional writers and booksellers in a modern heteropolis. Virginia Woolf's *Jacob's Room* (1922) repeats the phrase, once twentieth-century women writers may enter themselves in the book. In Godwin's milieu there was Joseph Johnson's room, in Paternoster Row, famous for its weekly dinners of mixed company, at one of which Godwin met Wollstonecraft on 13 November 1791 in an emblematic scene of writing–reading. In 1791 Godwin was at a critical stage of negotiations with Robinson the publishers over *An Enquiry concerning Political Justice* and wanted to buffer his work-in-progress from direct competition, specifically with Burke's *Reflections* and Paine's *Rights of Man*. Godwin's journal for 13 November 1791 records: 'Nov. 13 Su Correct. Dyson & Dibdin call; talk of virtue & disinterestedness. Dine at Johnsons with Paine Shovel & Wollstonecraft talk of Monarchy, Tooke Johnson Voltaire, pursuits & religion Sup at Holcrofts.'[25]

The shorthand is fairly accessible. Joseph Johnson was Mary Wollstonecraft's and Tom Paine's publisher. Tête-à-tête Sunday suppers were an institution with Godwin and Holcroft.[26] 'Correct' is Godwin correcting the pages of the work-in-progress to becoming *An Enquiry concerning Political Justice*. And the topics of 'good' talk are listed.

In *Memoirs of the Author* the daily record is re-membered:

It was in the month of November in the same year (1791), that the writer of this narrative was first in company with the person to whom it relates. He dined with her at a friend's[27] together with Mr Thomas Paine and one or two other persons. The invitation was of his own seeking, his object being to see the author of *The Rights of Man*, with whom he had never before conversed.

The interview was not fortunate. Mary and myself parted, mutually displeased with each other. I had not read her *Rights of Woman*.[28] I had barely looked into her *Answer to Burke*[29] and been displeased, as literary men are apt to be, with a few offenses against grammar and other minute points of composition. I had therefore little curiosity to see Mrs Wollstonecraft, and a very great curiosity to see Thomas Paine. Paine, in his general habits, is no great talker; and, though he threw in occasionally some shrewd and striking remarks, the conversation lay principally between me and Mary. I, of consequence, heard her, very frequently when I wished to hear Paine.[30]

Godwin attaches his first unfavourable impression of Wollstonecraft herself to an abortive reading of her 1790 and 1792 *Vindications*, and his later, amended impression to a reading of her *Letters Written . . . in Sweden*. His tortuous account of how he had *not* read the *Vindication of the Rights of Woman* (as yet five months short of publication), prevaricates with his jealousy of Wollstonecraft's early start of him. He approached personal relations with her crab-fashion. After meeting her at Johnson's he did not again speak with her until January 1796 at Mary Hays's. False starts are structural props of the *Bildüngsroman* of Godwin's London life up to the age of forty-two, a life in and out of phase with the mind's writing–reading of itself. These layered impressions imbricate sociable occasion, sexual attachment and textuality.

Although the focus on shared experience and private emotions is proper to the obituary memoir, Godwin's *Memoirs of the Author* (1798) has skewed critical perceptions, not only of the complexion of the Godwin marriage but of the epoch in Godwin's life and writing that the marriage was.[31] Mark Philp's *Godwin's Political Justice* (1986) is particularly striking in its emphasis on the marriage as a watershed. Philp writes the Godwin marriage into the plot of 'The Decline of Radicalism' (Philp's tenth and last chapter), and implicitly positions sex as epochal and disruptive: '[A] detailed discussion of the affair is warranted because of the role it, and its history (in Godwin's *Memoirs*), played in betraying some of the cracks which existed in radical circles.'[32]

Quoting the Augustan tag, 'the feast of reason and the flow of soul', Philp's chapter 7 contains a lively description of Godwin's premarital socializing with a select few talented women and a galaxy of rising men. A tessellation of venues ('in coffee-houses, at publishers' lunches, theatres, exhibitions, and at . . . numerous tea, dinner, and supper parties'), and a daily journal itemizing a large gallery of fellow debaters and discutants (and what Godwin's journal noted as *desiderati* – people he wished to meet[33]), mark up Godwin's 'highly sociable' 'extensive sociability', his 'entry into broader social circles' and the background influence to be found in 'the sociability of the culture into which Godwin increasingly moved, and in the self-conception it entertained' from December 1793 to the end of 1795.[34] Philp's sample of sixteen names plucked from Godwin's journal are as it happens all male, which extenuates an impression elsewhere that all Godwin's friends and contacts were writers, whether men or women.

In Philp's chapter 8, which is entitled 'Wollstonecraft and *Political Justice*', Godwin's circulation through London's social sets is abruptly curtailed, duplicating an ellipsis in Godwin's own text, which sublates the petty actualities of these months under the tremendous weight of Wollstonecraft's death. Philp tacitly upholds the impression (*in absentia* any contradicting text) that only Godwin's writing practice was quarantined, expressly and by mutual consent from the joint concern, and that inevitably marriage entailed a radical make-over of his everyday routines and social contacts. In fact, Godwin's sociable existence had continued much as before, not without some ructions with Wollstonecraft, intensifying when he left London to pay house visits to Samuel Parr and the Wedgwoods in June. It was her death not her presence that was a watershed. Fixed to his desk in what had been 'their' rooms, for the four months of composition, October to December 1797, under the Opie portrait of a faintly smiling pregnant Wollstonecraft, Godwin's memoir is post-mimetic, removing himself from social circulation in March to September 1797 to tell off the months marching down to the last days.

Mary Hays had published an obituary notice of Wollstonecraft in September 1797 in which she quoted from Wollstonecraft:

Those who are bold enough to advance before the age they live in, and to throw off, by the force of their own minds, the prejudices which the maturing reason of the world will in time disavow, must learn to brave censure. We ought not to be too anxious respecting the opinion of others. – I am not fond of vindications. – Those who know me will suppose that I acted from principle. – Nay, as we in general give others credit for worth, in proportion as we possess it – I am easy with regard to the opinions of the *best* part of mankind. – I *rest* on my own.[35]

This single paragraph, whether addressed to Hays in a private letter, or shown to her as a sample of Wollstonecraft's ongoing signature work, is a remarkable enunciation, matched elsewhere in Wollstonecraft's text in *Letters Written . . . in Sweden*, and fitfully recalled in the anguished soliloquys of her fictional protagonist Maria in the manuscript left unfinished at her death. It is at once personal and committed to the social weal, the collective 'we' – the unexpected phrase from the author of *A Vindication of the Rights of Woman*, 'I am not fond of vindications', suggestive of Keats's later formulation of the poet's 'Negative Capability', as the embedding of a poetic meditation in a private letter also is suggestive of Keats's practice.

In the course of reviewing the (mostly hostile) reviewers of *Memoirs of the Author*, and concerned to vindicate Godwin's integrity under this attack, Mark Philp picks up and twists the thread that ties Wollstonecraft to Hays in this woman-to-woman obituary. He writes, 'Mary Wollstonecraft expected censure, but she only braved it from the security which their marriage offered.'[36]

'AA'

Godwin's frequent correspondent from his native town Norwich during the 'off-season' months September to March was Amelia Alderson, who signed off all her letters 'AA' like a boon companion. In 1796 her letters were assiduous in pressing Godwin to read her manuscript play and help her to get it before the theatre managers Twiss and Richardson.[37]

In April, Amelia arrived in London for her annual dip in the metropolitan froth, where she sought out 'Mrs Imlay'.[38] Amelia returned to Norwich in late August, and wrote a winsome letter to 'Mrs Imlay', pressing boldly forward to claim Wollstonecraft as a fellow writer and creative free spirit. For Amelia, seeing was reading and authors wore the colours of their texts.

I remember the time when my desire of seeing you was repress'd by fear, – but as soon as I read your letters from Norway, the cold awe which the philosopher had excited, was lost in the tender sympathy call'd forth by the woman – I saw nothing but the interesting creature of feeling, & imagination . . . I saw you, & you are one of the few objects of my curiosity who in gratifying have not disappointed it also – you & the Lakes of Cumberland have exceeded my expectations – Mr Godwin disappointed them – .[39]

There is an intriguing forecast here of the tribute enshrined in Godwin's *Memoirs of the Author*, that by early 1796 he had fallen in love as a reader with the author of *Letters Written . . . in Sweden*.[40] A letter to Godwin from Alderson in Norwich on 1 November 1796 announces that her playscript is progressing in hopes:

Well – you will *receive* my play – cela va sans doute – But will you read it, &c – Soon? Will you deign to enter into the feelings of an impatient girlish [*cancelled*: author] parent, whose whole soul is wrapt up in the babe she has brought forth, & who, unlike the owl in the fable, does not think her offspring a beauty ^herself^ but is very desirous *others* should think it so? Will you assist at her bantling's toilette with all possible expedition? & let the anxious Mamma know whether you do not think Miss may grow up handsome when her features are more formed ? – . . . I have had thoughts of rewriting Egerton's character & borrowing for him Sir Hugh Tyrold's[41] bonhommie, & phraseology – & , if you say, such a loan would bear good interest I will undertake the task.

Alderson is anxious to make her male characters converse like the urbane characters of Fanny Burney, and like denizens of the London milieu to which she believes Godwin holds the key. Over to Godwin, then, with facetious exhortations to inseminate her with those nodes of social deportment that she calls 'bonhommie'. On the manuscript, Mary Jane Godwin adds a tart marginal note to the phrase 'if you say, such a loan would bear good interest I will undertake the task', to wit: 'Do not the words confound the sense?'[42]

'THEIR ^ PRECIOUS ^ CIRCLES'

The spring of 1797 brought Amelia Alderson to London as usual and planning a visit to the theatre for 19 April, to see a fashionable comedy, George Lillo's *The Will*. But this spring had brought a momentous change: and the next letter in the folder[43] is addressed to 'Mrs Godwin', and apologises for sending it to Mr Godwin's address, 'The direction will make you laugh, but I write it on the presumption that you, as Mrs Godwin were not known yet forgetting the *number* would point out y[r] house.'

It continues:

Mrs Hamilton, an aristocratic friend of mine, is very desirous of accompanying us to the play on Wednesday,[44] if you can spare her a place in your box – I believe I told you before that I hoped you would admit the beau who was to have accompanied Mrs Inchbald, & me – therefore you may think it unreasonable in me to request a third place, but as the box holds nine, & my friend will be contented with any seat, however bad, I trust that you will excuse this application. Mrs Philips is, I find, to join us there . . . Had I not been obliged to make some arrangements for the ball this evening, I should have called on you, instead of writing, but I have desired the bearer of this to wait for an answer – & so farewell!

A: Alderson

Three days after Mary Wollstonecraft died on 10 September 1797, Godwin wrote to Elizabeth Inchbald:[45]

I must endeavour to be understood as to the unworthy behaviour with which I charge you towards my wife. I think your shuffling behaviour about the taking places to the comedy of the Will, dishonourable to you. I think your conversation with her that night at the play, base, cruel & [*cancelled*: insolent] insulting. There were persons in the box[46] that heard it, & they thought as I do. I think you knew more of my wife than you were willing to acknowledge to yourself, & that you have an understanding capable of doing some small degree of justice to her merits. I think you should have had magnanimity & self respect enough to have showed this. I think that, while the Twisses & others were sacrificing to what they were silly enough to think a proper etiquette,[47] a person so out of all comparison their superior as you are, should have placed her pride in acting upon better principles, & in courting & distinguishing insulted greatness & worth. I think that you chose a mode of political conduct, when you might ^have^ chosen a conduct that would have done you immortal honour. You had not even their excuse. They could not (they pretended) receive her in to their ^precious^ circles. You kept no circles to debase & enslave you.

I have now been frank & explicit on this subject, & have done with it, I hope, for ever.

I thank you for your attempt at consolation in your letter of yesterday. It was considerate & well intended, though its connotations are utterly alien to my heart.

Sep. 13. 1797.   Wgodwin

I wish not to be misunderstood as to the circles above alluded to. I mean not to apply my idea to the sacrificers, for one or two of whom I feel more kindness than I can easily express – but to the idols.

Formerly an actor in the Kemble company, now retired, a celebrated novelist and successful playwright, Elizabeth Inchbald was in 1793 'competing with her friend Sarah Siddons in the literary press for the title of the Tenth Muse'.[48] Godwin had been quick[49] to enrol himself among the pretty widow Inchbald's circle of admirers in 1792 after the runaway success of her first novel, *A Simple Story*, while she was in the ascendant professionally and before he had come close enough to feel any heat from her expectations of him.

In the spring of 1797 Sarah Siddons and her sister and brother-in-law Twiss cut the acquaintance of Mary Wollstonecraft and William Godwin[50] when the announcement of their marriage made it no longer possible not to know that Wollstonecraft was the unmarried mother of three-year-old Fanny Imlay.[51] An alternative cause of disapproval was the bigamy if the French marriage to Gilbert Imlay had been valid. The concept that what was valid in revolutionary France was not so in reactionary England, does not seem to have counted for much. The 'formidable reputation for moral probity' that Gillian Russell assigns[52] to Siddons required regular upkeep, the more so that it was a collective fantasy conflating the person of a celebrity with her most applauded performances.

'I know that you do not like me to go to Holcroft's',[53] Wollstonecraft wrote to Godwin on Sunday 25 June 1797. The immediate context is Godwin's regular date at Holcroft's for supper on a Sunday, the immediate pathos Wollstonecraft's reminder to Godwin that she can no longer enjoy herself in Johnson's company, since 'Mr J–'s house and spirits were so altered', nor expect to be welcome as before 'every third Sunday at Twiss's': 'I am then, you perceive, thrown out of my track, and have not traced another.' Wardle's editorial note ventures to smooth off this rough edge, 'Godwin evidently felt . . . Mary should spend more time with her own friends.' I will pass up the temptation to adjudicate a married couple's tiff, only repeating that sociable interactions and competitive vying for the good fellowship of people worth knowing remained as potent for Godwin and as demonstrably a source of resentment on Wollstonecraft's part and pedantic insistence on his, during the marriage as before.

In 1797, at the peak of her second career as a writer, Inchbald's social standing was assured, but by no means invulnerable to Godwin's habit of denying the backdoor cruelties of gender inequity. With much at stake because she had been appearing in public with Godwin as her escort at the time he had contracted the secret marriage with Wollstonecraft, Inchbald administered 'the cut direct' that evening in the theatre. Godwin's letter of 13 September insists that Wollstonecraft was its object and victim. Such other evidence as we have points straight at *him*. He never points straight, and his postscript, excusing 'the sacrificers' but condemning the 'idols', leaves it vague as to whether these latter are Baconian abstractions – 'idols of the world' – or actual celebrities and *divas*. Inchbald could hardly choose between these poles.

What fascination with theatre box and theatre stage propelled Wollstonecraft and Inchbald to a face-off in Godwin's presence when all parties had advance notice of a looming 'scene'? No false pride in consistency had ever kept Godwin out of the theatre despite his strictures on 'theatrical exhibitions' but he was not (or not yet) *of* the theatre, whereas Inchbald and Holcroft and of course the Twiss and Siddons circle, were celebrated professionals. Amelia Alderson, as she herself admitted, was a tyro longing to break into theatre (she never did). Finally, Wollstonecraft, cutting a figure of somewhat scary fame as a radical philosopher of women's rights, had hitherto been too poor and too serious-minded to be a regular theatre-goer. Of all of them that evening, she was furthest outside her territory. The ceremony at St Pancras on 29 March was of the genre of 'the open secret' – since it could not conceal Wollstonecraft's second trimester pregnancy, it simply concealed itself, within the impression that the couple had been married for quite a long time before they chose to declare themselves on 19 April. This turned the screw for Inchbald, since the longer Godwin had been married the longer he had been using her as a beard.

Memoirs of the Author gave Godwin a second chance to vindicate his wife and put his signature on the epoch of their marriage. In accordance with the rest of his book, he superimposes the reader-writer relation on woman-to-woman relationships. He rules himself an invisible spectator of the social circles of idols and their sacrificers but returns as a judge of persons and literature to endorse and be endorsed by . . . Mrs Siddons: 'She [Mrs Siddons] very truly observes, in a letter now before me, that the *Travels in Norway* were read by no one, who was in possession of "more reciprocity of feeling, or more deeply impressed with admiration of the writer's extraordinary powers".' He continues:

Two of the persons, the loss of whose acquaintance Mary principally regretted upon this occasion, were Mrs Inchbald and Mrs Siddons. Their acquaintance, it is perhaps fair to observe, is to be ranked among her recent acquisitions. Mrs Siddons, I am sure, regretted the necessity, which she conceived to be imposed upon her by the peculiarity of her situation, to conform to the rules I have described. She is endowed with . . . rich and generous sensibility . . . [54]

The conformist 'rules . . . described' in his previous paragraph are such as allow a Wollstonecraft to be shunned by 'the supporters and the subjects of the unprincipled manners of a court', 'the dull and insolent dictators, the gamblers, and demireps of polished society'.[55] Provided Siddons does not identify her reputation with any such persons she can accept the proffered compliments to her sensibility and her literary taste without a qualm.

As these other women withdrew, 'Mary felt a transitory pang', and moved on, and now Godwin moves into the first person plural of the married couple, 'no two persons ever found in each other's society, a satisfaction more pure and refined'.[56] The auto/biographical claim of remembered happiness is incontestable, the paratactic movement from unsatisfactory women-to-women relationships to exclusive heterosexual couple, is generative for the *Memoirs of the Author*, and a deposition of the sex–gender dependence of the writing mind.

AFTERWARDS

In August 1798, the London *Monthly Magazine* carried an advertisement for a forthcoming work by Robert Merry on 'American manners'. In that month the recently widowed Godwin was at home in London struggling to digest the rejection of his proposals of marriage to Miss Harriet Lee of Bath (another actor's daughter turned playwright). Mary Shelley later wrote that on first meeting with her, he 'immediately wished to study her mind'.[57] He had wooed her with many letters starting with one in which he invited her to stay in his London house chaperoned by his young housekeeper.[58] This repeated with added emphasis his invitation (also declined) to Miss Amelia Alderson when she first visited for the London season in 1794, staying in unfashionable Southgate, far from the hub.[59]

Godwin pits conventional gender mores, which he labels and feminizes 'etiquettes', against masculine sexual agency; and thrusts his repressive will against sexuality. He puts both women's reputations in jeopardy with his invitations, all the more that he absolves himself of sexual designs on them. Mary Wollstonecraft in 1796 and Mary Jane Clairmont in 1801 did not wait to be invited, and Godwin was not able to absolve himself of either woman. The revisions to *Political Justice* continued until the last decade of his life, and his novels too repeatedly preponderated the balance between masculine ambition and familial and sexual ties, an agonistic dilemma revised by his daughter Mary Shelley's *Frankenstein*. The utopian longing circulating throughout *Political Justice*, and expressed in its miniature Appendix to Book VIII, 'Of Property'[60], images a Miltonic pendent world giving back the reflection of an invisible sun. An attempt to segregate 'the sexual commerce' from the sociable meeting place of minds and merits had patently failed when Godwin began his affair with Mary Wollstonecraft, but her death regenerated the writerly ambition of making good the promise of the 'generous soul' not to ask for its deposit back.

NOTES

For full citations see Bibliography.

1 I gratefully acknowledge Lord Abinger's kind permission to quote from the Abinger Shelley–Godwin manuscripts deposited at the Bodleian Library, Oxford.

2 Philp, *Godwin's Political Justice*, p. 177.

3 Dunlap, *Diary*, p. 255.

4 Abinger MSS Dep. b. 227/2 (d) lists a letter from 'an admirer of Political Justice, W. Dunlap, 1 Oct. 1795'.

5 Wollstonecraft, *Collected Letters*, pp. 331–94.

6 *Ibid.*, pp. 335, 347, 340, 361.

7 *Ibid.*, pp. 403–5 (p. 404), Wollstonecraft to Godwin (London, 4 July, 1797).

8 Abinger MS Duke University microfilm reel 5, letter from Godwin to Hays, 5 October 1797. St Clair, *Godwins and the Shelleys*, p. 537, identifies Godwin's letter to Hays of 27 October 1797 in Abinger MS Dep. b.227/8.

9 Tomalin, *Life*, p. 271 and St Clair, *Godwins and the Shelleys*, p. 174 agree that it was Wollstonecraft who insisted Miss Pinkerton be banned from the matrimonial home.

10 Abinger MS Duke University microfilm reel 5, Godwin letters to Hays of 10, 22, 27 October 1797.

11 Mary Hays's obituary notice of Wollstonecraft appeared in *Monthly Magazine*, September 1797, reprinted in *Annual Necrology 1797–8* (London, 1800): St Clair, *Godwins and the Shelleys*, p. 537. Favret, *Romantic Correspondence*, pp. 238–9, cites Mary Hays as author of 'Memorial for Mary Wollstonecraft Godwin', *Gentleman's Magazine*, 67 (1797), p. 894.

12 Cf. De Man, 'Shelley Disfigured', p. 68.

13 Pateman, *Sexual Contract*.

14 Sedgwick, *Between Men*.

15 Godwin, *Enquiry*, ed. Kramnick. Godwin relegates this discussion to Book viii, 'Of Property', chapter VIII, 'Objections to this System [of Equality] from the Inflexibility of its Restrictions', Appendix 'Of Co-operation, Cohabitation and Marriage': Godwin, *Enquiry*, pp. 754–6, 756–67. Kramnick's text is based on the revised 3rd edition 1798, with new footnotes by Godwin replying to the objections raised by readers of the first edition.

16 Quotation marks apparently quoting Hays.

17 St Clair, *Godwins and the Shelleys*, p. 180, n4, believes as well that Hays's public announcement that Godwin's 'abler hand' was currently writing a biography of Wollstonecraft had incensed Godwin.

18 Godwin, *Memoirs*, in Wollstonecraft and Godwin, *A Short Residence in Sweden* and *Memoirs*, p. 269.

19 Letter from Mary Shelley to Mary Hays, 20 April 1836, in Shelley, *Letters*, vol. II, p. 270.

20 Godwin, *Collected Novels*, vol. I. Philp, Introductory Note, p. *58*, states that the papers bear watermarks of various dates between 1796 and 1819.

21 Siskin, *Work of Writing*, pp. 2, 3, 8.

22 Godwin 'proposed' to Dr Alderson to put up the money, and Merry promised to pay it back once settled in America. Some recent critics have misread Godwin's carefully worded account and portray him as personally forking out the £200.

23 Godwin, *Collected Novels*, p. 51.

24 Godwin's letters to King in 1795 and 1796 cited in Kegan Paul, *Godwin*, vol. I, pp. 146–7, 154–57.

25 Godwin's journal entry as transcribed in Abinger MS Dep. c.606/1: 13 by Mary Shelley in 1836. In transcribing the journal entry, Mary Shelley has regularized the spelling of her mother's family name.

26 St Clair, *Godwins and the Shelleys*, p. 276: 'After Holcroft's return [from Germany] . . . in 1802, he and Godwin had again started to dine together nearly every Sunday, as they had done, with few interruptions, since 1786.'

27 'a friend's,' Joseph Johnson.

28 *A Vindication of the Rights of Woman*, not published until 23 April 1792. Paine published *Rights of Man*, Part i, February 1791, and Part ii, February 1792.

29 In December 1790 Mary Wollstonecraft's *A Vindication of the Rights of Men; In a Letter to the Rt. Hon. Edmund Burke*, was among the first published replies to Burke's *Reflections on the Revolution in France*, published November 1790.

30 Godwin, *Memoirs*, in *A Short Residence in Sweden* and *Memoirs*, pp. 235–6.

31 A distinguished recent article has been drawn to my attention too late for the preparation of this chapter: see Jacobus, 'Intimate connections'.

32 Philp, *Godwin's Political Justice*, p. 175.

33 St Clair, *Godwins and the Shelleys*, p. 38.

34 Philp, *Godwin's Political Justice*, pp. 164–6.

35 Wollstonecraft, *Collected Letters*, p. 413, Letter 346 To Mary Hays (?) (London, *c.* summer 1797). Wardle's conjectural date and question mark to the addressee.

36 Philp, *Godwin's Political Justice*, p. 189.

37 St Clair cites a reply from Godwin *c.* February 1796, 'I can no longer withhold from you the general information . . . that your comedy has, in my opinion, no inconsiderable merit' (*Godwins and the Shelleys*, p. 149, and n16).

38 Wollstonecraft, *Collected Letters*, p. 335, Wollstonecraft to Godwin.

39 Abinger MS Dep. b.210/6, Amelia Alderson to Mrs Imlay, 28 August (1796).

40 Godwin, *Memoirs*, p. 249: 'a book of travels that so irresistably seizes upon the heart . . . If ever there was a book calculated to make a man in love with its author, this appears to me to be the book.'

41 'Sir Hugh Tyrold' is a paternalistic head of the family in Frances Burney's *Camilla*, which Wollstonecraft reviewed for the *Analytical Review* in August 1796.
42 Abinger MS Dep. b.210/6, note, initialled 'MJG' in margin of letter from Amelia Alderson to Godwin, 1 November 1796.
43 Abinger MS Duke University microfilm reel 12, dated 29 Pollard Street – Monday (17 April 1797), letter from Amelia Alderson to Mary Wollstonecraft Godwin. Alderson is replying to a letter from Wollstonecraft dated by Wardle 'Tuesday Night [11 Apr. 1797]' (Wollstonecraft, *Collected Letters*, pp. 389–90).
44 19 April 1797 was a Wednesday.
45 Abinger MS Duke University microfilm reel 5, quoted in Kegan Paul, *William Godwin*, vol. I, p. 278. St Clair, *Godwins and the Shelleys*, p. 179, n3, cites a reply from Inchbald on 14 September quoted in Kegan Paul, *Godwin*, vol. I, p. 279.
46 St Clair, *Godwins and the Shelleys*, pp. 171–2 names the 'other friends' in the theatre box on 19 April 1797.
47 Cf. Wollstonecraft to Alderson, 11 April 1797: 'I shall be sorry to resign the acquaintance of Mr and Mrs Twiss ... but my conduct in life must be directed by my own judgment and moral principles' (Wollstonecraft, *Collected Letters*, p. 389).
48 St Clair, *Godwins and the Shelleys*, p. 149.
49 Just how quick is uncertain. Mary Shelley in Abinger MS Dep. c.606/1 casts doubt on a note in his papers to the effect that he met Inchbald in 1791 and was asked to read and comment on the manuscript of *A Simple Story*, at the same time that Holcroft did so.
50 Kegan Paul dates Godwin's acquaintance with Siddons to 1795 (Kegan Paul, *Godwin*, I, pp. 148–9). St Clair, *Godwins and the Shelleys*, p. 163 dates it to spring 1796 when Godwin had some dealings with theatre-manager Francis Twiss, her brother-in-law, and writes that Godwin introduced Wollstonecraft to Siddons, but leaves it open that Wollstonecraft may have been a guest at the Twiss's earlier than Godwin.
51 St Clair, *Godwins and the Shelleys*, p. 174.
52 GR/Gillian Russell, 'Siddons, Sarah', in McCalman (ed.), *Oxford Companion*, p. 705.
53 Wollstonecraft, *Collected Letters*, pp. 399–400, and ni, Letter 324, 25 June 1797, Wollstonecraft to Godwin.
54 Godwin, *Memoirs*, p. 261.
55 *Ibid.*, p. 61.
56 *Ibid.*, pp. 261–2.
57 Abinger MS Dep. b.228/4, Mary Shelley's posthumous memoir of Godwin.
58 Abinger MS Dep. b.228/4, letter from Godwin to Harriet Lee in March 1798.
59 St Clair, *Godwins and the Shelleys*, pp. 147–8.
60 Appendix: 'Of co-operation, cohabitation, and marriage': Godwin, *Enquiry*, pp. 756–67.

The Byronic woman:
Anne Lister's style, sociability and sexuality

Clara Tuite

> The commercial society imagined in the eighteenth century and
> realized in the wake of Waterloo was . . . a regime of effects without
> agents.[1]

In this chapter, I wish to propose the category of style as one of the primary categories of the 'commercial society' which Jerome Christensen
has argued has its *imaginary* phase in early eighteenth-century Britain –
the setting for Jürgen Habermas's 'blueprint' of the classical public
sphere – and is then *realized* in Britain in the 'culturally dominant
and economically profitable' system of Byronism.[2] Consolidated during the Romantic period as a way of regulating, classifying, individu-
alizing and historicizing the products of an intensifying literary culture
of professionalization and celebrity, style is a paradigmatic category of
the commercial society and its mediatized social, economic and cultural
mobilities. Style is a particularly enabling category for elaborating the
complicated relations between the social system and the literary system, sociability and textuality, social agency and textual effects, and
the corporeal and phantasmatic aspects of social subjectivity and social
performance.

A minor-canonical and late-Romantic statement on style as a national
and socially mobile category is Thomas De Quincey's 1840 essay 'Style'.
This was published in *Blackwood's*, the journal which produced its particular ideology of the literary aesthetic by, as Jon Klancher has suggested,
'erasing the journalistic world from which it arose'.[3] Informed by the
structuring anxiety of the Romantic literary marketplace that 'any distinction displayed in the public sphere was subject to counterfeit',[4] De
Quincey's essay elegizes the 'true English style' as an aristocratic ease under threat from the frantic mimicries of a vulgar, middle-class 'periodic'
or 'newspaper style'.[5] He locates the last vestiges of this style in the body
of the leisured female subject, cultivated yet free from 'the contagion

of bookishness', unmarried and over the age of twenty-five – 'the interesting class of women unmarried upon scruples of sexual honour' who through natural refinement and sexual abstinence embody the 'purity of female English' as both a corporeal and discursive purity of 'the mother tongue'.[6] The 'true English style' is emphatically non-reproductive and non-circulating, inscribed not in published writings but in the handwritten forms of private correspondence. De Quincey's essay asserts an originary aristocratic cultural priority over commercial culture by asserting nature through the body, corporealizing a style which cannot be counterfeited through commercial reproduction.

Like the genre of the letter, the journal is another paradigmatic genre of unpublished and unmarketed leisured female style. The journal writings of Anne Lister (1791–1840), the provincial gentry heiress in Halifax, West Yorkshire, who aspired to the status of published author, manifest neither aristocratic ease nor female purity. Not published during Lister's lifetime, Lister's extensive diaries – which run to almost four million words, with a significant part written in cipher – were first published from the late 1980s.[7] These writings flaunt a spectacular departure from De Quincey's paradigm of national, corporeal and generic hygiene, in their representation of Lister's extensive sexual activity with other women, in their elaboration of an acute sense of sartorial, corporeal and social unease, and in their habitual identification with and mimicry of the suspect models of social, sexual and literary style of Byron and Rousseau.[8] In this chapter, I wish to engage Anne Lister as a case study of Romantic style, sociability and sexuality. It has been argued by Katherine Binhammer that the 1790s is a critical moment for the history of sexuality in its 'social enforcement of compulsory heterosexuality',[9] underwritten by the enforcement of constructions of gender. I wish to engage the case of Lister to illuminate how the social enforcement of compulsory heterosexuality is consolidated in the post-Waterloo period at the level of social performance and social scandals of sexual publicity.

SOCIABILITY AND EMBODIMENT

In Jürgen Habermas's influential account of the development of the bourgeois public sphere, sociability is linked with the display and artifice of the *ancien régime*. According to Habermas, what distinguishes the bourgeois public sphere from an aristocratic culture of representative publicness is the way in which a bourgeois culture of publicity begins to 'shed its dependence on the authority of the aristocratic noble hosts and to acquire that autonomy that turns conversation into criticism and *bon mots* into arguments'.[10]

However, if bourgeois public culture is a culture of autonomy and critique, it is also one of dependence and imitation. A less utopic account of the bourgeois transformation of the public sphere would argue that 'commercial society' does not so much 'shed its dependence on ... aristocratic noble hosts' as acquire and accumulate newly phantasmatic forms of dependence, which reproduce the host and the residue of this dependence in the phantasmatic forms of commercial culture.[11] I am interested in engaging how aristocratic culture is called upon to host – as both patron and parasite – the bourgeois public sphere, in the form of the desired original that is reproduced in the counterfeited forms of commercial culture. We might call this noble aristocratic host 'Lord Byron', and 'Byronism' the paradigmatic form of this counterfeiting commercial culture. As Jerome Christensen argues: 'the literary system of Byronism ... was collaboratively organized in the second decade of the nineteenth century by coding the residual affective charge that still clung to the paraphernalia of aristocracy in order to reproduce it in commodities that could be vended to a reading public avid for glamour'.[12]

I wish to engage the 'literary system of Byronism' as a framework for examining the embodiments of Anne Lister's social, sociable and socially sexual performative style. In its simplest terms, 'Byronism' encompasses Lord Byron the historical subject, the author and Lord Byron's poetry. It works both to instantiate a distinction between the subject and the poetry and to provide an alibi for their conflation in a new culture of Romantic literary celebrity.[13] Both formulas of distinction and conflation are working for Lister in her response to the death of Lord Byron: 'Who admired him as a man? Yet "he is gone & forever!" The greatest poet of the age! And I am sorry.'[14] Lister's eulogy both distinguishes the man from the poetry (in the denunciation of Byron 'as a man') yet conflates these in mourning the death of the 'poet'. Unlike Christensen, as quoted in the epigraph to this chapter, I do not maintain an opposition between agents or subjects and effects or discourse. Rather, I see them as interimplicated. As Judith Butler has pointed out, subjectivity involves 'a fundamental dependency on a discourse we never chose but that, paradoxically, initiates and sustains our agency'.[15] The category of embodiment engages both social agency and textual effects, and it is a critical component of sociability. Byronism is a particularly useful category for understanding

Romantic sociability because it engages the fraught status of embodiment within the context of the bourgeois public sphere's displacement of court culture and its aristocratic forms of representative publicness.

The comportment of the body is critical to Lister's saga of style, sociability and sexuality. To begin this story, I want to begin with Lister's fashion story, which, from late summer 1817, is a perennial winter story. Lister's decision to wear black and only black all year round meets with a mixed reception. It has disastrous social consequences, for example, in 1823, in an episode I will discuss later in the essay, when Lister wears black at the height of summer, on the sands at Scarborough, holidaying with her lover, Mariana Lawton (née Belcombe, the 'M–' of the journals), Mariana's sisters and a clutch of social acquaintances who leave Lister to take her chances with the stares and whispers and other unkindnesses of strangers. However, at the moment that Lister in black makes her debut, in the late summer of 1817, at the age of twenty-six, she is triumphant:

Spent the whole of the morning vamping up a pair of old black chamois shoes & getting my things ready to go & drink tea at Cliff-hill. As soon as I was dressed, went to drink tea with the Miss Walkers of Cliff-hill. Went in black silk, the 1st time to an evening visit. I have entered upon my plan of always wearing black (Tuesday 2 September, 1817).[16]

The practice of wearing all black originates both from social levelling traditions and from the practical requirements of the northern English male gentry travelling on horseback.[17] In adopting the wearing of black as a fashionable style – and therefore as a socially distinguishing rather than socially levelling practice – Lister anticipates the Byronic hero of Edward Bulwer-Lytton's silver-fork novel *Pelham* (1828) by more than a decade.[18] More specifically, in adopting black as a fashionable style for young women, Lister anticipates Coco Chanel's 'little black dress' by just over a century. Undertaken by a young, single woman, Lister's performance and fashionable practice of wearing all black puts into circulation for her contemporaries a strange and perplexing social semiotic – particularly striking given that fashionable dresses worn by young women in this period were almost invariably all white.[19] Lister's black attire, combined with an unusual walking gait and 'mustaches' were part of a repertoire of effects which her contemporaries identified as masculine.[20]

Byronism is the code which makes Lister's masculinity legible. Whilst Lister differs from Byron in gender, rank, sexual practice, party-political identification, religion and region, her sociable performance is paradigmatically Byronic. A female, Tory and landed gentry performance of a male, radical aristocratic libertine Whig style, Lister's Byronism offers a leading example of the commodification of aristocracy which marks Romantic public culture: literally, a *gentrification* of Byron. In this way, Lister's Byronism also embodies the crossover between capital and landed gentry status. For if one way in which Byron instantiates nobility is by exploiting the prerogatives of what Norbert Elias has referred to as 'prestige-consumption' or the 'status-consumption ethos' to go into debt and to lose land, Lister enacts the gentry-based 'income-expenditure' model which involves keeping 'consumption below the level of income so that the difference can be invested in savings in the hope of increased future income'.[21] Lister's Byronic accoutrements – such as the volumes of Byron's poetry which are mobilized as tools of seduction and tokens of exchange to cement lovers' vows – are themselves entered into this table of expenditure.

Engaging the interrelations of class, rank, gender, sexuality, social and sociable style that are put into play by Lister's performance of Byronism enables us to ask what happens to the code of the gentleman when it is taken up by a gentlewoman? How preposterous is Lister's perfor- mance as the social persona she refers to as 'gentleman Jack'? What kind of social imposture is enabled and effected by Lister's mobilizations of Byron, by her elaborate rhetorical and corporeal prosthetic enact- ments as the Byronic woman? Lister's style of masculine embodiment is modelled on this elusive fetish of the gentleman, as she suggests in the following account of breakfast with Mrs Priestley, an older female acquaintance, talking politics: 'her sentiments republican, mine monar- chical . . . I twirled my watch about, conscious of occasionally bordering upon a rather gentlemanly sort of style'.[22] This masculinity also has a distinctly military inflection, as in this 1818 account of a haircut like a helmet worn by soldiers in the Napoleonic Wars. Parsons, Lister's York hairdresser, 'cut me close behind, & curled my hair like the crest of a helmet at the top of my head, as they wore it 8 or 10 years ago'.[23] Even on a bad hair day, Lister still calculates a military effect, as in an 1824 account of the handiwork of a Parisian hairdresser whom she 'paid . . . 2 francs for making me a terrible grenadier-like looking figure'.[24]

This military self-fashioning occurs at the level of corporeal, sociable and sexual embodiment, and as political and cultural identification with the chivalric ideology that was clearly embraced by Lister as a member of an old landed gentry military family. As this code was instantiated rather mournfully by Lister's father, Captain Jeremy Lister, a fourth son and soldier wounded in the American War of Independence, Anne for a time looked to her younger brother, Sam, an ensign in the army in Ireland, to revive the family cult: 'You my dear Sam, are the last remaining hope and stay of an old, but lately drooping family . . . Renovate its languid energies . . . Ah! let the well-ascended blood that trickles in your veins . . . prove it not degenerated from the spirit of your ancestors.'[25]

Two months after this letter was written, Sam was to die by drowning, and Lister's father continued to bear the unwitting burden of signifying this 'droop' in the Lister family fortunes. Largely absent in the diaries, Captain Lister cuts quite a figure of pathos in his most memorable appearance as the bumbling country squire on a trip with Anne to Paris via London, where Anne is 'shocked to death at his vulgarity of speech and manner [and] perpetually in dread of meeting anyone I know'.[26]

If Lister's father embodies the droop of military honour into vulgarity, Lister aimed to renovate the family's languid energies and strengthen the family's property holdings through the economic and social capital from the moneyed and titled women she hoped to dazzle in Britain, Paris and at the Swedish court. Eventually, Lister managed to consolidate the land holdings of Shibden estate through her clandestine marriage in 1834 to Anne Walker. As neighbouring heiress of a worsted-manufacturing fortune, Walker brought the mixed blessings of new economic capital and *nouveau-riche* social vulgarity to Lister's old Halifax wool-money and ancient status claims.

SEXUAL SOCIABILITY

If we were to use Lister to ask how sociable, if at all, is sex? – to take up the question raised in Judith Barbour's chapter in this volume – then it would seem to be very sociable. All the significant sites and practices of Lister's northern rural gentry sociability – tea; music after tea; dinners; supper parties; house visits and parties; shopping expeditions in Halifax or York; public lectures;[27] visits to or assignations in the local library; walks; church; balls – function doubly as exercises in sociability and sexual flirtation/seduction.

Operating in the interstices of homosocial and heterosocial modes of sociability in Halifax society, Lister cultivates a particular style of social performativity that I want to call sexual sociability. It combines masculine and feminine modes of sexual sociability – at once 'gallant' and coquettish – involving '[a]rrant flirting', '*double entendre*' and 'agreeablizing':

'I saluted her left cheek ... My manner was not quite so flirting this morning.'[28] The code of gallantry, with its military inflections, becomes a critical component of Lister's mode of sexual sociability. As the social and cultural historian Niklas Luhmann points out, 'under the guise of gallantry, courting can take place – and to a certain extent without obligation – in the presence of third parties. Gallant behaviour provides adaptive links both to intimacy as well as to sociability and can bridge differences in rank.'[29] Nonetheless, as Luhmann also goes on to point out, 'gallantry is rapidly superseded as the demands for an individual stylization of love increase and as the bourgeoisie begins to usurp the behavioural models of the nobility'.[30] Gallantry is a somewhat archaic social and sexual form, then, outmoded by Romantic love and the 'moral legitimation of emotion';[31] but both of these codes inform Lister's social performance of gentlemanly flirtation. Arguably, it is precisely its archaic nature which makes gallantry available to Lister, since the particular claims to social capital that Lister can make good in the community of Halifax are her ancient status claims as landed gentry heiress of an old wool-farming and military family.

A critical support of Lister's Byronic mode of social performance and sexual sociability is Lord Byron's poetry itself and its relationship to the construction – albeit tentative – of Lister's own literary subjectivity. This literary subjectivity is heavily implicated in Lister's sociable–sexual performance and operates as a critical component of Lister's social persona. Lister's literary ambition was well published amongst her acquaintants, as was a knowledge of her journals, the existence of which unnerved these same acquaintances with their threat of disclosure. Lister's superior status claims and self-modelling as a literary subject are mutually implicating alibis which enable her to enjoin Lord Byron's poetry for a performance of rakish gallantry. Lister habitually recruits the services of a volume of Byron as a subject of conversation and tool of seduction, as in this account of afternoon tea in April 1818:

Mending my gloves, the trimming of my black bombazine petticoat and all in readiness for this afternoon ... At ½ past 5, went to the Greenwoods' ... Miss Browne & her 2 friends ... arrived in about an hour ... Considering her situation in life, Miss Browne is wonderful – handsome, or rather, interesting ... I wonder what she thinks of me? My attention to her is sufficiently marked to attract her notice. Is she flattered? I think she is. I have thought of her all the way home, of writing to her anonymously and (as she said, when I asked her if she liked Lord Byron's poetry, 'Yes, perhaps too well') of sending her a Cornelian heart with a copy of his lines on the subject. I could soon be in love with the girl.[32]

Here, the figure of 'Lord Byron's poetry' functions with the 'conspic-uous visibility and cryptic formality of a code',[33] in this case, of sexual knowledge. Miss Browne's coy reply to Lister's question – 'Yes, perhaps too well' – is flirtatious and knowing, or at least performs the requisite knowingness that is the recognition and acknowledgement of a code. 'Lord Byron's poetry' is located, then, at the nexus of knowledge and desire – a trope of the unnameable as the nonetheless desirable. Miss Browne has to answer to 'liking' the poetry. What is required of her then is not the production or explicit naming of that knowledge or code – most definitely *not* this in polite company – but some pledge of affective relation to this metaphor of the unspeakable. Miss Browne's pledge – ringing with innuendo – doubles for Lister as the hint of reciprocated sexual interest. As Luhmann writes, 'the tactics of seduction centred pre-cisely on exploiting such signs as the basis for something more'.[34] There *was* something more, and Lord Byron's poetry becomes an intricate machine of sexual flirtation and deferral between Lister and Browne for the next two years. A few days after this exchange, they chance to meet at the Halifax library – both, as it would happen, in pursuit of a copy of *Childe Harold's Pilgrimage* (1812). From then on, Miss Browne undergoes an extended period as 'Anne's shadow' – as the wagging tongues of Halifax put it – before marriage in 1819, the year coincidentally that the first two cantos of *Don Juan* are published.

Three years after the initial exchange with Miss Browne, Byron appears as the far less successful social host and lubricant of a dinner-party conversation about improper reading matter, this time between Lister and a neighbouring married couple who fail to make the link between *Don Juan* and *Lallah Rookh* (1817), by Thomas Moore, Byron's co-confector of Oriental romance:

Mr Saltmarshe sat with us all the time after tea. Long talk about what books were improper & what not. They mentioned *Lallah Rookh* their not finding it out. I said I thought it as much so as ... the two first cantos of *Don Juan* ... I don't know how it is, I thought Emma a little under restraint on this subject before her husband & that he might be a little so, before his wife. I have often thought married people the best company when separated (30 March 1821).[35]

This scene of conjugal domestic sociability pantomimically enacts the Sedgwickean 'privilege of unknowing'[36] – a particular kind of norma-tive power of ignorance – maintained in this case through the grim conspiracy between each of the marriage partners to 'not finding it out'. In a parodic reversal of the previous scene of sociable reading with

Miss Browne, the sexual tension that informs the knowing operation
of the shared code is thoroughly evacuated here as Byron is forced to
circulate as a closed book rather than an open secret.

Such are the awkward social moments – often with the husbands of
Anne's past or present attachments – that Lister converts into opportunities for her particular brand of droll social satire. In Halifax society,
the 'oddity' of Lister's flirtations are to some extent licensed, or at least
tolerated, as the intense friendships that form a critical part of premarital
female homosociality. Outside that space, whether it be in York, alone,
or in a wider social setting, where the forms of sociability are far more
circumscribed as modes of display, Lister's social persona takes on a specific kind of visibility, oddity and sexual publicity of gender deviancy, and
is forced to instantiate scenarios of the unsociable, the anti-sociable, the
social failure and social outcast.

As Jill Liddington has suggested, Lister becomes subject to various
forms of 'rough music' – those traditional carnivalesque forms of popular social outrage and sociability directed against unpopular, irregular
or unnameable forms of social and sexual conduct.[37] Particularly after
Anne Walker comes to live with Lister at Shibden Hall, a whole repertoire
of enforcements of compulsory heterosexuality are brought to bear upon
Lister's gender deviance and the unnameable and unrepresentable form
of irregular social and sexual conduct which these new living arrangements imply. These enforcements take a range of forms. There is the
homophobic charivari of hoax marriage advertisements in the local paper, undertaken as part of the Whig campaign in the 1835 elections to
discredit Lister, an active Tory supporter during the elections. There are
recurrent rumours of Lister being burned in effigy in neighbouring pad-
docks. Finally, there are the regular occurrences of physical and verbal
abuse and sexual harrassment which Lister undergoes. A particularly
chilling example of this harrassment occurs in the form of a living effigy, when a man dressed in black approaches Lister walking home in
a country lane on her way back from a social call at the vicarage of
Halifax. He introduces himself as 'Joseph Lister of Shelf', and invites
her to get to 'know' him. Lister brushes this episode off as another of
'these ignorant impertinences', but it is clear that she had feared for her
safety, having to 'walk forwards at a smart pace'.[38] Lister is subjected
to repeated taunting that emphatically targets her masculinity, as, for
example, when a group of men in York hail her as she walks past with
'That's a man' and 'Does your cock stand?'[39] In answer to this eloquent
piece of Yorkshire rough music, we might say, with Judith Butler, that

Anne Lister's cock stands to 'repeat and displace through hyperbole, dissonance, internal confusion, and proliferation the very constructs by which [gender norms] are mobilized'.[40] Lister's hyper-embodiment and surplus corporeality as a gendered subject work to effigize that fetish of the gentleman *as* a construct of gender, class and status.

Lister, as the Byronic woman – a form of bionic woman whose Byronic prostheses work to rebuild and to remediate aristocratic glamour in gentrified, phantasmatic social forms – instantiates the eighteenth- and nineteenth-century social and literary occupation of self-modelling after the fetish of the gentleman.[41] In place of the missionary position – and that missionary position *manqué* that De Quincey attributes to 'the class of unmarried women above twenty-five . . . who, for mere dignity of character, have renounced all prospects of conjugal . . . life, rather than descend into habits unsuitable to their birth'[42] – Lister chooses the Byronic position. Lister, rather than Byron, because, as Christensen points out, 'the Byronic position . . . need not and finally cannot be occupied solely by Byron'.[43] And the question of position – social, sexual and Sapphic – is everything in Lister.[44] If, as Christensen argues, ' "Byron" is the transitional figure between an aristocratic culture of honor and a middle-class culture of commerce',[45] Lister's female gentrification of Byron embodies this transitional status at the level of gender and status position.

In the 1820s, in the wake of the French Revolution, Waterloo and Peterloo, and the consolidation of English radical culture into the parliamentary reform movement, the aristocracy's supposedly natural claims to rule are not self-evident; these claims have lost their grounding and are self-identical with the textual supplements and prosthetic supports of Edmund Burke's 'ensigns armorial'.[46] Lister's version of the gentleman – like her Byronism and like the Byronic position itself – is a 'remediation' of an already mediated effect.[47] These fetishes of aristocratic masculinity become the subject not only of discursive production, but of social enactment, social competition and commercial transaction. Lister's main social, sexual and economic rival is another Halifax landowner, Christopher Rawson. Rawson had run away to sea and returned to become the leading local banker, Deputy Lieutenant and county magistrate, and purchases for himself the medieval trappings of the Lordship of the Manor of Southowram.[48] Gender trumps class, and new gentry trumps old, as these public offices which might rightly be due to the heir of Shibden – that is, to Lister, were she a man – are bought by this masculine representative of new gentry profession and money.

Disqualified through gender from the race for patrimonial accoutrements and public offices, Lister's competition occurs at the level of
social performance, where success is measured by the degree to which the
performance can be said to command. The Byronic performance was of
course available to any old rake, any old contemporary Regency fashion
victim. But merely donning the clothes of the Don – 'à la milord Byron' –
is not enough for success, as Lister makes clear in her sardonic reading of
the performance of one Sir William Ingleby, an 'eccentric baronet [who]
walks about Ripley & Ripon . . . in his dressing gown, without smalls or
neckcloth on [and whose] naked throat, shirt-collar displayed à la milord
Byron, had a striking effect . . . the scarecrow impression'.[49] In this wry
account of the failed Byronic performance, Lister demonstrates that
vulgarity is not the exclusive preserve of the mercantile classes. Lister's
obsessive charges of vulgarity throughout the diaries launch pre-emptive
and retaliatory strikes against the snubs and slurs of her social equals,
superiors and inferiors. Lister's strategy is to discriminate amongst performances of style and vulgarity, pitting claims of status, rank and symbolic capital against those of gender and economic and political capital.
Lister's claims of status and rank can often – but not always – trump the
demands of gender.

Just as Lister's diaries might be said to instantiate the 'eye in search of
variance',[50] they also instantiate the eye in search of vulgarity – and with
a vengeance. No one, it seems, is safe from Lister's basilisk eye. (Certainly
not the middle-class British women whom Lister encounters in her travels to Paris between 1824 and 1826, finding 'not much style about any
of them'.[51]) Lister levels the charge of vulgarity against strangers, social snubbers, social and sexual rivals, family members and current and
prospective lovers alike. 'Vulgarity is a bad concern with me', Lister
intones ominously, reflecting on one Ellen Empson, who 'merely suited
me a little to flirt with . . . before she was married'.[52] The vulgar company of Ellen Empson is enough to dampen Lister's usually irrepressible
enthusiasm for *double entendre* and Byronic innuendo – her two favourite
modes of flirtation, after all – to such an extent that on one occasion she abstains from both: 'Ellen rather boisterously talkative & she
& Mrs Waterhouse had all the conversation, which they turned rather
towards the *double entendre* . . . Mrs Waterhouse asked me afterwards if
I had read *Don Juan*. I would not own it . . . I thought Ellen quite vulgar.'[53]
As Lister deliberates over the pros and cons of extending the flirtation
with 'the fair charmer' Miss Browne into a more lasting sexual relationship, and the social relationship it will necessarily entail, she muses,

'What sort of a connection am I forming?'[54] Even for Anne Walker, with whom Lister will eventually exchange vows in a clandestine marriage, it is irredeemable vulgarity at first sight: 'Miss Anne Walker & I were tête-à-tête ... Very civil, etc, but she is a stupid vulgar girl. Indeed, I scarce know which of the party is the least vulgar & I have no intention of ... letting the acquaintance go one jot further.'[55]

In Lister's parlance, 'éclat', together with style, is a particularly important category of social performance. Eclat is (1) brilliant display; dazzling effect. (2) social distinction; conspicuous success; universal approbation (*OED*). Eclat is the speculative social stock that lubricates Lister's social and sexual exchanges. It is socially capitalized style – the dazzling mirage shimmering in the skirts of so many eligible young women which so often turns out to be illusory, disguising its other of vulgarity or mere *in*distinction. (Even so, as Lister herself says, '[a] lady's dress always strikes me, if good or bad'.[56]) Too often, the charms of a beautiful young woman will conceal at home a drunken '*mater familias*', inclined 'to clip the King's English'[57] and indulge the vain hope of hitching the mercantile family wagon on to Lister's superior social capital, or hoping to make 'a stepping stone' or 'cat's paw of [her] to get into society'.[58] Lister will take but not give éclat. Except to Mariana: 'When I can give her éclat it will be very well.'[59]

One of the ways in which Lister hopes to 'give éclat' to Mariana is through a particular kind of social performance. This is the successful Byronic performance which – unlike the unsuccessful one enacted by the 'eccentric baronet' – transforms social awkwardness into social success, mere scandal into *succès de scandale*. Lister's Byronism aspires to the status of precisely such a magical conversion. To the extent that Lister's diaries offer no self-conscious declaration or articulation of an intention to imitate Byron, Terry Castle has argued that Lister's Byronism is 'unconsciously modeled' and the stuff of a 'subliminal Byronic fixation'.[60] However, even an unconscious or psychic form of 'modelling' is directed towards and legible only within the context of the larger social and cultural script. In this way, it would seem to be more productive to understand the mode of sociable–sexual performance I am calling Lister's Byronism as the habitual performative quotation of a widely circulating and disseminated code – an always already fetishized Byron – which crosses the literary system and the social system. As I suggested earlier, Byronism as both a literary system and a social system is implicated in Lister's aspirations for literary fame, elaborated in the early diaries. When Lister writes of having '[t]alked [to my aunt] of my ambition in the literary way, of my wish for a name in the world',[61] she engages literature as a mode of ambition and as a means of securing a 'name'. Literature is a way of transforming social notoriety into a prestigious form of social publicity or distinction. It provides Lister with the possibility of distinguishing herself from and amongst her provincial neighbours: 'Determined to devote myself solely to study and the acquirement of that literature which may make me eminent and more decidedly above them all hereafter.'[62]

More than literary fame itself, then, literature is a means of turning the social liability of Lister's 'oddity' into triumphant social capital. Literature is pursued as a form of symbolic capital to be translated into social capital. Indeed, given that Byronism crosses the literary system and the social system – and mediates crossings between these two registers – Lister's Byronism is more interesting and exemplary on account of the fact that Lister does *not* become a published writer, in that it demonstrates that the 'literary system' is positioned within and across the social system, has disjunctions and conjunctions with the social system. That the literary system can be used as a strategic system within the social system, and that it can be exceeded by the social system, is suggested by the ways in which Lister's literary ambition is overtaken in her later diaries by her landowning ambition.

ROUSSEAU 'FOR THE STYLE'S SAKE'

I have been arguing that Lister adopts a Byronic persona which is as much socially performative and sociable–sexual as literary. A more explicit model of specifically discursive or literary identification and imitation is offered in Lister's appropriation of Jean-Jacques Rousseau. The most significant generic precedent for Lister's journal writings was Rousseau's *Confessions* (posthumously published 1782–9, and translated into English in 1782 and 1786–90). As Lister writes in 1825: 'From 7–40 to 9½, reading aloud to myself from p. 42 to 50 (*very* carefully) vol. 1, Rousseau's Confessions. I read this work so attentively for the style's sake. Besides this, it is a singularly unique display of character.'[63]

Lister's appropriation of Rousseau 'for the style's sake' presents a significant rereading of Rousseau. It produces Rousseau's genre of the confession – predicated on sincerity against artifice – as a 'style' to be imitated. This imitation instantiates the fate of distinction in the public sphere to be subject to counterfeit.

That the most private, subjective and sincere of Romantic genres – the confession – can be reproduced as a style to be imitated and forged and displayed places Rousseau's 'sincerity' on the same level of cultivated artifice as Byron's repertoire of masks and personas. Lister's refiguration of the Rousseauvian genre of the sexual *Bildungsroman* produces not a private and subjective mode of sexuality, opposed to the social – and for Rousseau sexuality is definitely not sociable, or has no need to be[64] – but a highly socialized and sociable model of sexuality.

Lister's appropriation of Rousseau works to transform the French Revolutionary hero of simplicity and sincerity against aristocratic corruption, luxury and dissipation into a fetish of 'style'. This resignification of Rousseau as style subverts Rousseau by turning him into a specifically female affectation, a piece of decorative artifice, a supplement, like the phallus which appears in Lister's speculations on the sexuality of acquaintances and sometimes in her sexual fantasies. Rousseau is made over into an accessory of precisely the kind of landed, religious and feminine mode of culture that he opposed. Anglican and Tory, Lister engages Rousseau for style and as a model of a sexual *Bildungsroman*, but detaches from this prosthetic model Rousseau's radical Enlightenment cultural politics.

Lister's appropriation of Rousseau suggests how important sociability is for Romanticism, by demonstrating the extent to which the genre of the diary and the Rousseauvian sexual confession are performative, as well as socially constructed and sociable. Lister's diaries offer a paradigmatic instantiation of the Romantic confession after Rousseau, but they present a private subjectivity which we see in its social and sociable guises, going out into sociable sorties, both socially and textually performative. As Habermas suggests, '[s]ubjectivity, as the innermost core of the private, was always already oriented to an audience (*Publikum*). The opposite of the intimateness whose vehicle was the written word was indiscretion and not publicity as such.'[65] For Habermas, the diary is a critical genre for this practice of 'audience-oriented privacy'.

Such a conception of the public and socially oriented production of the private individual underlies Niklas Luhmann's formulation of the 'stylization' of the individual and the culture of 'affect-management'.[66] These ideas are predicated upon an understanding of the individual not as an isolate, but as a socially recognized entity who is required to perform his or her individuality within a repertoire of codes and modes of affect. These modes of 'audience-oriented privacy' and 'affect-management' are instantiated in Lister's emphasis on the 'unique display of character'. The 'display' of character foregrounds the performative function of character. To copy someone for the 'unique display of character' has the immediate effect of questioning the integrity of that 'character', through the fact that it is subject to 'display' and that the display is itself copied.[67]

Traditional histories of Romanticism have tended to invoke Rousseau's *Confessions* as the canonical model of Romantic autobiography, in order to corroborate a version of Romanticism which privileges subjectivization and individuation over socialization and social formation, locating a truth in an individual experience opposed to social experience. Whilst Rousseau does produce arguably the most extreme version of the Romantic anti-sociable – so extreme that, as Carol Blum points out, Rousseau formulated the category of pity in order 'to repudiate the idea that man is naturally sociable'[68] – this rhetoric is itself both 'audience-oriented' and sociably staged even in its anti-sociability.[69]

Another critical way in which Lister's diaries engage Rousseau is in the production of a particular rhetoric of Romantic love, predicated upon an opposition between the natural sincerity of the individual against the artifice of the social, of the true lover against the worldly beloved. Based on a language of sentiment,[70] this rhetoric is addressed to Mariana Lawton – Lister's dearest and most passionately beloved lover. It is elaborated most strenuously in an extended diary entry of 1824, written when the tempestuous relationship between the two has all but exhausted itself in the effort to sustain itself for almost ten years as a long-term, long-distance affair after the marriage of Mariana in 1815 to Charles Lawton. The entry is an extraordinarily sustained love lyric as elegy, which offers a 'display of character' and in which Lister's 'attentive' reading of Rousseau 'for the style's sake' appears to be paying off, so smooth is its rendition of the sentimental and Romantic Rousseauean lover:

She is too tamely worldly . . . She loves me, I do believe her, as well as she is capable of loving, yet her marriage was worldly . . . it never struck me as it does at this moment (Thursday 21 August, 3. 55 pm, 1823). It now opens upon me as the key of all, that all I have never yet been able to comprehend in her character . . . The time, the manner of her marriage. To sink January, 1815, in oblivion! . . . Suppliant at her feet, I loathed consent [to the marriage] but loathed the asking more . . . It was a coward love that dared not brave the storm &, in desperate despair, my proud, indignant spirit watched it sculk [*sic*] away. How few the higher feelings we then could have in common! The chivalry of heart was gone. Hope's brightest hues were brushed away. Yet still one melancholy point of union remained. She was unhappy. So was I. Love scorned to leave the ruin desolate; & Time & he have shaded it so sweetly, my heart still lingers in its old abiding place, thoughtless of its broken bowers, save when some sudden gust blows thro', & screeching memory is disturbed.[71]

The entry opens optimistically enough, with a reference to 'the erotics' of the previous night. However, as Lister begins to take stock of the considerable burden that Mariana's shame and social embarrassment about Lister places upon the relationship, she finds the burden is becoming intolerable: 'But oh! no more. "The heart knows its own bitterness" [a quotation from the Bible] it is enough.'

A repeated quotation from the *Confessions – je sens mon coeur, je sens mon coeur* (I know my own heart) – becomes the refrain in this Rousseauvian torch song in which Lister and Mariana enact the respective parts of 'chivalry of heart' and a 'coward love that dared not brave the storm'. 'Mary', Lister apostrophizes, 'your caution cheats the world out of its scandal.'[72]

This formulation begs a couple of questions. It asks, how sociable is scandal?, and, when does a scandal become a *succès de scandale*? It produces at least two very different meanings of scandal, both of which are attached to the scandal of sexual publicity. Lister's heroic invocation of scandal rhetorically converts the scandal of spectacle and dysphoric sexual publicity into the positive social value of a *succès de scandale*. The *succès de scandale* is the most Byronic and glamorous sociable animal, involving a socially outflanking mode of social and sexual publicity, visibility and notoriety. It is a socially distinguishing mode of spectacle that dares to assert its own authority, commands success and demands to be obeyed and imitated. Scandal inspires the begrudging recognition of superior symbolic capital achieved through the shock tactics of notoriety, a recognition manifested in the desire to emulate. For Lister, the *succès de scandale* is that miracle of the transubstantiation of her own social 'oddity' into a source of interest, social rivalry, sexual competition, gossip and glamour. In this way, Lister's heroic invocation of scandal casts Lister's inviolable 'heart' within the terms of a particular form of sociability and worldly interest – and does so at the very moment at which Lister repudiates Mariana's tainted love on account of its 'worldliness'. Even more than this, however, and with the same contradictory – because worldly – logic, the scandal itself becomes the unattainable object of desire.

Finally, as though all that remains without the prize of scandal is to respond in kind to the 'worldly' Mariana, the entry closes with a bathetic swerve away from an intensely subjective Romantic Rousseauvian persona to a socially preoccupied persona: 'Went downstairs at $8\frac{1}{2}$. Breakfasted ... took leave & off from the Belcombes ... Wrapt in musing. Thought of ... my manners and appearance. Building castles

about their improvement; elegance; engagingness, etc. the good society
I hope to get into.'[73]

In recounting the affair with Mariana Belcombe – Anne's *grande
passion* – the diaries tell a love story, of love both requited and unrequited. However, that love story is also a story of social mobility and
social performance. Paradoxically, a critical component of this social
performance is the Rousseauvian persona of the true and sincere lover
who repudiates worldliness and its social and sociable forms of artificiality
and hypocrisy.

In *Don Juan* (1819–24), the word 'scandal' circulates like a charm, a
dare, a command to be obeyed. It answers, recapitulates and recircu-
lates the *succès de scandale* of Lady Caroline Lamb's silver-fork *roman à
clef, Glenarvon* (1816), which novelized Lamb's brief affair with Byron and
functions as curtain-raiser to her ventriloquization of *Don Juan* in *New
Cantos* (1819). In September 1823, Lister's copy of *Glenarvon* is circulated
amongst acquaintances during a holiday at Scarborough with Mariana
and her two sisters, Lou and Eli, where Lister makes a scandalous spectacle of herself that is anything but a success. Here, as she writes, 'I
seem to have no proper dress. The people stare at me', 'I must manage
my appearance and figure differently.'[74] Lister's copy of Lamb's *succès
de scandale* is loaned to women of their acquaintance, who thank her for
it only to later snub her. Anne finds out later through a mutual social
acquaintance that they had heard 'that I was masculine ... they are
determined not to know me'.[75]

The Scarborough holiday involves acute dramas of sexual publicity,
enforced sociability and social unease. It is a particularly anxious time
for Anne and Mariana in the private and public negotiation of their
relationship, and for Anne herself in being without the toleration of her
oddity to which she is accustomed in Halifax society. The holiday is
initiated by an episode of extreme social mortification referred to by
Lister in the diaries as 'the 3 steps business'. It starts out simply enough:
the arrangement was for Anne to meet Mariana in Halifax and join her
on her journey, stay with her for one night in York and then return to
Halifax while M– went on to Scarborough, where Anne was to join her
later. However, instead of waiting for the coach to bring M– to Halifax,
Anne decides to set out from home in Shibden Hall across the moors 'to
be in time for the Manchester mail, to meet M– on whatever part of the
road she might be'.[76] Here she is, braving the wild country road which
will take her to the woman she loves:

Between the 9th & 10th milestone, passed the division stone between the coun-
ties of York & Lancaster. A dreary mountain moor-scene ... A countryman
observed in passing, 'It's but a wildish place, this.' The inn soon came in view ...
I had just determined to go in & order a little boiled milk ... when I spied the
carriage winding up the hill. It was a nameless thrill that banished every thought
but of M– ... It was just 11.50 as I reached the carriage, having walked about
10 ½ miles in 3 hours, 10 minutes.

When Lister meets the carriage, the reunion which should have been
carried off as a sociable meeting becomes instead a spectacle bordering
on scandal:

Unconscious of any sensation but pleasure at the sight of M– who, with Lou,
had been dozing, one in each corner of the carriage, the astonished, staring eyes
of the man & maid behind & of the post-boys walking by the horses were lost to
me & , in too hastily taking each step of the carriage & stretching over the pile
of dressing-boxes, etc., that should have stopped such eager ingress, I unluckily
seemed to M– to have taken 3 steps at once. I had still more unluckily exclaimed,
while the petrified people were bungling about the steps, that I had walked
all the way from Shibden. What with exclamation & with stride, the shock so
completely wrapt round M–'s heart it left no avenue to any other feeling than joy
that her friend, Miss Pattison, was not there! She would have been astonished &
M– horror-struck. Why did I say I had walked from Shibden? Never saw John's
eyes so round with astonishment; the postboys, too ... But the poisoned arrow
had struck my heart & M–'s words of meeting welcome had fallen like some
huge iceberg on my breast.[77]

Leaving the iceberg on Lister's breast in all its tragic glory just for
the moment, I want to stop first for another chance meeting in this
chapter between Lister and De Quincey over the mail. Lister, like
many of the women in De Quincey's writing, 'risk[s] being run over
by an English mail coach', as Mary Jacobus has put it. In Jacobus's
witty formulation, 'what De Quincey is worried about is that ... the
mechanology of style, gaining momentum of its own, might over-
run thought and cause a fatal accident in which the feminine (the
language of feeling) is the casualty'.[78] On this occasion, the casualty of the fatal accident is the ideal of the properly female sociable
style which is given the fatal blow by Lister's 'eager ingress', spurred
by the 'nameless thrill that banished every thought but of M– ...
[u]nconscious of any sensation but pleasure at the sight of M–'.[79] The
hidden casualty of this tragi-comic moment, jostled by the commotion of
the 'postboy's wonder' and 'the petrified people ... bungling about the

steps', is Lister's heart, struck by 'the poisoned arrow' of M–'s 'shocked astonishment', which makes Lister feel, 'yes, unutterable things ... "Shame, shame," said I to myself, "to be so overcome"'.[80]

As Anne joins Mariana and Lou in the coach for the ride to Leeds, the iceberg on Lister's breast appears to thaw, but in reality has merely plunged itself deeper into her heart: 'We were now all quite right & merry. Alas! I had not forgotten. The heart has a memory of its own, but I had ceased to appear to remember save in occasional joking allusions to *"the three steps"*.'[81] The heart's memory puts this moment into cold storage, snap-frozen into the euphemism of 'the three steps' to be retrieved painfully and obsessively from that point on as a nagging trope of both M–'s social shame of Lister – growing ever more visible and public – and Lister's knowledge that this shame must be confronted: 'This "3 steps" business haunts me like a spectre. I cannot throw it off my mind; it is my 1st thought in the morning & last at night. It teems with reflections that discomfort me.'[82] This chilly 'spectre' haunts Lister from the moment she arrives at Scarborough: 'Got to Scarbro' at 7. Eli received me. M– & Lou out walking. Eli & I went out to meet them just the cliff end of the street ... the "three steps" business so in my mind, I seemed coolish, I daresay, & formal.'[83]

Together with the figure of 'the postboy's wonder', the figure or spectre of the 'three steps business' is repeated in the account of the holiday. It haunts Anne's thoughts as well as the conversations between Anne and M–. In one conversation, M– says to Anne: 'You know, my Fred, I love you very dearly ... but ... I would not have you excite wonder, even in a postboy.'[84] To which Anne replies in her diaries with that familiar mode of apostrophe from her lofty position of wounded Romantic lover: 'Mary! Your friend had other things to think of than a postboy's wonder.' Referring to M–'s '*shame* that prouder circumstances did not attend me', Lister asks rhetorically: 'Had I driven up in my own chaise & four, I might have stepped with impunity, heedless of the world's opinion or the postboy's wonder. But she is worldly, therefore she is selfish.'[85] The term 'worldly' here denotes for Lister the pursuit of material wealth signified by the chaise and four, but it also refers to the worldliness of sociability. Shame is a form of worldliness which cuts right at the heart of identity. As Rita Felski suggests, '[s]hame ... is fundamentally connected to everyday sociability'.[86] The power of Mariana's shame to haunt Lister attests precisely to the way in which this poignant form of worldliness can cut to the quick of one's innermost core of identity – or 'inmost soul' as Lister puts it, referring to the resting point of the 'poisoned arrow' and 'huge iceberg' of Mariana's shamed 'welcome'. Lister bares 'the agitation of [her] inmost soul' to Mariana, only to be pierced anew by more of Mariana's shame over the most superficial of details: 'the awkwardness of the cut & curl of my hair'.[87] Somehow, we sense that a chaise and four would not have been enough to enable Lister to 'step with impunity' that fateful morning. Better to have stayed at home, as she had earlier in 1819, when she declined an invitation to meet M– at the mail-coach stop in Manchester so 'that she may get a sight of me': 'too forlorn in spirit & in wardrobe'.[88]

In staging complex dramas of sexual publicity, scandal, shame and visibility, Lister's diaries often illuminate sociability through its very absence. The 'three steps episode' at the inn between York and Lancaster and the sociable occasions of the holiday at Scarborough itself present a tableau of failed sociability, anti-sociability and dysphoric sexual publicity, of sociability gone horribly wrong as it veers uncontrollably into spectacle, and the twilight world of stares and whispers, of social cuts and social ostracism, and the overnight crash of hard-earned social-speculative stocks of éclat. Each of these occasions demonstrates the relations between sociability, gender performance and the social enforcement of compulsory heterosexuality, in quite different ways. The 'three steps episode' turns on an excess of intimacy in a social and sociable space. It is a moment in which sociability turns into a scandal available as a spectacle across classes, as the 'postboy's wonder' demonstrates.

In the ostensibly more fashionable, fluid and mobile space of the watering-hole at Scarborough, strict codes of gender nonetheless inform social performance and suggest gender as a critical component of the consolidation of compulsory heterosexuality as a regulatory category. Here, in this elite social space of fashionability and sociability, Lister embodies a particular kind of sexual publicity and gender deviancy, as she does in the streets alone in York faced with the taunts of groups of labouring-class men. In illuminating the social enforcement of compulsory heterosexuality which occurs through seaside gender performance amongst the British elite in the post-Napoleonic summer watering season, Lister's diaries are compelled to instantiate scenarios of failed sociability – to enact sociability's others of anti-sociability, social failure and shame that are her lot as a social oddity. As Felski suggests, '[t]he opportunities for experiencing shame increase dramatically with geographic and social forms of mobility, which provide an infinite array of chances for failure, for betraying by word or gesture that one does not belong to one's environment'.[89]

However, if Anne Lister's diaries suggest a consolidation of compulsory heterosexuality, they also suggest at the same time the instability of this regulatory category. They do this by suggesting how different spaces of sociability, such as the circles of Halifax society, work to tolerate and enable different degrees of gender and sexual deviance, different degrees of both witting and unwitting parody as a resistant strategy. Lister's diaries testify to the exploitation of a range of social and rhetorical spaces that enable the social performance of a particular kind of parodic female masculinity and female-to-female sexual sociability.

Michael Warner pointed out in the early 1990s that 'the energies of queer studies have come more from rethinking the subjective meaning of sexuality than from rethinking the social'.[90] This has to some extent been the case with much work on Anne Lister. Lister's explicit quotation of Rousseau, the writing in cipher, the staging of a subjective and solitary self, have made Lister available for recuperation within a particular model of Romantic subjectivity, a model of the literary or sexually deviant subject identified with sincerity, solitude and an expressivist model of writing which has underwritten not only much Romanticist studies but much lesbian and gay studies too.

In this chapter, I have attempted to engage Lister's writings to think about how we might make sense of the category of sociability as it is applied to a set of texts and practices which have until recently been understood in terms of subjectivization and solitude. By considering the confessional production of sociable style in the genre of the journal – that least sociable of literary genres – I wish to have suggested a more socialized account of the Romantic confessional genre. Indeed, Lister's journals, in their habitual instantiation of Byronic and Rousseauvian rhetorical prosthetics, necessitate an account of the Romantic confessional genre as a slavishly social and sociable beast. They also elaborate a leisured English gentry female style of rhetorical, social, sociable and sexual mobility which cuts against De Quincey's grain of compulsory – even if *in abstentia* – heterosexuality. Lister's negotiation of sociable and sexual opportunity is informed both by an extraordinary symbolic mobility and an acute anxiety about downward social mobility and the contaminating effects of bourgeois, specifically mercantile, vulgarity. In this way, Lister's diaries stage not so much the drama of unrequited love and unrealizeable desire – though they do this too, in spades, as a drama of often quite extraordinary pathos and within a scrupulously trained and habituated Rousseauvian vocabulary or 'style' of Romantic love – as the friction of clashing and competing tribadic class, social, sociable and sexual styles, that do not always rub one another the right way.

NOTES

My thanks to Susan Conley, Sarah Lloyd and Gillian Russell for their helpful comments and suggestions.

For full citations see Bibliography.

1 Christensen, *Lord Byron's Strength*, pp. xvi–ii.
2 *Ibid.*, p. xx.
3 Klancher, 'Prose', p. 285.
4 Christensen, *Lord Byron's Strength*, p. 12.
5 De Quincey, 'Style', p. 78.
6 *Ibid.*, pp. 66, 67.
7 See Lister, *Own Heart*; Lister, *No Priest*; Liddington, *Female Fortune*. All references in this chapter to Lister's diaries are to these published editions. For an excellent account of the long history of familial and scholarly suppression of the diaries, see Liddington, *Female Fortune*, pp. xiii–xxi and pp. 235–41, and 'Anne Lister'; Anderson, 'Historian's Notebook'.
8 For earlier readings of Anne Lister in relation to Byron and Rousseau, see Castle, 'Diaries', pp. 103–4, p. 101; Clark, 'Anne Lister's Construction', pp. 31, 37–8; Moore, *Dangerous Intimacies*, p. 127.
9 Binhammer, 'Sex Panic', p. 411. The term 'compulsory heterosexuality' was coined by Rich in 'Compulsory Heterosexuality'.
10 Habermas, *Structural Transformation*, p. 31.
11 In re-engaging Habermas's category of 'dependence', I am not arguing against bourgeois independence, or suggesting a straightforward process of imitation and emulation. Rather, I wish to stress that the bourgeois take on aristocratic culture occurs as a dialectic of imitation and differentiation.
12 Christensen, *Lord Byron's Strength*, p. xvi.
13 As Elfenbein points out, 'the celebrity [is distinguished] from merely famous people as a figure whose personality is created, bought, sold, and advertised through capitalist relations of production'; *Byron and the Victorians*, p. 47.
14 Lister, *Own Heart*, p. 344.
15 Butler, *Psychic Life of Power*, p. 2.
16 Lister, *Own Heart*, p. 14.
17 See Harvey, *Men in Black*, p. 27.
18 On *Pelham* and Byronism, see Elfenbein, 'Byronism.'
19 As William Hazlitt observes the following year in 1818, 'a white muslin gown is now the common costume of mistress and maid'; 'On Fashion,' in *Complete Works*, vol. XVII, p. 55.
20 Lister, *Own Heart*, p. 296. Recently, Judith Halberstam has claimed Anne Lister as an example of 'female masculinity', which she elaborates within a larger rubric of 'gender deviance'; see *Female Masculinity*, p. 46. Halberstam's

important formulation revises 'the unproblematic categorization of Lister and her desire as a lesbian', a view which is exemplified in Clark's 'Anne Lister's Construction of Lesbian Identity'. However, whilst Halberstam eschews this category of the lesbian for reasons of Foucauldian historical correctness, she seems to fashion nonetheless a somewhat essentialized and ahistorical version of masculinity for Lister to embody.

21 Elias, *Court Society*, p. 67.

22 Lister, *Own Heart*, p. 330.

23 *Ibid.*, p. 64.

24 Lister, *No Priest*, pp. 49–50.

25 Liddington, *Female Fortune*, p. 10.

26 Lister, *Own Heart*, p. 219.

27 See the chapter by Gillian Russell in this volume.

28 Lister, *No Priest*, p. 25; Lister, *Own Heart*, pp. 244, 136, 342.

29 Luhmann, *Love as Passion*, p. 76. I designate these codes as modes of sexual sociability to indicate their dual role in terms of sex and sociability, as sociable modes of sexual behaviour.

30 *Ibid.*, p. 78.

31 *Ibid.*

32 Lister, *Own Heart*, pp. 41–2. Lister's spelling of Miss Browne's name varies: She will be referred to here as Browne.

33 Christensen's pithy formulation for the 'method' of homosexual allusion which circulated between Byron, John Cam Hobhouse and Charles Skinner Matthews. See *Lord Byron's Strength*, p. 60.

34 Luhmann, *Love as Passion*, p. 72.

35 Lister, *Own Heart*, p. 151.

36 Sedgwick, 'Privilege of Unknowing', p. 23.

37 See Liddington, *Female Fortune*, pp. 247ff. For a general account of this social form, see Thompson, 'Rough Music'.

38 Lister, *Own Heart*, pp. 316–7.

39 *Ibid.*, p. 49.

40 Butler, *Gender Trouble*, p. 31.

41 On the 'recreation of the English gentleman', see Langford, 'Manners', pp. 294ff.

42 De Quincey, 'Style', p. 67.

43 Christensen, *Lord Byron's Strength*, p. 65. Christensen produces this formulation in honour of Percy Bysshe Shelley, for whom he reserves a privileged place in the Byronic position. Christensen withholds a seat in the Byronic position from Lady Caroline Lamb, choosing instead to present her with the somewhat proverbial and disappointing charge of 'vulgar Byronism', (p. 140).

44 Lister's diaries canvass a range of sexual positions. On these, and on a range of ideological and definitional positions on the subject of 'Saffic regard' and its relations to friendship and sexuality, and in relation to the question of sexual techniques and technologies, see esp. *No Priest*, pp. 31–2 and 49–50.

45 Christensen, *Lord Byron's Strength*, p. 72.

46 Burke, *Reflections*, ed. O'Brien, p. 121. Bourgeois culture may well be the 'phantom of aristocratic values', as Jean Baudrillard has suggested in *For A Critique*, p. 119, but it did turn conversation into critique by challenging the claim to nature of title.

47 Remediation refers to the process by which a single interface or mediating force is replaced by multiple interfaces (such as virtual reality or the filming of a novel). See Bolter and Grusin, *Remediation*. In this sense, performances of 'Byron' by, for example, Shelley, Lamb and Lister, are remediations of 'Lord Byron' as an already mediated textual and social effect.

48 Liddington, *Female Fortune*, p. 20.

49 Lister, *Own Heart*, p. 312. The 'scarecrow impression' clearly falls short of the intended 'Juan effect', celebrated by McGann and Christensen; see McGann, '*Don Juan*', p. 83 and Christensen, *Lord Byron's Strength*, pp. 214–15.

50 Jeanette Foster's is the original 'eye in search of variance'. See her pioneering account of 'sexual variance', lesbian representation and literature, *Sex Variant Women*.

51 Lister, *No Priest*, p. 12.

52 Lister, *Own Heart*, p. 185.

53 *Ibid.*, p. 131.

54 *Ibid.*, p. 74.

55 *Ibid.*, p. 189.

56 Lister, *No Priest*, p. 102.

57 Lister, *Own Heart*, p. 86.

58 Liddington, *Female Fortune*, pp. 92, 98.

59 Lister, *Own Heart*, p. 294.

60 Castle, 'Diaries', p. 103.

61 Lister, *Own Heart*, p. 82.

62 *Ibid.*, p. 46.

63 Lister, *No Priest*, p. 103.

64 On Rousseau's masturbatory model of sexuality, which is part of his asocial formulation of the natural man in *The Social Contract*, who is 'subject to few passions, [which can in any case be sufficed] unto himself', see Blum, *Rousseau*, p. 89. Rousseau's anti-sociability is also elaborated in the *Discourse on Inequality*, where Rousseau identifies sociability with effeminacy: 'in becoming sociable and a slave, [man] grows feeble, timid, servile; and his soft and effeminate way of life completes the enervation both of his strength and his courage', Part One, p. 86.

65 Habermas, *Structural Transformation*, p. 49.

66 Luhmann, *Love as Passion*, p. 17.

67 For a recommendation of the 'copying' of conversations of men of genius, see Disraeli, *Dissertation on Anecdotes*, p. 51.

68 Blum, *Rousseau*, p. 89.

69 Not only 'audience-oriented' but also sociably staged before actual audiences, the *Confessions* derived much of its impact from specifically sociable readings, when Rousseau would read out loud from the work. News of the

readings was often met with rage, however, by friends whose foibles were exposed, such as Mme Epinay, who asked the lieutenant of police to forbid further readings of the *Confessions*. See Blum, *Rousseau*, p. 84.

70 For a reading of the relationship between Lister's language of sentiment and her performance of masculinity, which suggests that Lister adopts the persona of the 'man of feeling', see Gloria Prentice, 'Anne Lister's Pilgrimage: Forging a Sexual Identity as a Masculine Woman in the Long Eighteenth Century', Hons. thesis, University of Melbourne, 2001, p. 25.

71 Lister, *Own Heart*, pp. 282–3.

72 *Ibid.*, p. 282.

73 *Ibid.*, p. 283.

74 *Ibid.*, pp. 295, 294.

75 *Ibid.*, pp. 294–5.

76 *Ibid.*, p. 277.

77 *Ibid.*, pp. 278–9.

78 Jacobus, *Romanticism, Writing and Sexual Difference*, p. 134.

79 Lister, *Own Heart*, p. 278.

80 *Ibid.*, p. 279.

81 *Ibid.*, p. 280.

82 *Ibid.*, p. 285.

83 *Ibid.*, p. 292.

84 *Ibid.*, p. 284.

85 *Ibid.*, p. 285.

86 Felski, 'Nothing to Declare', p. 39.

87 Lister, *Own Heart*, p. 279.

88 *Ibid.*, p. 102.

89 Felski, 'Nothing to Declare', p. 39.

90 Warner, 'Introduction', p. x.

Counter publics: shopping and women's sociability

Deidre Shauna Lynch

At stake in my chapter are two histories whose interconnections we have been reluctant to acknowledge: the history of 'the birth of a consumer society' and the history of 'the structural transformation of the public sphere'.[1] For more than a decade, scholars of eighteenth-century Britain's new forms of commercialized leisure have investigated the challenges this developing consumer culture posed to old mappings of social experience, the topography of public and private domains especially. Yet despite this scholarship there has been little alteration of the gendered framework we deploy as we sort out the relations between consumer spaces and public meanings.

An 1817 article entitled 'Remarks on the Progressive Improvements in Dress' can remind us of how we usually construe those relations. The issue of *La Belle Assemblée*, John Bell's upmarket fashion magazine, in which it appears was published two months after the Spa Fields Riots that shook London in December 1816. Perhaps some readers finished perusing the 'Remarks' and then went out to attend the trial of William Hone, the publisher whose vociferous support for reform had marked him out for government persecution. But we know in advance that if we read the issue for how it reflects this turbulent historical moment when monarchy appeared on the brink of collapse, and when other organs of British print culture were publicizing alternative forms of public solidarity and undergoing prosecution for those endeavours, we are preparing ourselves for disappointment. It does not, sadly, come as a surprise that the vignette the *Belle Assemblée*'s staff historian of fashion supplies when she arrives at another era of political crisis reduces historical change to the petty dimensions of a wardrobe crisis. 'In such governments [as Oliver Cromwell's protectorate]' the *Belle Assemblée* observes, 'feathers and flowers lose their honourable and elevated station, and seldom is a new hat or a new trimming invented during the epoch of republican triumph.'[2]

When she opens *The Proper Lady and the Woman Writer* with a point-by-point comparison of the *Gentleman's Magazine* and the *Lady's Magazine* (the fashion magazine that was the predecessor and chief competitor of *La Belle Assemblée*), Mary Poovey observes the same phenomenon: how civics lessons that target a female audience can seem in fact to lead women away from the public sphere, interpellating them instead as agents of private acts of acquisition – of self-adornment especially. In 1793 both journals opened the new year 'with a statement of purpose and response to the trial and death of France's Louis XVI'. Readers of the *Gentleman's Magazine* were warned that the fate of all of Europe was involved in the death vote taken by the Jacobins. Engaging those readers as individuals authorized to form opinions about public affairs, the editors retraced for their benefit the proceedings that had led up to parliament's recent passage of the Alien Act. By contrast, the *Lady's Magazine*, Poovey remarks, addressed its female readership in ways that fortified the gendered boundaries between public and private. It downplayed civic choices in favour of sartorial choices. 'That the *Lady's Magazine* is especially interested in the appearance of the king is borne out by this detailed description, which has no equivalent in the *Gentleman's Magazine*: "His hair was dressed in curls, his beard shaved; he wore a clean shirt and stock, a white waistcoat, black florentine silk breeches, black silk stockings, and his shoes were tied with black silk string."'[3]

Embedded in these turn-of-the-nineteenth-century examples, at least as I have served them up here, is an excessively familiar proposition: civic consciousness and fashion consciousness do not mix. The corollary to this proposition, one that renders it the scaffolding for a rigid conception of sexual difference, is a description of this period's social boundaries that takes it for granted that eighteenth- and nineteenth-century Englishwomen had no opportunity to think of themselves as public beings: civic consciousness and fashion consciousness do not mix, one is supposed to surmise, any more than in a culture regulated by the 'doctrine of separate spheres' the genders did. This chapter on women's sociability offers a modified view of the modishness pursued by the readership of the *Lady's Magazine* and the *Belle Assemblée* as it sets out to challenge these ways of using gender as the boundary marker that segregates participation in the marketplace on the one hand from public action and political activism on the other. To pursue this aim I follow recent readings of Jürgen Habermas's *Structural Transformation of the Public Sphere* and invoke the concept of a 'counter public'.

Habermas, one suspects, would have little patience with the interest in millinery these period examples ascribe to female Britons living in the so-called golden age of the public sphere. At the same time, there is no shortage of dissatisfaction over Habermas's lack of interest in women: over his readiness to applaud institutions – the eighteenth-century coffee-house notoriously – whose claims to serve as sites of an egalitarian and potentially all-inclusive publicness were not only contradicted by their exclusion of women, but predicated on that exclusion.[4] *The Structural Transformation of the Public Sphere* proposes that a new symbolic politics – a battle between 'public opinion' on the one hand and the arbitrary dictates and secret practices of the absolutist state on the other – came into being in the Enlightenment, when new sites of sociability and mechanisms of affiliation (coffee-houses, clubs, self-improvement societies, routinized periodical publishing) permitted bourgeois men to engage in rational debate over public measures. Habermas's best feminist critics have acknowledged the value of the utopian elements in this account: that it may be most useful when we treat it not as a historical description, but as a normative account of what democratic modes of association and discussion might achieve. They have also pointed out that the 'classical' public sphere whose institutions Habermas describes coexisted from the start with other sites for public deliberation and competing ways of articulating a horizon of intersubjectivity. Miriam Hansen and Nancy Fraser have used the term 'counter publics', coined by Terry Eagleton, to identify those alternative formations of publicity. They have cautioned that to pretend that there was a time when the classical public sphere was the only game in town, to overlook the existence of these discursive arenas in which 'members of subordinated social groups . . . formulate oppositional interpretations of their identities, interests, and needs', is to accept at face value the category error at the heart of Habermas's account: the identification of a particular (bourgeois, white, male) public as *the* public.[5]

At the same time that I take my cue from these feminist revisions of the Enlightenment's definitions of public action, I am also intent on challenging a second, somewhat neglected dimension of the gender politics underpinning Habermas's history. Proposing that after the eighteenth century the Enlightenment public sphere began to dissolve under the pressures of nineteenth-century consumer capitalism, Habermas chronicles a degenerative process leading from the 'classical' public sphere to the 'pseudo' or 'mass' public and from 'cultural discourse' to 'cultural consumption'. Like many legends of the Fall, this narrative has troubling implications for women. By and large, women's histories lie outside Habermas's purview – except, importantly, when he observes that the women who were excluded from the eighteenth-century political public did participate in the reading public that was the latter's staging ground, the crucible in which its ideals of critical judgement were elaborated. Yet in so far as it reworks the *Dialectic of Enlightenment* (reinstating Horkheimer and Adorno's identification of the 'culture industry' with the 'castration' of the worker), and in so far as it recycles, as well, the admonitions against unmanly commerce elaborated in the eighteenth-century discourse on luxury, Habermas's history does double duty as the story of a (bad) feminization of culture.[6] The women his historiography excludes do play a part. They are cast as the public sphere's inside saboteurs, a role they take up once they appear on the historic stage, in stereotypically feminine guise, as the subjects of consumption – as material girls.

I think it is possible to construe the relations between commerce, the public sphere and women's historical agency in a way that would deviate from Habermas's. True, he does not consistently cast those first two categories as antinomies. He concedes that from their beginnings his coffee-houses often metamorphosed into places of business (not only selling coffee, but serving as clearing-houses where stock jobbers kept up with the latest economic news). But Habermas also narrativizes the relationship between commerce and the public sphere – outlining a process in which commercialization represents the sad, feminized sequel to public sphere conversation. He thus takes away with one hand the concessions he offers with the other. To tell a different story, I shall concentrate on a fifty-year period that begins in the 1780s – the decade in which 'public opinion' first becomes a watchword of British print culture,[7] and in which 'shopping', according to the *Oxford English Dictionary* (which quotes Frances Burney's journals) also makes its earliest appearance in print. This is the decade, too, in which Burney – denied access to the very technologies of publicity and public opinion that fascinate her throughout her work – failed to publish a text that will be central to my argument. This is *The Witlings*, the play Burney wrote in 1779 and revised the next year, and which, because of the objections of her family, was never sent to the London theatre managers. What made *The Witlings* appear so risky a vehicle for the Burneys' social and literary ambitions was, I shall suggest, its dramatization of the debates over taste that engaged the republic of letters (deliberations that, as Peter Hohendahl claims, 'pave[d] the way for political discussion in the middle classes').[8] The metatheatre of Burney's comedy – Burney's staging of the literati staging themselves – brings to the fore the histrionic aspects of such deliberations. It demonstrates that the public use of reason at stake in the Enlightened salon involves not only the logical relations between arguments but also, since this reasoning is simultaneously a sociable practice, the passionate relations between persons. It involves communications with and from bodies as well as minds.[9] Burney goes a step further still. She also pointedly makes her characters' literary debates the mirror image of the fashion counselling and gossip sessions that engage the workers and clients on both sides of the counter in Mrs Wheedle's millinery shop.

Burney came of age at a moment when, thanks to developments in the architecture of retail space and changes in the protocols of buying and selling, the 'private' world of market exchange – of the apparel trades in particular – began to offer itself to Englishwomen as a stage on which they could produce themselves as public beings.[10] My chief aim in reconstructing her work as a Romantic theorist of the public is thus to recover the pun that Habermas's revisionists have concealed in that term 'counter' publics. Transactions over shop counters, I shall argue, could make that strange amalgam of female leisure and female work we call shopping into an occasion on which women of the English middle classes might acquire the ability to articulate certain aspects of their existence as 'public' issues. With relative impunity, they could within the homosocial space of the shop become 'public women'. They could acquire a group identity. In this way, the point of purchase could even become a launching pad for political activism. Habermas's example authorizes a mode of cultural history that makes room for speculation about utopian possibilities. And so I will conclude this chapter in a speculative vein as, turning to women's writings of the period 1798 to 1815, and to an era when sociability was politicized as never before, I begin to outline the terms of this activism: how the fashion-conscious counter public interacting in milliners' shops might have set about the process of realizing its utopian, and feminist, potential.

When Frances Burney's German fan, the novelist Sophie von La Roche, travelled to London in 1786 she kept a journal reporting her impressions not just of the authoress of *Evelina* and *Cecilia* but also of the institutions that made English civil society look enlightened. La Roche's ardour for England's public culture – for a land, she writes, where 'thought, tongue, pen and press are free' and where 'the public is the great tribunal by whom all judgments are made' – anticipates the most idealistic moments of *The Structural Transformation of the Public Sphere*. Her itinerary around London is designed accordingly. It takes her, for example, to a print shop (where the crowd, anticipating a favourite occupation of the late twentieth-century mass public, is contemplating cartoons depicting the 'life and marriage of the Prince of Wales'). Before that it takes her to a meeting of a debating society, 'where all topics of interest to an Englishman are discussed: 6d a person is the charge'. After La Roche notes that many Englishwomen were in attendance as the assembly debated the question, 'Whether it is useful or harmful to create a number of peers of the realm as has recently happened', she adds, 'This kind of pastime after tea and work is an added proof that common sense and reflection are very common in England.'[11]

La Roche had in fact arrived in London at a moment when debate was all the rage. As sponsors of 'rational entertainment and mental improvement', as sponsors too of the piquant thrills of social levelling, of opportunities to mingle with strangers who might be of any origin, debating societies had caught the fancy of a moneyed public. They sprang up across the city in the 1780s.[12] Held in tea rooms, ballrooms and taverns, their weekly meetings often attracted audiences in the hundreds. Included in these audiences – as the organizers were eager to point out – were growing numbers of women, who came not only to listen to the arguments but also, increasingly, to make them. The newspapers took considerable glee in reporting on the public appearance of these 'fair orators' (as well as in puffing the advent of the handful of debating clubs – among them one named 'the Female Congress' and another named 'the Belle Assemblée' – that for brief intervals in 1780, 1781 and 1788 admitted women exclusively). That the papers were quite taken with the novelty value of this diverting new mode of theatre (as historian Mary Thale observes, public disputation generally 'was a kind of theater') is clear.[13] They do not seem, by contrast, terribly intent on either asserting or querying the *social* value of women's participation in these public activities.

Sophie von La Roche's response to the debate she attends is more highminded. And one can imagine that, in some measure, her enthusiasm about public deliberation is directed towards the ways in which speech in this setting is hedged about with rules of order meant to make it 'free'. She admires what Michael Warner, in his work on print culture, identifies as the distinctive semiotic environment fostered in the public sphere, a context in which individual utterances acquire validity in so far as they testify to speakers' consciousness of the specialized medium in which all have consented to speak. '[T]hat consciousness of the medium is valued precisely because it remains unreconciled with the conventions of personal exchange.' Within the public sphere, linguistic exchange ceases to be a matter of relations between private individuals. Instead it is encountered as a vehicle that transforms those individuals, ridding them of their particular biases, enabling them to disappear behind the impersonal norms of public spiritedness.[14]

Indeed, to immerse oneself in writing by and on Habermas is quickly to learn that, in the project of publicness, disappearing acts are *de rigeur*. The metaphors that both critics and defenders of his liberalism summon to describe entry into the bourgeois public sphere often involve negation. We read, accordingly, of 'vanishing' and 'disembodiment' and a process of 'stripping away' that brackets the markers of social and economic inequality and leaves individuals who participate in this critical space purified – free to define the 'common interest' as they interact with one another in terms of what is purely 'human'. It is notorious, of course, that this concept of the public sphere as a zone where particularities *vanish* served to legitimate a form of class rule: a practice of domination that hinged on the transfiguration of the particular qualities of whiteness, masculinity and membership in the middle class that distinguished an emerging elite into the epitome of what was natural, normal and universalizable. For at the same time that certain men of property donned what (borrowing from Wordsworth) we might call 'a Coat of Darkness' emblazoned with 'the word / INVISIBLE', their concept of the universalist public made the bodies of others into 'glaringly visible signs of the particular, the self-interested, the merely private'.[15] The historical record makes it important to remember that the bourgeois public sphere has its own, historically specific regimes of value and taste, its own protocols of style.[16] It is salutary accordingly to discover that some debating clubs invited the men and women in attendance to don masks and dominos (the long loose cloaks worn to masquerades): in this way the clubs accommodated 'those who, from diffidence or any other objection, may be discouraged from appearing as public speakers'.[17] This sartorial device for transforming people into members of the rational public identifies public spirit with fancy dress, in a way that clarifies that reason, too, is a kind of style. It aligns the public sphere with other sites of dressing-up: theatres, for instance, or the shops that were home to the apparel trades – sites that are rather more overtly the haunts of the material girls, those putatively over-embodied citizens, whom Habermas exiles from the public sphere's official biography.

Remapping the late eighteenth century's sites of cultural congregation along the lines that realignment suggests can help us be more cagey

about the bourgeois public sphere's claims to stand outside the world
of commerce, fashionable appearances and fashionable sociability.
Reservations about those claims, both about whether they were achieved
and about whether they are desirable, may in turn make it easier for us to
grant authority to other, competing arenas of identification and deliberation – publics constructed by women included. Knowing that some
debaters of the 1780s were in the habit of donning fancy dress helps us acknowledge the performative dimensions of public sphere reason – how it
was, so to speak, materialized. Such an acknowledgement seems crucial
given recent criticism's tendency to bracket precisely these aspects of that
matrix of places, time and habits of speech and bodily disposition in which
ideas of publicness were first articulated. Michael Warner, for instance,
opts (following Habermas) to make the story of the public sphere's differentiation from state and civil society a story about the eighteenth-century
reading public primarily. His public is thus disembodied: first and fore-
most, a textual effect. However, to reiterate Habermas's emphases and
preferences in this way may anticipate subsequent developments that
are specific to the Romantic period. More important, such a response
to Habermas leaves unchallenged the ideological assumption that the
public sphere, a Romantic 'mental theatre' by definition, excludes
the material aspects of human existence.[18]

For this reason, it is important to note that a visit to a debating society
('crowded with all kinds of people') is not the sole occasion that sets Sophie
von La Roche musing on the topics of public access and participatory
parity. La Roche's proto-Habermasian statements about the maturity
of England's public institutions are also elicited at moments when she
considers herself the guest of a nation of shopkeepers and reports on
her shopping excursions. And La Roche is an inveterate shopper while
in London. For her, retail trade is another thing England does better:
'Every article is made . . . attractive to the eye . . . We especially noticed
a cunning device for showing women's . . . silks, chintzes, or muslins.' A
lamp-seller's shop inspires her to produce a piece of panegyric that – as
a mini-allegory of Enlightenment – does not, in its linkage of consumer
access to civic participation, sound so different from her description of
the debating society:

The highest lord and humble labourer may purchase here lamps of immense
beauty and price or at a very reasonable figure, and both receive equally rapid
and courteous attention. I stayed long enough to notice this, and was pleased
with a system which supplied the common need – light – in this spot, whether
for guineas or for pence, so efficiently.[19]

La Roche's tribute to the lamp shop also sounds disturbingly like modern-day advertisements, which likewise promote the cheery fiction that it is in the neutral zone of the shop floor that we who live in a stratified society can best realize the democratic promise of equality. (Everyone's money is good there, after all.) But before we turn in dismay from this shopper's guide, let us pause and ask what might justify extending the concept of publicness as La Roche's description of the lamp shop invites us to do. I wish to ground the answer to this question in historical specifics and to that end will pose a second question: what might La Roche have seen in the course of a London shopping excursion in 1786 that she could not have seen at home?

Here we might consider how often in Romantic-period Britain writers' preoccupation with the mechanisms of social integration – their interest, to cite Wordsworth's self-serving example in the Preface to the *Lyrical Ballads*, in how a poet could serve 'as the rock of defence for human nature; an upholder and preserver, carrying everywhere with him relationship and love' – manifested itself as fascination in particular with the money passing from hand to hand across shop counters, with the throngs of people, looking to spend or just looking, who were passing through the streets in the city's retail districts. 'At first I thought some extraordinary occasion must have collected such a concourse; but I soon perceived it was only the usual course of business.'[20] Even in Book 7 of *The Prelude*, a notably hostile account of urban crowds, Wordsworth's use of repetition suggests the surreptitious connections between his poetic ambition – to effect a new communal solidarity through poetry's 'moving' pictures – and the trading classes' desire – to create 'a world of moving objects', to speed up the mechanisms of communication and commerce that set commodities travelling and set people off in pursuit of them.[21] In fact, to many of Wordsworth's contemporaries the new 'shopping' – we should recall that for them the very word was a neologism – was notable for fostering cultural congregation, in ways that an older marketing had not.

Shops, Robert Southey wrote in 1807 in *Letters from England*, were no longer kept for the convenience of the people, but for their amusement. They were emphatically something more now than 'mere repositories of goods'.[22] In the *Letters from England*, Southey assumes the persona of a Spaniard exposed for the first time to the commercial mores of the big city of London. The choice of persona enables Southey's readers to indulge in some starry-eyed self-congratulation while they re-encounter the features of their retail modernity; it gives them a pretext for rehearsing what they already know about their recent history. Their history lesson brings

3. 'Harding, Howell, & Co.'s Grand Fashionable Magazine, No. 89, Pall-Mall' from R. Ackermann's *Repository of the Arts*, no. 3, vol. 1 (March 1809).

home to us, as well, the fact that by the end of the eighteenth century the arrangement and decoration of the shop had become important to retail practice in ways that would have seemed odd to the seventeenth-century peddler who moved from town to town or who had set up a stall in the market square, and odd, too, to the seventeenth-century customer who was likely used to doing business while standing in the street, dealing across the dressing board that might be set up in the window frame of a house that fronted the market square.[23] Southey's Spaniard applauds those shifts. He waxes so enthusiastic over the care London tradespeople take over the display of their wares that one can easily picture him pressing his nose against their show windows (themselves a new feature of retail architecture).[24] While he walks along Exeter Change ('a sort of street under cover . . . with a row of shops on either hand'), his eye is caught by 'a pair of shoes in one window floating in a vessel of water, to show that they were water-proof'; in another window display he sees 'busts painted to the life, with glass eyes, and dressed in full fashion to exhibit the wigs which are made within, in the very newest and most approved taste' (*Letters* vii, p. 54; xiii, p. 77).

Shops had become destinations for a sightseer like the Spaniard not simply because they were visually attractive and boasted a greater variety of articles for the visitor to inspect, but also because one *could* merely look. Gradually over the course of the eighteenth century a policy of obligation-free browsing had been introduced into London emporia; such a policy was in fact to be expected in a new-style 'monster shop' like 'Harding, Howell & Co.'s Grand Fashionable Magazine' (a Pall Mall haberdashery), a large-scale enterprise consistently so crowded that its forty employees could devote little time to individual customers (see fig. 3).[25] With fixed prices and even price-tags also becoming the norm, the social interactions that transpired in the interior of the shop could henceforth be various in nature. One could do something in a shop besides buy. Formerly the shopper had had to keep her wits about her, be ready to haggle with shopkeepers over the price of their wares. A different perceptual approach to the world and a different way of incorporating market exchange into everyday personal interaction fell into place once (to quote the Spaniard) 'the usual morning employment of English ladies [was to] go a-shopping . . . that is, to see curious exhibitions. This [the English ladies] do without actually wanting to purchase any thing' (*Letters* xi, p. 69). Shops had become public sites in which a woman might be seen herself and see, and network with, other women. Shopping could now serve as a pretext for and mechanism of sociability: a licence to join the crowd.

Feminist scholarship has taken a rather jaundiced view of efforts to claim that this transformation in consumer behaviour epitomizes human progress. It has, for a start, highlighted what is troublesome about the habitual association of shopping with female leisure and pleasure – just the association Southey is helping to codify. (As Meaghan Morris observes, a shopping expedition, like the related activity of the 'family holiday', may be more accurately described as a case of 'women's work in leisure' and as such associated with a range of moods that extend beyond pleasure: 'anger, frustration, sorrow, irritation, hatred, boredom, fatigue ... moments of ... sceptical, if not paranoid assessment'.)[26] Yet at the same time feminists have also noted that, in contradistinction to an old-style marketing, which involves the satisfaction of needs ('stocking up' on that which is 'indispensable'), shopping implies 'a more leisurely examination of the goods', a selection of one object rather than another, and 'behaviours ... more directly determined by desire'. Although there is no disputing that they come at a cost, opportunities for women's agency and self-invention do inhere in that concept of choice on which shopping pivots. As shoppers we can mentally 'try on' the goods on display and be transported into new identities. We can achieve, that is, a mode of mental if not social mobility, even if, in doing so, we inevitably confront the discrepancies between this imaginative power, our spending power and our earning power.[27]

However, in highlighting this refashioning of subjectivity, feminist commentary has largely neglected how the 'birth of a consumer society' might also have instituted a new horizon of intersubjectivity. But shopping facilitates various kinds of 'social work'. A dialogue published in 1807 by William Gilpin, a figure better known as a theorist of the picturesque and of a rather different mode of 'just looking', expounds on those social meanings. One of the parties engaged in Gilpin's comparison of 'The Advantages of a Town Life and a Country Life', warns of the noxious influences to which young men are exposed in the metropolis. This Mr Willis spotlights the technologies of publicity that had recently been adopted by radical politicians. Gilpin writes, of course, at a moment when the debating society no longer appeared a modish diversion (as in the 1780s) but instead looked to be the chief engine of what his contemporaries liked to call 'the wholesale trade in sedition'. What is startling in the dialogue is how Willis's expression of anxiety over the effects on men of 'pamphlets in shop windows' and 'clubs and meetings – where ... licentious speeches are ... applauded', is juxta-posed with a derisive account of women's shopping – a lament that modern shops supply the setting for women's extradomestic sociability.[28] Willis proposes to his interlocutor that 'a censor ... be appointed by authority, at the corner of every street, to question each lady passenger, on what errand she was bent'. Sir Charles commends the scheme, despite his status as the dialogue's spokesman for the advantages of urbanity. He is particularly approving when he figures out that censors might prevent 'fair itinerant[s]' from 'going a-shopping':'It would keep many a gadding female out of mischief – it would save the shopkeeper much trouble – it would make the streets more comfortable, and commodious for those who had real business –; and, above all, it would keep mothers from misleading their daughters.'[29]

This reference to the shopkeeper's 'trouble' suggests that women who chose browsing over spending could still in 1807 be blamed for violating proper customer behaviour (the ethnography of shopping in *Letters from England* notwithstanding).[30] Part of the social work involved in Romantic-period shopping lay, indeed, in just this style of bad behaviour. It is worth scrutinizing with care the lady who spent her days 'cheapening' and 'routing over every body's best goods' and who then went home without making a purchase (or who, even worse, left the shop with the goods but – ready to abuse the credit system that shopkeepers in the higher end of the market maintained well into the nineteenth century – did so without the least intention of paying for them).[31] For this woman was for-tifying the boundaries of social class. She was teaching haberdashers and milliners their place. (This was a popular pastime. Edward Copeland as-serts that in women's fiction of the period the petty shopkeeper represents the 'universal scapegoat'.)[32] In studies of the eighteenth-century and early-nineteenth-century marketplace, Elizabeth Kowaleski-Wallace and Adela Pinch have suggested that the disorderly female shopper (the woman who shopped too much or, waiting too long to pay, turned shop-ping into theft) should be viewed less as a figure of individual pathology and rather more as an adept of certain social knowledges and rituals of so-cial control.[33] Everyday intimacies between the lady and the shopkeeper could be said, that is, to have the same kind of impact on the 'nation of shopkeepers' as the covert electioneering that the most aristocratic ladies managed to engage in (despite their formal disenfranchisement) when they flexed their consumer muscles at election time and cultivated their connections with the voting tradespeople. In each case, the shopping in question is far from being a purely private act of self-gratification.

It is, of course, through considering precisely this aspect of female con-
sumerism that Gilpin's dialoguing gentlemen find *their* common ground.
Both Sir Charles and Mr Willis assert that one might draw a firm line
between women's 'business' and the putatively 'real business' engaging
men (who, we are to presume, never shop); they concur that the city is
no place for ladies; and so they agree to call in the censors and send the
gadding females home. At a moment not long after the Pitt government
had introduced restrictions on public assembly, when the governing elite
was stepping up its struggle to control and define the forms of political sociability, Gilpin's gentleman-spokesman frets aloud over what his
womenfolk might get up to, not simply when they leave the precincts of
the home, but when they go into public spaces *together*.

In 1807, when Gilpin published his *Dialogues*, the bourgeois project of
publicness (needing to be insulated as never before from the buffeting it
would get in the crowd) was commencing its retreat to 'the virtual space
of print' – and so to the safety of the domestic interior. Eventually, Kevin
Gilmartin notes, the exercise of public reason would be almost wholly
reinvented in de-socialized terms – exemplified for Robert Southey 'by
the individual reader at his "breakfast table," absorbing a newspaper
"while he sips his coffee"'.[34] It might be useful to qualify Gilmartin's
picture of domestic dissociation, however, by emphasizing that as policies of obligation-free browsing became the norm the shop was being
reinvented too: as a woman-friendly site of assembly, perhaps partak-
ing of some qualities of that other object of Gilpin's gentlemen's fear,
the debating club. Indeed, as something besides a theatre of buying and
selling, the shop might have served – if only *in potentia* – as a theatre for
deliberating and debating.

The Romantic-period audience for the drama had long been acquainted with plays that required their spectators to think through these
relations between sorts of 'theatre' – between the building the spectators
enter to watch the show and other 'scenes' of public action. That audience therefore was possibly quite adept at negotiating the confusions
Gilpin produces when he aligns the street life of his female consumers
with the political life of his endangered young men. After all, theatre,
as Julie Carlson remarks, 'subverts [the eighteenth and nineteenth century's] burgeoning domestication of sexual difference'. Accounts that
differentiate the sexes by segregating private spaces from public ones
are dramatically self-cancelling when they occur on stage, for 'the body,
the masquerade, the spectacle that is associated with "woman" fuels the
house but disrupts the home'.[35] One might think here of the scene in

The Country Wife that is set among the booths of the New Exchange (an urban space that was in some ways a prototype for the pedestrian mall, and was largely reserved for female-owned businesses – haberdashery, needlework, perfume-making). Getting the jokes that cluster around the fact that Margery Pinchwife's escape from rural domesticity leads her to the 'Change depends on our knowing about the interchangeability of various 'public' or 'professional' women – the female entrepreneur, the prostitute and, of course, the actress – in the Restoration imagination. And Oliver Goldsmith's *She Stoops to Conquer*, which hinges on Marlow's mistaken belief that he has arrived in a public inn when he is in fact in a private home, should also be seen as engaging in a kind of metatheatre – reminding its audience of how plays depend on their publics' willingness to subject private affairs to public scrutiny and to see the public space of the stage as a metaphor for private interiorized space.[36]

But when, in 1779, Frances Burney set the first act of *The Witlings* in 'a milliner's shop', and supplied the stage direction 'A Counter is spread with Caps, Ribbons, Fans & Band Boxes. Miss Jenny & several young Women at Work', she did something surprising.[37] Margaret Doody remarks on how 'striking' a piece 'of stage naturalism' Burney supplied in opening the play in this manner.[38] I think that it is even more remarkable how, on being ushered into the interior of Mrs Wheedle's shop, the audience enters a place with a double nature. It functions as a gynaeceum, a site that as such makes male characters in the play such as Beaufort and Censor anxious about their exposure to 'a ridiculous and unmanly situation' (I, 92); and, at the same time, it represents a kind of news room, a data processing centre. The male characters see Mrs Wheedle's establishment as a zone of female mysteries, 'a wilderness of frippery' (I, 419), and are made fretful by the hermetic nature of the seamstresses' sartorial vocabulary. (Aghast, Censor rolls his tongue over words such as 'furbelows', 'pompoms' and 'falaldrums' (I, 112–15; 329).) By the end of Act One, nonetheless, it is clear that the shop cannot in any simple way be associated with trade mysteries or feminine arcana (shop talk or girl talk), idioms stigmatized by the period's boosters of plain English. Despite its dedication to style, the shop is not the nexus, either, of the sort of sensualized language *mondaine* that (as Landes suggests) was attacked by late-eighteenth-century exponents of democratic publicness as the idiolect of women of the court.[39] Instead, Burney takes pains to demonstrate that the milliner's shop functions as a public crossroads for both people and intelligence, indeed, as a public sphere. Articles that are too spoiled to sell go into the show window, where they disseminate the fashions. Mrs Wheedle puts a 'tippet' on display for this reason. She notes (with some asperity, to be sure, as well as insight into the insecurity of her trade) that 'there the Miss Notables who Work for themselves may look at it for a Pattern' (I, 27–9). Mrs Voluble goes to Mrs Wheedle's shop to hear the latest news, and no one seems to mind that hunger for information, rather than the desire to buy, motivates her daily visits. Bending the ear of every shop assistant who will listen, she announces that 'it's the greatest treat in the World to me to spend an Hour or 2 here in a morning: One sees so many fine things and so many fine folks' (I, 43–6); and 'I'm sure you've a pleasant life of it here, in seeing so much of the World' (I, 464–5).

Over the course of Act One of *The Witlings*, in keeping with Mrs Voluble's insistence that she is at the nexus of a news culture, almost all the important pieces of intelligence that move Burney's plot find their way to the shop. For instance, the milliners, who are charged with making the trousseau, gossip with Mrs Voluble about the upcoming wedding of the play's heroine, Cecilia Stanley. This conversation ends prematurely with the arrival of Beaufort's half-brother, Jack, a character whom Burney pointedly portrays as a late-eighteenth-century descendant of the newshounds of *The Tatler* and *The Spectator*, figures whose frenzied ways of posting from one coffee-house to another, distributing the talk of the town, made them into human versions of the very newsletters they sought.[40] In a bravura way, Burney also arranges over the course of the first act for almost every one of her characters (or messages representing them) to circulate through the shop. The act closes with the entrance of Mrs Voluble's son, Bob, who comes in pursuit of his mother and whose lines make clear to the spectators the challenge the play has already posed to notions of women's natural affinities with domestic space: 'Why Lord, mother, you've been out all the morning, and never told Betty what was for Dinner!' (I, 475).

In the succeeding acts Burney launches her romantic comedy's storyline. Once more in the role of emissary, Jack hears news, which he instantly spreads, about a bankruptcy of which 'every body was talking' at the Exchange (II, 512). Cecilia's fortune, we learn, is involved in the banker's downfall, and it is likely that, having learned this, Beaufort's aunt, Lady Smatter, will use her power over her nephew's purse-strings to forbid their marriage. In shifting the scene as she sets this plot going, Burney makes another bold move. The sociable circle centred on Mrs Wheedle's shop counter has a genteel equivalent, we discover, in a second sociable circle which calls itself the 'Esprit Club' and which includes

Lady Smatter, a certain Mrs Sapient (already encountered ordering an apron from Mrs Wheedle), Jack's father, Mr Dobson, and a poetaster named Dabler. It exists (as Beaufort explains in some cancelled lines) 'for the discussion of literary subjects'.[41] The Club provides a test audience for Dabler's verse and also, in the manner of both the bluestocking salon and the modish debating society of the 1780s, a forum for discussions in which its members abide by certain rules as they engage a set topic. As business hours at Mrs Wheedle's shop become the occasion for sociability, so in the final two acts of *The Witlings* we again see the whole cast brought together on stage by an evening session of the Club, which takes place in Act Four in the 'Club Room' at Lady Smatter's house and is reconvened in Act Five in a parlour at Mrs Voluble's. (Mr Dabler, as it happens, has lodgings there.) Margaret Doody and Barbara Darby describe how, in creating this parallel, Burney confronts us with two different economies: 'everyone has something for sale'.[42] If in the first act, ribbons, ruffles, caps and aprons are exchanged, amongst the Witlings who give Burney her title the 'pseudo-currency is words; they are handled, tried on, palmed off, and advertised. They are even made, like the caps, in full view of the audience'.[43] Much as nothing is wasted by Mrs Wheedle's seamstresses (the goods they spoil end up in the window or are shipped off to City clients, whose ignorance of the mode makes them easy to please), so the prevention of waste is a constant concern within the precincts of Lady Smatter's talk-manufactory: Dabler 'never destroyed a Line he ever wrote in his life' (I, 275).

The ironies that Burney generates by aligning these two discursive arenas may be assessed in terms a bit different from those Doody and Darby employ, especially if we recall that in his account of the structural transformation of the bourgeois public sphere, Habermas made large claims for literary circles like the Witlings'. Literary criticism represents for Habermas a trial version – one, importantly, that could engage women and servants as well as men of property – of the new processes of rational discussion that converted intimate identities into public ones. In literary criticism, we see 'a rational-critical debate in the world of letters within which the subjectivity originating in the family, by communicating with itself, attained clarity about itself'.[44] In eighteenth-century reading clubs particularly, Habermas suggests, discussion proceeds as if among equals: differentials of status are suspended. As they forge the collective norms of 'good taste', these people who talk about literature – about, for instance, the conduct of Goethe's Charlotte 'in admitting the visits of Werter' (the Westminster Forum's topic of debate for October 1786) – are supposed

to be in the vanguard of Enlightened civil society.[45] This is why it is so
provocative that Burney, savvy to questions about the 'worth' of words
and mindful of the overlap between the bourgeois public sphere and the
commercial arena, levels the distinction between being a member of this
literary public and being a customer musing over a selection of ribbons.

And however much the Witlings themselves (not to mention the
milliners and their clientele) fall short of the heights of public spirit, rationality, or egalitarianism – instead, showing themselves to be ruthlessly
self-seeking and ready to come to blows when it comes to evaluating one
another's literary credentials – much within the play predicts the interest
that Burney's subsequent works will take in the mechanisms of social integration and public opinion. The later works seem increasingly marked
by one of the chief consolatory fantasies that attended on the Romantic
era's new modes of popular authorship: the fantasy, namely, that if public
opinion is not in one's favour it must be because that public is not public
enough, that an impersonal, self-regulating marketplace of ideas can be
relied on to judge rightly, except when it is insufficiently impersonal. As
the narrator of the last novel, *The Wanderer, or, Female Difficulties* (1814),
claims, shifting to a utopian register at the moment when that novel's
heroine has finally lost any credit she once possessed in the community,
'The public at large is generally just, because too enormous to be in-
dividually canvassed; but private circles are almost universally biassed
by partial or prejudiced influence.' (Wordsworth's insistence on differ-
entiating 'the People, philosophically characterized' from 'the Public'
alters the terms but makes a similar distinction.)[46] Within Burney's later
novels this idealizing of the public tribunal has odd effects on the characterization, turning particular characters into allegories of the social,
engendering what Catherine Gallagher calls the novels' 'attempt[s] to
generate a universal subjectivity ... to escape from the particulars of
novelistic "character"'. [47] A comparable endeavour – but one that in
this instance fails, to comic effect – seems to be at stake in *The Witlings* in
the description Censor gives of Mrs Sapient, who is the oddest Witling
because of her thoroughgoing muddling of the voice of universal opinion and her own particular voice. In Sapient's lines personal and doxic
effects are entangled: as Censor puts it, 'she retails all the opinions she
hears, and confidently utters them as her own' (I, 221–2).

Lady Smatter asks similarly discomfiting questions about the terms on
which the private can be connected to the public. When Cecilia dodges
a question about her accomplishments with the modest disclaimer that
'my pursuits, whatever they may be, are too unimportant to deserve

being made public', Lady Smatter responds in terms that, freighted with proto-Bourdieuvian insights into the public sphere's economy of prestige, blow the cover on the normally invisible ironies of publicness. When talk on topics that are ostensibly of common concern functions as a marker of one's own distinction, one might well have an interest in disinterestedness: 'if my pursuits were not made public, I should not have any at all, for where can be the pleasure of reading Books, and studying authors, if one is not to have the credit of talking of them?' (II, 16–17; 23–5).

Burney's characterization of Lady Smatter and Mrs Sapient proved controversial. Her mentors, her father, Charles, and the family advisor 'Daddy' Crisp, were convinced that the bluestocking circle headed by Elizabeth Montagu would see themselves as the originals for those characters. Consequently, *The Witlings* never received a reading outside Burney's family: in effect, Charles Burney and 'Daddy' Crisp warned Frances that if she published, she would perish. They urged her to keep 'not only the whole piece, but [also] the plot . . . secret, from every body'.[48] Ironically, however, within *The Witlings*, it is the process of going public – of divulging secrets, and not to select individuals, but broadcast to all and sundry – that salvages the play's romantic storyline. After Beaufort has in vain pointed out to his aunt that if she blocks his marriage to Cecilia, she will be condemned by 'the judgement of the World at large[, which] is always impartial' (II, 121–2), Censor succeeds in blackmailing Lady Smatter into giving her nephew's marriage her blessing. His strategy involves a threat to move into print – to deposit lampoons against Lady Smatter 'in every coffeehouse' and to supply epigrams for all the daily papers (V, 831). Lady Smatter's plan to use the law to prevent this publicity would merely, Censor says with a smirk, produce more publicity (V, 824). Publication – the mobilizing of public opinion – saves the day, reminding us that *The Witlings* is the product of a moment wont to make much of the supervisory principle that distinguished its bourgeois public sphere – 'that very principle which demands that proceedings be made public'.[49]

Censor is thus the *deus ex machina* of the play, but he is throughout an unpleasant figure (as his name suggests). It is annoying how this man trumps the other characters with his 'ability to make himself heard effectively' and with his control 'over personal reputation and instruments that can influence it, like the press and public gathering places'.[50] As Barbara Darby implies, through her portrayal of this ambiguous figure Burney anticipates the insights of those feminist critics who, correcting for

Habermas's blindspots, have analyzed how the genderings of bodies and statements function as ways of controlling the flow of information – how gendered constraints dictate which individuals can go public at all. There is a second feminist element to Burney's play I would like to underline. I do not think we should dismiss the sociability we see in Mrs Wheedle's shop: the potential that this space (which, more so than the salon, is open to all) has to provide the setting for a 'counter public' that might articulate 'oppositional interpretations of [women's] identities, interests, and needs'. It is worth recalling, with Rachel Bowlby and Rosalind Williams, that in late nineteenth-century France consumer leagues and feminist movements were considered natural allies, and worth recalling, with Erika Rappaport, that in late nineteenth-century London the project of facilitating feminine access to the public spaces of the metropolis was a goal held dear both by the feminist founders of women's clubs and by retail magnates such as Selfridge, who incorporated the female club within the spaces and meanings of their department stores.[51] Could a story of comparable alliances or collusions be told of Romantic-period Englishwomen and their shopping? Let me conclude with some speculations about the historical materials that would enable one to tell it.

When in *The Witlings* the news of Cecilia Stanley's bankruptcy first gets abroad, Lady Smatter muses that 'Nothing is so difficult as disposing of a poor Girl of Fashion . . . She has been brought up to nothing, – if she can make a Cap, 'tis as much as she can do' (II, 554–8). For a moment it seems possible that Cecilia, born a lady, but now penniless, may have to cross to the other side of the shop counter and turn milliner too. That plot turn is one Burney implemented in earnest in *The Wanderer*, begun in 1802, and a document of an era when women's economic insecurity became in new ways a public rather than a private issue. By the time Burney published her chronicle of 'female difficulties' in 1814, the reading public was well acquainted with stories of ladies who found themselves plunged from affluence by the death or desertion of a parent or husband: stories deliberately designed to convey readers from the front of the shop counter, where cold-hearted 'votaries of fashion' might expect to buy a cambric shirt for ten shillings, to the back of the shop, where the shirtmaker was revealed earning a mere threepence a day for her labours.

Through the 1790s particularly, and then for the next twenty years, writer after writer – essayists such as Priscilla Wakefield, author of *Reflections on the Present Condition of the Female Sex* (1798), and Mary Ann Radcliffe, author of *The Female Advocate* (1799), as well as the anonymous content-providers for the *Lady's Magazine* and *La Belle Assemblée* – pointed to how often women of all classes could find themselves suddenly depending on the needle for survival.[52] These writers demonstrated the high stakes of style decisions: how the choice to wear a plain sleeve rather than an embroidered one, to affix a train to a court dress rather than omit it, though to some women a mere matter of fashionable appearances, could for others spell the difference between employment and destitution. These women also excoriated the 'man milliner'. To do so they adopted (as Wollstonecraft had in her first *Vindication*) the tones of manly (and homophobic) republicanism and proved themselves the better men while decrying modern effeminacy. The targets of their rhetorical assault were those fops and dandies who, lisping 'fine phrases to females of distinction', compromised the period's gender norms as they usurped employments that properly, 'by right', belonged to women (see fig. 4).[53]

This feminist politicking 'stresse[d] the connections among women and depict[ed] as arbitrary the economic circumstances that produce[d] distinctions' between the female consumer and the woman who supplied her articles of consumption.[54] The writers who developed this rhetoric turned women's shared gender – and the female consumer's and female worker's encounter within the precincts of the milliner's shop – into the organizing principle for a new politics, using print culture to make issues that might be dismissed as particular, private matters count as matters of *common* concern. They projected new forms of public solidarity for women – and cast the market as the arena in which that solidarity might best be discovered and manifested.

Priscilla Wakefield thus scolds ladies who 'patronize such a brood of effeminate beings in the garb of men' – men who measure 'linen, gauze, ribbons and lace . . . displaying their talent in praising the elegance of bonnets and caps' – 'when sympathy with their humbler sisters should direct [ladies] to act in a manner exactly opposite'. Wakefield calls for a consumer boycott – 'women of rank and fortune . . . should frequent no shops that are not served by women; they should wear no clothes that are not made by them' – and concludes with an attempt to subordinate consumption patterns to the public good: 'For once let fashion be guided by reason, and let the mode sanction a preference to women.'[55] Mary Lamb's essay 'On Needle-Work', published pseudonymously in the *British Lady's Magazine* in 1815, also responds to the economic vulnerability of women in the needle trades. Lamb not only stresses these cross-class connections between women. In her vision of female solidarity she makes it a tricky business to distinguish the woman who extends her patronage from the one who receives it. In this argument about

4. C. Williams, 'The Haberdasher Dandy', 1818.

why needlework should never be a fashionable pastime but instead be
preserved as one of the few remunerative employments open to women,
moneyed ladies turn out to be at once the employers and the debtors
of working-class milliners. For Lamb proposes to the lady who (despite
this polemic) cannot resist plying her needle that she should give the
'money so saved to poor needlewomen belonging to those branches of
employment from which she has *borrowed* these shares of pleasurable
labour'.[56]

A Habermasian narrative, which casts 'the displacement of embodied
spectacle . . . as the crucial condition of modern sociability',[57] and which
is set up to identify women's presence in any manifestation of the public
as a sign of the public's post-Enlightenment decadence, makes it hard
to acknowledge how the milliner's shop and the debating society belong to the same historical moment. It makes it easy to forget that the
debating society had its own protocols of style – its own ways of encour-
aging showing off and dressing up. And it makes it difficult to associate
the shop with new modes of public consciousness – difficult to see, what
the writings of figures such as Lamb and Wakefield nonetheless imply
when they project new alliances between shoppers and shopgirls, how
the homosocial spaces created by the late eighteenth-century culture
of shopping might have functioned as 'bases and training grounds for
agitational activities directed toward wider publics'.[58] Certainly there
are risks in allowing the marketplace to supply us our definition of real
social relations, our interdependency. In classic liberal fashion, 'society'
can end up appearing the mere byproduct of the arrangements people
undertake to satisfy their individual interests; it is the desire to obtain
property, and not, for example, compassion, or an ethos of mutual care,
that takes precedence in this scheme. Still, it is risky, too, for a feminist
not to take her publics where she can find them.

NOTES

Preliminary versions of this chapter were, by turns, presented under the
auspices of the Society for Critical Exchange at the 1997 Modern Language
Association convention and read by the Enlightenment Focus Group of the
University of California, Santa Barbara. I would like to thank that M. L. A.
audience – especially Mark Osteen – and my hosts at Santa Barbara, as well
as Tom Keirstead, Julia Saville and the editors of this volume, for many
helpful suggestions.
For full citations see Bibliography.
1 McKendrick *et al.*, *Birth*; Habermas, *Structural Transformation*.

2 Anon., 'Remarks on the Progressive Improvements in Dress', *La Belle Assemblée* (January 1817), p. 275.

3 Poovey, *Proper Lady*, pp. 16, 17.

4 See Landes, *Women and the Public Sphere*.

5 Hansen, 'Unstable Mixtures', p. 207; Fraser, 'Rethinking', p. 14. These feminist responses to Habermas converge, as well, with histories that reconstruct how working-class politicians were equally excluded when the protocols for rational debate were codified by and targetted at property-owning men: see, e.g., Gilmartin, *Print Politics*.

6 See Hansen, 'Unstable Mixtures', p. 191; and Landes, 'Public and the Private Sphere', p. 93.

7 Klancher, Introduction, p. 524.

8 Hohendahl, *Institution*, p. 52.

9 For a good account of how the bluestocking doyennes attempted in the 1770s and 1780s to invent new settings for the sociable exercise of reason, see Heller, 'Bluestocking Salons'.

10 See Mui and Mui , *Shops*, pp. 234–5.

11 Roche, *Sophie in London*, p. 292 (10 October); p. 262 (2 October); p. 229; p. 230 (23 September).

12 There were nine London debating societies in 1779 and an astonishing thirty-five in 1780, when parliamentary reform, Catholic emancipation and the war in America were alike in the news; they declined in number after that and then flourished once more during the period 1785–92 (until suppressed in the aftermath of Pitt's Gagging Bills). See Andrew's Introduction to *London Debating Societies*, p. x; also her 'Popular Culture', and Thale's 'Women in London Debating Societies'.

13 Thale, 'Women in London Debating Societies', p. 10.

14 Warner, *Letters*, p. 40.

15 *1805 Prelude*, Book 7, lines 304; 309–10 in *The Oxford Authors: William Wordsworth*, ed. Gill; Robbins, 'Introduction', *Phantom Public Sphere*, p. xvi. Subsequent references to *The Prelude* are to book and line number and follow the text of this edition.

16 See Mackie, *Market*, p. ix: 'Bourgeois taste seems affronted by stylistic reminders of difference that threaten its ideals of equality, an equality dependent on a promise of access to the dominant culture that is actually a demand for assimilation into that culture.'

17 Advertisement for Academy of Sciences and Belles Lettres, *London Courant*, 2 February 1780, in Andrew, *London Debating Societies*, p. 66.

18 See MacArthur, 'Embodying the Public Sphere', esp. p. 68.

19 Roche, *Sophie in London*, p. 87 (5 September); p. 142 (11 September).

20 Wordsworth, Preface to *Lyrical Ballads* (1802) in *The Oxford Authors: William Wordsworth*, p. 606. Southey, *Letters*, Letter vii, p. 50.

21 The phrase 'world of moving objects' is J. G. A. Pocock's: see 'The Mobility', p. 109. Book 7 of *The Prelude* is, of course, famous for the corrosive terms it uses to depict a world where human relations have been reduced to the

cash nexus. Yet, in lines 172–5, a preposition is all that differentiates, a line break all that separates, a vision of communication or even conviviality – 'The Comers and the Goers face to face' – from the poet-*flâneur*'s memory of the commercial environment as an unremitting succession of objects and of de-individuated people reduced-to-objects – 'Face after face; the string of dazzling Wares, / Shop after shop'. As John Plotz remarks, Wordsworth both imagines 'that these city crowds pose a threat to poetry' and imagines that they 'provide a new sort of power that allows poetry to go on': *The Crowd*, p. 42. Among many recent discussions of Book 7 see, in addition to Plotz's *The Crowd*, chapter 1, Pascoe, *Romantic Theatricality*, chapter 5, and Galperin, *Return*, chapter 4.

22 Southey, *Letters*, Letter xi, p. 68. Subsequent references to Southey's *Letters* appear parenthetically in the text.

23 See Walsh, 'Shop Design'.

24 See Davis, *Fairs*, p. 191.

25 Mui and Mui, *Shops*, p. 239. See fig. 3 Harding, Howell, & Co.'s Grand Fashionable Magazine, No. 89, Pall-Mall. R. Ackermann's *Repository of the Arts*, no. 3, vol. 1 (March 1809). The *Repository* informs us that 'there is no article of female attire or decoration, but what may be here procured in the first style of elegance and fashion'.

26 Morris, 'Things to Do', pp. 219, 217.

27 Friedberg, *Window Shopping*, p. 57. See also Kowaleski-Wallace, *Consuming Subjects*, pp. 79–98, 145–58; Bowlby, *Just Looking*; Lynch, *Economy of Character*, pp. 164–206.

28 Gilpin, 'The Advantages', p. 163. See also Gillian Russell's chapter in this volume.

29 Gilpin, 'The Advantages', p. 153.

30 For other Romantic-era accounts of the disorderly female shopper, see, e.g. Hunt, 'Of the Sight of Shops'; Egan (attrib.), *Real Life*, vol. II, chapter 9.

31 On 'ladies cheapening' see Charles Lamb, Letter to Thomas Manning, 28 November 1800, in *Selected Prose*, p. 300; on 'routing over every body's best goods', see Burney, *Camilla*, p. 611.

32 Copeland, *Women Writing*, p. 85.

33 Kowaleski-Wallace, *Consuming Subjects*, pp. 79–98; Pinch, 'Stealing Happiness', pp. 122–49.

34 Gilmartin, *Print Politics*, p. 30.

35 Carlson, 'Impositions', p. 152.

36 See Turner, "News"; and Russell, *Theatres of War*.

37 Burney, *Witlings*, pp. 6–101. Subsequent references to *The Witlings* are keyed to act and line number in this edition and appear parenthetically in the text.

38 Doody, *Frances Burney*, p. 78.

39 See Landes, *Women and the Public Sphere*, p. 45, on 'the strong association of women's discourse and their interests with "particularity"' and 'the artificial style and language of le monde'.

40 See Mackie, *Market*, p. 220, for an account of how Addison and Steele used this figure to meditate on an emergent market in information from which they tried to distance themselves.

41 The line, which was to have been placed around 1, 195, is restored in a footnote in Sabor's edition, p. 12.

42 Darby, *Frances Burney*, p. 27.

43 Doody, *Frances Burney*, p. 80.

44 Habermas, *Structural Transformation*, p. 51.

45 *The Morning Herald*, 14 October 1786, in Andrew, ed., *London Debating Societies*, p. 188.

46 Burney, *The Wanderer*, p. 319; Wordsworth, 'Essay, Supplementary to the Preface (1815)', in *The Oxford Authors: William Wordsworth*, p. 662.

47 Gallagher, *Nobody's Story*, pp. 233–4.

48 Letter from Charles Burney, quoted in Doody, *Frances Burney*, p. 95.

49 Habermas, 'The Public Sphere: An Encyclopedia Article', quoted in Warner, *Letters*, p. 41.

50 Darby, *Frances Burney*, pp. 36–7. See also Thompson's 'Evelina's Two Publics'.

51 Bowlby, *Just Looking*, p. 20; Williams, *Dream Worlds*; Rappaport, *Shopping*, p. 107.

52 See Copeland, *Women Writing* and Hofkosh, *Sexual Politics*, chapter 3.

53 The quotation is from Mary Robinson's portrait of the man-milliner in the penultimate instalment of her anonymous essay series 'Present State of the Manners, Society, & c., & c. of the Metropolis of England': *Monthly Magazine* 10 (October 1, 1800), p. 221. Men-milliners are also under attack in *The Lady's Magazine* 27 (October 1796), p. 455 and in a short story, 'Men-Milliners' in *La Belle Assemblée* 5 (1808), pp. 217–19.

54 Hofkosh, *Sexual Politics*, p. 74.

55 Wakefield, *Reflections*, pp. 153, 154.

56 Lamb, 'On Needle-Work', p. 50; emphasis added. See Aaron, *Double Singleness*, p. 79.

57 Thompson, 'Evelina's Two Publics', p. 155.

58 Fraser, 'Rethinking', p. 15.

Bibliography

Anon., *Advice to a Certain Lord High Chancellor, Twelve Judges, 600 Barristers, 700 English and 800 Irish Students of Law, 30,000 Attornies!* (London, 1791).

Anon., *Equality, As Consistent with the British Constitution, In a Dialogue between a Master-Manufacturer and one of his Workmen* (London, 1792).

Anon., *Freymaureren. Glizzirt im Lichte der Wahrheit* (Frankfurt-am-Main, 1785).

Anon., *Modern Poets, a satire: to which is prefixed a dedication to the Monthly, the Critical and the Analytical reviewers* (London, 1791).

Anon., *Secession; or True Blue separated from Buff. A Political-Satirical-Panegyrical Poem, Humbly inscribed to his Royal Highness The Prince of Wales. By Churchill-minor* (i.e. Anon) (London, 1793), Huntington Library, no. 315362.

Aaron, Jane, *A Double Singleness: Gender and the Writings of Charles and Mary Lamb* (Oxford, 1991).

Abbott, S. (ed.), *Fictions of Freemasonry: Freemasonry and the German Novel* (Detroit, MI, 1991).

Abinger MS, Duke University, Durham, NC.

Abinger Shelley – Godwin MS, Bodleian Library Oxford.

Account of the Proceedings of a Meeting of the London Corresponding Society, held in a field near Copenhagen House . . . (London, 1795).

Adams, M. Ray, 'Robert Merry, Political Romanticist', *Studies in Romanticism* 2 (1962), pp. 23–37.

Aikin, John, 'To Gilbert Wakefield, A.B. on his Liberation from Prison', *Monthly Magazine* (June 1801), p. 422.

Aikin, John, *Poems* (London, 1791).

Aikin, Lucy, *Memoir of John Aikin, M.D.*, 2 vols. (London, 1823).

The Works of Anna Laetitia Barbauld, with a Memoir, 2 vols. (London, 1825).

'To the Memory of Gilbert Wakefield', *Monthly Magazine* (October 1801), pp. 220–1.

Alger, John Goldworth, *Paris in 1789–94: Farewell Letters of Victims of the Guillotine* (London, 1902).

Ali Ibn Abi Bakr, Burhan al-Din, al-Marghinani, *The Hedàya, or Guide: a Commentary on the Mussulman Laws: translated by order of the Governor-General and council of Bengal, by Charles Hamilton* (London, 1791).

Altick, Richard D., *The Shows of London* (Cambridge, MA, 1978).

American Universal Magazine.

Analytical Review.

Anderson, Benedict, *Imagined Communities: Reflections on the Origins and Spread of Nationalism*, rev. edn (London, 1991, first pub. 1983).

Anderson, Olive, 'Historian's Notebook: The Anne Lister Papers', *History Workshop Journal* 40 (1995), pp. 190–2.

Andrew, Donna T. 'Popular Culture and Public Debate: London 1780', *Historical Journal* 39 (1996), pp. 405–23.

'The Code of Honour and Its Critics: the Opposition to Duelling in England, 1700–1850', *Social History* 5 (1980), pp. 409–34.

London Debating Societies, 1776–1799 (London, 1994).

Annual Necrology 1797–8 (London, 1800).

Annual Register.

Armour, Richard W. and Raymond F. Howes, *Coleridge the Talker: A Series of Contemporary Descriptions and Comments* (New York and London, 1969).

Armstrong, Isobel, 'The Gush of the Feminine: How Can We Read Women's Poetry of the Romantic Period?', in *Romantic Women Writers: Voices and Countervoices*, ed. Paula Feldman and Theresa M. Kelley (Hanover, NH, 1995), pp. 13–32.

Aske, Martin, 'Critical Disfigurings: The "Jealous Leer Malign" in Romantic Criticism', in *Questioning Romanticism*, ed. John Beer (Baltimore, MD, 1995), pp. 49–70.

Aston, Nigel, 'Horne and Heterodoxy: The Defence of Anglican Beliefs in the Late Enlightenment', *English Historical Review* 108 (1993), pp. 895–919.

Austen, Jane, *Mansfield Park* (1814), ed. Tony Tanner (Harmondsworth, 1966).

Baillie, Joanna, *A series of Plays on the Passions*, in *The Dramatic and Poetical Works* (Hildesheim and New York, 1976).

Baker, Herschel, *William Hazlitt* (Cambridge, MA, 1962).

Barbauld, Anna Letitia, *An Address to the Opposers of the Repeal of the Corporation and Test Acts*, 2nd edn (London, 1790).

Remarks on Mr Gilbert Wakefield's *Enquiry into the Expediency and Propriety of Public or Social Worship*, 2nd edn (London, 1792).

Civic Sermons to the people (London, 1792).

The Poems of Anna Letitia Barbauld, ed. William McCarthy and Elizabeth Kraft (Athens, GA, 1994).

Barish, Jonas, *The Antitheatrical Prejudice* (Berkeley, CA, 1981).

Barker, Hannah and Elaine Chalus (eds.), *Gender in Eighteenth-Century England: Roles, Representations and Responsibilities* (London, 1997).

Barker-Benfield, G. J., *The Culture of Sensibility: Sex and Society in Eighteenth-Century Britain* (Chicago, IL, 1992).

Barrell, John, *Imagining the King's Death: Figurative Treason, Fantasies of Regicide, 1793–1796* (Oxford, 2000).

Bate, Jonathan, *Shakespearean Constitutions: Politics, Theatre, Criticism 1730–1830* (Oxford, 1989).

Baudrillard, Jean, *For A Critique of the Political Economy of the Sign* (St Louis, MO, 1981).

Beattie, J. M., 'Scales of Justice: Defence Counsel and the English Criminal Trial in the Eighteenth and Nineteenth Centuries', *Law and History Review* 9 (1991), pp. 221–67.

Beaudry, Harry R., *The English Theatre and John Keats* (Salzburg, 1973).

Beloe, William, *The Sexagenarian; or the Recollections of a Literary Life*, 2 vols. (London, 1817).

Bewell, Alan, '"Jacobin Plants": Botany as Social Theory in the 1790s', *The Wordsworth Circle* 20 (1989), pp. 132–9.

Bewley, Christina, *Gentleman Radical: A Life of John Horne Tooke, 1736–1812* (London, 1998).

Binhammer, Katherine, 'The Sex Panic of the 1790s', *Journal of the History of Sexuality* 6 (1996), pp. 409–34.

Binns, John, *Recollections of the Life of John Binns* (Philadelphia, PA, 1854).

Birmingham City Library, MS Letter written from Nantes, 17 October 1792, James Watt Jr to his father, JWP, w/6.

Blake, William, *For the Sexes. The Gates of Paradise* (London, 1793), Huntington Library no. 57439.

Bloom, Edward A., and Lillian D. Bloom (eds.), *The Piozzi Letters: Correspondence of Hester Lynch Piozzi, 1784–1821 (formerly Mrs Thrale)*, 3 vols. (Newark, NJ, 1989).

Blum, Carol, *Rousseau and the Republic of Virtue: The Language of Politics in the French Revolution* (Ithaca, NY, 1986).

Boaden, James, *Memoirs of the Life of John Philip Kemble Esq. Including A History of the Stage, from the Time of Garrick to the Present Period*, 2 vols. (London, 1825).

Bolter, Jay David and Richard Grusin, *Remediation: Understanding New Media* (Cambridge, MA 1999).

Bond, Donald F., (ed.), *The Spectator*, 5 vols. (Oxford, 1965).

The Tatler, 3 vols. (Oxford, 1987).

Booth, Alan, 'Popular Loyalism and Public Violence in the North-West of England, 1790–1800', *Social History* 8 (1983), pp. 295–313.

Borsay, Peter, '"All the Town's a Stage": Urban Ritual and Ceremony, 1660–1800', in *The Transformation of Provincial Towns, 1600–1800*, ed. Peter Clark (London, 1984), pp. 228–58.

The English Urban Renaissance: Culture and Society in the Provincial Town, 1660–1770 (Oxford, 1989).

Bourdieu, Pierre, *Language and Symbolic Power*, trans. Gino Raymond and Matthew Adamson (Cambridge, MA, 1991).

Bowlby, Rachel, *Just Looking: Consumer Culture in Dreiser, Gissing, and Zola* (New York, 1985).

Bradley, James E., *Religion, Revolution and English Radicalism: Nonconformity in Eighteenth-Century Politics and Society* (Cambridge, 1990).

Brewer, John, 'Commercialization and Politics', in *The Birth of a Consumer Society: The Commercialization of Eighteenth-Century England*, ed. Neil McKendrick, John Brewer and J. H. Plumb (London, 1982), pp. 197–262.

'This, That and the Other: Public, Social and Private in the Seventeenth and Eighteenth Centuries', in *Shifting Boundaries: Transformations of the Languages of Public and Private in the Eighteenth Century*, ed. Dario Castiglione and Lesley Sharpe (Exeter, 1995), pp. 1–21.

The Pleasures of the Imagination: English Culture in the Eighteenth Century (London, 1997).

Bright, Henry A., 'A Historical Sketch of Warrington Academy', *Transactions of the Historic Society of Lancashire and Cheshire* 11 (1859), p. 22.

Brightwell, Cecilia Lucy, *Memoir of Amelia Opie* (London, 1855).

British Library MSS ADD 35345.

Bromwich, David, *Hazlitt: The Mind of a Critic* (New York and Oxford, 1983).

Brown, Ford K., *The Life of William Godwin* (London, 1926).

Burke, Edmund, *A Letter from the Right Honourable Edmund Burke to a Noble Lord* (London, 1796).

Reflections on the Revolution in France, ed. C. C. O'Brien (Harmondsworth, 1969; first published 1790).

Letter to a Noble Lord, in *The French Revolution 1790–1794*, ed. Leslie G. Mitchell (1989), vol. VIII of *The Writings and Speeches of Edmund Burke*, gen. ed. Paul Langford, 9 vols. (Oxford, 1989–97).

Reflections on the Revolution in France, in *The French Revolution 1790–1794*, ed. Leslie G. Mitchell (1989), vol. VIII of *The Writings and Speeches of Edmund Burke*, gen. ed. Paul Langford, 9 vols. (Oxford, 1989–97).

Burney, Frances, *Camilla, or, A Picture of Youth*, ed. Edward A. Bloom and Lillian D. Bloom (Oxford, 1983).

The Wanderer; or, Female Difficulties, ed. Margaret Anne Doody, Robert L. Mack and Peter Sabor (Oxford, 1991).

The Witlings, in *The Complete Plays of Frances Burney*, 2 vols., ed. Peter Sabor (London, 1995), vol. I, pp. 6–101.

Burroughs, Catherine B., *Closet Stages: Joanna Baillie and the Theater Theory of British Romantic Women Writers* (Philadelphia, PA, 1997).

Butler, Judith, *Gender Trouble: Feminism and the Subversion of Identity* (London, 1990).

Bodies that Matter: On the Discursive Limits of 'Sex' (London, 1993).

The Psychic Life of Power: Theories in Subjection (Stanford, CA, 1997).

Butler, Marilyn, *Romantics, Rebels and Reactionaries: English Literature and its Background, 1760–1830* (Oxford, 1982).

Butler, Marilyn (ed.), *Burke, Paine, Godwin, and the Revolution Controversy* (Cambridge, 1984).

Byron, Lord George Gordon, *'Famous in My Time': Byron's Letters and Journals*, ed. Leslie A. Marchand, *Vol. II 1810–1812* (London, 1973).

The Complete Poetical Works, ed. Jerome J. McGann and Barry Weller, 7 vols. (Oxford, 1980).

Capellen, Joan Derck van der, *Brieven van en ann Joan Derck van der Capellen de Pool*, ed. W. H. De Beaufort (Utrecht, 1879).

Cappe, Newcombe, *Discourses on Devotional Subjects, to which are prefixed Memoirs of his Life, by Catherine Cappe* (London, 1805).

Carlson, Julie A., 'Impositions of Form: Romantic Antitheatricalism and the Case against Particular Women', *ELH* 60 (1993), pp. 149–79.

In the Theatre of Romanticism: Coleridge, Nationalism, Women (Cambridge, 1994), pp. 134–75.

'Forever Young: Master Betty and the Queer Stage of Youth in English Romanticism', *SAQ* 95 (1996), pp. 575–602.

Carnall, Geoffrey, 'The Surrey Institution and its Successor', *Adult Education* 26 (1953), pp. 197–208.

Castle, Terry, 'The Diaries of Anne Lister', in *The Apparitional Lesbian: Female Homosexuality and Modern Culture* (New York, 1993), pp. 92–106.

Cervantes, Fernando, *The Devil in the New World: The Impact of Diabolism in New Spain* (New Haven, CT, 1994).

Cestre, Charles, *John Thelwall: A Pioneer of Democracy and Social Reform in England During the French Revolution* (London, 1906).

Chandler, James, *Wordsworth's Second Nature: A Study of the Poetry and Politics* (Chicago, IL, 1984).

England in 1819: The Politics of Literary Culture and the Case of Romantic Historicism (Chicago, IL, 1998).

Chard, Leslie F., 'Joseph Johnson: Father of the Book Trade', *Bulletin of the New York Public Library* 79 (1975), pp. 65–6.

Christensen, Jerome, *Lord Byron's Strength: Romantic Writing and Commercial Society* (Baltimore, MD, 1993).

Claeys, Gregory, (ed.), *Political Writings of the 1790s*, 8 vols. (London, 1995).

Clark, Anna, 'Anne Lister's Construction of Lesbian Identity', *Journal of the History of Sexuality* 7 (1996), pp. 23–50.

Clark, J. C. D., *English Society, 1660–1832* (Cambridge, 2000).

Clark, Peter, *The English Alehouse: A Social History, 1200–1800* (London, 1983).

British Clubs and Societies 1580–1800: The Origins of an Associational World (Oxford, 2000).

Clayden, P. W., *The Early Life of Samuel Rogers* (London, 1887).

Clayton, C. A., 'The Political Career of Richard Brinsley Sheridan', Oxford University D. Phil thesis, 1992.

Cohen, Michèle, *Fashioning Masculinity: National Identity and Language in the Eighteenth Century* (London, 1996).

Coleridge, Samuel Taylor, *The Complete Poetical Works of Samuel Taylor Coleridge* ed. E. H. Coleridge (Oxford, 1912; 1978 rpt.).

Collected Letters of Samuel Taylor Coleridge, ed. Earl Leslie Griggs, 6 vols. (Oxford, 1956–71).

The Collected Letters of Samuel Taylor Coleridge, ed. E. L. Griggs, 6 vols. (Oxford, 1956–71).

The Collected Works of Samuel Taylor Coleridge, 16 vols. (*Vol.* VII *Lectures 1808–1819 on Literature*, 2 vols.) ed. R. A. Foakes (London and Princeton, NJ, 1987).

Notebooks of Samuel Taylor Coleridge ed. Kathleen Coburn, 4 vols. (London, 1957–1990).

Biographia Literaria, ed. James Engell and W. Jackson Bate (2 vols. 1983), vol VII of *The Collected Works of Samuel Taylor Coleridge*, gen. eds. Kathleen Coburn and Bart Winer, 16 vols. (London and Princeton, NJ, 1971–).

The Collected Works of Samuel Taylor Coleridge, 16 vols. (*Vol.* II *Lectures 1795 on Politics and Religion*) ed. Lewis Patton and Peter Mann (London and Princeton, NJ, 1971).

Table Talk, ed. Carl Woodring (2 vols. 1990), vol. XIV of *The Collected Works of Samuel Taylor Coleridge*, gen. eds. Kathleen Coburn and Bart Winer, 16 vols. (London and Princeton, NJ, 1971–).

Conner, Clifford D., *Jean Paul Marat: Scientist and Revolutionary* (Atlantic Highlands, NJ, 1997).

Copeland, Edward, *Women Writing about Money: Women's Fiction in England, 1790–1820* (Cambridge, 1995).

Cornell, Drucilla, 'The Violence of the Masquerade: Law Dressed Up as Justice', *Cardozo Law Review*, 11 (1990), pp. 1047–70.

Cowan, Brian, 'What was Masculine about the Public Sphere? Gender and the Coffeehouse Milieu in Post-Restoration England', *History Workshop Journal* 51 (2000), pp. 127–57.

Cox, Jeffrey N., *Poetry and Politics in the Cockney School: Keats, Shelley, Hunt and their Circle* (Cambridge, 1998).

Critical Review.

Darby, Barbara, *Frances Burney, Dramatist: Gender, Performance, and the Late-Eighteenth-Century Stage* (Lexington, KT, 1997).

Dartmouth, Earl of, *The Manuscripts of the Earl of Dartmouth, prepared by the Historical Manuscripts Commission, Great Britain* ed. G. A. Billias, 3 vols. (Boston, MA, 1972).

Darwin, Erasmus, *The Botanic Garden. Part II. Containing The Loves of the Plants. A Poem. With Philosophical Notes*, 2nd edn (London, 1790).

Davidoff, Leonore, and Catherine Hall, *Family Fortunes: Men and Women of the English Middle Class, 1780–1850* (London, 1987).

Davis, Dorothy, *Fairs, Shops, and Supermarkets: A History of English Shopping* (Toronto, 1966).

Davis, Michael T., '"That Odious Class of Men Called Democrats": Daniel Isaac Eaton and the Romantics 1794–95', History 84 (1999), pp. 74–84.

De Bolla, Peter, *The Discourse of the Sublime* (Oxford, 1989).

De Boom, Ghislaine, *Les Ministres Plenipotentiaires dans les pays-bas autriciens principalement Cobenzl*, in *Academie royale de Belgique. Memoires*, 10th series, 31 (1932), pp. 63–6.

De Certeau, Michel, *Practice of Everyday Life*, trans. Steven Rendall (Berkeley, CA, 1984).

De Man, Paul, 'Shelley Disfigured', in *Deconstruction and Criticism*, ed. Harold Bloom *et al.* (London, 1979).

De Quincey, Thomas, 'Style' (1840), rpt. in *De Quincey as Critic*, ed. John E. Jordan (London, 1973).

Derrida, Jacques, 'Force of Law: the "Mystical Foundation of Authority"', *Cardozo Law Review*, 11 (1990), pp. 921–1039.

Dictionary of National Biography.

D'Israeli, Isaac, *A Dissertation on Anecdotes* (London, 1793).

Vaurien: or, Sketches of the Times, 2 vols. (London, 1797).

Ditchfield, G. M., 'The Priestley Riots in Historical Perspective', *Transactions of the Unitarian Historical Society* 20 (1991), pp. 3–16.

Doody, Margaret Anne, *Frances Burney: The Life in the Works* (New Brunswick, NJ, 1988).

Dülmen, Richard van, *The Society of the Enlightenment: The Rise of the Middle Class and Enlightenment Culture in Germany*, trans. Anthony Williams (London, 1992).

Dunlap, William, *Diary of William Dunlap (1766–1839): The Memoirs of a Dramatist, Theatrical Manager, Painter, Critic, Novelist, and Historian* (New York and London, 1969).

Durey, Michael, *Transatlantic Radicals and the Early American Republic* (Lawrence, KS, 1997).

Dwyer, John, 'Enlightened Spectators and Classical Moralists: Sympathetic Relations in Eighteenth-Century Scotland', in *Sociability and Society in Eighteenth-Century Scotland*, ed. John Dwyer and Richard B. Sher (Edinburgh, 1993), pp. 96–118.

'The Imperative of Sociability: Moral Culture in the Late Scottish Enlightenment', *British Journal for Eighteenth-Century Studies* 13 (1990), pp. 169–84.

Dyer, George, *Poems by George Dyer*, 2 vols. (London, 1800).

Eagleton, Terry, *The Function of Criticism: From The Spectator to Post-Structuralism* (London, 1984).

Egan, Pierce, (attrib.), *Real Life in London*, 2 vols. (London, 1821–2).

Eger, Elizabeth, 'The Nine Living Muses of Great Britain (1779): Women, Reason, and Literary Community in Eighteenth-Century Britain', Cambridge University Ph.D thesis, 1999.

Eger, Elizabeth, Charlotte Grant, Clíona Ó Gallchoir and Penny Warburton (eds.), *Women, Writing and the Public Sphere 1700–1830* (Cambridge, 2001).

Eley, Geoff, 'Nations, Publics, and Political Cultures: Placing Habermas in the Nineteenth Century', in *Habermas and the Public Sphere*, ed. Craig Calhoun (Cambridge, MA, 1992), pp. 289–339.

Elfenbein, Andrew, 'Byronism and Homosexual Performance', *MLQ* 54 (1993), pp. 535–66.

Byron and the Victorians (Cambridge, 1995).

Elias, Norbert, *The Court Society* (1969), trans. Edmund Jephcott (Oxford, 1983).

Ellis, Grace, *Memoir, Letters, and a Selection from the Poems and Prose Writings of Anna Laetitia Barbauld*, 2 vols. (Boston, MA, 1874).

Ellis, Markman, 'Coffee-women, "The Spectator" and the Public Sphere in the Early Eighteenth Century', in *Women, Writing and the Public Sphere 1700–1830*, ed. Elizabeth Eger, Charlotte Grant, Clíona Ó Gallchoir and Penny Warburton (Cambridge, 2001), pp. 27–52.

Elster, Jon, *Alchemies of the Mind: Rationality and the Emotions* (Cambridge, 1999).

Emsley, Clive, 'An Aspect of Pitt's "Terror": Prosecutions for Sedition during the 1790s', *Social History* 6 (1981), pp. 155–84.

'Repression, "Terror" and the Rule of Law during the Decade of the French Revolution', *English Historical Review* 100 (1985), pp. 801–25.

Enfield, William, *A Funeral Sermon, Occasioned by the Death of the Late Rev. John Aikin, D.D.* (Warrington, 1781).

Epstein, James, 'Radical Dining, Toasting and Symbolic Expression in Early Nineteenth-Century Lancashire: Rituals of Solidarity', *Albion* 20 (1988), pp. 271–9.

Radical Expression: Political Language, Ritual, and Symbol in England, 1790–1850 (Oxford, New York, 1994).

Erdman, David V., *Commerce des Lumières. John Oswald and the British in Paris, 1790–1793* (Columbia, MO, 1986).

European Magazine.

Evening Mail.

Everest, Kelvin, *Coleridge's Secret Ministry: The Context of the Conversation Poems 1795–1798* (Brighton, 1979).

Farington, Joseph, *Diary*, ed. Kenneth Garlick, Angus Macintyre and Kathryn Cave, 16 vols. (New Haven, CT, 1984).

Favret, Mary A., *Romantic Correspondence: Women, Politics, and the Fiction of Letters* (Cambridge, 1993).

Felski, Rita, 'Nothing to Declare: Identity, Shame, and the Lower Middle Class', *PMLA* 115 (2000), pp. 33–45.

Ferguson, Moira, *Subject to Others: British Women Writers and Colonial Slavery, 1670–1834* (London, 1992).

Field, William, *Memoirs of the Life, Writings, and Opinions of the Rev. Samuel Parr, LL.D.*, 2 vols. (London, 1828).

Finn, Margot, 'Women, Consumption and Coverture in England, *c*. 1760–1860', *Historical Journal* 39 (1996), pp. 703–22.

Fish, Stanley, *Doing What Comes Naturally: Change, Rhetoric, and the Practice of Theory in Literary and Legal Studies* (Durham, NC, 1989).

Fliegelman, Jay, *Declaring Independence: Jefferson, Natural Language & the Culture of Performance* (Stanford, CA, 1993).

Foote, George A., 'Sir Humphry Davy and his Audience at the Royal Institution', *Isis* 43 (1952), pp. 6–12.

Foster, Jeannette Howard, *Sex Variant Women in Literature: A Historical and Quantitative Survey* (London, 1958).

Fraser, Nancy, 'Rethinking the Public Sphere: A Contribution to the Critique of Actually Existing Democracy', in *The Phantom Public Sphere*, ed. Bruce Robbins (Minneapolis, MN, 1993), pp. 1–32.

Friedberg, Anne, *Window Shopping: Cinema and the Postmodern* (Berkeley, CA, 1993).
Fruchtman, Jr, Jack, *Thomas Paine and the Religion of Nature* (Baltimore, MD, 1993).
Furniss, Tom, 'Nasty Tricks and Tropes: Sexuality and Language in Mary Wollstonecraft's *Rights of Woman*', *Studies in Romanticism* 32 (1993), pp. 177–209.
Gallagher, Catherine, *Nobody's Story: The Vanishing Acts of Women Writers in the Marketplace, 1670–1820* (Berkeley, CA, 1994).
Galperin, William H., *The Return of the Visible in British Romanticism* (Baltimore, MD, 1993).
Gentleman's Magazine.
George, Eric, *The Life and Death of Benjamin Robert Haydon: Historical Painter 1786–1846*, 2nd edn with additions by Dorothy George (Oxford, 1967).
Gifford, William, *The Baviad and the Maeviad*, 8th edn (London, 1811).
Gilmartin, Kevin, *Print Politics: The Press and Radical Opposition in Early Nineteenth-Century England* (Cambridge, 1996).
Gilpin, William, 'The Advantages of a Town Life and a Country Life, Compared', in *Dialogues on Various Subjects* (London, 1807).
Ginter, Donald E., 'The Financing of the Whig Party Organization, 1783–1793', *American Historical Review* 71 (1966), pp. 421–40.
Godwin, William, *An Enquiry concerning Political Justice, and its Influence on General Virtue and Happiness*, 2 vols. (London, 1793).
'Of English Style', in *The Enquirer: Reflections on Education, Manners, and Literature* (London, 1797).
Enquiry Concerning Political Justice and Its Influence on Morals and Happiness, 3 vols., 3rd edn, ed. F. E. L. Priestley (Toronto, 1946).
Uncollected Writings (1785–1822) by William Godwin, ed. Jack W. Marken and Burton R. Pollin (Gainesville, FL, 1968).
Enquiry Concerning Political Justice and its Influence on Modern Morals and Happiness, ed. Isaac Kramnick (London, 1976, 3rd edn 1798).
Things as They Are or The Adventures of Caleb Williams, ed. Maurice Hindle (Harmondsworth, 1988).
Collected Novels and Memoirs of William Godwin, gen. ed. Mark Philp, 8 vols. (London, 1992).
Political and Philosophical Writings of William Godwin, gen. ed. Mark Philp, 7 vols. (London, 1993).
Godwin's diary, Abinger Collection, Bodleian Library, Oxford.
Golinski, Jan, *Science as Public Culture: Chemistry and Enlightenment in Britain, 1760–1820* (Cambridge, 1992).
Goodman, Dena, 'Public Sphere and Private Life: Toward a Synthesis of Current Historiographical Approaches to the Old Regime', *History and Theory* 31 (1992), pp. 1–20.
Goodwin, Albert, *The Friends of Liberty: The English Democratic Movement in the Age of the French Revolution* (Cambridge, MA, 1979).
Goveia, E. V., *The West Indian Slave Laws of the 18th Century* (London, 1970).
Grylls, Rosalie Glynn, *William Godwin and his World* (London, 1953).

Guillory, John, 'The English Common Place: Lineages of the Topographical Genre', *Critical Quarterly* 33:4 (1991), pp. 3–27.

Habermas, Jürgen, *The Structural Transformation of the Public Sphere: An Inquiry into a Category of Bourgeois Society*, trans. Thomas Burger with Frederick Lawrence (Cambridge, MA, 1989).

Hadley, David, 'Public Lectures and Private Societies: Expounding Literature and the Arts in Romantic London', in *English Romanticism: Preludes and Postludes. Essays in Honor of Edwin Graves Wilson*, ed. Donald Schoonmaker and John A. Alford (East Lansing, MI, 1993), pp. 43–58.

Halberstam, Judith, *Female Masculinity* (Durham, NC, 1998).

Hamilton, Paul, 'Coleridge and Godwin in the 1790s', in *The Coleridge Connection: Essays for Thomas McFarland*, ed. Richard Gravil and Molly Lefebure (Houndmills, Basingstoke, 1990), pp. 41–59.

Hans, N., *New Trends in Education in the Eighteenth Century* (London, 1951).

Hansen, Miriam, 'Unstable Mixtures, Dilated Spheres: Negt and Kluge's *The Public Sphere and Experience*, 20 Years Later', *Public Culture* 5 (1993), pp. 179–212.

Hargreaves-Mawdsley, W. N., *The English Della Cruscans and Their Time, 1783–1828* (The Hague, 1967).

Harvey, John, *Men in Black* (London, 1995).

Hay, Douglas, 'Property, Authority and the Criminal Law', in *Albion's Fatal Tree: Crime and Society in Eighteenth-Century England*, ed. Douglas Hay *et al.* (London, 1975), pp. 17–63.

Hayden, John O., *The Romantic Reviewers 1802–1824* (Chicago, IL, 1968).

Haydon, Benjamin Robert, *The Diary of Benjamin Robert Haydon*, ed. Willard Bissell Pope, 2 vols. (Cambridge, MA, 1960).

Hazlitt, William, *Hazlitt on Theatre*, ed. William Archer and Robert Lowe (New York, 1895).

    Complete Works, ed. P. P. Howe, 34 vols. (London, 1930–4).

    The Spirit of the Age (1825) (London, 1966).

    Selected Writings, ed. Jon Cook (Oxford, 1991).

Heller, Deborah, 'Bluestocking Salons and the Public Sphere', *Eighteenth-Century Life 22* (1998), pp. 59–82.

Herzog, Don, *Poisoning the Minds of the Lower Orders* (Princeton, NJ, 1998).

Highfill Jr, Philip H., Kalman A. Burnim and Edward A. Langhans, *A Biographical Dictionary of Actors, Actresses, Musicians, Dancers, Managers & Other Stage Personnel in London, 1660–1800*, 16 vols. (Carbondale, IL, 1973–93).

Hill, Bridget, *The Republican Virago: The Life and Times of Catharine Macaulay, Historian* (Oxford, 1992).

Hitchcock, Tim and Michèle Cohen, *English Masculinities, 1660–1800* (Harlow, 1999).

Hodgson, William, *The Case of William Hodgson* (London, 1796).

Hofkosh, Sonia, *Sexual Politics and the Romantic Author* (Cambridge, 1998).

Hohendahl, Peter Uwe, *The Institution of Criticism* (Ithaca, NY, 1982).

Holcroft, Thomas, *The Theatrical Recorder* (1805), 2 vols. (New York, 1968).

Hone, J. Ann, *For the Cause of Truth: Radicalism in London, 1796–1821* (Oxford, 1982).

Hont, lstvan, 'The Language of Sociability and Commerce; Samuel Pufendorf and the Theoretical Foundations of the "Four-Stages Theory"', in *The Languages of Political Theory in Early-modern Europe*, ed. Anthony Pagden (Cambridge, 1987), pp. 253–76.

Howe, P. P., *The Life of William Hazlitt*, 2nd edn (New York, 1923).

Howell T. B., and T. J. Howell (eds.), *A Complete Collection of State Trials*, 33 vols. (London, 1809–26).

Hughes-Hallett, Penelope, *The Immortal Dinner: A Famous Evening of Genius & Laughter in Literary London, 1817* (London, 2000).

Hunt, Leigh, 'Of the Sight of Shops', in *Essays by Leigh Hunt*, ed. Edmund Ollier (London, 1890), pp. 199–209.

   Leigh Hunt's Dramatic Criticism 1808–31, ed. Lawrence Huston Houtchens and Carolyn Washburn Houtchens (New York, 1949).

Hunt, Lynn (ed.), *The French Revolution and Human Rights: A Brief Documentary History* (Boston, 1996).

Huntington Library, HM 31201, Anna Maria Larpent's diary.

Huntington Library, HM 4829, 27 July 1800.

Huntington Library, MS BN 454, 16 June 1815, Helen M. Williams to her friend in America, Ruth Baldwin Barlow.

Huntington Library, Sydney Smith MSS, HM 30430, HM 30431, HM 30433, HM 30449, HM 30453.

Hutton, Catherine, *Reminiscences of a Gentlewoman of the Last Century: Letters of Catherine Hutton*, ed. C. H. Beale (Birmingham, 1891).

Hutton, William, *The Life of William Hutton, including a particular account of the Riots at Birmingham in 1791*, 2nd edn (London, 1817).

Jacob, Margaret C., 'Radicalism in the Dutch Enlightenment', in *The Dutch Republic in the Eighteenth Century: Decline, Enlightenment, and Revolution*, ed. Margaret C. Jacob and Wijnand W. Mijnhardt (Ithaca, NY, 1992), pp. 224–40.

Jacob, Margaret C., *The Radical Enlightenment: Pantheists, Freemasons and Republicans* (London, 1981).

   Living the Enlightenment: Freemasonry and Politics in Eighteenth-Century Europe (New York, 1991).

Jacobus, Mary, *Romanticism, Writing and Sexual Difference: Essays on 'The Prelude'* (Oxford, 1989).

   'Intimate Connections: Scandalous Memoirs and Epistolary Indiscretion', in *Women, Writing and the Public Sphere 1700–1830*, ed. Elizabeth Eger, Charlotte Grant, Clíona Ó Gallchoir and Penny Warburton (Cambridge, 2001), pp. 274–89.

Jerningham, Edward, *Edward Jerningham and his Friends: A Series of Eighteenth-Century Letters*, ed. Lewis Bettany (London, 1919).

Jewson, C. B., *The Jacobin City: A Portrait of Norwich in its Reaction to the French Revolution 1788–1802* (Glasgow and London, 1975).

John Rylands Library, Manchester, MS 570, 26 February 1792, to Mrs Piozzi.

John Rylands Library, Manchester, MS 570.

Johnson, Claudia, *Equivocal Beings: Politics, Gender, and Sentimentality in the 1790s: Wollstonecraft, Radcliffe, Burney, Austen* (Chicago, IL, 1995).

Jones, Stanley, *Hazlitt: A Life. From Winterslow to Frith Street* (Oxford, 1989).

Kahan, Gerald, *George Alexander Stevens & The Lecture on Heads* (Athens, GA, 1984).

Keach, William, 'A Regency Prophecy and the End of Barbauld's Career', *Studies in Romanticism* 33 (1994), pp. 569–77.

'Barbauld, Romanticism, and the Survival of Dissent', in *Romanticism and Gender*, ed. Anne Janowitz (Leicester, 1998), pp. 44–61.

Keane, John, *Tom Paine: A Political Life* (Boston, MA, 1995).

Keate, William, *A Free Examination of Dr Price's and Dr Priestley's Sermons, with a post-script containing some strictures upon 'An Address to the Opposers of the Repeal of the Corporation and Test Acts'* (London, 1790).

Keats, John, *The Letters of John Keats 1814–1821*, ed. Hyder Edward Rollins, 2 vols. (Cambridge, 1958).

Keele University, Wedgwood MS W/M21.

Keele University, Wedgwood MSS, W/M 1112, fo. 159.

Keen, Paul, *The Crisis of Literature in the 1790s: Print Culture and the Public Sphere* (Cambridge, 1999).

Kegan Paul, Charles, *William Godwin: His Friends and Contemporaries*, 2 vols. (London, 1876).

Kelly, Gary, 'Bluestocking Feminism', in *Women, Writing and the Public Sphere 1700–1830*, ed. Elizabeth Eger, Charlotte Grant, Clíona Ó Gallchoir and Penny Warburton (Cambridge, 2001), pp. 163–80.

Kiernan, V. G., *The Duel in European History: Honour and the Reign of Aristocracy* (Oxford, 1988).

Klancher, Jon P., *The Making of English Reading Audiences, 1790–1832* (Madison, WI, 1987).

Introduction to 'Romanticism and Its Publics: A Forum', *Studies in Romanticism* 33 (1994), pp. 523–25.

'Prose', in *An Oxford Companion to the Romantic Age: British Culture 1776–1832*, ed. Iain McCalman (Oxford, 1999), pp. 279–86.

'Lecturing', in *An Oxford Companion to the Romantic Age: British Culture 1776–1832*, ed. Iain McCalman (Oxford, 1999), p. 581.

Klein, Lawrence E., *Shaftesbury and the Culture of Politeness: Moral Discourse and Cultural Politics in Early Eighteenth-Century England* (Cambridge, 1994).

'Sociability, Solitude, and Enthusiasm', *The Huntington Library Quarterly* 60 (1998), pp. 153–77.

Knight, David, *Humphry Davy: Science and Power* (Oxford, 1992).

Kowaleski-Wallace, Elizabeth, *Consuming Subjects: Women, Shopping, and Business in the Eighteenth Century* (New York, 1997).

La Belle Assemblée.

Lacan, Jacques, *The Seminar of Jacques Lacan*, Book VII: *The Ethics of Psychoanalysis 1959–60*, trans. Dennis Porter (New York, 1986).

Lady's Magazine.

Lamb, Charles, *Works*, ed. E. V. Lucas, 7 vols. (London, 1903–5).

The Complete Works and Letters of Charles Lamb (New York, 1935).

The Letters of Charles and Mary Anne Lamb, ed. E. W. Marrs, 3 vols. (Ithaca, NY, 1975).

Selected Prose, ed. Adam Phillips (Harmondsworth, 1985).

Lamb, Mary, 'On Needle-Work', in *British Literature, 1780–1830*, ed. Anne K. Mellor and Richard E. Matlak (Fort Worth, TX, 1996).

Landes, Joan B., 'The Public and the Private Sphere: A Feminist Reconsideration', in *Feminists Read Habermas: Gendering the Subject of Discourse*, ed. Johanna Meehan (New York, 1995), pp. 91–116.

Women and the Public Sphere in the Age of the French Revolution (Ithaca, NY, 1988).

Langford, Paul, *A Polite and Commercial People, 1727–1783* (Oxford, 1989).

'Manners and the Eighteenth-Century State: The Case of the Unsociable Englishman', in *Rethinking Leviathan: The Eighteenth-Century State in Britain and Germany*, ed. John Brewer and Eckhart Hellmuth (Oxford, 1999), pp. 281–316.

Englishness Identified: Manners and Character, 1650–1850 (Oxford, 2000).

Leask, Nigel, 'Salons, Alps and Cordilleras: Helen Maria Williams, Alex von Humboldt and the Discourse of Romantic Travel', in *Women, Writing and the Public Sphere, 1700–1800*, ed. Elizabeth Eger, Charlotte Grant, Cliona Ó Gallchoir and Penny Warburton (Cambridge, 2001), pp. 217–35.

Leaver, Kristen, 'Pursuing Conversations: *Caleb Williams* and the Romantic Constitution of the Reader', *Studies in Romanticism* 33 (1994), pp. 589–610.

Le Breton, Anna Letitia, *Memoir of Mrs Barbauld* (London, 1874).

Memories of Seventy Years, ed. Mrs Herbert Martin (London, 1883).

Lee, Richard 'Citizen', *Songs from the Rock to Hail the Approaching Day, Sacred to Truth Liberty and Peace* (London, nd (1795)).

Lefebure, Molly, *Samuel Taylor Coleridge: A Bondage of Opium* (London, 1974).

Lewis, Gordon K., *Main Currents in Caribbean Thought: The Historical Evolution of Caribbean Society in its Ideological Aspects, 1492–1900* (Baltimore, MD, 1983).

Liddington, Jill, 'Anne Lister of Shibden Hall, Halifax (1791–1840): Her Diaries and the Historians', *History Workshop Journal* 35 (1993), pp. 45–77.

Female Fortune: Land, Gender and Authority. The Anne Lister Diaries and Other Writings, 1833–1836 (London, 1998).

Lillywhite, Bryant, *London Coffee Houses* (London, 1963).

Lister, Anne, *I Know My Own Heart: The Diaries of Anne Lister, 1791–1840*, ed. Helena Whitbread (London, 1988).

No Priest But Love: The Journals of Anne Lister, 1824–1826, ed. Helena Whitbread (New York, 1992).

Litchfield, R. B., *Tom Wedgwood: The First Photographer* (1903: rpt. New York, 1973).

Lloyd, Sarah, 'Pleasing Spectacles and Elegant Dinners: Conviviality, Benevolence and Charity Anniversaries in Eighteenth-Century London', forthcoming *Journal of British Studies*.

London Gazette.

Luhmann, Niklas, *Love as Passion: The Codification of Intimacy*, trans. Jeremy Gaines and Doris L. Jones (Stanford, CA, 1986).

Lynch, Deidre Shauna, *The Economy of Character: Novels, Market Culture, and the Business of Inner Meaning* (Chicago, IL, 1998).

MacArthur, Elizabeth J., 'Embodying the Public Sphere: Censorship and the Reading Subject in Beaumarchais's *Mariage de Figaro*', *Representations* 61 (1998), pp. 57–77.

Mackie, Erin, *Market à la Mode: Fashion, Commodity, and Gender in* The Tatler *and* The Spectator (Baltimore, MD, 1997).

Magnuson, Paul, 'Romanticism and its Publics', *Studies in Romanticism*, special issue 33 (1994), pp. 523–88.

Reading Public Romanticism (Princeton, NJ, 1998).

Manchester Herald.

Marshall P. J., and Glyndwr Williams, *The Great Map of Mankind. Perceptions of New Worlds in the Age of Enlightenment* (Cambridge, MA, 1982).

Marshall, Peter H., *William Godwin* (New Haven, CT, 1984).

McCalman, Iain, 'Ultra-Radicalism and Convivial Debating-Clubs in London, 1795–1838', *English Historical Review* 102 (1987), pp. 309–33.

'Newgate in Revolution: Radical Enthusiasm and Romantic Counterculture', *Eighteenth-Century Life* 22 (1998), pp. 95–110.

Radical Underworld: Prophets, Revolutionaries and Pornographers in London, 1795–1840 (Cambridge, 1988).

McCalman, Iain (ed.), *An Oxford Companion to the Romantic Age: British Culture 1776–1832* (Oxford, 1999).

McCann, Andrew, *Cultural Politics in the 1790s: Literature, Radicalism and the Public Sphere* (Houndmills, Basingstoke, 1999).

McCarthy, William, '"We Hoped the Woman was Going to Appear": Repression, Desire, and Gender in Anna Letitia Barbauld's Early Poems', in *Romantic Women Writers: Voices and Countervoices*, ed. Paula Feldman and Theresa M. Kelley (Hanover, NH, 1995), pp. 113–37.

McDonagh, Josephine, 'Barbauld's Domestic Economy', in *Romanticism and Gender*, ed. Anne Janowitz (Leicester, 1998), pp. 62–77.

McFarlane, Anthony, 'Identity, Enlightenment and Political Dissent in Late Colonial Spanish America', *Transactions of the Royal Historical Society*, sixth series, 8 (1998), pp. 325–27.

McGann, Jerome, *'Don Juan' in Context* (Chicago, IL, 1976).

The Poetics of Sensibility: A Revolution in Literary Style (Oxford, 1996).

McKendrick, Neil, John Brewer and J. H. Plumb, *The Birth of a Consumer Society: The Commercialization of Eighteenth-Century England* (Bloomington, IN, 1985, first pub. 1982).

McLachlan, H. J., 'Mary Priestley: A Woman of No Character', in *Motion Toward Perfection: The Achievement of Joseph Priestley*, ed. A. Truman Schwartz and John McEvoy (Boston, MA, 1990), pp. 251–64.

McLachlan, H., *Warrington Academy: Its History and Influence* (Manchester, 1943).

McNeill, Mary, *The Life and Times of Mary Ann McCracken, 1770–1866* (Belfast, 1960).

Mee, Jon, 'The Political Showman at Home: Reflections on Popular Radicalism and Print Culture in the 1790s', in *Radicalism and Revolution in Britain 1775–1848: Essays in Honour of Malcolm I. Thomis*, ed. Michael T. Davis (Houndmills, Basingstoke, 2000), pp. 41–55.

Enthusiasm, Romanticism, and Regulation (Oxford, forthcoming).

Meehan, Michael, *Liberty and Poetics: Liberty and Poetics in Eighteenth-Century England* (London, 1985).

Mellor, Anne, 'The Female Poet and the Poetess: Two Traditions of British Women's Poetry, 1780–1830', *Studies in Romanticism* 36 (1997), pp. 261–76.

Merry, Robert, *Diversity: A Poem* (London, 1788).

The Laurel of Liberty (London, 1790).

Ode for the Fourteenth of July, 1791 (London, 1791).

Proposals for Printing by subscription . . . the work, complete, in verse and prose of Robert Merry (London, 1796).

The Pains of Memory (London, 1796).

Miller, P. N., (ed.), *Joseph Priestley: Political Writings* (Cambridge, 1993).

Money, John, *Experience and Identity: Birmingham and the West Midlands 1760–1800* (Manchester, 1977).

Monthly Magazine.

Monthly Review.

Moore, Charles, *A Full Inquiry into the Subject of Suicide. To which are added . . . Two Treatises on Duelling and Gaming*, 2 vols. (London, 1790).

Moore, Lisa L., *Dangerous Intimacies: Toward a Sapphic History of the British Novel* (Durham, NC, 1997).

Moorman, Mary, *William Wordsworth: A Biography: The Later Years 1803–1850* (Oxford, 1965).

Morning Chronicle.

Morning Post.

Morris, Meaghan, 'Things to Do with Shopping Centres', in *Grafts: Feminist Cultural Criticism*, ed. Susan Sheridan (London, 1988), pp. 193–225.

Mui, Hoh-Cheung, and Lorna H. Mui , *Shops and Shopkeeping in Eighteenth-Century England* (London, 1989).

Mullan, John, *Sentiment and Sociability: The Language of Feeling in the Eighteenth Century* (Oxford, 1988).

Nead, Lynda, 'Mapping the Self: Gender, Space, and Modernity in Mid-Victorian London', in *Rewriting the Self: Histories from the Renaissance to the Present*, ed. Roy Porter (London, 1997).

Neugebauer-Wölk, M., *Esoterische Bünde und Bürgerliche Gesellschaft: Entwicklungslinien zur modernen Welt im Geheimbundwesen des 18. Jahrhunderts* (Wolfenbüttel, 1995).

New York Public Library, uncatalogued Dyer letter, no. 101, 5 February, n.d.

Newlyn, Lucy, *Reading, Writing, and Romanticism* (Oxford, 2000).

Northern Star.

Oldham, James, *The Mansfield Manuscripts and the Growth of English Law in the Eighteenth Century*, 2 vols. (Chapel Hill, NC, 1992).

Olney, Clark, *Benjamin Robert Haydon: Historical Painter* (Athens, GA, 1952).

Oswald, John, *The Cry of Nature; or an appeal to Mercy and to Justice on behalf of the persecuted animals* (London, 1791).

Oxford Magazine.

Paine, Thomas, *The Writings and Speeches of Thomas Paine*, ed. Moncure Daniel Conway, 4 vols. (London, 1894–6).

  Rights of Man (1791–2), in Thomas Paine, *Rights of Man, Common Sense, and Other Political Writings*, ed. Mark Philp (Oxford, 1995).

Paris, John Ayrton, *The Life of Sir Humphry Davy* (London, 1831).

Pascoe, Judith, *Romantic Theatricality: Gender, Poetry and Spectatorship* (Ithaca, NY, 1997).

Pateman, Carole, *The Sexual Contract* (Cambridge, 1988).

Phillipson, Nicholas, 'The Scottish Enlightenment', in *The Enlightenment in National Context*, ed. Roy Porter and Mikuláš Teich (Cambridge, 1981), pp. 26–30.

Philp, Mark, *Godwin's Political Justice* (London, 1986).

  'Vulgar Conservatism, 1792–3', *English Historical Review* 110 (1995), pp. 42–69.

Pigott, Charles, *Persecution. The Case of Charles Pigott: Contained in the Defence He had Prepared and Would Have Delivered . . .* (London, 1793).

  A Political Dictionary (London, 1794).

Pinch, Adela, 'Stealing Happiness: Shoplifting in Early Nineteenth-Century England', in *Border Fetishisms*, ed. Patricia Spyer (London, 1997), pp. 122–49.

Pincus, Steven, '"Coffee Politicians Does Create": Coffeehouses and Restoration Political Culture', *Journal of Modern History* 67 (1995), pp. 807–34.

Piozzi, Hester Lynch, *The Piozzi Letters: Correspondence of Hester Lynch Piozzi, 1784–1821 (formerly Mrs Thrale)*, ed. Edward A. Bloom and Lillian D. Bloom, 3 vols. (Cranbury, NJ, 1989–93).

Plotz, John, *The Crowd: British Literature and Public Politics* (Berkeley, CA, 2000).

Pocock, J. G. A., 'Edmund Burke and the Redefinition of Enthusiasm', in *The Transformation of Political Culture, 1789–1848*, vol. III of *The French Revolution and the Creation of Modern Political Culture*, ed. François Furet and Mona Ozouf (Oxford, 1989), pp. 19–43.

  'The Mobility of Property and the Rise of Eighteenth-Century Sociology', in *Virtue, Commerce, and History: Essays on Political Thought and History* (Cambridge, 1985), pp. 103–23.

'Virtues, Rights, and Manners: A Model for Historians of Political Thought', in *Virtue, Commerce, and History: Essays on Political Thought and History* (Cambridge, 1985), pp. 37–50.

Pointon, Marcia, *Strategies for Showing: Women, Possession, and Representation in English Visual Culture, 1665–1800* (Oxford, 1997).

Poovey, Mary, *The Proper Lady and the Woman Writer: Ideology as Style in the Works of Mary Wollstonecraft, Mary Shelley, and Jane Austen* (Chicago, IL, 1984).

Porter, Roy, 'The Enlightenment in England', in *The Enlightenment in National Context*, ed. Roy Porter and Mikuláš Teich (Cambridge, 1981), pp. 8–18.

'Material Pleasures in the Consumer Society', in *Pleasure in the Eighteenth Century*, ed. Roy Porter and Marie Mulvey Roberts (London, 1996), pp. 19–35.

Prentice, Gloria, 'Anne Lister's Pilgrimage: Forging a Sexual Identity as a Masculine Woman in the Long Eighteenth Century', Hons. thesis, University of Melbourne, 2001.

Priestley letters held in Warrington Library (typescript, British Library, 10902. i. 8).

Priestley, Joseph, *A Farewell Sermon*, ed. J. Wordsworth (Oxford, 1989).

PRO (Public Record Office), TS 11/944 [3433], crown brief.

PRO (Public Record Office), TS 11/962/3508, SCI Minute Book, vol. II, 1791–4; TS 11/3505/2; 'J. F.' [John Frost] to Horne Tooke, Paris, 20 September. 1792, in TS 11/951/3495.

Public Advertiser.

Pyne, W. H., and W. Combe, *The Microcosm of London*, 3 vols. (London, 1904, first published 1808).

Quarterly Review.

Radcliffe, Evan, 'Revolutionary Writing, Moral Philosophy, and Universal Benevolence in the Eighteenth Century', *Journal of the History of Ideas* 54 (1993), pp.22–40.

Rappaport, Erika D., *Shopping for Pleasure: Women in the Making of London's West End* (Princeton, NJ, 2000).

Raven, James, 'New Reading Histories, Print Culture and the Identification of Change: the Case of Eighteenth-Century England', *Social History* 23 (1998), pp. 281–5.

Reynolds, Frederic, *The Life and Times of Frederic Reynolds*, 2 vols. (London, 1828).

Rich, Adrienne, 'Compulsory Heterosexuality and Lesbian Existence', in *Women: Sex and Sexuality*, eds. Catherine R. Stimpson and Ethel Spector Person (Chicago, IL, 1980), pp. 62–91.

Riede, David G., *Oracles and Hierophants: Constructions of Romantic Authority* (Ithaca, NY, 1991).

Robbins, Bruce (ed.), *The Phantom Public Sphere* (Minneapolis, MN, 1993).

Roberts, W., *Memoirs of Hannah More*, 4 vols., 2nd edn (London, 1834).

Robinson, Eric, 'An English Jacobin: James Watt, Junior', *Cambridge Historical Journal* 2 (1953–5), pp. 349–55.

Robinson, Henry Crabb, *Henry Crabb Robinson on Books and their Writers*, ed. Edith J. Morley, 3 vols. (London, 1938).

The Diary of Henry Crabb Robinson. An Abridgement, ed. Derek Hudson (Oxford, 1967).

Robinson, Mary, 'Present State of the Manners, Society, &c., &c. of the Metropolis of England', *Monthly Magazine* 10 (1 October 1800), p. 221.

Poems (London, 1791).

Roche, Sophie von la, *Sophie in London 1786: being the Diary of Sophie v. la Roche*, trans. Clare Williams (London, 1933).

Rodgers, Betsy, *Georgian Chronicle: Mrs Barbauld and her Family* (London, 1958).

Roe, Nicholas, *Wordsworth and Coleridge: The Radical Years* (Oxford, 1988).

John Keats and the Culture of Dissent (Oxford, 1997).

Rogers, Nicholas, 'Pigott's Private Eye: Radicalism and Sexual Scandal in Eighteenth-Century England', *Journal of the Canadian Historical Association/ Revue de la societé historique canadienne*, new series, 4 (1993), pp. 247–63.

Crowds, Culture and Politics in Georgian Britain (Oxford, 1998).

Rose, R. B., 'The Priestley Riots of 1791', *Past and Present* 18 (1960), pp. 68–88.

Ross, Marlon, 'Configurations of Feminine Reform: the Woman Writer and the Tradition of Dissent', in *Re-visioning Romanticism: British Women Writers, 1776–1837*, ed. Carol Shiner Wilson and Joel Haefner (Philadelphia, PA, 1994), pp. 91–110.

Rousseau, Jean-Jacques, *A Discourse on Inequality* (Harmondsworth, 1987).

Russell, Gillian, *The Theatres of War: Performance, Politics, and Society, 1793–1815* (Oxford, 1995).

Russell, Martha, 'On the Birmingham Riots', from Adam Matthew Publications, *Women's Language and Experience, 1500–1940: Women's Diaries and Related Sources* ed. A. Vickery. Part II, Reel 19.

Rutt, J. T., *The Theological and Miscellaneous Works &c of Joseph Priestley*, 25 vols. (New York, 1972).

Ryan, Robert M., *The Romantic Reformation: Religious Politics in English Literature 1789–1824* (Cambridge, 1997).

Saunders, Julia, '"The Mouse's Petition": Anna Laetitia Barbauld and the Scientific Revolution', forthcoming in *Review of English Studies*.

Schofield, Robert E., *The Enlightenment of Joseph Priestley: a Study of His Life and Work from 1733 to 1773* (Philadelphia, PA, 1997).

Scrapbook of Political Broadsides, British Library [pressmark 648.c. 26].

Scrivener, Michael, 'The Rhetoric and Context of John Thelwall's "Memoir"', in *Spirits of Fire: English Romantic Writers and Contemporary Historical Methods*, ed. G. A. Rosso and Daniel P. Watkins (London and Toronto, 1990), pp. 112–30.

Sedgwick, Eve Kosofsky, *Between Men: English Literature and Male Homosocial Desire* (New York, 1985).

'Privilege of Unknowing: Diderot's The Nun', *Tendencies* (Durham, NC, 1993), pp. 23–51.

Shaftesbury, Anthony, Earl of, *Characteristicks of Men, Manners, Opinions, Times* 3 vols., 4th edn (London, 1732).

Shapin, Steven, *A Social History of Truth: Civility and Science in Seventeenth-Century England* (Chicago, IL, 1994).

Shelley, Mary Wollstonecraft, *The Letters of Mary Wollstonecraft Shelley*, ed. Betty T. Bennett, 3 vols. (Baltimore, MD, 1983).

Shields, David S., *Civil Tongues and Polite Letters in British America* (Chapel Hill, NC, 1997).

Shteir, A. B., 'Botany in the Breakfast Room: Women and Early Nineteenth-Century British Plant Study', in *Uneasy Careers and Intimate Lives: Women In Science, 1789–1979*, ed. Pnina G. Abir-Am and Dorinda Outram (New Brunswick, NJ, 1987), pp. 31–43.

'Linnaeus' Daughters: Women and British Botany', in *Women and the Structure of Society*, ed. Barbara J. Harris and JoAnne K. McNamara (Durham, NC, 1984), pp. 67–73.

Simmel, Georg, 'Sociability', in *The Sociology of Georg Simmel*, trans. Kurt H. Wolff (Glencoe, IL, 1950), pp. 40–57.

Simpson, Michael, *Closet Performances: Political Exhibition and Prohibition in the Dramas of Byron and Shelley* (Stanford, CA, 1998).

Siskin, Clifford, *The Historicity of Romantic Discourse* (New York, 1988).

The Work of Writing: Literature and Social Change in Britain (Baltimore, MD, 1998).

Smith, Adam, *Theory of Moral Sentiments*, ed. D. D. Raphael and A. L. Macfie (Oxford, 1976).

Smith, Nowell C. (ed.), *The Letters of Sydney Smith*, 2 vols. (Oxford, 1953).

Smith, Sydney, *The Works of the Rev. Sydney Smith*, 3 vols. in one (New York, 1871).

Smyser, Jane Worthington, 'The Trial and Imprisonment of Joseph Johnson, Bookseller', *Bulletin of the New York Public Library* 77 (1974), pp. 418–35.

Somers, Margaret R., 'Citizenship and the Place of the Public Sphere: Law, Community, and Political Culture in the Transition to Democracy', *American Sociological Review* 58 (1993), pp. 596–7.

'Rights, Relationality, and Membership: Rethinking the Making and Meaning of Citizenship', *Law and Social Inquiry* 19 (1994), pp. 63–112.

Southey, Robert, *Letters from England*, ed. Jack Simmons (London, 1951).

St Clair, William, *The Godwins and the Shelleys: The Biography of a Family* (London, 1989).

Stallybrass, Peter, and Allon White, *The Politics and Poetics of Transgression* (Ithaca, NY, 1986).

Surrey Institution, (Various circular letters, cards of admission etc. relating to the Surrey Institution) London, 1808–23. British Library 822.1.9

Swartz, Richard G., '"Their terrors came upon me tenfold": Literacy and Ghosts in John Clare's Autobiography', in *Lessons of Romanticism: A Critical Companion*, ed. Thomas Pfau and Robert F. Gleckner (Durham, NC, 1998), pp. 328–46.

Sweet, Nanora, '"Lorenzo's" Liverpool and "Corrine's" Coppet: The Italianate Salon and Romantic Education', in *Lessons of Romanticism: A Critical Companion*, ed. Thomas Pfau and Robert F. Gleckner (Durham, NC, 1998), pp. 244–60.

Taylor, Tom (ed.), *Life of Benjamin Robert Haydon*, 3 vols. (London, 1853).

Thale, Mary, 'London Debating Societies in the 1790s', *Historical Journal* 32 (1989), pp. 57–86.

'Women in London Debating Societies in 1780', *Gender & History* 7 (1995), pp. 5–24.

'The Case of the British Inquisition: Money and Women in Mid-Eighteenth-Century London Debating Societies', *Albion* 31 (1999), pp. 31–48.

Thale, Mary, (ed.), *Selections from the Papers of the London Corresponding Society 1792–1799* (Cambridge, 1983).

The Cabinet, by a Society of Gentlemen, 3 vols. (London, 1795).

The Complete Reports of the Committee of Secrecy of the House of Lords and Commons . . . (London, 1794).

The First and Second Report from the Committee of Secrecy: Together with their Appendix to the Second Report . . . Huntington Library, no. 287835 (London, 1794?).

The Florence Miscellany (Florence, 1785).

The Genuine Trial of Thomas Paine . . . (London, 1793).

The Indicator 2 (20 October 1819).

The Library of the Grand Lodge, The Hague, MS 41:8, fo. 26.

The Life of John Thelwall. By his Widow (London, 1837).

The Poetry of the World, 4 vols. (London, 1788–91).

The Trial of John Frost, for Seditious Words . . . (London, 1794).

The World.

Thelwall, John *The Peripatetic*, 3 vols. (London, 1793).

The Natural and Constitutional Right of Britons to Annual Parliaments, Universal Suffrage, and the Freedom of Popular Association (London, 1795).

An Appeal to Popular Opinion, Against Kidnap and Murder (London, 1796).

Prospectus of a Course of Lectures (London, 1796).

Selections and Original Articles, for Mr Thelwall's Lectures on the Science and Practice of Elocution (Birmingham, 1806).

'Prefatory Memoir' in *Poems Written Chiefly in Retirement 1801* (Oxford, 1989).

The Politics of English Jacobinism: Writings of John Thelwall, ed. Gregory Claeys (Philadelphia, PA, 1995).

Thieme, John A., 'Spouting, Spouting-clubs and Spouting Companions', *Theatre Notebook* 29 (1975), pp. 9–16.

Thomas, Peter D. G., *John Wilkes: A Friend to Liberty* (Oxford, 1996).

Thompson, E. P., 'Hunting the Jacobin Fox', *Past and Present*, 142 (1994), pp. 94–140.

'Rough Music', in *Customs in Common: Studies in Traditional Popular Culture* (New York, 1991), pp. 467–538.

The Making of the English Working Class (London, 1963).

Thompson, Helen, 'Evelina's Two Publics', *The Eighteenth Century: Theory and Interpretation* 39 (1998), pp. 147–67.

Thompson, Judith, 'An Autumnal Blast, a Killing Frost: Coleridge's Poetic Conversation with John Thelwall', *Studies in Romanticism* 36 (1997), pp. 427–56.

The Times.

The Times Literary Supplement.

Tomalin, Claire, *The Life and Death of Mary Wollstonecraft* (London, 1985, first published 1974).

Triber, Jayne E., *A True Republican: The Life of Paul Revere* (Amherst, MA, 1998).

Tuite, Clara, *Romantic Austen: Sexual Politics and the Literary Canon* (Cambridge, 2002).

Turner, James Grantham, '"News from the New Exchange": Commodity, Erotic Fantasy, and the Female Entrepreneur', in *The Consumption of Culture, 1600–1800: Image, Object, Text*, ed. Ann Bermingham and John Brewer (London, 1995), pp. 419–39.

Turner, Michael, 'The Limits of Abolition: Government, Saints and the "African Question," *c*. 1780–1820', *English Historical Review* 112 (1997), pp. 319–57.

Turner, William, 'Historical Account of the Warrington Academy', *Monthly Repository* 8 (1813), p. 169.

'Mrs Barbauld', *The Newcastle Magazine* 4 (1825), p. 230.

Tyson, Gerald P., *Joseph Johnson: A Liberal Publisher* (Iowa City, IA, 1979).

Van Kley, Dale K., *The Religious Origins of the French Revolution: From Calvin to the Civil Constitution, 1560–1791* (New Haven, CT, 1996).

Vickery, Amanda, 'Golden Age to Separate Spheres? A Review of the Categories and Chronology of English Women's History', *Historical Journal* 34 (1993), pp. 383–414.

The Gentleman's Daughter: Women's Lives in Georgian England (New Haven, CT, and London, 1998).

Wahrman, Dror, 'Public Opinion, Violence and the Limits of Constitutional Politics', in *Re-reading the Constitution: New Narratives in the Political History of England's Long Nineteenth Century*, ed. James Vernon (Cambridge, 1996), pp. 83–122.

Wakefield, Gilbert, *Memoirs* (London, 1792).

'To John Aikin, M. D.', *Monthly Magazine* (July 1801), p. 513.

Wakefield, Priscilla, *Reflections on the Present Condition of the Female Sex; with Suggestions for its Improvement* (London, 1798).

Walpole, Horace, *Letters of Horace Walpole*, ed. Pagett Toynbee, 19 vols. (Oxford, 1925).

Walsh, Claire, 'Shop Design and the Display of Goods in Eighteenth-Century London', *Journal of Design History* 8 (1995), pp. 157–76.

Warner, Michael, 'Introduction', in *Fear of a Queer Planet: Queer Politics and Social Theory*, ed. Michael Warner (Minneapolis, MN, 1993).

The Letters of the Republic: Publication and the Public Sphere in Eighteenth-Century America (Cambridge, MA, 1990).

Watts, Michael R., *The Dissenters*, 2 vols. (Oxford, 1978).

Webb, R. K., 'Rational Piety', in *Enlightenment and Religion: Rational Dissent in Eighteenth-Century Britain*, ed. K. Haakonssen (Cambridge, 1996), pp. 287–311.

Weber, Samuel, *Return to Freud: Jacques Lacan's Dislocation of Psychoanalysis*, trans. Michael Levine (Cambridge, 1990).

Weindling, Paul, 'Science and Sedition: How Effective Were the Acts Licensing Lectures and Meetings, 1795–1819?', *The British Journal for the History of Science* 13 (1980), pp. 141–53.

Weintraub, Jeff, 'The Public/Private Distinction', in *Public and Private in Thought and Practice: Perspectives on a Grand Dichotomy*, ed. Jeff Weintraub and Krishan Kumar (Chicago, IL, and London, 1997), pp. 1–42.

Werkmeister, Lucyle, *The London Daily Press, 1772–1792* (Lincoln, NB, 1963).

A Newspaper History of England, 1792–3 (Lincoln, NB, 1967).

White, Daniel E., 'The "Joineriana": Anna Barbauld, the Aikin Family Circle, and the Dissenting Public Sphere', *Eighteenth-Century Studies* 32 (1999), pp. 511–33.

Whyman, Susan E., *Sociability and Power in Late-Stuart England: The Cultural Worlds of the Verneys 1660–1720* (Oxford, 1999).

Williams, Raymond, *Culture and Society 1780–1950* (New York, 1983, first published 1958).

Williams, Rosalind H., *Dream Worlds: Mass Consumption in Late Nineteenth-Century France* (Berkeley, CA, 1982).

Wilson, Kathleen, *The Sense of the People: Politics, Culture and Imperialism in England, 1715–1785* (Cambridge, 1995).

Wollstonecraft, Mary, *Letters Written During a Short Residence in Sweden, Norway, and Denmark* (London, 1796).

Collected Letters of Mary Wollstonecraft, ed. Ralph M. Wardle (Ithaca, NY, 1979).

The Works of Mary Wollstonecraft, ed. J. Todd and M. Butler, 7 vols. (London, 1989).

Wollstonecraft, Mary, and William Godwin, *A Short Residence in Sweden* and *Memoirs of the Author of 'The Rights of Woman'*, ed. Richard Holmes (Harmondsworth, 1987).

Woodfall, William, *Monthly Review* 48 (1773).

Wordsworth, William, *The Prose Works*, ed. W. J. B. Owen and J. W. Smyser, 3 vols. (Oxford, 1974).

The Prelude, 1799, 1805, 1850, ed. Jonathan Wordsworth, M. H. Abrams and Stephen Gill (New York, 1979).

The Oxford Authors: William Wordsworth, ed. Stephen Gill (Oxford, 1984).

Wykes, David L., '"The Spirit of Persecutors exemplified": The Priestley Riots and the Victims of the Church and State Mobs', *Transactions of the Unitarian Historical Society* 20 (1991), pp. 17–39.

Yorke, Henry, *These are the Times that Try Men's Souls! A Letter to John Frost Prisoner in Newgate* (London, 1793).

Index